Whites and Reds

Whites and Reds

*A History of Wine in the Lands
of Tsar and Commissar*

STEPHEN V. BITTNER

OXFORD
UNIVERSITY PRESS

Great Clarendon Street, Oxford, OX2 6DP,
United Kingdom

Oxford University Press is a department of the University of Oxford.
It furthers the University's objective of excellence in research, scholarship,
and education by publishing worldwide. Oxford is a registered trade mark of
Oxford University Press in the UK and in certain other countries

First Edition published in 2021

Impression: 3

Published in the United States of America by Oxford University Press
198 Madison Avenue, New York, NY 10016, United States of America

British Library Cataloguing in Publication Data
Data available

Library of Congress Control Number: 2020948159

ISBN 978–0–19–878482–1

DOI: 10.1093/oso/ 9780198784821.001.0001

Printed and bound in Great Britain by
CPI Group (UK) Ltd, Croydon, CR0 4YY

For my parents

Table of Contents

Introduction

Identity

Wine and Civilization

In an otherwise scholarly essay on wine as a metaphor in eighteenth- and nineteenth-century Russian poetry, Mikhail Stroganov, famous for his explorations of place through the lens of literature (so-called 'literary local studies'), strayed to humorous reminiscence.

> During Andropov's campaign against drunkenness, when the sale of alcohol was prohibited before 2.00 p.m., when cops raided the beer halls, collaring the muzhiks found drinking during work hours, when the vineyards of Crimea and the North Caucasus were uprooted, I happened to stop by a liquor store with my wife to get something to go. Because the populace did not yet realize what was happening, there was no line. In order to protect the goods and salesclerks from the suffering and thirsty, steel grating had been installed, enclosing the counter and creating a substantial setback from their lustful looks. At this blessed moment, we witnessed a miracle: among the vodkas were two bottles of wine with different labels. Such a thing never happens! 'Tell me, what kind of wine do you have?' we asked the salesclerk. 'What kind of wine? It's wine!' the salesclerk answered ungraciously. 'Ah, we understand, but what is it called?' 'What does it matter what it is called? Wine is wine!' the lady moralized, as if we, stupid people, did not understand this utterly true premise.[1]

Stroganov's story can be read in different ways. On a scholarly level, it helps draw attention to the apparent contradiction that is the focus of his essay. In popular discourse, wine was anonymous and interchangeable, and not only during the Andropov years. Despite the fact that the Russian word for wine is a cognate— *vino*—and despite the fact that *vino* appears in some of the earliest known Russian-language texts, it is far more ambiguous in its meanings than the Latin original (*vinum*). Until the Soviet period, Russian *vino* was often preceded by the adjective form of 'grape' to avoid confusion. Until the late nineteenth century, *vino* was shorthand for vodka. The inelegant word *vinzavod* (a commonly used compound word meaning wine factory) might refer to a winery or distillery,

---

[1] M. V. Stroganov, 'Ob upotreblenii vina: Pushkin i drugie', in *Literaturnyi tekst: problemy i metody issledovaniia, 8. Motiv vina v literature*, ed. I. V. Fomenko (Tver, 2002), 24.

Whites and Reds: A History of Wine in the Lands of Tsar and Commissar. Stephen V. Bittner, Oxford University Press (2021).

which reflects the shared etymology of *vino* and the compound word for distillation, *vinokurenie*. The latter captures the act of putting wine to flame, thus creating distillate for brandy. Even I often encountered persons in the course of my research who thought it a great tragedy that I excluded Estonian apple wine (a cider, from the German *Apfelwein*), Ukrainian raspberry wine (a fortified raspberry-flavoured juice), and a host of other so-called wines from my analysis. In short, *vino* encompasses a great deal in everyday usage, far more than wine. Yet in Russian poetry, *vino* is of the conventional sort—made from grapes, poured from a bottle. In the works of Pushkin, Derzhavin, and others, wine is a metaphor for the fullness of life (the full bottle), a life cut short (the half-drunk bottle), the fieriness of youth (champagne), or an allusion to the restlessness of mind and soul (which wine purports to cure, at least temporarily). Wine's versatile ambiguity in popular usage is accompanied by a rich, varied, and highly particularistic literary usage.

Stroganov's story can also be read as satire, in which the salesclerk's unsophisticated palate and rudimentary understanding of wine is held up for ridicule by Stroganov's erudite readers. Nearly every Soviet citizen would have recognized the social type represented by the salesclerk—working-class, brusque, lacking in the insincere niceties that define customer service in other parts of the world, perhaps revelling in the power that comes from selling an item in short supply. As the final chapter will show, this type of wine writing was common in the Soviet Union during the 1970s and 1980s. Despite its outward snobbery, it conformed to long-standing cultural tropes in which the intelligentsia served as the country's arbiter of taste, as the chief determiner of highbrow and lowbrow. Yet this is perhaps an ungenerous and incomplete reading, because Stroganov accepted the salesclerk's 'utterly true premise': wine was, in fact, wine. To put it differently, even the lowliest Soviet wines—the sweet and fortified ports that were ubiquitous in the late-Soviet marketplace, or the low-quality Bulgarian and Algerian imports that Soviet consumers sometimes found on store shelves—signified something important. In a country noted for its affinity for vodka—and for all the deleterious health effects that stemmed from that affinity—wine was aspirational. As another scholar noted in an essay in the same volume about wine in Pushkin's one-act play, *A Feast in the Time of Plague*, wine was a hallmark of the Russian intelligentsia's 'European consciousness'.[2] Even Stroganov's salesclerk, who saw first-hand which customers preferred wine to the more potent and ubiquitous vodka, may have understood this to be true.

*   *   *   *   *

[2] O. G. Lazaresku, 'Vino i traditsii evropeiskogo soznaniia (kul'turnogo "samoopredeleniia") v "Pire vo vremia chumy"', in *Literaturnyi tekst: problemy i metody issledovaniia, 8. Motiv vina v literature*, ed. I. V. Fomenko (Tver, 2002), 30–8.

Like a study of panda bears in Patagonia or dolphins in the Sahara, this book is devoted to what may seem an entirely incongruous topic—the history of wine and winemaking in the Russian Empire and the Soviet Union. Wine evokes images that are alien in a place more often associated with arctic weather, vodka, and an economy of shortages: trellised vineyards on warm Mediterranean hills; wealthy connoisseurs with prized cellars of dusty, ageing bottles. Yet by the mid-1970s, the Soviet Union was the world's fourth largest producer of wine by volume, trailing only Italy, France, and Spain.[3] As in the tsarist period, most Soviet wine originated in regions near the Black Sea: the Dniester and Prut river valleys in Moldova (Bessarabia) and the southern Ukrainian steppe, Crimea, and the valleys and lowlands of the Caucasus. In these areas wine was deeply embedded in local economies and cultures many millennia before the Russian annexation in the late eighteenth and nineteenth centuries.

While this book begins with wine's appearance in the *Primary Chronicle*, a twelfth-century source that describes the origins of Kievan Rus three centuries earlier, and ends with Vladimir Putin's 2006 embargo on Georgian and Moldovan wine during the lead-up to Russia's war in Georgia, its central focus is on the nineteenth and twentieth centuries. During these years, domestic production slowly eclipsed, and then during the Soviet years replaced almost entirely imports of wine from Europe. Chapters are ordered chronologically, but they are episodic in structure. They describe the ideas, controversies, political alliances, technologies, business practices, and international networks that shaped the history of Russian and Soviet wine production and consumption. This book thus bears little resemblance to the 'commodity' histories that have become a popular genre in recent years—about cod, salt, coffee, and so on.[4] Wine has pride of place, but always as a prism that refracts other phenomena: science, empire, revolution, nationalism, Stalinism, the Cold War, and the myriad failures of a failing socialist system.

Each chapter is bound by its own arguments, but several threads run throughout. First, wine was domesticated in the Russian Empire by virtue of imperialism. The principal settings for the chapters that follow—Moldova (Bessarabia), southern Ukraine, Crimea, and the Caucuses—were incorporated into the Russian Empire during the late eighteenth and early nineteenth centuries through imperial rivalry, great-power intrigue, warfare, and diplomatic treaty. With the exception of Cossack communities in Ukraine and the north Caucasus, in none of these territories were Russians or Russian-speakers particularly numerous at the moment of

---

[3] G. G. Valuiko, *Vinogradnye vina* (Moscow, 1978), 4–5. There is good reason to be sceptical about production statistics published in the Soviet Union. Yet in the case of wine, published statistics may have understated true levels of production. Behind closed doors, Soviet industry officials spoke about being the world's third largest producer of wine in the early 1970s, with an annual volume exceeding that of Spain: see Rossiiskii gosudarstvennyi arkhiv ekonomiki [Russian State Archive of Economics, hereafter RGAE], f. 468, o. 1, d. 2807, ll. 70–77.

[4] See, for instance, Mark Kurlansky, *Cod: A Biography of the Fish that Changed the World* (New York, 1998); Mark Kurlansky, *Salt: A World History* (New York, 2003).

incorporation, although that would change rapidly in the decades that followed. In all of these territories, tsarist administrators encountered long-standing vini-cultural economies and cultures, which they sought to fold into Russian political structures and economic networks. Consequently, there is a great deal in this book that will be familiar to historians of Russian and Soviet imperialism: state-led, ideologically driven attempts to control, categorize, and modernize the empire's vinicultural populations, not to mention a good deal of imperial grief about the apparent intransigence of non-Russian viniculturalists.[5] Yet this book is also concerned with something different. It shows how a by-product of imperial-ism became embedded in the daily lives of Russian and Soviet citizens, a line of analysis recently pioneered by Erik Scott in his study of the Georgian diaspora in the Soviet Union.[6] Raising questions about who was acculturating whom, persons far from the vineyards of Georgia, Crimea, and Bessarabia experienced empire, in part, through the consumption and appreciation of wine. The history of Russian and Soviet wine production and consumption thus shows that the currents of imperialism flowed not only from the Russian core outward, but in the opposite direction as well.

Second, this book seeks to understand Russia's post-Petrine embrace of European norms and culture in light of these imperial relationships. As Willard Sunderland has noted in a history of the settlement of the southern Russian steppe, Russian imperialism was peculiar in the European context because it served as an anvil upon which Russian society was reforged in a European fashion.[7] During the two centuries of tsarist, Soviet, and post-Soviet rule that followed the annexation of the Black Sea territories, the production and consumption of wine became an important marker of status—as European, aristocratic, bourgeois, and *kul'turno* (meaning appropriately cultured, in Stalinist jargon). The absorption into the Russian Empire of the Black Sea wine cultures was thus part of what Norbert Elias has termed the 'civilizing process', the diffusion of behavioural norms and modes of etiquette and consumption in post-medieval Europe.[8] Catriona Kelly has observed that the 'civilizing process' in Russia and the Soviet Union nearly

---

[5] The relevant literature is large and growing. See, for instance, Francine Hirsch, *Empire of Nations: Ethnographic Knowledge and the Making of the Soviet Union* (Ithaca and London, 2005); Terry Martin, *The Affirmative Action Empire: Nations and Nationalism in the Soviet Union, 1923–1939* (Ithaca, 2001); Ian W. Campbell, *Knowledge and the Ends of Empire: Kazak Intermediaries and Russian Rule on the Steppe, 1731–1917* (Ithaca and London, 2017); Robert Geraci, *Window on the East: National and Imperial Identities in Late Tsarist Russia* (Ithaca, 2001); Kelly O'Neill, *Claiming Crimea: A History of Catherine the Great's Southern Empire* (New Haven, 2017); Paul Werth, *At the Margins of Orthodoxy: Mission, Governance, and Confessional Politics in Russia's Volga-Kama Region, 1827–1905* (Ithaca, 2001).

[6] Erik R. Scott, *Familiar Strangers: The Georgian Diaspora and the Evolution of the Soviet Empire* (Oxford, 2016).

[7] Willard Sunderland, *Taming the Wild Field: Colonization and Empire on the Russian Steppe* (Ithaca and London, 2004), 5.

[8] Norbert Elias, *The Civilizing Process*, vol. 1: *The History of Manners*, trans. E. Jephcott (Oxford, 1978); Vadim Volkov, 'The Concept of *Kul'turnost'*: Notes on the Stalinist Civilizing Process', in *Stalinism: New Directions*, ed. Sheila Fitzpatrick (London and New York, 2000), 210–30; Vadim Volkov

always meant assimilation to values imported from the West.[9] Yet winemaking and its elaborate cultures of consumption had native roots in the Russian Empire, albeit in territories peripheral to the imperial core. This tension—between viniculture and winemaking as a European practice and a mark of refinement, on the one hand, and the places it occurred and the people who engaged in it, on the other—is a central theme. Upon arriving for tours of duty in Simferopol, Tiflis (Tbilisi), Odessa, and Kishinev (Chişinău), many tsarist officials discovered that there was something admirable about their new neighbours. In short, the history of wine sheds light on the unusual Orientalism of the Russian and Soviet empires. It simultaneously reveals Russian and Soviet anxieties vis-à-vis Europe and non-Russian compatriots.[10]

Third, this book argues that the history of wine over the late-tsarist and Soviet periods underscores powerful continuities between the pre- and post-revolutionary eras. Before the 1870s, wine was sufficiently unusual on the Russian table that the word for wine almost always referred in popular usage to vodka. Yet in the decades that followed, the values attributed to good domestic wine and its consumption outside the vinicultural territories—as a luxury item to be savoured and reserved for special occasions, as a mark of refinement preferred by the intelligentsia, as an object deserving of connoisseurship—remained remarkably uniform, even though there was very little about the tsarist wine industry that should have endeared it to the Bolsheviks. The industry was obsessed with status, its wines were often more expensive than high-quality imports from France, and it was dominated by wealthy aristocrats and foreign investors, such as the Roederer family from Champagne-Ardenne, who produced sparkling wine in Odessa. Yet in the 1930s and beyond, Soviet wine found powerful patrons in the Kremlin, particularly Anastas Mikoyan, who was among the cohort of Bolsheviks from Transcaucasia who owed their careers to Stalin. My point is not that viniculture and winemaking were unscathed by the events of 1917. In fact, quite the opposite was true, which is the subject of chapter 4. Rather, the reasons why it was seen as important to foster domestic winemaking and consumption did not fundamentally change

and Catriona Kelly, 'Kul'turnost'' and Consumption', in Constructing Russian Culture in the Age of Revolution, ed. Catriona Kelly and David Shepherd (Oxford, 1998), 291–313.

[9] Catriona Kelly, Refining Russia: Advice Literature, Polite Culture, and Gender from Catherine to Yeltsin (Oxford, 2001), xxvii–xxviii.

[10] On the peculiarities of Russian Orientalism, see David Schimmelpenninck van der Oye, Russian Orientalism: Asia in the Russian Mind from Peter the Great to the Emigration (New Haven, 2010); Nathaniel Knight, 'Grigor'ev in Orenburg, 1851–1862: Russian Orientalism in the Service of the Empire?', Slavic Review 59, no. 1 (Spring 2000): 74–100; Adeeb Khalid, 'Russian History and the Debate over Orientalism', Kritika: Explorations in Russian and Eurasian History 1, no. 4 (Fall 2000): 691–9; Nathaniel Knight, 'On Russian Orientalism: A Response to Adeeb Khalid', Kritika: Explorations in Russian and Eurasian History 1, no. 4 (Fall 2000): 701–15; Maria Todorova, 'Does Russian Orientalism Have a Russian Soul? A Contribution to the Debate between Nathaniel Knight and Adeeb Khalid', Kritika: Explorations in Russian and Eurasian History 1, no. 4 (Fall 2000): 717–27.

across the 1917 caesura. Pierre Bourdieu has argued that consumption practices correlate with class aspirations.[11] For many important persons in the vanguard party of the ascendant Soviet proletariat, the consumption of wine encapsulated the victory of 1917.

Finally, and tightly interwoven with previous threads, this book traces long-standing linkages between consumption and identity in the Russian Empire and the Soviet Union. In recent years, consumption has proven to be fertile ground for historians working on the Soviet period and the communist periods in Eastern Europe. The upsurge in scholarly interest comes after many decades of neglect, during which production was understood to be the paramount shaper of socialist identity. The big rubrics of Soviet social history, after all—worker, peasant, and *intelligent*—were formed through production. Yet consumption also shaped identity, sometimes in ways that confirmed the older identities, and sometimes in ways that cut across them. For instance, a worker in the late 1920s who attended a so-called *rabfak*, an equivalency programme for persons lacking conventional credentials for university admission, and who was subsequently promoted into the ranks of engineers or the party apparat, was expected to show a level of *kul'turnost'* appropriate to life's new station—proper clothing had to be purchased, culturally enriching concerts attended, restorative vacations planned, and perhaps—if one was truly blessed—a single-family apartment tastefully decorated. In an economy characterized by minimal choice, limited access, and frequent shortage, consumption was inherently political, because it situated one along axes of privilege and exclusion, compliance and rebellion, conformity and individuality.[12]

For historians working in the tsarist period, the connections between consumption and identity are an older insight, linked to scholarship from the 1960s about the 'Westernization' of the post-Petrine aristocracy. As Arcadius Kahan writes about the eighteenth-century gentry, 'exogenous factors', by which he means the demands of an activist, modernizing state, 'gradually imposed upon the gentry a new pattern and rising level of consumption'. Among other things, this entailed the purchase of European 'dress, cuisine, home furnishings, services,

---

[11] Pierre Bourdieu, *Distinction: A Social Critique of the Judgment of Taste*, trans. Richard Nice (Cambridge, MA, 1984).

[12] The literature on Soviet-era consumption is large and growing, as historians apply insights from the Stalin period to the decades that followed. See, in particular, Ann Ivanova, *Magaziny 'Berezka': paradoksy potrebleniia v pozdnem SSSR* (Moscow, 2017); Nataliia Lebina, *Sovetskaia povsednevnost': normy i anomalii ot voennogo kommunizma k bol'shomu stiliu* (Moscow, 2016), 13–166; Amy E. Randall, *The Soviet Dream World of Retail Trade and Consumption in the 1930s* (New York, 2008); Lewis H. Siegelbaum, *Cars for Comrades: The Life of the Soviet Automobile* (Ithaca and London, 2008); Christine Varga-Harris, *Stories of House and Home: Soviet Apartment Life during the Khrushchev Years* (Ithaca and London, 2015); Diane P. Koenker, *Club Red: Vacation Travel and the Soviet Dream* (Ithaca and London, 2013); Steven E. Harris, *Communism on Tomorrow Street: Mass Housing and Everyday Life after Stalin* (Washington DC and Baltimore, 2013). The collection of articles in *Communism Unwrapped: Consumption in Cold War Eastern Europe*, ed. Paulina Bren and Mary Neuburger (Oxford, 2012) is a particularly good introduction to similar analyses in communist-era Eastern Europe.

education, travel, and the like'. Although Kahan is most interested in the impact the costs of Westernization had upon serfs, who were the principal source of gentry wealth, he is describing a process of identity formation that was fundamentally rooted in consumption. The Russian gentry came to understand itself as European, at least in part, by consuming in ways that were recognizably European. This 'new pattern' diverged sharply from the experience of Muscovy, where there was a small degree of social and material differentiation between the majority of the provincial gentry and the peasants from whom they 'fed'. In recent years, historians of tsarist Russia have widened their analytical gaze to the consumption patterns of other social groups to call into question long-standing consensuses about the Russian Sonderweg, such as the idea that Russia's emerging urban middle class differed sharply in values and outlook from its counterparts in Western Europe.[13]

Wine thus stood as an important component of Russia's European embrace. Rooted in the sixteenth century and magnified many times over by Peter the Great at the beginning of the eighteenth, the turn toward Europe became a permanent feature of Russia under the Romanovs. Even persons most committed to the idea of Russian exceptionalism—such as the Slavophile nationalists who pined for a collectivist Byzantine utopia that supposedly existed before the Petrine corruption—were deeply reliant on ideas and ideologies of European origin while imagining that utopia. Likewise, the assumption that wine was important because it was a marker of identity became an article of faith in Russia—first among wealthy persons in the eighteenth and nineteenth centuries, who spent significant fortunes so that fine French and German wines and champagnes might grace their tables; then by domestic vintners, who struggled mightily and with no small degree of embarrassment to produce wines decent enough to win European accolades and respect; and even by a new Bolshevik government, which had little common cause with the wine-drinking public. For all of these persons, wine was an important component of the good life, sometimes its central component. Because wine indicated civilizational identity in a place where civilizational anxieties were never far from the surface, it was freighted with a significance in Russia that it lacked elsewhere. Even in France, where wine came to be understood in the late nineteenth century as a distinctive national achievement, it lacked the civilizational pedigree that it offered to Russia.[14] Stroganov's salesclerk was correct:

[13] Arcadius Kahan, 'The Costs of "Westernization": The Gentry and the Economy in the Eighteenth Century', *Slavic Review* 25, no. 1 (March 1966): 40–66. For more recent approaches, see Louise McReynolds, *Russia at Play: Leisure Activities at the End of the Tsarist Era* (Ithaca, 2002); Tricia Starks, *Smoking under the Tsars: A History of Tobacco in Imperial Russia* (Ithaca, 2018); Sally West, *I Shop in Moscow: Advertising and the Creation of Consumer Culture in Late-Tsarist Russia* (DeKalb, IL, 2011); Christine Ruane, *The Empire's New Clothes: A History of the Russian Fashion Industry, 1700–1917* (New Haven, 2009).

[14] On wine as a distinctively French achievement, see Van Troi Tran, 'Grapes on Trial: Wine at the Paris World's Fairs of 1889 and 1900', *Food and Foodways: Explorations in the History and Culture of*

even Soviet wine was wine, meaning a palpable linkage between the bare store shelves of Tver in the early 1980s, where Stroganov miraculously found two bottles of unknown wine, and the cellars and vineyards of Tuscany and Loire, which Stroganov could scarcely have imagined. The rest of this introduction, and the remainder of this book follow from this 'utterly true premise'.

*   *   *   *   *

Russia knew wine long before it mastered viniculture. The latter likely dates to the mid-1630s, when Persian merchants on their way to the Austrian court stopped in Astrakhan, which had been incorporated into Russia during the reign of Ivan IV eighty years earlier. Located at 46 degrees north latitude, roughly the same as Bordeaux, and near the mouth of the Volga, Astrakhan was an unfamiliar climate: summers were exceedingly hot and arid, which reflected proximity to the deserts of Central Asia. The merchants reputedly shared with local monks the wine they carried and taught them how to cultivate vines.[15] The Russian familiarity with wine, however, is considerably older. The entry in the *Primary Chronicle* for the year 969 notes that Sviatoslav, son of Oleg, preferred the city of Pereiaslavets on the Danube to Kiev, because of the availability of 'gold, brocades, wine, and various fruits'. According to Horace G. Lunt, the *Primary Chronicle* uses the verb 'drink' in conjunction with water in two passages, with wine in three, and with wine and mead jointly in seven more. The great villain of Kievan Rus, the fratricidal Sviatopolk, loved to drink wine while listening to string music. Ivan Pryzhkov, the nineteenth-century author of a colourful history, based on primary sources, of the traditional Russian pub (*kabak*), noted that 'grape wine' was widely available in Kievan Rus by the tenth century, and not terribly expensive. The Hypatian Chronicle indicates that Sviatoslav, prince of Iziaslav, had 80 amphorae (*korchagi*) of wine in his house in 1146, an amount equivalent to roughly 2,000 litres. The *Tale of Igor's Campaign*, which likely dates from the late twelfth century, soon after the events it narrates, indicates that 'there was much to drink, mead and kvass, wine'. The relative ubiquity of wine in Kievan Rus reflected southern trading routes that linked the Dnieper basin with Greek civilization in Constantinople and proximity to (non-Slavic) vinicultural communities on the north shore of the Black Sea and Crimea. Wine was likely less common than mead and kvass, but it predated the arrival of vodka or any distilled alcohol by more than 500 years.[16]

Human Nourishment 21, no. 4 (2013): 267–87; George Durand, 'Vine and Wine', in *Rethinking France: Les Lieux de mémoire*, vol. 3, ed. Pierre Nora, trans. David P. Jordan (Chicago and London, 2009), 193–231.

[15] V. V. Vlasov, *100 let dorogoiu V. E. Tairova* (Odessa, 2005), 6; Mikhail Ballas, *Vinodelie v Rossii: istoriko-statisticheskii ocherk*, vol. 1 (St Petersburg, 1895), 193.

[16] Horace G. Lunt, 'Food in the Rus' *Primary Chronicle*', in *Food in Russian History and Culture*, ed. Musya Glants and Joyce Stetson Toomre (Bloomington, 1997), 23–4; I. G. Pryzhkov, *Istoriia kabakov v Rossii* (Moscow, 2009), 9.

Yet if wine was relatively abundant during the Kievan period, it became less so in the centuries that followed, as Russian civilization shifted to the north-east, and as the trade routes across the Black Sea atrophied. It helped that medieval Orthodox peasants rarely took communion; given the absence of *Vitis vinifera*, the common wine grape, in Russia prior to the seventeenth century, where the wine originated when they did take communion is not known, although the Rhine region, which carried on trade with Novgorod, is one possibility. The Soviet-era wine writer Mechislav Peliakh notes that the Treaty of Pereiaslavl, which brought Ukraine into the Russian fold in 1654, was a crucial moment for Russian viniculture. Ukrainian monasteries were the source of grapes that were planted in the tsar's garden at Izmailovo on the outskirts of Moscow in subsequent decades. In his study of the seventeenth-century Russian economy, Richard Hellie identified 148 transactions for wine. This is a comparatively large data set, although Hellie recognized that most of the transactions likely involved vodka, given the indeterminacy of *vino* in Russian. Yet some transactions were clearly for wine: *vino* that was labelled as 'Rhine', 'church', or 'Spanish' sold for about three times more per *vedro* than vodka. Given the scarcity of grapes in Russia, prices for wine rose over the course of the century by an annualized rate of 0.73 per cent. As Peter the Great's early correspondence reveals, at the end of the seventeenth century, wine from Bordeaux and the Rhône, some of which was designated for the Eucharist, entered Russia via the port at Archangel. Brandy, which was made from distilled wine, was also present in the seventeenth century (six transactions), and very much coveted because it had higher alcohol content than vodka. Likewise, in the household inventories of Mikhail Tatishchev and Vasillii Golitsyn, who were among the wealthiest men of Muscovy, Hellie found wine from the Rhine, Romania, and elsewhere.[17]

It was Peter the Great who brought wine fully back to the elite Russian table after nearly a half-millennium hiatus. Nearly every memoirist and biographer of Peter mentions his love of wine; some the hijinks that ensued from wine. Johann Georg Korb, secretary to the Austrian ambassador in Moscow in 1699, described in his journal the celebratory feast that followed the executions of the treasonous *strel'tsy*:

> The banquet was remarkable for the sumptuous cookery and the costly and precious wines, which the well-stored cellar brought forth: for there was Tokay, red Buda, dry Spanish, Rhenish, red French, another as well that they call Muscatel, a great variety of hydromel [mead] and beer of various descriptions, and that complement which is not the least prized by the Muscovites, brandy.

---

[17] M. Peliakh, *Rasskazy o vinograde* (Kishinev, 1974), 36; Richard Hellie, *The Economy and Material Culture of Russia, 1600–1725* (Chicago, 1999), 85, 105–106, 579; *Pis'ma i bumagi Imperatora Petra Velikago*, vol. 1 (1688–1701) (St Petersburg, 1887), 546. My thanks to Scott Kenworthy and Nadieszda Kizenko for details about Orthodox peasants and communion.

Yet Korb also recorded the drunken and blasphemous debauchery that so often characterized court politics during the Petrine years. During the 'consecration' of Franz Lefort's palace in Moscow, Peter staged a celebration in honour of Bacchus, the Greek god of the grape harvest. The festivities included a 'sham Patriarch', 'a complete set of scenic clergy dedicated to Bacchus', a 'stark naked' and lascivious Bacchus, and of course, 'great bowls full of wine'. 'Who would believe that the sign of the cross—that most precious pledge of our redemption—was held up to mockery?' Korb wrote in his journal. In a scholarly biography of Peter, Lindsey Hughes has written that wine consumption was often a form of hazing in the Petrine court. When one of Peter's closest advisors, Aleksandr Menshikov, was caught in 1721 with wine from the Rhine, in contravention of Peter's expressed preference for Hungarian wine, Menshikov was forced to drink as punishment two bottles of the strong wine in rapid succession. Similar juvenile punishments were meted out to the persons who missed an important court funeral. Even Voltaire, writing in the 1750s and 1760s about the family strife that characterized Peter's early years, and about rumours that Peter's half-sister Sofia had tried to poison him, noted that Peter's 'true poison was the wine and brandy, in which, trusting too much to the strength of his constitution, he frequently indulged to excess'.[18]

Peter's familiarity with wine stemmed from his prodigious travels and interest in all things European. From his first incognito trip abroad, in 1697 to 1698, visits to famous wineries and wine cellars were regular parts of his itineraries. According to the historian Dmitrii Tsvetaev, who reconstructed Peter's travels in France for the journal *Russkoe obozrenie* in 1894, Peter loved to drink 'cold white wine and red wine of Nuits, but not sweet wine'. Nuits was likely Nuits-Saint-George in Burgundy, which would have meant that Peter's preferred varietals were Chardonnay and Pinot Noir. Conversely, Jakob von Staehlin, a Swabian German by birth and an important figure in Catherinian-era politics, noted in a 1788 account based on stories that contemporaries told that Peter preferred the wine of 'Cahors and Medoo [Médoc]; but having been ordered Hermitage wine [from the northern Rhône] by his physician, Mr. Areskin, on account of a diarrhoea [sic], of which he had an attack, he continued to drink it in the presence of all others.' Peter was reputedly impressed by the winemaking skills of the European clergy, whose industriousness gave him pretext to criticize the indolence of Orthodox priests back home. After being offered an especially delicious wine during a visit with an English merchant, Peter asked that the merchant's forty remaining bottles be given to him as a gift. ' "Spare them to me," said the Czar: "you cannot be without other wine equally good to give to your guests." '

[18] F. L. Glaser, ed., *Scenes from the Court of Peter the Great: Based on the Latin Diary of John G. Korb, a Secretary of the Austrian Legation at the Court of Peter the Great* (New York, 1921), 68, 126; Voltaire, *History of the Russian Empire under Peter the Great*, vol. 2 (Paris, 1901), 196; Lindsey Hughes, *Peter the Great: A Biography* (New Haven and London, 2002), 157, 187.

Peter was also generous with his own wine. He ordered that visitors to the Kunstkamera 'be offered, in my name, and at my expense, a dish of coffee, a glass of wine, or some other refreshment, in this repository of curiosities'. Peter was known to refuse the generosity of others when it suited his purposes. While Peter was visiting Karlsbad in 1711 and 1712, Charles VI, the Holy Roman Emperor, sent 960 bottles of Rhenish wine. Peter declined the gift, publicly because it was not 'conducive to the diet for using the waters', and privately because he was offended that the gift had been addressed to 'His Royal Highness' rather than 'His Imperial Highness'. After Charles properly addressed a later gift of Bohemian wine, Peter gave the wine to a local musketeer club in Karlsbad to use as a competition prize. Predictably, Peter then won the club's marksmanship contest, and shared his trophy wine with fellow club members.[19]

While discussing Mikhail Pogodin's so-called 'tragedy'—an 1831 essay that Pogodin wrote about Russia's corruption during the Petrine period—the historian and eventual anti-Bolshevik émigré Evgenii Shmurlo quoted Pogodin's famous description of the depth of the Petrine transformation: Peter's influence ranged from calendar to wardrobe, from language to table setting, from civil rank to canal dredging. Even the wine, Pogodin wrote, 'reminds us of Peter; we had no wine before him'. After the latter sentence, Shmurlo added a parenthetical, disapproving question mark, like a professor who is confused by a non sequitur in a student paper. Shmurlo likely understood that the latter part of Pogodin's statement was untrue: wine had been present in Russia long before Peter, and thus could not be couched as a symptom of corruption.[20] Regardless, both Pogodin and Shmurlo knew that the royal example was powerful. Much of the initial success of Tokaji, for instance, stemmed from its popularity among European autocrats—Peter the Great, Catherine the Great, Louis XIV, Maria Theresa, Franz Joseph, and others. From 1733 to 1800, the Russian government employed a purchasing agent in Bodrogkeresztúr to oversee shipments of Hungarian wine back to court at St Petersburg.[21] A few decades after Peter's death, Voltaire noted the shift in consumption patterns that Peter had initiated: the preferred drink of the Russian gentry had traditionally been mead, but 'of late, wine; though even with them brandy always makes a part of every repast.' Voltaire was describing what Tatiana Zabozlaeva, in her popular history of champagne in Russian culture and politics, has called the 'French landing in Russia': language, culture, consumption

[19] D. V. Tsvetaev, *Petr velikii vo Frantsii* (Moscow, 1894), 619; Jakob von Staehlin, *Original Anecdotes of Peter the Great, Collected from the Conversation of Several Persons of Distinction at Petersburgh and Moscow* (London, 1788), 64, 96, 353–4; K. L. Kustodiev, *Petr velikii v Karlsbad 1711 i 1712. Istoricheskiia vospominaniia* (Budapest, 1873), 21.

[20] E. Shmurlo, *Petr velikii v russkoi literature (Opyt istoriko-bibliograficheskago obzora)* (St Petersburg, 1889), 60. The historian Evgenii Anisimov cites a similar, albeit not identical passage from Pogodin about wine: see Evgenii Anisimov, *The Reforms of Peter the Great: Progress through Coercion in Russia*, trans. and intro. John T. Alexander (London and New York, 1993), 3.

[21] Alex Liddell, *The Wines of Hungary* (London, 2003), 271.

patterns, and of course, wine. Given the tiny size of the Russian aristocracy, the 'French landing' was a far more momentous development for Russia than for France. According to Kahan, Russia remained a 'marginal, even unimportant' factor in the French economy during the eighteenth century, given Russia's limited ability to absorb goods that France produced.[22]

As the nature of great Russian wealth began to shift at the end of the eighteenth century, from the old capital aristocracy and court favourites, who had long family histories close to power, towards persons whose income derived from commerce, industry, and tax farming, wine became a hallmark of the nouveau riche. Akakii Demidov, whose family wealth originated in the Petrine-era metal- lurgical industry in the Urals, built a wine cellar at his estate near Nizhnyi Novgorod with vintages from the Rhine and Hungary that stretched back nearly a century. For Demidov, wine was part of an eccentric, Westernized, almost hedon- istic lifestyle that was still unusual in the Russian provinces in the eighteenth cen- tury. Demidov spoke Russian poorly, 'like a foreigner', because of a childhood spent in boarding school in Holland. He was infamous for presenting huge quan- tities of food and wine to his guests, and for overseeing compulsory feasts that lasted for days. The forced consumption of the Petrine court was a clear prece- dent. Yet wine might also connote very different values. For Nikolai Mordvinov, who was a favourite of Catherine, Paul, and Alexander, as well as a self-made man and ambitious autodidact who served for three years on British naval vessels in the War for American Independence as a form of maritime apprenticeship, wine consumption was consonant with his Anglophilia, economic liberalism, and sober industriousness. In 1794 Catherine the Great awarded Mordvinov a vini- cultural estate in the Yalta Valley for his 'zealous service to the fatherland'. While in London in 1780, Nikolai Karamzin was treated to an 'authentically English' lunch with friends in Hyde Park—'roast beef, potatoes, pudding, and glass after glass of Claret and Madeira'. Karamzin wondered why his 'well-raised' English friends refused to speak French with him, given his own limited abilities in English: 'What difference is it to them?...In our so-called *good society* you would be deaf and dumb without French language.' Yet so engrained was the idea that European wine was a hallmark of cultured dining that Karamzin did not think to ask what specifically was English about the French and Portuguese wines on the table. While the revolutionary era in France—and the resulting prohibitions on the import of French wine that Catherine the Great and Paul I confirmed—made foreign wine consumption more difficult at home, Russian wine drinkers were eventually rewarded for the principal role their government played in the Bourbon Restoration. No friend of republicanism or of the economic duress

---

[22] Voltaire, *History of the Russian Empire*, vol. 2, 170; T. B. Zabozlaeva, *Shampanskoe v russkoi kul'ture* (St Petersburg, 2007), 52–76; Arcadius Kahan, *The Plow, the Hammer, and the Knout: An Economic History of Eighteenth-Century Russia*, ed. Richard Hellie (Chicago, 1985), 212.

caused by the Continental System, the house of Veuve Clicquot-Ponsardin sent an entire ship of champagne to Russia to celebrate Napoleon's defeat and the end of the revolutionary era.[23]

At the Durnovo house on the English Embankment in St Petersburg, the principal focus of Yuri Lotman and Jelena Pogosjan's study of elite dining in nineteenth-century Russia, wine from abroad was kept on display on the sideboard in the dining room. Members of the old Russian nobility, with familial connections to the Tolstoys and Demidovs, the Durnovos were part of St Petersburg's highest society, an elite that was fully Westernized in every way except politics. The Durnovo patriarch, Pavel Dmitrievich, remained a staunch defender of serfdom to the end of his life; the younger Durnovo reputedly entertained liberal ideas when young, but grew more conservative with age. The Durnovos lived in an opulent house, restored to its original eighteenth-century style, which fronted the Neva River, and which included a second-floor conservatory. In the summer, they found refuge from the urban heat at a family dacha, built in the neo-classical style, a short distance outside of St Petersburg. As Lotman and Pogosjan write, the Durnovos were among St Petersburg's 'Europeans'. Even though family life was characterized by only modest amounts of drinking, as was characteristic of the age, the Durnovos' quarterly wine shipments included 120 bottles from Château Margaux and 60 bottles of vin de Graves, both from Bordeaux, as well sherry and dessert wines from Spain. In the family cellar were rare wines purchased in large quantities on trips abroad, and prized vintages, such as 1811, when a comet seemed to herald an especially auspicious harvest. (Pushkin alluded to wine of the latter vintage in *Evgenii Onegin*, chapter 1, stanza 16.) When in Paris, the Durnovos purchased wine from the merchant Tailleur, who had many old bottles from the cellars of royalists who had fled abroad during the revolution. Yet if the Durnovos preferred French wine, they drank wine in the traditional English style, undiluted with water. (Darra Goldstein indicates in her annotations to the Lotman text that diluting wine with water was fading as practice in France as well.) Moreover, in the Durnovo house wine was consumed according to an elaborate code of connoisseurship. Soup was served with sherry. The fish course was followed by a Médoc or a Château Lafite. Roast beef was served with Port wine, turkey with a Sauterne, and veal with a Chablis. Champagne went with everything, because its presence signified formality rather than an appropriate food pairing. Lotman and Pogosjan acknowledge, nonetheless, that a 'true gourmet' would never drink champagne before the roast was served, hence Stiva Oblonsky's question about champagne to Levin in *Anna Karenina*, 'What? At the beginning?' There were different glasses for different wines on the Durnovo table; different

---

[23] Zabozlaeva, *Shampanskoe*, 129; N. M. Karamzin, *Pis'ma russkogo puteshestvennika* (Leningrad, 1984), 338; N. A. Kovalevskaia, 'Rol' vina v istoricheskikh protsessakh', in *Dionis-Vakkh-Bakhus v kul'ture narodov mira*, vyp. 2, ed. V. P. Kazarin (Simferopol, 2005), 49–50.

ways to present different wines; and certain wines, such as sweet wines from Italy and Spain, that were considered too lowbrow to ever appear on the table. Wine appreciation had come a long way in Russia in the century since Peter the Great had used excessive drinking as a form of punishment.[24]

The wine-drinking parallel between the Durnovos and the fictional Onegin is apt, because they occupied the same rarefied air of St Petersburg high society. Lotman and Pogosjan note that Onegin also drank undiluted red wine, which served to underscore his prodigality and careless wealth in the eyes of his frugal neighbours. Dinner with Lenskii began: 'Of Veuve Clicqout or of Moet / the blessed wine / in a befrosted bottle for the poet / is brought at once to the table.' But the champagne upset Onegin's stomach. In the following stanza, Pushkin indicated that bubbles born in Aÿ were a less sophisticated man's pleasure. 'For Ay I'm no longer fit / Ay is like a mistress / glittering, volatile, vivacious / and wayward, and shallow.' Instead there was the wine of Bordeaux: 'But you, Bordeaux, are like a friend / who is, in grief and in calamity / at all times, everywhere, a comrade, ready to render us a service / or share our quiet leisure.' In his commentary on *Onegin*, Vladimir Nabokov noted that Pushkin lapsed into autobiography when describing wine. These passages indicated Pushkin's own familiarity with the increasingly elaborate semiotics of wine consumption in high society. Literarily, they accomplished a sort of culinary foreshadowing of the strife that would eventually lead to Lenskii's death. Whereas Onegin had outgrown the 'shallow' pleasure of champagne, the more provincial Lenskii had not. In the final, pre-conversation stanza, after Onegin has switched to Bordeaux, Pushkin wrote 'the bright goblet / amid the table fizzes yet'. Pushkin again juxtaposed cosmopolitan sophistication and provincial aspiration at Tatiana's name-day feast, where dinner was accompanied not by an expensive French champagne that Onegin had already deemed superficial, but worse, by an inexpensive sparkling wine from the Don region, Tsimlianskoe.[25]

The significance of wine in *Evgenii Onegin* lies not so much in the fact that it is present—Pushkin's poetry is filled with wine references, and in the case of *The Bacchus Song*, which Rimsky-Korsakov put to music, with a toast for drinking wine.[26] Rather, *Onegin* shows that by the late 1820s, wine consumption had become a prism that refracted precise gradations of social status—from the worldly pretentiousness of Onegin to the earnest pretentions of the Larins. Lenskii, a graduate of a German university, occupied a middle ground—he knew

---

[24] Yuri Lotman and Jelena Pogosjan, *High Society Dinners: Dining in Tsarist Russia*, trans. Marian Schwartz, ed. and intro. Darra Goldstein (Devon, 2014), 50, 67, 141–7.

[25] Aleksandr Pushkin, *Eugene Onegin: A Novel in Verse*, vol. 1, trans. Vladimir Nabokov (Princeton, 1964), 196–7 (ch. 4, stanzas 45–7), 219 (ch. 5, stanza 32).

[26] On wine in Pushkin's writings, see Stroganov, 'Ob upotreblenii vina', 23–9; I. V. Aleksandrova and N. V. Karpenko, ' "Vina charuiushchaia sila" (Vina v lirike A. S. Pushkina i poetov pushkinskoi pleiady)', in *Dionis-Vakkh-Bakhus v kul'ture narodov mira*, vyp. 2, ed. V. P. Kazarin (Simferopol, 2005), 63–72; G. V. Priakhin and V. N. Baklanov, *Zazdravnaia chasha* (Moscow, 1996), 372–3.

the easy pleasure of French champagne, and he understood that its consumption identified him as a nobleman of a certain outlook, but he was oblivious to the more subtle pleasure of a fine Bordeaux. These were all 'Europeans', in the sense that Lotman and Pogosjan used the word; wine allowed Pushkin to disaggregate provincial aspiration from cosmopolitan weariness.

As the Larins' Tsimlianskoe suggests, the wine on Russian tables was no longer bound to be European in origin. The annexation of the Black Sea territories meant that Russia too made wine in sizeable quantities, even though connoisseurs like Onegin were prone to thumb their noses at it. Lermontov's narrator in *A Hero of Our Time* shared a bottle of Kakhetian wine with Maksim Maksimych in Vladikavkaz in the moments before Pechorin's carriage arrived. The wine helped compensate for the meagre food rations and dull the sadness surrounding the narrator's departure from the Caucasus. It was also unintentional proof of the narrator's unvoiced assessment of Maksim Maksimych, formed while listening—with some disapproval—to his tale about Bela: 'I could not help being struck by the capacity of the Russian to adapt himself to the customs of that people among which he happens to be living.'[27] The consumption of local wine thus alludes to the privations of military service in the Caucasus, which are dutifully suffered, and to the shallow imprimatur of European refinement that characterized even the officer corps. Pushkin first tried Kakhetian wine in 1829, en route to Arzrum (Erzurum) in eastern Anatolia during the Russo-Turkish War. His assessment was more positive, anticipating much of the optimism and sanguine comparison that surrounded domestic winemaking a half century later. 'Georgians do not drink in our fashion and are surprisingly strong', Pushkin wrote in his travel diary. 'Their wines do not stand up to export and quickly spoil, but here they are wonderful. Kakhetian and Karabakhian wines resemble some Burgundies.' Pushkin then described the unusual way Georgians stored wine—in 'huge jugs buried in the ground'—and the unfortunate fate of a Russian dragoon who drowned in one of these kvevris, when he tried to abscond with some of the wine inside.[28] Similarly, in Tolstoy's *Anna Karenina*, a delicious Crimean white wine—rather than a European wine—underscored the rustic fare on Levin's country table, which the visiting Oblonsky did not often encounter: 'herbed vodka (*travnik*), bread and butter, and especially, smoked goose, mushrooms, nettle *shchi*, and chicken with white sauce.'[29]

For Russia's ambitious and upwardly mobile, wine became something that one learnt, a sign of cultural refinement that was brought into high polish, like proper French pronunciation. Writing in *My Past and Thoughts*, Alexander Herzen

[27] Mikhail Lermontov, *A Hero of Our Time*, trans. Vladimir Nabokov, in collaboration with Dmitrii Nabokov (Ann Arbor, 1958), 28.
[28] A. S. Pushkin, *Sobranie sochinenii v 10 tomakh*, vol. 5 (Moscow, 1960), 431–2.
[29] L. N. Tolstoi, *Sobranie sochinenii v 22 tomakh*, vol. 8 (Moscow, 1981), 179.

recalled youthful dinners with the circle of 'Nikolais'—Ogarev, Satin, Ketcher, and Sazonov. Each brought to the meal a provision from a different store. The wine always came from the Deprez cellar on Moscow's Petrovka Street. 'Our inexperienced taste went no further than champagne', Herzen admitted, 'and was so young that we sometimes even exchanged *Rivesaltes Mousseux* for champagne'. Later in life, as an exile in the West, Herzen encountered the same inexpensive wine from the Pyrenees in a Parisian restaurant. By then, his palate had evolved beyond the tastes of his youth, and not even fond memories of Moscow helped him 'drink more than one glass'. Post-dinner conviviality with the circle of Nikolais involved even more wine: deeply philosophical and earnest discussions about how to make a proper punch—with champagne or Sauternes?[30] One did not need to be a conservative Slavophile like Pogodin to find something distasteful about Russians' efforts to educate themselves about wine. During an 1858 visit to Russia, the French poet Théophile Gautier wrote, with evident disdain, that the 'best wines of France and purest juice from our harvests are located in Russia; the best allotments from our cellars are destined for the gullets of these northerners, who pay no attention to the prices of things they drink'. Even at the Bologoe station near Tver, on the railroad line between Moscow and St. Petersburg, Gautier found Château Lafite, Château d'Yquem, Veuve Clicquot, Moët, and Sauternes. His criticism bore some semblance to Onegin's distaste for champagne: Russians were gauche, drinking French wine not out of any greater appreciation of it, but because they had the money to do so.[31]

As a result, by the end of the nineteenth century, the cultural valences of wine began to shift in ways that were sinister. Anton Chekhov, for instance, wrote two works in the late 1880s entitled 'Champagne'. The first was a darkly comical ode, which Chekhov subtitled 'Thoughts from the New Year's Hangover', and which was published in the satirical journal *Oskolki* in January 1886, just a few days after the author's supposed hangover would have faded. 'Don't believe in champagne', Chekhov warned readers.

> It sparkles like a diamond; it is clear like a forest brook; it is sweet like nectar; it is more preciously valued than the labor of a worker, the song of a poet, the caress of a woman. But…stay far away from it! Champagne is a brilliant courtesan, mixing its charm with the lies and impudence of Gomorrah, that gilded coffin full of the bones of the dead and every kind of impurity. A person drinks champagne and suffers hours of grief, sorrow, and visual deception.

It is tempting to dismiss Chekhov's sketch as pure satire, the dark musings of a writer who drank too much on New Year's Eve. Yet the following year, Chekhov

---

[30] Alexander Herzen, *My Past and Thoughts*, trans. Constance Garnett, intro. Isaiah Berlin (Berkeley and Los Angeles, 1982), 111.

[31] Kovalevskaia, 'Rol' vina v istoricheskikh protsessakh', 47; Zabozlaeva, *Shampanskoe*, 185.

published a short story with the same title and a similar theme. On New Year's Eve at a remote railroad station on the south-western steppe, a small spill of Veuve Clicquot, barely enough to fill a glass, leads to a wife's omen of misfortune in the coming year, and to the stationmaster's honest admission to himself that if that misfortune should be his wife's death, 'Even that would not be terrible. I cannot hide from my conscience: I do not love my wife!' The stationmaster, of aristocratic birth, is already unhappy in a life that has diverged from youthful plans: how can it get any worse, he asks. Only small pleasures—such as the sight of a beautiful woman on a passing train—puncture the monotony of his days. In Chekhov's formulation, the New Year's champagne is destabilizing because it brings to the surface long buried restlessness and desires; it is the snake that entices Eve, as Chekhov wrote in the initial comical sketch. A second bottle of Clicquot is opened a short while later to celebrate the unexpected arrival of the wife's aunt, the long-suffering spouse of an abusive husband. At first glance, the stationmaster can see that this woman will be his partner in adultery: 'That our guest was easy, I understood from her smile, from her smell, from the manner in which she batted and played with her eyelashes, and from the tone she used with my wife, a respectable woman.' An assignation and proclamations of love quickly follow, which are set in prose to the lyrics of 'Dark Eyes'. The affair sweeps away the stationmaster's wife, career, home, and eventually even his lover, leaving him abandoned on a dark street: 'Tell me now: what misfortune can still await me?'[32]

Part of the reason for the shift in cultural valences surrounding wine was growing concern at the end of the nineteenth century about the social toll of alcohol in Russia. As a physician, Chekhov would have seen first-hand the effects of alcoholism. Indeed, at least one biographer has noted that Chekhov's older brothers, Nikolai and Aleksandr, were alcoholics.[33] Even the allusion in Chekhov's comical sketch to Eve's temptation in the Garden of Eden would become a common trope in later temperance writings, albeit one not often associated with Chekhov, as 'Green Snake' was a Soviet-era metaphor for alcohol's seductive powers. According to Zabozlaeva, Chekhov used champagne as 'the kiss of Judas, as a symbol of treachery, hypocrisy, sycophancy'.[34] Yet there was far more at stake in Chekhov's writings than alcohol's destructiveness. Fine European wine spoke to instabilities in Russia that vodka could not, particularly the tension between a narrow elite that had been acculturated over the course of two centuries to Western patterns of consumption, and broad masses that remained oblivious to them. For Chekhov's short-story narrator, champagne was a noble birthright. The two bottles of Veuve Clicquot that he opened on New Year's Eve, however, were won in a wager. Their

---

[32] A. P. Chekhov, 'Shampanskoe (mysli s novogodnego pokhmel'ia)', in *Polnoe sobranie, sochinenii i pisem*, vol. 4 (Moscow, 1976), 282; A. P. Chekhov, 'Shampanskoe', in *Polnoe sobranie, sochinenii i pisem*, vol. 6 (Moscow, 1976), 12–17.

[33] Ronald Hingley, *A New Life of Anton Chekhov* (New York, 1976), 74–5, 104.

[34] Zabozlaeva, *Shampanskoe*, 232.

cost would have exceeded his modest stationmaster's salary. Since the time of Peter, European wine had embodied the aspirations and outlooks of Russia's elite; Chekhov used champagne to highlight the restless hearts and daily miseries of the downwardly mobile, the aristocrats without wealth.

As fine wine came to symbolize a Europeanized elite, it became the target of popular rage. Its destruction, theft, or misappropriation was a powerful manifestation of social antagonism and disorder. In Pushkin's account of the Pugachev Rebellion, wine was evidence of the pretender's great wealth: 'Our father has a lot of wine', Pugachev's soldiers told Cossacks outside of Orenburg, as if the sheer quantity of wine established Pugachev's identity as Peter III, Peter the Great's grandson and the rightful tsar whom Catherine the Great had murdered in 1763. But wine was also a reminder of oppression among the Yaik Cossacks, because its sale was monopolized by the state. And, of course, wine was a potential distraction and cause of mayhem among Pugachev's followers. Pushkin wrote that Pugachev 'smashed the barrels of wine in his *izba*, preventing drunkenness and confusion. Wine ran through the streets.' The usual caveat applies here about the indeterminacy of the Russian word *vino*, although Pushkin likely had in mind conventional wine rather than vodka in at least the final passage about smashed barrels. Nearly a century and a half later, *pogromshchiki* in Odessa were nearly as keen to loot the city's wine cellars as they were to attack their Jewish neighbours during the unrest in the fall of 1905. Robert Weinberg writes that many *pogromshchiki* started killing Jews, got distracted by the unguarded wine cellars, and then drunkenly plundered even Russian homes. For those who were politically apathetic—unaligned with either the socialist left or monarchical right—none of these actions showed much premeditation. Instead, wine, Jewish neighbours, and wealthy Russians were convenient targets for an amorphous, poorly defined rage. Even in Estonia, where in 1905 class-based grievances intersected aspirations for national liberation, workers attacked a local distillery, carrying into the street wine that was destined to become cognac. Stores that sold wine and vodka were also ransacked; bottles were smashed or handed out free of charge to passers-by. There was a carnivalesque element in much of this—for a short time, at least, the slaves would drink from the goblets of their masters.[35]

As chapter four will show, Russia's 'passage through Armageddon'—the more than six years of war, revolution, and civil war—nearly spelt the end of Russian viniculture and winemaking. It was an even greater disaster for Russia's private wine cellars, which were almost impossible to evacuate in the context of civil war, and prone to looting during moments of chaos and expropriation by Soviet authorities. By the end of the nineteenth century, one of the most valuable wine

---

[35] Aleksandr Pushkin, *Istoriia Pugacheva* (Moscow, 2019), 65–6, 112; Robert Weinberg, *The Revolution of 1905 in Odessa: Blood on the Steps* (Bloomington, 1993), 182; Ia. K. Pal'vadre, *Revoliutsiia 1905–1907 gg. v Estonii* (Tallinn, 1955), 120, 163.

cellars in the world belonged to the Russian royal family. 'All of the [royal family's] wines were exceptional', wrote Aleksandr Mosolov, the director of the household's chancellery. 'But there was a special "reserve" cellar, which contained, as it was said, the best vintages.' During the reign of Nicholas II, the special cellar at the Winter Palace was zealously guarded by Count Pavel Benkendorf, one of Nicholas's closest advisors. Access of any sort required great guile, because Benkendorf himself had to approve. 'The perfect pretext had to be found', Mosolov wrote: saints' days, family celebrations, various holidays and anniversaries. Nicholas II drank wine with nearly every meal: Madeira with breakfast, and red and white wine with lunch and dinner, all of which Nicholas insisted on pouring himself when at the intimate family table. Nicholas's father, Alexander III, brought European wines to the table only for visiting heads of state and diplomats. In more familiar settings, Alexander preferred domestic wines, many of which were from so-called 'crown estates', vineyards such as Massandra, Ai-Danil', and Abrau-Diurso, which were directly owned by the royal family, and whose revenues went to the family's upkeep. Alexander's 'wine nationalism' marked a sharp departure from the experience of his father, Alexander II, who drank only foreign wines. Perhaps familiar with Peter's hijinks, Mosolov admitted that wine no longer played the same role at court as it had during the eighteenth century. But one ancient wine ritual had survived. During coronation dinners, the palace *Oberschenk*—the senior cellar-master—gave the new tsar a golden coronation cup overflowing with wine and announced, 'His Majesty wishes to drink.' At that moment, all foreigners including diplomats, had to leave, 'because at the feast in the Palace of Facets [in the Moscow Kremlin] only His Majesty's true subjects can be present'.[36]

Shortly after the Provisional Government surrendered to the Bolsheviks, the royal family's special 'reserve' cellar was ransacked. The wine that was not destroyed or consumed in the cellar was carried out on the square, where 'the bodies of drunk persons lay about in piles'. On that night, at least, if Mosolov is to be believed, the relatively bloodless October Revolution produced a scene that 'looked like a real field of wounded soldiers'. A less ignominious fate appears to have befallen the wine in Mathilda Kshesinskaia's cellar. The lover of Tsar Nicholas II before his marriage and before he ascended to the throne, and the prima baller-ina absoluta at the Mariinsky Theatre, Kshesinskaia regularly hosted dinners in her cellar for wine lovers. Fearing retribution from the crowds, Kshesinskaia went into hiding in February 1917. Before fleeing abroad in July, she drove past her old home. In the garden was Alexandra Kollontai, wearing an ermine jacket that Kshesinskaia had left behind.[37]

Whether Mosolov's tale about the royal cellar's destruction is true is perhaps less important than the fact that he told it: the soldiers who seized the Winter

---

[36] A. A. Mosolov, *Pri dvore poslednego imperatora* (Moscow, 2014), 232–3.
[37] Christina Ezrahi, *Swans of the Kremlin: Ballet and Power in Soviet Russia* (Pittsburgh, 2012), 1–2.

Palace on that fateful night in October 1917 lacked the sophistication and erudition to appreciate the wines they drunkenly guzzled and destroyed. All the misfortune that befell Russia in subsequent years could be foreseen at that moment. As subsequent chapters will show, Mosolov's assessment was not exactly true. After the fever of revolution and civil war broke, the new Soviet government was keenly aware of the treasures hidden in private and commercial wine cellars. During the 1920s, the contents of many cellars—whose owners had fled abroad, perished, or were just trying to live modestly in the new political climate—were seized by Vintorg, the Soviet agency that administered the wine trade, and sold to the public in an orderly fashion (and at prices commensurate with values) to raise money for the domestic wine industry. Moreover, despite the fact that early Bolshevism was suffused with the values of temperance, the new Soviet state lifted the wartime prohibition on wine sales in 1920, five years before full-strength vodka was legalized. In an industry that was administered largely—but not entirely—by holdovers from the tsarist period, the idea that wine was a hallmark of civilization and that consumers should be acculturated to appreciate fine wine was never seriously questioned. To the contrary, many industry officials—regardless of class background—welcomed the possibility of a more activist, regulatory state, which would protect growers and producers from the vicissitudes of the free market. They got their wish in the late 1920s and 1930s, first when the so-called 'Great Break' destroyed the remnants of the free market, and then when Stalin himself embraced champagne as part of the good life of socialism.

During the 1930s and 1940s, wine became an important component—perhaps the central component—in a popular fascination with Georgian foodways that lasted until the end of the Soviet period. Stalin, in turn, became the Soviet Union's most eloquent toastmaster, its *tamada*-in-chief, most famously in May 1945 when he raised a glass to the central role of the Russian people in the Soviet victory over Nazi Germany. Notwithstanding the generalissimo's Georgian upbringing and rumours that his favourite wines were Khvanchkara and Kindzmarauli, both semi-sweet reds, one famous visitor to the Kremlin reported that Stalin drank red wine in the Russian fashion—diluted with vodka.[38] In the more relaxed environment of the 1960s and 1970s, foreign visitors to the Soviet Union discovered that endless toasting in the Georgian style—first to virtuous goals such as world peace and friendship among peoples, and then as the flush of alcohol took hold, to spouses, children, pets, and any number of absurdities—was a rite of passage, even when the drink du jour was more potent than wine. Wine toasting was grist for comedy in Leonid Gaidai's 1967 film, *Prisoner of the Caucasus, or Shurik's New Adventures*. The movie's title irreverently alluded to more serious works by

---

[38] Scott, *Familiar Strangers*, 87–8, 99–100; Milovan Djilas, *Conversations with Stalin* (San Diego, 1962), 77.

Pushkin and Tolstoy; its dialogue provided one of the most commonly recited toasts of the final Soviet decades:

> My great-grandfather says, 'I have the desire to buy a house, but I do not have the ability. I have the ability to buy a goat, but I do not have the desire.' Let's drink to our abilities always corresponding to our desires.

Toasting—along with excessive alcohol consumption in general—became a common subject of ridicule in the satirical journal *Krokodil*. A cartoon entitled 'When a Cheat Sheet is Customary' lampooned a New Year's toastmaster, presumably drunk, who had to scrawl the new date on his palm: 'Friends, I wish you a happy nineteen…sixty…sixty…' Likewise, toasting to the self-evident inadequacies of Soviet life, always in ways that were outwardly sincere, was the template for an oft-repeated, easily adaptable joke: 'To the wonderful floor', the toastmaster at a housewarming party declared, standing amid broken parquet.[39]

In the post-Stalinist decades, as domestic wine production grew rapidly, industry officials readily acknowledged that bad wine remained the rule rather than the exception. The poor quality of commercial wine in Georgia was dramatized in Otar Iosseliani's 1966 film *Falling Leaves*.[40] Iosseliani juxtaposed a young winemaker's refusal to approve for bottling wine he knew to be undrinkable with an opening montage of traditional Georgian production methods and wine consumption: harvest by hand, a barefoot crush, fermentation in underground clay amphorae (kvevris), and the drunken male revelry of the *supra*. The implication was that the idealistic winemaker was defending the cultural heritage of Georgia. As Iosseliani's film suggested, the tsarist-turned-Soviet civilizing process had been half successful: 'grape wine' of poor quality was produced in great quantity, yet it was comparatively scarce on store shelves in the big cities of the north (which explains Stroganov's surprise at encountering it), and per capita consumption was modest, about 12 litres per person per year (compared to 104 litres per person in France and 110 litres per person in Italy).[41] While these statistics likely understate consumption, because they do not account for household production in Georgia and elsewhere in the south, the divergence between production and consumption was real. It can be explained partly by the export of Soviet wine, which began in earnest in the 1960s and 1970s, mostly to reliable allies in Eastern Europe, but also on occasion to points farther west (a topic in chapter 6). It stemmed principally, however, from the Soviet practice of strengthening and sweetening finished wines with grain alcohol, beet sugar, and fruit juice. Referred to colloquially as *bormotukha* (from the verb 'mumble') and *chernila* (ink), these

---

[39] E. Shcheglov, 'Kogda privyk pol'zovat'sia shpargalkoi', *Krokodil* 36 (1967): 15; I. Sychev, 'Novosel'e', *Krokodil* 8 (1977): 3.
[40] *Giorgobistve*, dir. Iotar Iosseliani, 1966.   [41] Valuiko, *Vinogradnye vina*, 5–6.

adulterated wines were much beloved by Soviet consumers. The fact that industry officials elided *bormotukha* from per capita consumption might be considered a mild form of subversion: Soviet citizens deserved better, even if they did not realize it themselves.

Despite these difficulties, the dream of turning the Russian Empire, and later the Soviet Union, into a wine superpower, and Russian and Soviet citizens into wine drinkers sophisticated enough to discern good from bad, never died. The Durnovo family in St Petersburg, 'Europeans' in Lotman and Pogosjan's description, thus found counterparts a century and a half later among Soviet diplomats and cultural figures who discovered in their travels abroad wines that had once been commonplace in Russia. Tsarist Russia's most prolific wine writer, Mikhail Ballas, offered inspiration to an unlikely and eclectic cohort of late-Soviet connoisseurs and wine writers, who penned works extolling wine's sublime and ineffable characteristics for readers all too familiar with the scourge of vodka. Prince Lev Golitsyn, the chief vintner for the southern crown estates and an indefatigable champion of elitist, artisanal ways in the face of the democratizing impulses of modern oenology, had a kindred spirit in Pavel Novichkov, who was chief winemaker at Massandra's wine factory no. 1 before his arrest in 1951, and who insisted on building his own barrels out of a belief that better wine would result. These persons, and many others, animate the seven chapters that follow.

Chapter one, '*Terroir*', examines the landscapes of winemaking in late-imperial Russia through the writings of Mikhail Ballas, a Bessarabian nobleman and wine-maker who won the Emperor Alexander III Prize in Viniculture for a magisterial six-volume set that exhaustively chronicled the persons, places, and histories of winemaking within the empire. While Ballas was sceptical that a sense of *terroir* existed in Russia—in large part because consumers more often saw wine as an interchangeable commodity rather than a singularity linked with place of provenance—he described something in his writings that resembled the way *terroir* would come to be understood a century later: a mutually constitutive relationship between vine, soil, weather, culture, and winemaker. Chapter two, 'Science', reconstructs the international commercial and scientific networks that brought phylloxera—the so-called 'great wine blight'—to Russia in the 1870s and 1880s, as well as a flawed technology for combatting it. Central to Russia's anti-phylloxera campaign was Aleksandr Kovalevskii, a pioneering natural scientist whose distinctively Russian reading of Darwin's speciation theory made him sceptical of the only sure-fire cure for the blight, grafting imperilled European scions onto immune American rootstock. Chapter three, 'Authenticity', follows debates around the turn of the century between Prince Lev Golitsyn, Russia's most bombastic and critically acclaimed vintner, and Vasilii Tairov, a provincial upstart and the influential editor of *Vestnik vinodeliia* (Winemaking Bulletin), about the defining characteristics of wine. Was wine artisanal by nature, a 'natural' product diminished by any form of adulteration and remediation? Or was wine the result of myriad forms of unnatural, human intervention? Chapter four, 'Commerce', examines the fate, in the first decade after the revolution, of Russia's winemakers, hardly a lot noted for their socialist sympathies, who found a *modus vivendi* with a Soviet state that promised to regulate a wine trade that for many years had benefitted merchants and harmed producers. Wine made for strange bedfellows during that first Soviet decade. Chapter five, 'Hospitality', describes the investigation and arrest of several winemakers in Crimea for the 'misuse' of wine in the years after the Second World War. It argues that winemakers were participants in a 'gift economy', sharing wine in gratis tastings with old allies and new friends. Chapter six, 'Taste', follows the travels of a prominent American connoisseur and vinicultural scientist, Maynard Amerine, through the Soviet Union's vinicultural territories during the early 1970s, and the return of the Soviet Union, after a fifty-year hiatus, to international tasting competitions. It argues that these interactions constituted a highly unusual front in the Cold War, as the Soviet Union's wine producers sought critical approbation from persons whose values diverged sharply from their own. Chapter seven, 'Quality', traces efforts to improve the quality of Soviet wine in the 1970s and 1980s in hopes of mitigating the allure of vodka and its deleterious health effects. During these years, a small number of wine writers produced a literature of connoisseurship that sought to acculturate Soviet citizens to subtleties of fine wine. Finally, the book ends with a conclusion that assesses the place of wine in post-Soviet Russia and its 'near abroad', and the future of winemaking in places once seen as so promising.

1

Terroir

The Landscapes of Winemaking

Perched on a hill high above the Alazani river plain, with views of the snow-capped Caucasus to the north, the red-tiled roofs and rough-hewn, brick and stone buildings of Sighnaghi (see Figure 1.1) might pass on first glance for a village in Veneto or Piemonte. Nearly 600 metres below Sighnaghi, the Alazani plain widens from a narrow canyon in the north-west, where the river's churning waters turn placid as the terrain flattens, to about twenty kilometres in the south-east, where Georgia meets Azerbaijan. From there the Alazani drains into the Mingachevir reservoir in eastern Azerbaijan; its waters then descend to the Caspian Sea via the Kura River. Along the axis of the Alazani, on the valley floor, the land slopes imperceptibly toward the river and the soils are alluvial, rich with nutrients deposited from mountain aeries. Lining the Alazani are many of the most famous locations of Georgian winemaking—Tibaani, Mukuzani, Telavi, Gurjaani, Napareuli, Tsinandali. Archaeological evidence indicates that the Alazani plain was the cradle of viniculture, where humans first mastered the grape at least 6,000 years before the common era. The local harvest festival, Rtveli, when grapes are crushed and must is poured into clean kvevris for fermentation and storage, is thought to be scarcely younger.

In an empire more often associated with taiga, tundra, and steppe, Kakheti was unfamiliar landscape. Like the southern shore of Crimea and the Dniester and Prut river valleys in Bessarabia, which drew sanguine but not entirely unmerited comparisons in the nineteenth century to Languedoc-Roussillon, Mosel, and even California, Kakheti was blessed with dramatic scenery, temperate weather, and vinicultural traditions that predated the Russian encounter by many millennia.[1] The wine of Kakheti thus served as a synecdoche for the geographical and climatic diversity of the empire, bottled proof that not all of the tsar's lands were in winter's grip. As Mark Bassin has argued about the popular fascination with the Amur region in the mid-nineteenth century, geographical imagination tends to say more about the imaginers than the lands being imagined, an observation that

---

[1] Andreas Schönle, 'Garden of the Empire: Catherine's Appropriation of Crimea', *Slavic Review* 60, no. 1 (Spring 2001): 1–23; L. A. Orekhova, '"Krym skoro zastavit zabyt', chto est' Shampan' i Bordo": stranitsy istorii krymskogo vinodeliia', in *Dionis-Vakkh-Bakhus v kul'ture narodov mira*, vyp. 2, ed. V. P. Kazarin (Simferopol, 2005), 16–34; Ruben Guliev, Robert Guliev, Aleksandr Prilipko, and Valentin Stremiabin, *Vino, vlast' i obshchestvo* (Kyiv, 2006), 12.

Whites and Reds: A History of Wine in the Lands of Tsar and Commissar. Stephen V. Bittner, Oxford University Press (2021).
© Stephen V. Bittner. DOI: 10.1093/oso/9780198784821.003.0002

Figure 1.1. Sighnaghi in the 1870s. Miriam and Ira D. Wallach Division of Art, Prints and Photographs: Photography Collection, The New York Public Library, 'Kakhetia. Town of Signakh' (n.p., 1870–79).

holds true for the empire's vinicultural territories, and for the writers who sought to describe them.[2] Yet places like Kakheti, where the imperial gaze might have discerned a palimpsest of Europe in traditions of winemaking that were older than Russia itself, also confounded the type of Orientalist arrangements that concern Bassin and other scholars. It was almost as if the vineyards of Bessarabia, Crimea, and Georgia offered Russia a more ideal version of itself, a version where the civilizing process did not entail the slavish imitation and adoption of European modes of consumption, but the cultivation of characteristics intrinsic to the empire. Not even the most patriotic Slavophile could have imagined the irony.

Kakheti and places like it were also potentially destabilizing, because they suggested that the currents of imperialism flowed not only from the centre outwards, via the state's efforts to catalogue, control, and modernize its non-Russian populations, but in the opposite direction as well, through consumption and

[2] Mark Bassin, *Imperial Visions: Nationalist Imagination and Geographical Expansion in the Russian Far East, 1840–1865* (Cambridge, 1999), 5–8.

acculturation. This and the following two chapters examine different aspects of the tension that arose between the idea that wine production was a European characteristic, and the reality of where and how wine was made in the Russian Empire. By the end of the nineteenth century, it had become an article of faith among ambitious Russian vintners that fine wines reflected the ecological subtleties of the places they were made. This probably reflected awareness of French winemaking's elaborate geographical hierarchies, which would coalesce in the early twentieth century in the *appellation d'origine contrôlée* system, and the idea of *terroir* as something essential to the production of grapes, an association that dates to the thirteenth century. Food and place have become so inextricably linked in French culture, and *terroir* such a prominent expression of that linkage that other languages have produced no equivalent word, using the French term instead.[3]

The significance of *terroir* to fine wine, even questions about whether it exists, remain the subject of endless debate in the world of wine. Kolleen M. Guy notes that as early as the sixteenth century the meanings of *terroir* had moved beyond the ecological prerequisites for viniculture to the link between soil and the sensory experience of wine. During the eighteenth century, *terroir* became medicalized, encompassing a host of strengths and maladies—in people as well as comestibles—that were linked to place of provenance.[4] The Franco-Prussian defeat in 1870, which was blamed in popular discourse on the health of the nation, thus became one of the pretexts for codifying a hierarchy of *terroir* in the AOC system. While *terroir* is now invoked in the affirmative—fine wine is distinguished by a *goût de terroir*—for much of its history it was a pejorative for flawed wine; it referred to unsavoury tastes and smells that were thought to have emanated from the soil. In the twentieth century, as vinicultural scientists began to question the principles underlying *terroir*, such as the idea that grapevines 'transmutated' the soil into berries, much like an alchemist producing gold, *terroir* gradually widened its definitional arc. It came to express the unquantifiable and often indescribable interactions, over long periods of time, between soil, climate, vine, and winemaker. Wines with the most acclaimed *terroir*—such as the blends of Grenache, Syrah, and Mourvédre that have made a village outside of Avignon famous—invariably had histories that stretched back many centuries. In Châteauneuf-du-Pape and similar places, viniculturalists painstakingly bred varietals perfectly suited for local soil and climate; winemakers, in turn, honed a set of practices that accentuated those varietals. Success was gauged by trial and error, over very long periods of time. It was almost as if *terroir* turned into an anthropological concept, into a 'theory of how people and place, cultural tradition and landscape ecology, are mutually constituted over time', at precisely the moment natural science began to

---

[3] Thomas Parker, *Tasting French Terroir: The History of An Idea* (Berkeley, 2015), 3.
[4] Kolleen M. Guy, *When Champagne Became French: Wine and the Making of a National Identity* (Baltimore, 2003), 42–3.

undermine its conceptual foundations. It is for this reason that *terroir* is often couched as an ineffable quality, best expressed in spiritual or poetic terms. 'In the end', the vinicultural scientist and *terroir* sceptic Mark A. Matthews writes,

> terroir is a shibboleth that establishes an in-group in a world unto itself. This isn't wine appreciation, and it certainly doesn't reflect interest in the grapevine; it is more like wine snobbery.[5]

The purpose of this chapter is not to challenge or affirm the reality of *terroir* as a characteristic manifest in fine Russian wine. It shows instead that the idea of *terroir* existed among Russian vintners at the end of the nineteenth century, and that its existence says something important about vintners' aspirations and the localities where they made wine. However, if the idea of *terroir* existed, the reality of *terroir* in the bottle, by consensus, did not. Indeed, in Russia's long dalliance with French language and culture, few imported ideas have proven more frustrating. Coming into Russia's vinicultural lexicon at the end of the nineteenth century, *terroir* was almost always invoked to refer to something that Russia lacked: consumers who appreciated the ecological subtleties and serendipities of winemaking enough for winemakers to cultivate those characteristics.[6] Even in coveted vinicultural regions such as the south shore of Crimea, where vineyards were planted with an eye toward the microclimates created by mountains, valleys, and the sea, the difficulty that most growers and producers had in turning a profit suggested that the burgeoning Russian middle class, contrary to the aristocracy, did not much care for wine made in the European fashion. Consumers instead preferred the sugared and fortified concoctions that merchants blended in their stores and warehouses, and that comprised the vast majority of late-tsarist Russia's domestic wine sales. In Russia's marketplace for wine, *terroir* was often an advertising challenge for unprincipled merchants, who sought to conjure not only desirable varietals but the regions where grapes were grown: whites from Crimea, reds from Kakheti, and dessert wines from distant Santorini. The absence of formal protections for *terroir*, in the form of guarantees of truth in advertising, was thus a central component of the so-called 'crisis in winemaking' that preceded the passage in 1914 of Russia's short-lived wine purity law (the topic of chapter 3). Perhaps characteristic of their predicament, Russian vintners could not agree on a

---

[5] Heather Paxson, 'Locating Value in Artisan Cheese: Reverse Engineering *Terroir* for New-World Landscapes', *American Anthropologist* 112, no. 3 (September 2010): 444; Mark A. Matthews, *Terroir and Other Myths of Winegrowing* (Berkeley, 2015), 163, 204–205. Sophus A. Reinert has recently used the idea of *terroir* as a way of understanding the geographies of the Enlightenment: see Sophus A. Reinert, 'Northern Lights: Political Economy and the *Terroir* of the Norwegian Enlightenment', *Journal of Modern History* 92, no. 1 (March 2020): 78–115.

[6] A. Volzhenikov, *Sovremennoe polozhenie vinodel'cheskogo khoziaistva na IuBK* (Simferopol, 1901), 1–4.

standard transliteration of the thing they lacked, sometimes rendering it *terruar* and *terrua* in the same pages.[7]

While few ambitious Russian vintners could have imagined any affinity with the wine forgers who nearly drove them out of business, they shared a view about the importance of place. For vintners, wine drinkers needed to be acculturated to subtleties of place and the premiums place commanded, in large part because of the labour and investment that were required to cultivate those subtleties; for wine forgers, place was a culinary challenge that required blending the right proportions of inexpensive, low-quality, and geographically non-descript table wine (so-called chikhir) with sugar, grain alcohol, dye, and a whole variety of different herbs and spices. In short, for neither vintner nor forger was wine an interchangeable commodity; wine's diversity reflected the localities where wine was made. Drawing on the works of the chef Patric Kuh and the food historian Rachel Laudan, the anthropologist Paul Manning has underscored a similar valuing of locality in recent decades in California. The emergence of a distinct Californian epicurean culture, in which wine has played a prominent part, was predicated upon a 'semiotic transition from the "large" California, the California of the Central Valley, California as Agricultural Conglomerate, to the "small" California of wine labels and Chez Panisse menus'. In the context of foodways that were increasingly standardized and industrialized, this amounted to a 'reverse engineering' of *terroir*, a recreation of artisanal ways and small geographies of production, such as the appearance after 1980 of more than fifty legally defined and sharply demarcated viticultural areas, which stretched from Temecula in the desert northeast of San Diego to the foggy Sonoma coast. To borrow Rachel Laudan's formulation, the values of production in California winemaking shifted from an egalitarian and industrialized 'Culinary Modernism' to an elitist and artisanal 'Culinary Luddism'.[8]

Russian vintners did not attempt to 'reverse engineer' *terroir* in the sense of their New World counterparts a century later. There were no modern foodways against which they were rebelling, no 'Culinary Luddism' to be reclaimed in an economy of standardized wine production. In fact, as chapter 3 will show, quite the opposite was true: many of the same growers and vintners who were most optimistic about the possibilities of Russian winemaking were proponents of a set of scientifically-informed best practices that promised to standardize grape growing and winemaking, and thus make good wine more plentiful and less expensive. Yet in privileging locality as an essential characteristic of fine wine, Russian vintners were undermining claims about the universalism of their scientific arsenal.

[7] Saistorio tsentraluri arkivi [Central State Archive of Georgia, hereafter STA], f. 243, o. 7, d. 355, l. 27 and pamphlet after l. 50.

[8] Paul Manning, *The Semiotics of Drink and Drinking* (London, 2012), 23; Patric Kuh, *The Last Days of Haute Cuisine: America's Culinary Revolution* (New York, 2001); Rachel Laudan, 'A Plea for Culinary Modernism', *Gastronomica* 1, no. 1 (Winter 2001): 36–44.

Some places were just better than others when it came to wine, and no amount of vinicultural or oenological expertise could rectify the inequality of location.

This is where the instability lay: the growing emphasis on locality as the essential characteristic of great wine raised questions about the role of science in viniculture and winemaking. In an empire where wine production and consumption were understood to be European traits, where the economies and cultures of winemaking existed principally in the non-Russian periphery, and where the imperial core generally lacked long-standing familiarity with wine, science was Russia's contribution to domestic winemaking. The emerging sense of *terroir* undermined the importance of this contribution.

The latter tendency was especially evident in the work of late-tsarist Russia's most prominent wine writer—Mikhail Konstantinovich Ballas, who despite using the term only twice, and only in reference to wines spoiled by an unsavory *goût de terroir*, described something that resembled the ways *terroir* would come to be understood in the latter half of the twentieth century.[9] Long before *terroir* took an anthropological turn, Ballas wrote about the geographical and climatic diversity of empire, the vinicultural possibilities inherent in that diversity, and most important, the ways that human activity and ecology intersected in vineyards to produce fine wine. Unlike his counterparts in the small world of Russian wine writing, who underscored above all the modernizing and civilizing role that the tsarist government played in the vinicultural belt, Ballas's work could be read in subversive ways. Wine that reflected the subtleties of place and the localized skills of the people who made it often came from the imperial newcomers—typically wealthy Russian estate owners who were the beneficiaries of state policies to encourage winemaking, and who were the harbingers of vinicultural and oenological modernity. But it also came from unexpected places.

*   *   *   *   *

In 1913, a book entitled *A Jubilee Historical and Artistic Commemoration of the 300th Anniversary of the Reign of the Sovereign House of Romanov* was published in Moscow. Clumsy title aside, the book was meant to be a collector's item. The embossed cover showed portraits of the first Romanov tsar, Michael, whose election by the Assembly of the Land spelt the end of the Time of Troubles, and the man who would very soon turn out to be the last Romanov tsar, Nicholas II. Surrounding their portraits were gilded frames, set below the two-headed eagle that symbolized Russia's connection to the lost Orthodox civilization of Byzantium. Below was a pedestal, painted to look as if it were marble—the solid foundations of the house of Romanov. The book offered a snapshot of Russian officialdom and high society at its apogee. After surveying the history of the

---

[9] Mikhail Ballas, *Vinodelie v Rossii*, vol. 6 (St Petersburg, 1903), 173, 179.

Romanov family, the book included brief biographies of the leaders of church and state, and prominent persons in the military, sport, industry, commerce, and finance. These were the luminaries of the Russian Empire, the beneficiaries of the benevolent and wise rule of the Romanovs. Inclusion in the volume was an honour, proof of one's standing in Russian society.

Among the biographies of regional administrators was an entry for Mikhail Ballas. Formally posed in the accompanying photograph in a charcoal business suit, whose cut revealed a matching vest, long necktie, and a white shirt with a high collar, the aristocratic Ballas appeared considerably younger than his years. His hair, though receding, was still dark and his moustache drooped stylishly, a bit like Taras Shevchenko's. Ballas's jubilee biography indicated that he was born in 1857, although other accounts date his birth to 1851. After attending Moscow University, Ballas entered state service as an assistant to an ober-secretary in the courts, eventually becoming a civil magistrate in St Petersburg. At the time of the Romanov anniversary, Ballas was a privy councillor, the third civil rank, and marshal of the nobility in Akkerman uyezd in southern Bessarabia, where Ballas owned two estates, Iash-Murza and Varatik. There his family, which was of Greek origin, had deep roots: his grandfather, one of just five noblemen in all of Akkerman in the 1820s, was active in local administration and helped organize the construction of the famous Greek-revival cathedral in nearby Izmail. Ballas was a long-time contributor to the journal *Vestnik vinodeliia* (Winemaking Bulletin) and a member of the Imperial Society for Agriculture in Southern Russia, which met in a building off the municipal garden on Deribasevskaia Street in nearby Odessa. According to later accounts, Ballas died 'circa 1918', around the time that the Kingdom of Romania annexed Bessarabia in the wake of the Treaty of Brest-Litovsk. Ballas's fortune—and indeed the autocracy's fortune—had fallen far in the five years since the jubilee.[10]

Ballas's biographer mentioned only in passing that Ballas had won the Emperor Alexander III Prize in Viniculture for his six-volume set, *Vinodelie v Rossii* [Winemaking in Russia], which was published in St Petersburg between 1895 and 1903. In terms of ambition and breadth, Ballas's work was without precedent in tsarist Russia. Ballas devoted a volume to each of the six winemaking regions in the empire: Crimea, the steppe portion of Tauride guberniya, the Don, and Astrakhan; the western Caucasus; the eastern Caucasus; the northern Caucasus; southern Russia, Bessarabia, Kherson, Podolsk, and Ekaterinoslav; and Asiatic Russia. He exhaustively chronicled the history of viniculture and winemaking in each region, from its earliest, pre-Russian instantiations to recent decades, when viniculturalists began to replant their vineyards with European varietals.

---

[10] *Iubileinoe istoricheskoe i khudozhestvennoe izdanie v pamiat' 300-letiia tsarstvovaniia der-zhavnogo Doma Romanovykh* (Moscow, 1913), n.p.; M. A. Peliakh and N. S. Okhremenko, *Rasskazy o vinogradariakh i vinodelakh* (Kishinev, 1982), 23.

He provided tables that showed growth in the area of plantings and the volume of production from about the mid-nineteenth century. He described local growing conditions, including soil characteristics, weather, forms of cultivation, common varietals, common types of pestilence and disease, and typical harvest dates and practices. Unusual for his day, Ballas devoted an entire chapter to the quality of wine that emanated from many of the regions, linking it to the volume of sales, the prices wines commanded, land values, and ultimately the profitability of viniculture as a profession in late-tsarist Russia. The late-Soviet wine writer, Mechislav Peliakh, who like Ballas wrote for both specialist and non-specialist audiences, and the Magarach vintner Nikolai Okhremenko described Ballas's work as a 'unique encyclopaedia of viniculture and winemaking'. The six-volume set was such a rare, invaluable source on viniculture that Konstantin Frank, who trained as a winemaker in Odessa, worked in inter-war Soviet Georgia, and became one of the principal architects of winemaking in New York's Finger Lakes region, carried the books out of Odessa as he fled the advancing Red Army in the waning months of the Second World War. That set, one of the few that exists in North America, now resides in Special Collections at Cornell University's Mann Library. The marginalia in Frank's hand suggests that Ballas's collected wisdom reverberated far beyond the borders of the old tsarist empire.[11]

Yet if Ballas's encyclopaedia was unique in terms of ambition and scale, it belonged to a certain style of wine writing in nineteenth-century Russia. Almost as soon as the vinicultural economies of the south were brought into the imperial fold, self-identified men of science began to document the region's landscapes, their potentials, and the traditions of their vinicultural denizens in ways that were part farmer's almanac and part rudimentary ethnography.[12] Nowhere was this more evident than in Crimea, which quickly became the empire's most described and analysed vinicultural territory. In 1839, for instance, the Imperial Society for Agriculture in Southern Russia commissioned a report on winemaking in the Alma Valley, just north of Sevastopol. Unlike other regions along the Crimean coast, temperatures in the Alma Valley often dipped low enough in the winter months for snow to accumulate. Here Greek and Karaite viniculturalists had devised an arsenal for unforgiving winter weather that bore some resemblance to late-Soviet vinicultural practices in Ukraine, where vines were trained to be flexible enough to be detached from trellises in the autumn and buried beneath the ground. Greek and Karaite growers built seasonal mounds around their vines, which ranged in height from twelve *vershki* (approximately a half metre) to a full *arshin* (three-quarters of a metre). In the spring, when the ground was free of

[11] Peliakh and Okhremenko, *Rasskazy*, 21. On Frank, see Tom Russ, *Finger Lakes Wine and the Legacy of Dr Konstantin Frank* (Charleston, SC, 2015).

[12] On the domestication of Crimea's vinicultural economy, see Kelly O'Neill, *Claiming Crimea: A History of Catherine the Great's Southern Empire* (New Haven, 2017), 219–58.

snow—which was the only 'mistake-free barometer'—the vines were freed from the mounds so they could blossom. The first buds generally appeared between 2 and 10 April, the first pruning two or three weeks later. To protect grape clusters from rot, the remaining, unpruned stalks were wound around 'wooden forks' that stood three-quarters of an *arshin* high. In the lower reaches of the Alma Valley, vineyards benefitted from irrigation systems; at the upper end of the valley, there was either sufficient rain or the land was too rocky for excavation. During harvest, which generally fell between 22 and 25 September, grapes were crushed in the 'Tatar fashion' (*po tatarski*), by one or two pairs of bare feet, before fermentation and barrelling. Indicative of the general primitive state of winemaking in Crimea, barrels of new wine were stored outside, rather than in cellars, and then sold to merchants from Kharkov, Poltava, and Romny (north-eastern Ukraine).[13]

The Imperial Society's investigation of the Alma Valley was an early example of the scientific tilt of vinicultural writing in nineteenth-century Russia, yet it embodied several of the characteristics that would come to define the genre in the decades preceding the publication of Ballas's work. First, in his attention to the heights of mounds and wooden forks and the dates of bloom and harvest, the Imperial Society's investigator diligently measured and quantified everything that could be measured and quantified. He was not alone. The year before, in 1838, 'state councilor Steven', who was likely Christian von Steven, the Finnish-born botanist who was one of the founders and the first director of the Nikitskii Botanical Garden outside of Yalta, tried to gauge the total volume of wine production in Kherson guberniya and the average prices for which it sold. In Steven's early years as director, the Nikitskii Botanical Garden became a centre for experimental and practical viniculture, despite suffering from such dire labour shortages that Steven petitioned the tsarist government for the right to purchase fifty serfs. He was offered convicts and orphans instead. Steven wrote prodigiously about silk making, viniculture, and horticulture; many of his 'observations' and 'short essays' comprise the foundation of the botanical garden's library. A decade later, Fr. Dombrovskii counted the total number of vineyards in Tauride guberniya in 1832 and 1848 (1,219 and 2,801, respectively), vines (5,846,205 and 35,577,000), volume of production (482,735 and 822,330 *vedra*, or roughly 5.9 million and 10.1 million litres), revenue from that production (1.1 million and 2.3 million silver roubles), and for 1832, the number of vineyard landowners (370), who owned about 60 per cent of all vines in the guberniya. (Presumably, the remaining 40 per cent were under a form of Tatar collective ownership—*cemaat*—which was similar to the Russian peasant commune.) Dombrovskii then disaggregated his tallies for each uyezd within the guberniya.[14]

---

[13] *Pribavleniia k listkam Obshchestva sel'skogo khoziaistva iuzhnoi Rossii, vinodelie v Alminskoi doline v Tavricheskoi gubernii* (Odessa, 1839), 37–9.

[14] St. sov. Steven, *Shchelkovodstvo, vinodelie i sadovodstvo iuzhnykh gubernii Rossii v 1838 godu* (n.p., n.d.), 6–7; Peliakh and Okhremenko, *Rasskazy*, 6–7; Fr. Dombrovskii, *Vzgliad na sostoianie*

Similar efforts to count and collate had been underway in Bessarabia since at least the early eighteenth century, when Dimitrie Cantemir, who would become a member of the Royal Academy of Berlin, described the role viniculture played in local peasant life, and how it linked peasants to international commercial networks. In the decades after the Treaty of Bucharest in 1812, which brought Bessarabia into the empire of the tsars, Karl Tardan (Tardent), the son of the founder of Shabo (Chabag), the Swiss vinicultural colony near the mouth of the Dniester, became one of the leading vinicultural scientists and pedagogues of the day. Among Tardan's many published works was an authoritative manual on and guidebook to viniculture in the Dniester and Prut valleys. Russian ampelography— the science of vine classification and description—has similarly deep roots. It dates to at least 1802, when the Prussian botanist Simon Pallas, who three years earlier had likely produced Crimea's first sparkling wine on his south shore estate, published a description of the vineyards in Astrakhan guberniya. Later ampelographic work was undertaken by Petr Keppen, who travelled the backroads of Tauride guberniya in the 1820s and 1830s as a silk inspector, carefully cataloguing the vines that he encountered. Even at the end of the nineteenth century, the crown vinicultural estates in the Caucasus, whose revenues went directly to the maintenance of the royal family, were investing in infrastructure to gather raw meteorological data.[15] These and dozens of similar studies produced sufficient data about viniculture that the Central Statistical Committee in St Petersburg produced an authoritative chronicle in 1877, which tallied and collated virtually every imaginable category of vinicultural data going back to the 1820s: plantings, production volumes, revenues, topographies, altitudes, average temperatures, the average number of days with precipitation, all-time high and low temperatures, common varietals by village, the costs of vineyard maintenance, sugar contents, and so on. If, as Ian Campbell has argued about the tsarist empire in distant Central Asia, the lack of basic data—the 'lifeblood of the state'—produced a sort of imperial blindness in the late eighteenth and early nineteenth centuries, then the vineyards of Crimea and Bessarabia and later the Caucasus stand out for being comparatively well-probed and catalogued. Here the Russians counted, compiled, and collated.

Second, in his description of winter mounds, wooden forks, and a crush that occurred barefoot, in the 'Tatar fashion', the Imperial Society investigator helped

vinodeliia i sadovodstva v Tavricheskoi gubernii v 1848-om godu (Simferopol, 1849), 5–9, 21. On cemaat, see O'Neill, *Claiming Crimea*, 183.

[15] Dimitrii Kantemir, *Opisanie Moldavii* (Kishinev, 1973), 34–5; K. I. Tardan, *Vinogradarstvo i vinodelie* (Odessa, 1862); Peliakh and Okhremenko, *Rasskazy*, 8–9, 21; I. Bok and G. Ershov, eds., *Vinogradarstvo i vinodelie v Rossii v 1870–73 godakh*, Statisticheskii vremmenik Rossiiskoi imperii, seriia II, vyp.15 (St Petersburg, 1877); STA, f. 351, o. 1, d. 2, l. 47; Ian W. Campbell, *Knowledge and the Ends of Empire: Kazak Intermediaries and Russian Rule on the Steppe, 1731–1917* (Ithaca and London, 2017), 1, 13–30.

exoticize local and often indigenous vinicultural traditions for an audience that assumed a priori that there was a scientifically informed set of best practices, and that these practices were of European origin and Russian transmission. A. Volzhenikov, who was among the most eloquent champions around the turn of the century for the cultivation of distinct Crimean *terroirs*, thus declared that it was impossible to speak about viniculture prior to Mikhail Vorontsov, the Cambridge-educated governor of New Russia who took a special interest in the creation of a domestic wine industry in the 1820s and 1830s. Despite many millennia of vinicultural experience in the Caucasus and elsewhere, wine before Vorontsov's benevolent patronage was made in 'old fashioned, primitive ways, and the resulting product was not suitable for sale beyond the local population'. Bok and Ershov, the editors of the 1877 statistical chronicle, began with a similarly dubious assertion that Crimean viniculture was sustained after the fifteenth century, when the peninsula came under Turkish suzerainty, only by Jews, Armenians, and Greeks. They presumably had in mind viniculture that produced, in their view, decent grapes, because they later detailed the backwardness of contemporary Tatar practices. Tatar vineyards, which often had only half the number of plantings per desyatin as non-Tatar vineyards, were inefficient. Tatars did not properly prune their vines. Tatars planted vines in small holes rather than in the scientifically proven *plantage* (trenching) style. Dombrovskii complained that Tatar growers near Perekop, in northernmost Crimea, were impervious to outside advice and assistance, despite the fact that they cultivated a region far more prone to drought and inhospitable weather than coastal areas.

> We will not lay blame for the harmful resistance of some Tatars, who seem to be prejudiced against everything that promises to destroy their age-old negligence in almost all economic activities and endeavors. Because they are at the lowest level of material, mental and moral development, some Tatars are not amenable to economic improvement.[16]

Bigotry aside, there were clear misrepresentations in Russian accounts of Tatar viniculture. Crushing grapes by foot in the 'Tatar fashion', for example, remained common in parts of Western Europe, such as the Portuguese Douro, well into the twentieth century. The practice was mechanized because of rising labour costs, not because of misplaced concerns about hygiene or sanitation. Moreover, the

---

[16] Volzhenikov, *Sovremennoe* polozhenie, 13–14; Bok and Ershov, *Vinogradarstvo i vinodelie*, 78–9, 109; Dombrovskii, *Vzgliad na sostoianie vinodeliia*, 16. On Vorontsov, see Anthony L. H. Rhinelander, *Prince Michael Vorontsov: Viceroy to the Tsar* (Montreal and Kingston, 1990). On viniculture in Crimea during the Ottoman period, see O. Halenko, 'Wine Production, Marketing and Consumption in the Ottoman Crimea, 1520–1542', *Journal of the Economic and Social History of the Orient* 47, no. 4 (2004): 507–47. Kelly O'Neill, *Claiming Crimea*, 30, has argued that the acculturation of Tatars was a distinguishing characteristic of Russian imperial policies in Crimea, and is the reason 'Crimea was viewed by Russia neither primarily as a colonization project nor as an internal resettlement project'.

modern alternative that Russian observers promoted in the nineteenth century, the wine press, was in fact ancient itself. It dates to at least the second century BCE, when Cato described a lever press in *De agri cultura*.[17] Russia's wine writers may have understood that vinicultural backwardness had its advantages, which is why they devoted so much time and effort lamenting it. At the turn of the century, Tatar growing costs were thought to be only half of a typical vinicultural estate's, because the latter was prone to engage in expensive vineyard maintenance—vine training, pruning during dormancy, irrigation, removal of ancillary blooms, and so on. If the point of viniculture was to turn a profit, Tatar growers and the legions of small-scale vintners who turned their grapes into wine at very low cost were among the most savvy and successful on the peninsula. Tatar viniculture may have been primitive, but it was widely understood to be a contributing factor to the difficulty many vinicultural estates had in turning a profit. Both stood to gain from growing consumer demand for Crimean wines, but one did so at half the cost.[18]

The conflation of ethnicity and vinicultural acumen was a common trope in Russia's nineteenth-century wine literature. It likely had some traction among consumers as well. Carol Stevens has recently described the premium commanded by wines from the Swiss community at Shabo. Other communities of European colonists around Odessa, such as Liustford, which was settled by families from Württemberg and Bavaria, likely benefitted from a similar wine ethnophilia.[19] Yet the association between ethnicity and skill was not perfect, which meant that Tatar viniculturalists did not have a monopoly on bad practice. In Feodosia and Simferopol, centres of Russian life on the peninsula, grape must was fermented in round or four-cornered vats (*tarapany*), which were rarely cleansed of the rotten residue from previous harvests. In Kherson guberniya, the vinicultural techniques were so rudimentary that they contributed to the general difficulty peasants had eking out a profit. Many peasants tore out their vineyards and planted grain instead, which was more predictable and easier to maintain. In 1882, a commission to promote viniculture in the hills outside of Sevastopol noted that profitability depended on the adoption of modern modes of cultivation and winemaking: 'It is still the case that we use techniques that we have inherited from the ancient inhabitants of Crimea'—mixing wine with water (sometimes from the sea!), storing in clay vessels, and using flavour additives. The author of an 1896 tourist guidebook to Tauride guberniya, which included not

---

[17] See A. Dinsmoor Webb, 'Crushing', in *The Oxford Companion to Wine*, ed. Jancis Robinson (Oxford, 3rd ed., 2006), 217; Jeremy Paterson, 'Press', in *The Oxford Companion to Wine*, 545.

[18] Volzhenikov, *Sovremennoe polozhenie*, 21.

[19] Carol B. Stevens, 'Shabo: Wine and Prosperity on the Russian Steppe', *Kritika: Explorations in Russian and Eurasian History* 19, no. 2 (Spring 2018): 292–8; K Shul'tsa, 'Neskol'ko slov o vinogradarstva v Odesskom uezde', in *Trudy komiteta vinogradarstva Imperatorskogo obshchestva sel'skogo khoziaistva iuzhnoi Rossii*, vyp. 1, 1898–1900 (Odessa, 1901), 172–3.

only Crimea but a broad swathe of the mainland from Kherson to Berdiansk, advised readers that the quality of winemaking in the region was 'primitive'. 'Educated viniculturalists' made great wine, he wrote; the vast majority of viniculturalists in the region, simple peasants, did not.[20] Iakov Bank, an early Russian champion of training vines to grow *en chaintres* (a pre-trellising technique, where vines developed two long oblique arms that ran parallel to the ground), and the author of a vinicultural and real-estate primer for wealthy individuals who were seduced by the romance of Crimean winemaking, was even more frank: 'You want to buy an estate on the south shore of Crimea? Mercy, for what reason am I asking such a question? Who does not yet know that Crimean estates are unprofitable and lead to ruin?' Investors in a vineyard estate could expect to find 'buildings, which are not always luxurious, extensive park lands, which are more or less neglected', as well as 'bad roads, irrigation systems that have no water, and ancient vineyards, recognizable by their pathetic, sickly vines that long ago stopped producing grapes'.[21] The reality of an estate vineyard in Crimea in the 1880s remained a far cry from the famous châteaux of Bordeaux. Compared to the posh vacation culture of Yalta, the amenities of a vinicultural estate were spartan.

Finally, despite Bank's plea for realistic expectations, embellishment about landscape and climate was a common trope in Russia's nineteenth-century wine literature. From almost the moment of first contact with the Black Sea littoral, Russia's wine writers drew comparisons between the empire's vinicultural territories and more famous *terroir* elsewhere. Behind the patriotic bombast was genuine wonder that large-scale viniculture was possible in the Russian Empire, and excitement about the possibilities. In January 1853, a speaker at the Imperial Society for Agriculture in Southern Russia noted that the steppe of New Russia, after a dry summer, bore some resemblance to the savanna of southern Africa. Even Bank underscored the climatic similarity between the south shore of Crimea and the region around Bologna and upper Provence, which were at roughly the same latitude. 'Winter, in the narrow sense of the word, with ice and blizzards, occurs only in places distant from the coast or poorly protected by the yayla ridge.' In sixteen years of meteorological observation, the Nikitskii Botanical Garden recorded only one freeze in October (1861), and two in April (1861 and 1875). The average daily temperature in Yalta was 13.6 degrees Celsius; in Sevastopol, 11.6. Here some varietals could be left to ripen on the vine until late October. Even the southern shore's marginal soil, which was so rocky that pickaxes were often needed to clear it for cultivation, proved to be an unexpected blessing, as vines that struggled to put down roots were thought to produce

---

[20] Bok and Ershov, *Vinogradarstvo i vinodelie*, 111; Steven, *Shchelkovodstvo*, 7; S. Mokrzhetskii, *Iz ekskursii po vinogradnikam Tavricheskoi gubernii* (Odessa, 1896), 5; *Doklad komissii po razvitiiu vinodeliia v okrestnostiiakh Sevastopolia* (Sevastopol, 1882), 5.

[21] Iakov Bank, *O primenenii novogo sposoba razvedeniia vinogradnikov v razstilku (en chaintres) k mestnym usloviiam iuzhnogo berega Kryma* (Moscow, 1885), 1.

superior wine. Dmitrii Mendeleev, who in addition to his career as chemist and inventor was a public advocate for domestic winemaking, wrote that

> more so than any other European country, [Russia] is blessed with lands suitable for viniculture…The production of wine is of such immense value and significance that all warm countries engage in it. Among these countries, our south still does not occupy its proper place, but in time it will play the leading role in all of Europe.[22]

Amid these riches of landscape and climate, the principal challenge was pairing varietal to location. In Crimea, botanists at the Nikitskii Botanical Garden had been 'crossing' varietals, in effect creating new ones, since the 1830s and 1840s. Yet contrary to the Soviet period, there was little belief that Crimea needed its own types of grapes. Nor was there any conviction that Crimea's indigenous grapes, grown by Tatars and others, were superior. Instead, European varietals were always thought to be best. Thus, Bok and Ershov argued that the south shore of Crimea was better suited for Burgundies—Pinot, Chardonnay, Gamay, and Aligoté—than Burgundy itself, especially when it came to producing wines with high enough alcohol contents to prevent spoilage. 'Crimean Burgundies significantly surpass in alcohol content single-estate French wines, and thus resemble something between a Burgundy and wines from farther south.' In Bessarabia, the verdict about which varietals were ideal was more equivocal. While Bok and Ershov noted that Shabo and a handful of aristocratic estates made high-quality wines from European grapes—Chasselas, Pinot, Muscat, Gamay, and Pinot gris— the majority of grapes in the guberniya were of local origin, or so far 'degenerated' from their European original as to be unrecognizable. Each peasant village grew just a few types of grapes that had been brought to the region in the distant past, and whose names had long ago been forgotten. They were called 'ordinary' grapes, 'Bessarabian red or white' grapes, or 'simple' grapes. Yet because the varietals had been cultivated to the peculiarities of their locations, they gave reasonably good wine. Peasants' chief concern was always productivity—how many grapes each vine produced—rather than varietal. This meant that vineyards were often a mishmash of different types of grapes. Once an older vine was deemed unproductive, it was uprooted and replaced with a younger vine, regardless of varietal.[23]

Prior to the publication of Ballas's six-volume masterpiece, this was the clearest description of the promise of Russian viniculture. The Russian Empire was better suited for some European varietals than the famous vinicultural regions in which

---

[22] Mendeleev is quoted without attribution in Peliakh and Okhremenko, *Rasskazy*, 13. *Vstupitel'naia beseda o sel'skom khoziaistve Novorossiiskogo kraia, 12 ianvaria 1853 goda* (Odessa, 1853), 5–7; Bank, *O primenenii novogo sposoba*, 2–3; V. Grossman, *Kratkii ocherk sovremennogo vinodelia* (Feodosia, 1861), 2–3.

[23] Bok and Ershov, *Vinogradarstvo i vinodelie v Rossii*, 12, 16.

they originated. Moreover, viniculture in the Russian Empire had developed its own beneficial peculiarities, in large part because of its historic isolation and impoverishment. In a land where there was a great deal of pessimism that *terroir* existed as a bottled characteristic, this was a recipe for something different. It took the prodigious talents of Mikhail Ballas to draw out its implications.

*   *   *   *   *

Ballas's first volume, which was devoted to Crimea, the steppe portion of Tauride guberniya, the Don, and Astrakhan, was published in 1895. For many decades already, Crimea had been the most celebrated vinicultural region of the empire. Its winemaking history—as Ballas's bibliography attests—was well-documented at the time of writing. Moreover, Crimean viniculture had the makings of a good tale of government beneficence. From almost the moment of annexation, Crimean viniculture benefitted from the patronage of powerful persons in St Petersburg, Odessa, and elsewhere. Grigorii Potemkin, who later arranged Catherine the Great's famous trip to the peninsula, received Joseph II's permission in 1785 to bring an Austrian vintner to Crimea to cultivate Tokaji, which had been a favourite in the Russian court since the time of Peter. In 1798, an official delegation visited the peninsula to ascertain what steps might be taken to encourage viniculture. Among its recommendations was the founding of a vinicultural field school, which opened in the Sudak valley in 1804 at the behest of Victor Kochubei, then Alexander I's Interior Minister. Until 1809, the school was led by the Prussian botanist Simon Pallas. In 1824, Alexander I visited the school, famously sketching the surrounding landscape from its balcony. The Nikitskii Botanical Garden was founded in 1811 with the patronage of Duc de Richelieu, who was governor of New Russia before returning to France during the Bourbon Restoration. One of Richelieu's successors in Odessa, Vorontsov, oversaw the founding of the Magarach Institute in Yalta in 1828, supporting it with funds gathered from an annual levy on Tatars. Between 1846 and 1853, Magarach sent over 650,000 vines to the Caucasus, Transcaucasia, and Bessarabia. Under Vorontsov's stewardship, more than four million European vines—from France, Spain, Greece, and the Rhine—were planted along the southern shore. Parallel investments were made in infrastructure—such as the pier at Yalta—and in laws that regulated the sale of alcohol to promote Crimea's rapidly growing wine industry.[24]

More than any other region of the empire, consequently, the patterns of viniculture in Crimea came to resemble those of Bordeaux and other prestigious wine regions in France and Italy, where a wealthy class of estate owners cultivated grapes side-by-side with peasants. In Crimea especially, grape growing and winemaking became something of a wealthy man's hobby. Ballas estimated that in

---

[24] Mikhail Ballas, *Vinodelie v Rossii: istoriko-statisticheskii ocherk*, vol. 1 (St Petersburg, 1895), 13–17, 20.

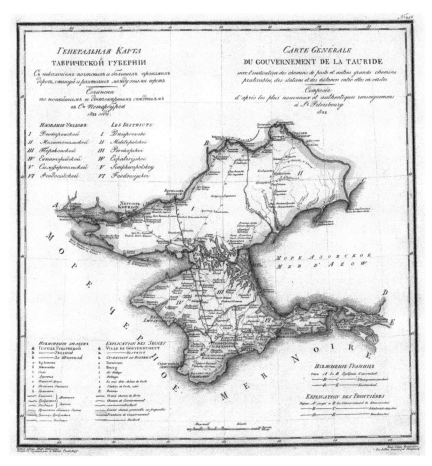

Figure 1.2. Map of Tauride guberniya, 1822, before construction of a road along the southern shore west of Sudak. *General'naia karta Tavricheskoi gubernii s pokazaniem pochtovykh i bol'shikh proezzhikh dorog stantsii i razstoianiia mezhdu onymi verst* (St Petersburg, 1822). Library of Congress. Geography and Map Division.

1823 there were between two and five Russian landowners who were engaged in viniculture on the entire southern shore (see Figure 1.2). By 1837, there were 105, an increase that was encouraged by the construction of a road between Alushta and Foros. 'Only after this time', Ballas writes, 'did there appear an array of luxurious villas, palaces, and cottages, and the beginning of proper cultivation'. The coastal strip from Alushta to Feodosia, where the mountains sloped more gently to the sea, was even more intensely cultivated, despite the absence of a modern road. Here Ballas counted 300 vineyards in the 1830s, including an estate that Vorontsov had spent a sizeable fortune to develop. Among the new arrivals on the southern shore were many of the empire's most famous aristocratic names— the Potemkins, Naryshkins, Golitsyns, Demidovs, even the family of the wife of

Alexander I, who was comfortably ensconced in Oreanda. In the hills near Sevastopol, Inkerman, and Balaclava, where there was a large military presence, viniculture became a popular pastime for high-ranking officers. There were foreign colonists who cultivated grapes, the descendants—often many generations removed—of foreign settlers who cultivated grapes, foreigners in the service of the tsar who cultivated grapes, and even just foreigners, who saw in Crimean viniculture a good business opportunity. In 1805, one grower on the southern shore, Ruv'e, enticed two vintners from Málaga to move with their families and a nursery of vines to Crimea. After Sudak was determined to be inappropriate, the Spaniards planted twenty desyatins (roughly twenty-two hectares) near Laspi, where steep mountains would protect the Spanish and Italian varietals from the cold winds of the steppe. In the Sudak valley, Greek varietals were planted near the end of the eighteenth century on the lands surrounding Prince Nassauskii's dacha. They had been carried to Crimea from the Greek islands by a vintner named Kebak. One of Magarach's first vintners was Frants (Frantz) Gaske, who with his family moved from France to Yalta in 1836 to oversee the production of table wines. By the mid-1840s, Gaske was producing under the Magarach label Riesling, Claret (a Bordeaux-style blend), Pedro, Port wine, and later Cabernet, Pinot gris, Traminer, Verdelho (traditionally a Madeira varietal), Muscat, and Albillo (a Spanish varietal traditionally grown in the Ribera del Duero region north of Madrid). Gaske would remain at Magarach for twenty-seven years. In Simferopol, which prior to the 1830s was a bit of a vinicultural backwater, a trio of German merchants and 'Father Wyman' (*pater Viman*) planted vineyards along the Salhir River. German colonists in Kronental, west of Simferopol, planted grapes, as did foreigners in Alma valley. At the time Ballas published his first volume, the largest growers in Simferopol uyezd, tending between 30,000 and 100,000 vines, were a hodgepodge of different ethnicities: Meier, Kazi, 'the descendants of Papalaksy', Revelioti, Aleksiano, Bardak, Kakoraki, and others. To oversee the storage and sale of Crimean wine in Simferopol, Vorontsov hired a Frenchman. This may have been Francois Nouveau, a Frenchman who opened a wine store on 'Rue de Ribas' (Deribasevkaia Street) in 1842, and then moved his operations to the Caucasus in 1847, soon after Vorontsov made the same move.[25]

The results were good. Reflecting on the quality of Crimean viniculture in the 1890s, after roughly a century of Russian involvement on the peninsula, Ballas wrote that 'climate, the appropriate selection of varietal for the underlying soil, the conditions of cultivation, and the way the wine was made' were the chief determinants of quality. He noted the marginal-soil paradox common to viniculture—namely, that gravelly and stony soils produced better wine than black soil (*chernozem*), which is why the dramatic landscape of the southern shore was ideal. Ballas gave his top endorsement to the Magarach vintners at the Nikitskii Botanical Garden. Over forty years Magarach had produced consistently good wines, as determined in *degustatsii* where tasters assessed strength (*krepost'*), richness (*gustota*), alcohol (*spirtuoznost'*), and bouquet. (*Krepost'* was a straightforward quantitative measure of alcohol content by volume; *spirtuoznost'* appears to have been a qualitative measure of the taste or burn of alcohol on the palate.) Magarach's best bottles tended to be fortified wines made from Muscat or in the style of Lacrima Christi, a wine traditionally made from several different varietals grown on the slopes of Mount Vesuvius. These were the Russian wines that showed best in international exhibitions. At the 1873 Vienna World's Fair, a fortified wine made from Traminer and Muscat grown at the Nikitskii Botanical Garden won top honours. Trailing not far behind were wines from the estates of princes Vorontsov, Kniazhevich, and Funduklei. According to Aleksei Ermolov, who would later become Minister of Agriculture and State Property, Russian wines showed so well in Vienna that many foreigners were caught off guard. Among dry wines, Ballas singled out an 1891 Muscat and Sauternes (Sémillon) made from grapes grown at Oreanda, and an 1890 'Lafite', a Bordeaux-style blend made from Cabernet and Pinot Franc grapes grown at Magarach.[26]

Vineyard prices in Crimea reflected proximity to quality. Vineyards that had an established record of producing good wine sold at a premium, as did neighbouring vineyards, regardless of past successes. At the time Ballas was writing, vineyards near Yalta and Alushta (which lay on opposite sides of the Nikitskii Botanical Garden), and near Balaklava fetched the highest prices when they came to market, as much as 4,000 roubles per desyatin (1.1 hectare), and sometimes more depending on location. Uncultivated land on the southern shore could sell for as much as a 1,000 roubles per desyatin, particularly if the parcel was situated close to town and ocean. Over the course of the nineteenth century, land prices on the southern shore had increased many times over, partly because of investments made in viniculture, partly because of the development of transportation infrastructures that made the southern shore in particular and Crimea in general more readily accessible, and partly because of growing demand for the lifestyle that the southern shore afforded. In 1817 Richelieu purchased 140 desyatins near Gurzuf for 750 roubles. In 1834, Vorontsov purchased forty of those same desyatins, on which Richelieu had built a manor house, for 25,000 roubles. Only in less prestigious Simferopol uyezd had vineyard prices remained more or less stable at the end of the century, selling in the mid-1890s for roughly the same prices as they had in the 1870s, 800–1,200 roubles per desyatin. Explaining why vineyards

---

[26] Ballas, *Vinodelie v Rossii*, vol. 1, 115–21.

near Yalta, Alushta, and Balaclava commanded such astronomical prices, Ballas wrote that 'here a great deal of money and labor have been invested in expensive knowledge, mastery, and careful cultivation not only by prosperous, educated landowners, but small-scale Tatar proprietors as well, who own 738 desyatins of vineyards in Yalta uyezd'. Ballas could have been writing about Châteauneuf-du-Pape, or any place in the Rhône or Tuscany or Mosel where human ingenuity and ecology intersected to produce fine wine. In a land where *terroir* was thought to be mostly absent as a characteristic manifest in bottles, Ballas was describing *terroir* as it would come to be understood a century later.[27]

To be sure, the story that Ballas told—about the Russian presence generally being favourable to the local vinicultural economy and to the quality of wine it produced—would have been familiar to readers. 'Influenced by the special care of the government and thanks to a whole array of deeply thoughtful measures', Ballas wrote in conclusion to the Crimean volume, 'starting at the beginning of this century and especially in the 1830s Crimean viniculture grew with particular strength and energy'. Russian wine writers had been saying similar things from almost the moment Crimea was brought into the imperial fold. Yet there were also unsettling components in Ballas's tale. The conflation of ethnicity and vinicultural acumen was less absolute in his telling than in earlier accounts. Tatars had become something more than a foil for benevolent imperial power and the policies it engendered. Tatars still grew, in great abundance, grapes that became wine of poor quality. In Yalta uyezd, however, they were no longer the embodiment of stubborn backwardness against which the Russian harbingers of modern viniculture and oenology could be juxtaposed. Moreover, wealthy and educated Russian producers, though present in increasing numbers on the southern shore, were just one part of the ethnic and confessional hodgepodge that comprised Crimea's vinicultural economy—foreign businessmen, colonists from Germany, grape growers from Málaga, and estate owners many generations removed from family origins elsewhere in Europe. To play upon a question that Lenin would famously ask a few decades later, *kto kogo*? Who was acculturating whom when it came to wine expertise? Indeed, Ballas wrote that the largest impediment to Crimean viniculture at the end of the century lay not in Crimea proper, but in the Russian lands to the north, where inexperienced consumers—lacking the knowledge to differentiate between good and bad wine, and unfamiliar with the regions where grapes were grown—were prone to manipulation and forgery. Adulterated concoctions based on inexpensive wines from Feodosia uyezd or from the far western regions of Crimea, which misleadingly bore the southern shore label, were immensely popular among consumers because of their low prices and high alcohol contents. The chief problem that Crimean winemaking faced was not so

---

[27] Ballas, *Vinodelie v Rossii*, vol. 1, 134–5.

much the ubiquity of backward vinicultural practices, Ballas argued, but the unrefined tastes and credulity of the Russian drinking public: if it was labelled 'southern shore', it must be good.[28]

The growth of viniculture in Crimea in the nineteenth century roughly paralleled developments in other parts of the empire where there were large Russian populations. In these regions, according to Ballas, foreign expertise and the patronage of powerful persons were decisive. Thus, in the southern Don and Azov region, where viniculture had origins among the ancient Greeks who settled on the shores of the Azov Sea in the seventh and sixth centuries BCE, and where local Cossack communities had produced wine for their own consumption prior to the Russo-Turkish wars that led to Russian annexation, Peter the Great played a central role. After winning the Azov Fortress in peace negotiations with the Ottoman Empire in 1700, Peter ordered vines from France, Hungary, and Astrakhan to be planted in the region. In 1711, the same year that the Ottomans regained control of the fortress, Peter brought a Frenchman from Berlin, Possuet, to oversee the cultivation. After a state visit to Paris in 1718, Peter sent several barrels of Pousset's wine as a gift to French military invalids. In the decades that followed, many of the same names that figured prominently in the development of Crimean viniculture—Pallas, Nassauskii, and others—lent their wealth and expertise to viniculture along the shores of the Don River and Azov Sea. Catherine the Great's successor, the ill-fated Paul, ordered an expedition to the Don around the turn of the century. Among other things, it recommended the formation of a regional vinicultural school. In 1808, the government of Alexander I decreed a tariff on foreign wine imports, with the intention of pumping up demand for domestic wines from the Don and elsewhere. During these years, the Ministry of Internal Affairs enticed a number of growers from the Rhine to sign ten-year contracts with the Don Host. After Western travellers wrote favourably about the quality of wine that came from the Don—'white wine that differs little from champagne, and red that reminds one of the best varietals from Bordeaux'—the Don Host intensified efforts to capitalize on the region's vinicultural potential. It first invited French winemakers to move to the region. Rebuffed, it later decided to send young Russian vintners to Champagne and Burgundy on two-year apprenticeships. After a series of weather-related disasters in the early 1840s and growing competition from Crimea, the Don Host again proposed sending young winemakers abroad for study.[29]

In the western and northern Caucasus, regions that were notable for having sizeable Muslim populations (which was not always a contraindicator of wine consumption), vinicultural development required a similar mixture of foreign input and Russian wealth. Ceded to Russia in stages over the late eighteenth and

---

[28] Ballas, *Vinodelie v Rossii*, vol. 1, 152–6.   [29] Ballas, *Vinodelie v Rossii*, vol. 1, 164.

early nineteenth centuries in wars with the Ottoman Empire, and not fully pacified until long after that, viniculture here remained relatively rudimentary, even at the end of the nineteenth century. Ballas described the Black Sea coast from Tuapse to Sochi as a jungle of untamed vines at the moment of annexation, evidence perhaps of a lost vinicultural past, of proximity to the place where *Vitis vinifera* was thought to have originated, or just neglect. Viniculture was common among state peasants who settled in the region, and in Abkhazian and Terek Cossack communities. The latter was depicted in the 1961 Soviet film *Cossacks*, which was based on Leo Tolstoy's 1863 novella of the same name. The film portrays Cossack girls picking grapes from un-trellised vines that were wound around sticks planted upright in the ground. Among the few exceptions to the general underdevelopment of the region were the crown estates Dagomys, near Sochi, and Abrau (later Abrau-Diurso), near Novorossiysk. The key figure in the development of both was Grand Prince Mikhail Nikolaevich, the fourth and final son of Tsar Nicholas I, and governor general of Caucasus from 1862 to 1882. In 1871, Mikhail Nikolaevich planted 2,000 vines from Kakheti. After two-thirds of the vines perished, he sent a local horticultural official abroad to purchase 20,000 Riesling and Blauer Portugieser vines for planting at Abrau, Dagomys, and a local vine nursery. By 1892, Abrau had ninety-two desyatins of vines under cultivation; in 1895, the vineyard area had grown to 133 desyatins, after a sizeable investment in Crimean vines. 'The influence of Abrau winemaking on the development of this branch of agriculture in the region is undeniable', Ballas wrote, as it became a school for local growers and winemakers. During the 1890s, as the Black Sea coast became an increasingly popular destination for wealthy Russians, numerous other estate vineyards were built near Sochi and Novorossiysk, the latter encouraged by a new rail link with Rostov-on-Don.[30]

In Astrakhan, which had been incorporated into Russia in the sixteenth century and was thus the empire's oldest vinicultural territory, the story was similar, albeit with a less auspicious ending. Positioned along a major trade corridor between Persia and Europe, the first wine varietals were likely brought by passing merchants and cultivated by local monks. Ballas writes that Persian travellers brought Georgian varietals to Astrakhan at the beginning of the seventeenth century; other sources credit German merchants and European varietals. Adam Olearius, who passed through Astrakhan in 1636 on his way to Isfahan, wrote that local gardens were provisioning the table of the tsar himself. 'I am in doubt

---

[30] Ballas, *Vinodelie v Rossii*, vol. 2 (St Petersburg, 1896), 20, 23–5; *Kazaki*, directed by Vasilii Pronin, 1961. On viniculture and wine consumption in the North Caucasus, see Thomas M. Barrett, *At the Edge of Empire: The Terek Cossacks and the North Caucasus Frontier, 1700–1860* (Boulder, CO, 1999), 98–100, 136–7; Austin Jersild, *Orientalism and Empire: North Caucasus Mountain Peoples and the Georgian Frontier, 1845-1917* (Montreal and Kingston, 2002), 44. On railroads as a spur for viniculture, see Z. D. Adalova, 'Vliianie stroitel'stva zheleznoi dorogi na razvitie vinodeliia v Dagestane v kontse XIX—nachale XX vv.', *Voprosy istorii* no. 11 (November 2011): 150–3.

whether [the fruit] of the Holy Land could be better; so delicious were the Melons and Peaches, and the Kernels of the Grapes were as big as Nuts.' Several decades later, Peter the Great ordered the cultivation of Hungarian varietals and brought Possuet from Azov to oversee production. Possuet would remain in Astrakhan for thirty-seven years. In the mid-eighteenth century, a Serbian formerly in the service of the Holy Roman Empire, Ivan Parobich, was named director of the State Bureau for Horticulture in Astrakhan. Parobich enlisted the help of an Italian vintner, Rizzo, who made wine according to 'French and Italian methods'. The adoption of tax farming (*otkup*) on alcohol in 1767 spelt the end of the monopoly on winemaking that the State Bureau on Horticulture enjoyed. Thereafter, the locus of Astrakhan winemaking shifted to a handful of wealthy estate owners, such as the writer Nikita Beketov, a favourite of Empress Elizabeth and the governor of Astrakhan during the 1760s and 1770s. Using Turkish prisoners of war, Beketov built an estate on Turtle Island, a short distance from Astrakhan, that included a wine cellar large enough to accommodate production from the 90,000 vines he cultivated. Beketov enticed a cooper from Germany to travel to Astrakhan to teach local agronomists about wine storage and how wine matures in the barrel. In 1794, the year of Beketov's death, Simon Pallas came to Turtle Island to advise on the planting of 60,000 additional vines.[31]

Ballas admitted that Beketov's results were modest.

> It is necessary...to note that these first experiments in producing mature wine...were not successful. In the impartial judgement of the local director of the economy, von Radingh, Beketov himself recognized that Hungarian wine made from vines sent from Tokaj and Persian raisin wine did not resemble their prototypes...Von Radingh saw the reason for the wine's poor quality in inexperience and in the characteristics of the soil, which contained a significant quantity of salt.

Ballas also emphasized climatic difficulties and costs inherent in them: hot and dry summers and autumns that made viniculture impossible without expensive investments in irrigation. Indeed, around the turn of the century, facing competition from Kizliar growers, many Astrakhan viniculturalists turned their attention to table grapes, which were thought to be less risky. Astrakhan viniculture then went into protracted decline. By the 1840s, many growers were letting their grapes

---

[31] Ballas, *Vinodelie v Rossii*, vol. 1, 193–8; Adam Olearius, *The Voyages and Travels of the Ambassadors from the Duke of Holstein to the Great Duke of Muscovy and the King of Persia*, trans. John Davies (London, 1662), 169; N. D. Chekulaev, 'Dvortsovoe khoziaistvo v Derbente v nachale XVIII v.', *Voprosy istorii* no. 5 (May 2010): 154–6. On *otkup* in the nineteenth century, see Yanni Kotsonis, *States of Obligation: Taxes and Citizenship in the Russian Empire and Early Soviet Republic* (Toronto, 2016), 68. On Beketov and Turtle Island, see Boris Merkulov, *Selo Nachalova, Cherepakha tozh, 1766–2016* (Astrakhan, 2016), 32–47. My thanks to Rachel Koroloff for sharing the latter text with me.

rot on the vine rather than harvest crops that had no buyers. The Ministry of State Property tried to encourage viniculture among Kalmyks and state peasants in the steppe portion of Astrakhan guberniya, but it never convinced more than a few persons to invest in vineyard construction. A vineyard census in the 1850s revealed just a few dozen planting sites resulting from the endeavour. By the 1850s, Astrakhan had become known chiefly as a supplier of chikhir, a low-quality white wine that was prone to spoilage because of low alcohol content, and was thus not suitable for cellaring or transportation to the markets of the north without adulteration. 'The condition of Astrakhan viniculture at the beginning 60s was lamentable', Ballas wrote. While this proved to be the pre-war and pre-revolution nadir for viniculture in Astrakhan—the advent of steamship passage on the Volga was already helping stimulate a revival, Ballas noted—the empire's first vinicultural territory would never be its most important.[32]

Given Ballas's penchant for sanguinity, his unsparing description of the downward trajectory of viniculture and winemaking in Astrakhan, over nearly a century, stands out in his six-volume work. It was indicative of the sad state of affairs in Astrakhan that Ballas devoted only four chapters to it; Crimea, in contrast, got fourteen. Neither the Don nor Astrakhan merited a separate chapter on the quality of wine. However, despite running counter to the triumphalism that is central to much of Ballas's narrative, Astrakhan's vinicultural history shared certain features with more celebrated regions, such as Crimea: foreign expertise was an indispensable factor in its development, but not the singular factor, since it was paired with an activist state and wealthy (mostly Russian) estate owners who were determined to turn Russia into a vinicultural power.

*   *   *   *   *

It was in Georgia and Bessarabia where the Crimean developmental pattern was most clearly shattered. In neither region was there a sizeable class of wealthy Russian estate owners, who served as conduits for modern vinicultural and oenological science, who planted European varietals, and who produced wine of comparatively high quality. Like Crimea, both regions were beneficiaries of tsarist policies meant to encourage viniculture. Yet in Georgia, where these policies were most pronounced, Ballas wrote that they had only modest impacts, and the quality of wine remained overwhelmingly poor even at the end of the nineteenth century. Nearly a hundred years of coexistence had mainly proven that Georgia's ancient wine culture, in which viniculture was ubiquitous and wine a dietary staple, was not easily or quickly transformed. In Bessarabia, to the contrary, the

---

[32] Ballas, *Vinodelie v Rossii*, vol. 1, 199–200, 204–205. On the history of Kizliar viniculture, see N. N. Garunova, *Ocherki istorii vinodeliia i kon'iachnogo proizvodstva na kizliarshchine v XVII–XXI vv.* (Makhachkala, 2009).

story was different. As it turned out, the Bessarabians did not need Russian help to make fine wine.

Georgia was incorporated into the Russian Empire with its largely Christian population in 1801 to fortify the southern border against Persian and Ottoman threats. Ballas wrote that the earliest textual evidence of viniculture in Georgia came from the fifth-century BCE account of Xenophon; he could not have imagined subsequent archaeological findings that dated viniculture's origins to the seventh millennium BCE. From the first centuries of the common era, Georgian wine could be found in the markets of the Near East, evidence of a commercial ubiquity that would fade in the modern era. Even in the nineteenth century, the residue of ancient winemaking was evident. At the time Ballas was writing, a monastery near Telavi, which was constructed in the fifth century, was thought to be using wine storage vessels (not kvevris, in Ballas's description) that were part of the original structure. A visitor to Tiflis in the 1840s noted that many vineyards had been in the possession of single families for more than 500 years, a continuity that was unusual in Russia's young wine industry.[33]

Russia moved quickly to support the vinicultural economy in Georgia after annexation. More than ninety vineyards were brought under state control. In 1807, the main tsarist administrator for Georgia, Prince Ivan Gudovich, ordered the Hungarian director of the Tiflis Academy to find ways to improve the quality of wines that came from state vineyards, in large part to inspire local Georgian and Armenian vintners to undertake similar measures. When Christian von Steven visited Georgia in 1811 to conduct a survey of local agriculture, he noted that the Alazani river plain in Kakheti was cultivated almost entirely with grapes—an unbroken swathe of vineyards—and that viniculture comprised the primary source of economic wealth in the region. At the invitation of the tsarist government, the first German colonists—486 families from Württemberg—arrived in Georgia in 1817, splitting into a number of different vinicultural settlements. In 1828, the tsarist government formed a 'Special Committee' to investigate ways to disseminate modern vinicultural practices among the local population, to establish a 'model farm' in Kakheti, and to promote the sale of Georgian wines in Russia. State efforts to encourage and modernize viniculture intensified in 1844, when Mikhail Vorontsov, who had played a seminal role in the development of the Crimean wine industry, was named viceroy to the Caucasus. Vorontsov ordered the creation of two nurseries to help familiarize local populations with the latest in vinicultural technologies, and to distribute—free of charge—European

---

[33] Ballas, *Vinodelie v Rossii*, vol. 3 (St Petersburg, 1897), 1–2, 5–6. For a non-scholarly history of Georgian wine and present-day fascination with traditional Georgian production methods, see Alice Feiring, *For the Love of Wine: My Odyssey through the World's Most Ancient Wine Culture* (Lincoln, NE, 2016); Darra Goldstein, *The Georgian Feast: The Vibrant Culture and Savory Food of the Republic of Georgia* (Berkeley, rev. ed., 2018), 62–78: pages 68–78 of this edition of *The Georgian Feast* comprise an essay by Alice Feiring, 'The Spirit of Georgian Wine'.

vines. Between 1846 and 1850, roughly 680,000 vine cuttings were sent from Crimea to Georgia at Vorontsov's request; students went in the opposite direction to Magarach and to the Bessarabian Horticultural Academy to study the latest in vinicultural science. In the late 1840s, the Caucasian Society for Agriculture formed in Tiflis (Tbilisi); modelled on its counterpart in Odessa, the Imperial Society for Agriculture in Southern Russia, it took an immediate interest in viniculture.[34]

Yet progress was slow. Viniculture in Georgia was never as important to tsarist administrators as the campaign to capture Shamil and pacify Dagestan, which was the chief reason Vorontsov was called from Odessa. Transportation infrastructure remained rudimentary until the 1870s, which hindered the growth of commercial demand (see Figure 1.3). Local suspicion of the new Russian administrators and their intentions ran deep. Russian administrators responded

Figure 1.3. Bullock-cart for transporting grapes on the estate of Prince Mukhranskii (Mukhrani), 1870s. Miriam and Ira D. Wallach Division of Art, Prints and Photographs: Photography Collection, The New York Public Library, 'Arby dlia podvoza vinograda v imenii Kn. Mukhranskago' (n.p., 1870–79).

---

[34] T. N. Chernova-Deke, 'Nemetskie poseleniia na Kavkaze, 1816–1914 gg', *Voprosy istorii* no. 3 (March 2010): 92–105; Ballas, *Vinodelie v Rossii*, vol. 3, 9, 11–13, 20–21.

with frustration at the apparent obduracy of Georgian peasants, who like the Tatars of Crimea appeared adept at ignoring even the most well-intentioned advice. Even Ballas was prone to moments of exasperation with and disparagement of persons who did not, in his view, grasp the importance of their endeavour.

> The predominance of peasant ownership cannot help but be reflected in the character of winemaking in Tiflis guberniya. The majority of the population, belonging to the Georgian nationality, shows little inclination toward industry or trade because of its patriarchal morals. With the exception of a small number of regions, where winemaking is perceived as an important branch of industry, the majority of the population looks at wine as part of a rather unpretentious diet; as a result of this view, it has a very different motive for engaging in viniculture.[35]

Nonetheless, by the 1850s, Kakheti alone was producing two million *vedra* of wine (nearly 25 million litres). Much of this wine—90 per cent, Ballas wrote, presumably not having tasted it himself—was suitable only for consumption 'on site, where its mass consumers, the common people and natives (*prostoliudiny-tuzemtsy*) do not have demanding tastes'. In a place where a great deal of wine was drunk, but little wine was sold to the world beyond the Caucasus, improvements in quality came indirectly. In 1871, a railroad was completed between Tiflis and Poti, a port on the Black Sea. The year before, the construction of a modern road traversing the Gombori Pass shortened the distance between Tiflis and Telavi, in the heart of Kakheti, by nearly seventy kilometres compared to the old route through Sighnaghi. Although a shipment of wine from Telavi to Tiflis could still take as long as eight days to arrive, the new road helped open Kakhetian winemakers to the lure of Russian and foreign commercial fairs, which were the central venues in tsarist Russia's wine trade. Amid the legions of peasant vintners, who produced poor quality kvevri wine for their own consumption (see Figure 1.4), were a very small number of standouts—typically aristocrats and foreigners who grew European vines and embraced modern forms of production: Prince David Chavchavadze, whose Napareuli estate later became part of the Kakhetian crown estate; the German settlements; Prince Amatuni; Prince Vachnadze; and the Bagrationi family, who were descendants of the last kings of Kartli and Kakheti. Comprising just a fraction of Georgia's overall production, the wines that came from these communities and estates helped introduce Russian consumers to Georgia.[36]

It was Ballas's native Bessarabia, however, which was incorporated into Russia in the wake of the Napoleonic Wars, and then repartitioned in response to the

---

[35] Ballas, *Vinodelie v Rossii*, vol. 3, 44.   [36] Ballas, *Vinodelie v Rossii*, vol. 3, 21–3, 26–7.

Figure 1.4. Kakhetian peasant with kvevris, 1870s. Miriam and Ira D. Wallach Division of Art, Prints and Photographs: Photography Collection, The New York Public Library, 'Kakhetiia. Kuvshiny (kvevri) v kotorykh sokhraniaiut vino' (n.p., 1870–79).

Crimean (1853–6) and Russo-Turkish Wars (1877–8), that diverged most completely from the vinicultural patterns in the Russian parts of the empire. Viniculture here had roots nearly as deep as in the Caucasus. While Ballas wrote that the earliest evidence of Bessarabian viniculture could be found in the writings of Herodotus, viniculture had already existed in the region for centuries by the time ancient Greeks colonized the northern Black Sea coast. During the period of Turkish rule, from the late fifteenth century to 1812, viniculture was sustained by Orthodox monasteries, which received a special dispensation to make wine, by Moldovan villagers, and in the southern Budjak region along the sea, by Turkish, Armenian, and Tatar villagers. By the late eighteenth century, Bessarabian wine, fortified and preserved with local wine distillate, was being carted all the way to markets in Cracow and Moscow; European travellers noted that Akkerman—the Turkish fortress near the mouth of the Dniester—'was distinguished by a healthy climate' and was already famous for its vineyards.[37]

---

[37] Ballas, *Vinodelie v Rossii*, vol. 5 (St Petersburg, 1899), 5–6; vol. 3, 1–2. On the history of viniculture in Moldova, see M. Peliakh, *Istoriia vinogradarstvva i vinodeliia Moldavii* (Kishinev, 1970); N. I. Vinokurov, *Vinogradarstvo i vinodelie antichnykh gosudarstv severnogo prichernomor'ia*

While the Treaty of Bucharest in 1812 extended the Russian Empire's territory south-westward to the banks of the Danube and westward to the Prut, it gave Russia no great demographic trophy. The entire population of the newly constituted Bessarabian oblast was only about 240,000 persons in 1812. It had been decimated by war, by an outbreak of the plague from 1812 to 1814, and darkly presaging the traumas of the twentieth century, by population transfer. Turks followed the retreat of the Ottoman Empire west and south. Nogais were resettled east into the steppe of Crimea and the Kuban. By 1855, the population of Bessarabia had grown to just under one million persons; it reached nearly 1.8 million at the end of the century. In the southern region of Budjak, which had been almost entirely depopulated in 1812, growth was bolstered by the settlement of Cossacks from the east, who formed the Ust-Danube Host; by several waves of Bulgarians fleeing Ottoman power in Thrace; by Germans from the Duchy of Warsaw; by French-speakers from Switzerland; by Greeks from the islands of the Aegean; and by Romanian-speaking Moldovans, who returned after the trauma of war had passed. 'All of these non-Russian (*inorodcheskie*) elements, familiar with the cultivation of grapes in their own lands, made possible to a significant extent its development in the southern region of Bessarabia.' Greeks and Bulgarians, in particular, settled in Izmail, Reni, and Akkerman, producing a 'Greek revival', and spurring the planting of large vineyards. Russians came too, but from a different world entirely than the wealthy aristocrats who found in Crimea a warm-weather getaway. They were refugees from serfdom, religious dissenters, and criminals on the run. Like foreign colonists, who received the inheritable right to use the land 'in perpetuity' in lieu of formal ownership, Russian settlers found in Budjak a mostly empty land, littered with the remnants of former residents: overgrown vineyards and orchards, fountains, irrigation wells and channels. Even Ballas, born in the 1850s, recalled a childhood spent among the remains of Ottoman civilization.[38]

To the north, on the Kodry highlands that lay between the Prut River, the border with the vassal principality of Moldavia to the west, and the Reut, a tributary of the Dniester that bisected central Bessarabia, viniculture was a Moldovan affair, sustained by monasteries and villagers. Historically isolated from the Turkish presence farther south, and lacking the tempering effect of the sea, Kodry was no match for Budjak when it came to wine. The former had black soil (*chernozem*) in

(Simferopol and Kerch, 2007), 48–50; Denis Deletente, 'Genoese, Tatars and Rumanians at the Mouth of the Danube in the Fourteenth Century', *The Slavonic and East European Review* 62, no. 4 (October 1984): 511–30; F. W. Carter, 'Cracow's Wine Trade (Fourteenth to Eighteenth Centuries)', *The Slavonic and East European Review* 65, no. 4 (October 1987): 550.

[38] Quote is from Ballas, *Vinodelie v Rossii*, vol. 5, 8. On colonists in Besssarabia, see D. Brandes, *Von den Zaren adoptiert. Die deutschen Kolonisten und die Balkansiedler in Neurußland und Bessarabien 1751–1914* (Munich, 1993); Olivier Grivat, *Les Vignerons suisses du Tsar* (Chapelle-sur-Moudon, Switz., 1993).

abundance, which was ideal for everything except viniculture; the latter had chalky, stony, and sandy soils that drew comparisons to Champagne-Ardenne. A nineteenth-century French traveller, whose account Ballas cited, described Bessarabian wine as 'course, bitter, and acidic with little bouquet'. The French traveller presumably had in mind the wine of central Bessarabia, because the wine that came from Akkerman drew an entirely different description from him: 'These wines are extraordinarily good, especially the whites. They are robust. They have bouquet, power, and pleasing strength, which make them worthy wines.'[39] In 1825, Prince Paravichini, a state counsellor and 'head forest officer' (*oberforstmeister*) was put in charge of the construction of an imperial garden near Akkerman. Of Sardinian descent, Paravichini bore principal responsibility for the invitation that brought Ivan Karlovich Tardan (Louis-Vincent Tardent) and five families from the Swiss Vaud to Bessarabia in 1822. As a winemaker and cellar master, Paravichini was convinced that Akkerman had the potential to produce sublime wine. The 1825 vintage, made from grapes grown in state-owned vineyards around Akkerman, was proof of concept:

> I have an extremely pure champagne, probably by origin from the *Iaidzhi* varietal [this was most likely a Chasselas], and a Burgundy...without any additives, from a single cuvée...which proves, at the very least, that in recent years, with appropriate effort and favorable summer weather, Akkerman wine compares favorably with the very best French wines.[40]

To be sure, as Paravichini's role suggests, the Russian state was by no means complacent about viniculture and winemaking in Bessarabia. From almost the moment of annexation, Russian officials used population politics to fortify a borderland region that had been depopulated by war and imperial retreat, and to solve a pressing agricultural problem—how to preserve an agricultural infrastructure that the Turks had devoted considerable resources to building, and then abandoned in the wake of the Treaty of Bucharest. The latter was the principal motive behind Paravichini's charge to build an imperial garden, presumably akin to the Nikitskii Botanical Garden outside of Yalta—'to restore the vineyards that had come into the possession of the state from the Turks'. Similarly, in 1832, Vorontsov decreed the formation of a state horticultural and vinicultural school on the grounds of the Akkerman gardens. After three years of struggle, the

---

[39] Ballas, *Vinodelie v Rossii*, vol. 5, 11.

[40] Paravichini is quoted in Ballas, *Vinodelie v Rossii*, vol. 5, 11–12. On Paravichini, see Vladimir Tarnakin and Tat'iana Solov'eva, *Bessarabskie istorii: Istoriko-kraevedcheskie zhurnalistskie rassledovaniia* (Chişinău, 2011), 154; Petr Keppen, *O vinodelii i vinnoi torgovle v Rossii* (St Petersburg, 1832), 148. According to *Ukazatel' Vserossiiskoi promyshlenno-khudozhestvennoi vystavki* (Moscow, 1882), 132, a bottle of *Iaidzhi* in the exhibit was in fact a Chasselas, one of the most common varietals for table wines in France.

school's gardens and vineyards were transferred to Shabo, with the understanding that Tardan would continue to educate aspiring viniculturalists, and that half the revenue from the wine the school produced would go to state coffers. Yet even Tardan's school failed, because of the 'mistaken opinion of the administration that private initiative in Akkerman uyezd was so strong that oversight was not necessary'.[41]

Despite the missteps, Bessarabian viniculture grew rapidly during these years, becoming one of the hallmarks of the region (see Figure 1.5). Between 1838 and 1848, the German and Bulgarian colonists planted, on average, 200,000 vines per year; in Akkerman and Kishinev, the average was 100,000 and 50,000 new vines, respectively. Only in northern Khotinsk, Jassy, and Sorokskii uyezds was the growth in plantings negligible. Many of the new plantings were European varietals, which helped establish a commercial connection that would prove catastrophic a few decades later, as phylloxera spread eastwards, between the empire's viniculturalists and nurseries in Germany, Hungary, the Danubian principalities, and Austria. General Ponse (Poncet) planted foreign vines at his Leont'evo estate in 1825. The Sikardy family, the owners of the Vadului-voda estate, put in French vines in 1829. On the twenty-seven desyatins (roughly 30 hectares) that he received upon moving to Bessarabia, Tardan planted 40,000 local vines and 15,000 vines that he sent for from abroad. In the 1830s, Prince Muruzi planted Hungarian and Romanian vines at this estate along the banks of the Prut. The private landowner Zhurmal-Popov planted 20,000 Cabernet and Riesling 'noble vines', meaning that they were propagated from the cuttings of individual vines known to produce high-quality grapes. Zhurmal-Popov later purchased a modern grape press from France, reputedly the first in all of Bessarabia. According to Ballas, these were the 'pioneers', persons who amid the 'overall low level of winemaking in Bessarabia...tried to raise it from common routine and find new beginnings'.[42]

In the view of Ballas and others, quality correlated with varietal: persons who grew European vines tended to embrace practices that resulted in better wine. Yet efforts to transition growers to European vines were costly. In the middle of the nineteenth century, Bessarabian authorities worked with horticulturalists at the Nikitskii Botanical Garden to create a vine nursery near Akkerman that would distribute vine seedlings and cuttings to local growers free of charge. While the numbers of distributed vines were never large—probably less than 50,000 total over several years—the varietals tended to be European: Mourvèdre, Pinot Franc, Traminer, Riesling, Tokaji, and others. Ballas himself put in Sémillon and Sauvignon blanc that he purchased from nurseries in Magarach, Oreanda, and Gurzuf. Of the 10,500 vines that the Akkerman section of the Russian

---

[41] Ballas, *Vinodelie v Rossii*, vol. 5, 13–14.   [42] Ballas, *Vinodelie v Rossii*, vol. 5, 16, 18–19.

Figure 1.5. Souvenir card from 1856 for Bessarabia guberniya that identifies vineyards as one of the province's distinctive characteristics. Russia lost Budjak, the southernmost region of Bessarabia, later in 1856 as a result of the Crimean War, and regained it in 1878 after the Russo-Turkish War. 'Bessarabskaia guberniia', in *Novaia natsional'naia i podrobnaia geografiia Rossiiskoi imperii* (St Petersburg, 1856), 36. Library of Congress.

Horticultural Society purchased from Crimea in 1894, only the Saperavi vines might have been considered indigenous. The others—Malbec, Pedro Jimenez (used for Sherry), Muscat, Sémillon, Cabernet—had roots in Europe.[43]

Despite the fact that the late 1880s and 1890s were consumed by phylloxera—the subject of the following chapter—the incremental improvements in vinicultural and winemaking techniques over nearly a century bore undeniable fruit.

> The infertile soil, unsuitable for any other purpose, demanded not only extraordinary strength, labor, many years of endurance and effort, and a huge investment in capital and savings from generation to generation, but also the energy to tend to all aspects of a vineyard.[44]

Writing in the early 1900s, Ballas noted that the area around Akkerman had become one of the empire's best vinicultural regions, on a par with Crimea. In nearly every village lived some persons engaged in viniculture. In large swathes of the Akkerman and Pridniestrovskii uyezds, viniculture was a primary economic activity; in a few areas, it was the only economic activity. To be sure, Akkerman enjoyed a clear advantage on areas farther north, because of its proximity to the markets and transportation facilities of Odessa. Yet Ballas wrote about Akkerman in ways that anticipated *terroir*'s anthropological turn.

> For people not familiar with its practical dimensions, the cultivation of vineyards in sandy, gravely soil seems like a minor undertaking, but the example of the tedious growth of viniculture on the Oleshky Sands [a geological feature of southern Ukraine and Bessarabia] suggests the opposite. The constant battle with May bugs [cockchafers], the necessity of occasionally replanting vines that are, by comparison, scraggly because they need better soil, the significant percentage of unsuccessful plantings: all of this means local viniculture will be difficult, and will require resources that are unknown in the other regions of Bessarabia. But these very circumstances are the main reason for the relatively high level of vinicultural technique, compared to other southern regions (with the exception of Crimea). Here is the clear example of enlightened winemakers—Tardent, Charenton, Dantz, and Corey—who brought from their native lands of France and Switzerland already tested approaches and techniques that were not without result.[45]

In southern Bessarabia, painstaking effort, persistence, and ingenuity got the best of environmental constraint. Even in the 1860s, when most Bessarabian wine was made 'under the skies', nearly every large-scale producer near Akkerman built

---

[43] Ballas, *Vinodelie v Rossii*, vol. 5, 18, 21, 42.   [44] Ballas, *Vinodelie v Rossii*, vol. 5, 38.
[45] Ballas, *Vinodelie v Rossii*, vol. 5, 39.

proper cellars and indoor production facilities. Many used equipment purchased from western Europe. Here viniculture was an all-encompassing endeavour: men, women, children, and even domestic servants worked in vineyards, especially during the rush surrounding harvest. Over time, individual winemakers, micro-regions, and entire communities built reputations for quality. The recently deceased P. E. Leonard, who is a minor character in the following chapter, and who grew Merlot, Cabernet, and Pinot gris on his estate near Bender, was known as 'one of the best [winemakers] in all Bessarabia, famous for his reds'. Semen Pozdniakov, the elder in Palanskaia volost, Akkerman uyezd, was a 'wonderful viniculturalist, who on eight desyatins produces good wine'. In Talmazskaia volost, Akkerman uyezd, a handful of vinicultural families 'built the reputations of wines: the now deceased elder Germanson, the Brunovskii brothers, Mordvinov, Savari, Loran, Klodts, and others'. In Izmail uyezd, the best wines came from vineyards in the dry Kopannaia and Kholodnaia river beds. Among their owners was the former Austrian consul to Izmail.[46] In the steppe around Akkerman, wine made by German colonists was allegedly a better bet than wine made by their Bulgarian neighbours, even though the Bulgarians, who were more numerous, had 2,000 more desyatins of vineyards under cultivation. German colonists planted vineyards on slopes and high places to maximize sun exposure, and they invested in the 'best varietals'. While the quality of wine gradually diminished to the north as the soil turned black, there were exceptions. Near Kishinev, Baron Stuart's wines—made from local indigenous white varietals—'had nothing in common with the rough reputation of Kishinev wines'. Likewise, the grower Mikhail Bliumenfel'd trained his Merlot, Cabernet, Pinot, and Verdot vines to grow on trellises, which was still a bit of a novelty in the Russian Empire at the end of the nineteenth century. Near Mileshty station, just south of Kishinev, Petr Kazimir 'achieved great success and strengthened his reputation as a vinicultural-ist' after planting varietals from Bordeaux and Burgundy in the 1860s and 1870s. At the time Ballas was writing, the vineyards that Kazimir planted more than two decades earlier constituted the 'only nursery in all of central and northern Bessarabia for obtaining the best, authentically European grapevines'.[47]

To be sure, Ballas was not uniformly positive about viniculture in his native Bessarabia. For every 'pioneer' who adopted proven techniques and equipment from the West, and for every winemaker who built a reputation for quality over many vintages, by trial and error and at no small cost, there were dozens of others who made wines that were mainly suitable for home consumption, adulteration, or distillation. Bad wine, in Ballas's judgment, remained the rule in all regions of the empire, Bessarabia and Crimea included, rather than the exception. Drawing on the verdict of a local scholar, Professor Murzakevich, Ballas wrote that the

---

[46] Ballas, *Vinodelie v Rossii*, vol. 5, 39–40, 45–6, 52–4.
[47] Ballas, *Vinodelie v Rossii*, vol. 5, 48, 57–8.

'majority of Bessarabian growers make wine of such low quality, that only they themselves might drink it, tasting in it the sweet fruit of their own labors'. Sarcastic word play aside, even in the early 1870s, when Bessarabian vineyards were producing more than a million *pudy* (roughly 16.3 million kilograms) of grapes annually, the rudimentary transportation system linking Bessarabia to the rest of the empire, and the rising cost of grain (which drove up demand for domestic cargo space), meant that most of Bessarabia's wine was consumed locally by necessity—by the families and neighbours of the persons who made it.[48]

Yet in Bessarabia, like in Crimea, the geography of winemaking increasingly resembled geographies of winemaking in western Europe, where wine had long ago ceased to be an interchangeable commodity. There were broad differences in the prices of vineyards in Bessarabia that correlated not to the productivity of the vines that grew there, but to the perceived quality of wine that emanated from those vines. Based on the period for which Ballas had data, 1889–1893, a desyatin in the sandy soils of Akkerman uyezd could be expected to produce between 20 and 145 *vedra* (255 and 1,782 litres) of wine, with an average of about 90 *vedra* (1,106 litres) per year. Productivity rose—by a factor of two, three, and even four times—in the vineyards of Kishinev and Orgeev uyezds. Yet the 'scraggly' vines that grew in the sandy soils of Akkerman uyezd fetched a considerably higher price—up to 1,000 roubles per desyatin—than the more productive vines near Bender (350 to 450 roubles), Kishinev (350 to 600 roubles), Orgeev (100 roubles) to the north. The reason, of course, was that the wines of Akkerman commanded higher prices in the marketplace, trading at the end of the century for a 20 to 25 per cent premium on the wines from nearby Shabo by standard unit of volume. Wines from Izmail and Bolgrad, located near the Danube, also commanded enviable prices. But prices there were calculated for the Moldavian *vedro* (which was 20 per cent larger than a Russian *vedro*), and showed greater range. A wine salesman sensitive to the high prices that Akkerman vintners demanded might still find wine trading above a rouble per *vedro* in Kishinev, Orgeev, and Bender uyezds, but the price floor there fell precipitously, to around 20 kopecks per *vedro*.[49] The *terroir* that Russian vintners could not taste in their bottles, was instead in their bank accounts and wallets.

*   *   *   *   *

Writing a century after Ballas's death, the American winemakers Tim Patterson and John Buechsenstein observed that every glass of wine worth raising has flavour, but a few extraordinary wines have 'meaning'. Borrowing from the wine writer Matt Kramer, Patterson and Beuchsenstein described the latter as a sense of 'somewhereness', a grounding in place that all great wines supposedly have.

[48] Ballas, *Vinodelie v Rossii*, vol. 5, 26–7.   [49] Ballas, *Vinodelie v Rossii*, vol. 5, 244, 251–5, 258.

On first glance, Kramer's coinage appears to have resonated among Russia's nineteenth-century wine writers. Since its advent in the Black Sea territorial annexations, Russian wine writing was preoccupied with 'somewhereness', with cataloguing the diverse landscapes and climates, the soil types and drainage patterns of the places where grapes were grown. This was almost certainly part of the broader project of imperial incorporation. As Kelly O'Neill has argued about a crucial part of Russia's new vinicultural belt, Crimea, political possession required spatial cognition, 'placing Crimea' in historical maps and chronologies.[50]

Yet on second glance, there is something trite about Patterson and Buechsenstein's use of 'somewhereness'. Wine had meaning in Russia long before it had identifiable taste, which is precisely why so much time and money was exhausted cataloguing the empire's vinicultural territories. The fact that many of the territories comprising the Russian Empire had long vinicultural histories—stretching back, in the case of Bessarabia, Crimea, and Georgia, many millennia—turned on its head the 'civilizing process' that had been part of Russian politics and culture since the time of Peter. The production and consumption of wine was a European characteristic, yet Russia was cultivating characteristics intrinsic to the empire in its pursuit of fine wine. As chapter 3 will show, prominent persons in late-tsarist Russia's wine industry were aware of the paradox: many millennia earlier, the territories that would one day comprise the Russian Empire gave Europe wine, which was then deracinated and returned to Russia as part of the civilizing process. As Dmitrii Mendeleev confidently predicted, Russia—with its immense vinicultural territories—would very soon take its place at the head of European winemaking.

Just as the history of viniculture in the Russian Empire confounded a narrative about Russia's post-Petrine embrace of European culture that was often unflattering, so too did it challenge ideas about who was acculturating whom within Russia. Crimea provided a celebrated template for vinicultural development that largely conformed to broader trajectories of Russian imperialism. There, an activist state and wealthy, principally Russian estate owners transformed viniculture over the course of the nineteenth century, remedying Tatar backwardness with modern vinicultural and oenological science. In the process, they often found the recipe for very fine wine. Yet in Ballas's recounting, there were cracks in the template: Tatar viniculturalists were not always intransigent objects of and impervious to well-intended Russian policies; foreigners played an outsized role in the development of Crimean winemaking, as they did in all the vinicultural territories; and bad wine remained the rule in Crimea, rather than the exception, because consumers in the big cities of the north had not been acculturated to demand better.

---

[50] Tim Patterson and John Buechsenstein, *Wine and Place: A Terroir Reader* (Berkeley, 2018), 8; O'Neill, *Claiming Crimea*, 10–31.

In other parts of the empire, however, the template broke down completely. The acme of viniculture in Astrakhan was sometime around the year 1800; it then went into long decline—due in large part to a hot, dry climate and competition from elsewhere—despite state policies meant to encourage growth. In Georgia, where viniculture was the central agricultural pursuit, and where the unbroken swathe of Kakhetian vineyards had astounded early visitors such as Christian von Steven, peasants looked sceptically upon the initiatives of the tsarist government, seeing wine not as an item for external trade and personal enrichment, but as an unpretentious staple of their daily diets not worthy of reflection or investment. Even at the end of the century, Ballas noted that good Georgian wine was exceedingly rare, emanating from a small number of princely estates and foreign settlements. Ballas's native Bessarabia made good wine in comparative abundance, particularly in the region around Akkerman, where the combination of bad soil and good viniculturalists produced some of the Russian Empire's best bottles and barrels. While vineyard prices in Akkerman were comparatively inexpensive, by Crimean standards, they displayed the same correlation between price and wine quality (rather than productivity) that characterized Crimean viniculture. Contrary to Crimea, however, Bessarabia did not have a sizeable class of wealthy Russian estate owners. Good wine came from aristocratic estates, villages, foreign settlements, and numerous small producers who mastered, by trial and error, the secrets of the 'Oleshky Sands'.

It is not clear whether Ballas—who presented himself as Russian patriot and wine optimist, and who was in many ways a beneficiary of tsarist politics—understood that his narrative about Bessarabia could be read in subversive ways. He was describing what would one day be identified as the essential characteristic of great wine—the mutually constitutive relationship between people, place, and vine. Yet Ballas found these relationships in a part of the empire where wealthy Russians—whom he often presented as the vessels of civilization and modernity elsewhere—were few in number, where colonists from Bulgaria, Germany, and Switzerland cultivated vines according to traditions from their homelands, where scraggly vineyards in dry, rocky river beds produced better wines than lush vineyards in the black soils to the north, where the remnants of Ottoman-era viniculture were ubiquitous, and where the imprint of tsarist policies meant to encourage viniculture was far from indelible.

2
Science

The Great Wine Blight in Late-Tsarist Bessarabia

On 20 June 1886, Afanasii Pogibko arrived at the Teleshov train station, twenty-five kilometres north of Kishinev in the Orgeev uyezd. A student in the natural sciences at Novorossiysk University in nearby Odessa, Pogibko spent the summer months as an inspector for the Bessarabian Phylloxera Commission. For weeks at a time, Pogibko travelled the potholed tracks near the middle Dniester and its right-bank tributaries. When he found vineyards, he presented his credentials to landowners and peasants, most of whom spoke little Russian, and asked that they allow him to spend a few hours walking among their vines. Similar inspectors had been at work in adjacent areas of Bessarabia and Kherson guberniyas since 1883. No one had ever found any evidence of the vine louse, which was a good thing because Bessarabia accounted for nearly 20 per cent of the Russian Empire's wine production. But in the vineyards on the estate of G. I. Kristi, his destination on 20 June, Pogibko found almost three contiguous hectares of dead and dying vines. As he had been trained in Odessa, Pogibko used a shovel to reveal the diseased vines' upper roots. Amid black soil that fed the most productive vineyards in Bessarabia, Pogibko found the cause of destruction. Phylloxera *vastatrix*—phylloxera the devastator—was feeding on root sap, in the process injecting a poison that prevented the vine from healing. Despite many years of prevention, surveillance, and quarantine, the 'great wine blight' had arrived in Bessarabia.[1]

Pogibko was not the first person to find phylloxera in the Russian Empire. The aphid's presence was confirmed on the south shore of Crimea in 1879, when 22 hectares of vineyards suddenly wilted. It appeared in both wild and cultivated vines at a coastal estate near Sukhumi in 1881. It was found in the Kuban in 1883, and near Tbilisi and the city of Quba in Baku guberniya in 1884. Moreover,

---

[1] For figures on wine production by region, see F. R. Ungern-Shternberg, 'O vinodelii na Iuzhnom beregu Kryma', in *Istoriia vinodeliia Kryma: Sbornik*, vyp. 2, ed. V. V. Mitiaev (Massandra, 2001), 218; Anon., *Doklad komissii po razvitiiu vinodeliiu v okresnostiiakh Sevastopolia* (Sevastopol, 1882), unnumbered insert. On soil conditions and production levels by vine and desyatin in Bessarabia, see I. Bok and G. Ershov, eds., *Vinogradarstvo i vinodelie v Rossii v 1870–73 godakh*, Statisticheskii vremmenik Rossiiskoi imperii, seriia II, vyp.15 (St Petersburg, 1877), 7, 21. On Pogibko, see Derzhavnyi arkhiv Odes'koï oblasti [State Archive of the Odessa Oblast, hereafter DAOO], f. 5, o. 1, d. 1521, ll. 79ob–80; A. Pogibko, 'O zashchite vinogradnikov ot filloksery v Rossi i zagranitsei', in *Otchet i trudy Odesskago otdela Imperatorskogo Rossiiskago obshchestva sadovodstva za 1893 god* (Odessa, 1894), 22–39. On the wine blight, see George Ordish, *The Great Wine Blight* (New York, 1972); George Gale, *Dying on the Vine: How Phylloxera Transformed Wine* (Berkeley, 2011).

Whites and Reds: A History of Wine in the Lands of Tsar and Commissar. Stephen V. Bittner, Oxford University Press (2021).
© Stephen V. Bittner. DOI: 10.1093/oso/9780198784821.003.0003

during the early 1880s the blight spread rapidly through the vineyards of the Danube river valley and its tributaries in neighbouring Romania, fuelling persistent worries in Bessarabia about the adequacy of domestic prevention when international borders were so close.[2] The upshot was that the events of 20 June 1886 came as little surprise. Since the early 1880s, provincial authorities in Odessa and the local scientific establishment had been mobilizing against a vine epidemic that seemed all but inevitable.[3] When news of Pogibko's discovery arrived in Kishinev and Odessa, authorities put in motion a plan that had been honed for many years in vineyards in Switzerland and laboratories in France. The executive members of the Bessarabian Phylloxera Commission converged on Teleshov to survey the damage. Their closer inspection revealed nine hectares of infected vines. They traced the provenance of blight to vines purchased from a nursery in Erfurt in 1875 or 1878. They designated 1,008 roubles for the oversight of twelve other sites where Kristi had planted vines from abroad. And they ordered the immediate destruction of the infected vines by uprooting and incineration, and the subsequent 'disinfection' of the soil by chemical fumigation. These were the commission's 'radical measures' (*radikal'nye mery* or *radikal'nyi metod*), its most aggressive tool to halt the spread of phylloxera.

Radical measures ultimately failed in Bessarabia, as they did in all the empire's wine-producing regions except Crimea, where topography and the relative paucity of vineyards were conducive to quarantine. By 1892, phylloxera had infected 88,642 hectares in Bessarabia, roughly three-quarters of the total vineyard area. Three years later, 100,000 hectares—1,000 square kilometres—were sick. The fact that most infections occurred in new vineyards, typically among Loire and Burgundy varietals like Chasselas, Pinot, and Gamay, made the losses all the more painful. Public dismay over the ineffectiveness of radical measures led to the emasculation of the Bessarabian Phylloxera Commission in 1895. By then, 4.2 million roubles had been spent across the south-western fringe of the empire in an unsuccessful attempt to stem the spread of blight. Even greater were the costs to goodwill and reputation.[4]

This and the following chapter examine the relationship between wine, science, and tsarist politics around the turn of the century. As late as the 1870s, the Russian Empire had hardly any wine expertise outside of the indigenous vinicultural economies along the Black Sea. This reflected a domestic market for wine in the

---

[2] DAOO, f. 22, o. 1, d. 614, ll. 67, 133, 138; M. Peliakh, *Istoriia vinogradarstvva i vinodeliia Moldavii* (Kishinev, 1970), 114; N. A. Demchenko, *Vinogradarstvo i vinodelie Moldavii v XIX—nachale XX v.* (Kishinev, 1978), 8–25.

[3] D. E. Liukasa, 'K sokhraneniiu nashikh vinogradnikov ot povrezhdeniia filokseroiu', in *Otchet i trudy Odesskago otdela Imperatorskogo Rossiiskago obshchestva sadovodstva za 1885 god* (Odessa, 1886), 12–32.

[4] Em. Belen-de-Balliu, untitled essay, in *Trudy Komiteta vinogradarstva Imperatorskogo obshchestva sel'skogo khoziaistva iuzhnoi Rossii*, vyp. 3, ed. V. V. Bychikhin (Odessa, 1908), 111; Peliakh, *Istoriia vinogradarstva*, 114.

core territories that was small, as it was limited almost entirely to the aristocracy, and a domestic market for domestic wine that was even smaller yet. Russia did have a sizeable scientific establishment, however, which from the 1880s to the end of the Soviet period played an outsized role in determining the trajectory of the wine industry. In the decades following the incorporation of Crimea into the empire in 1783, many of Russia's first vintners presented themselves as men of science, dutifully recording meteorological data and soil characteristics as they struggled to grow grapes. In truth, they were natural philosophers who sought to catalogue the world they inhabited. They had much in common with the 'enlightened bureaucrats' of the Nicolaevan era: for them, science embodied a positivistic worldview and empirical discipline, all infused with values that were decidedly Western in orientation.[5] As a separate, highly specialized vocation, Russian science was first called into action on behalf of the vinicultural economy to combat phylloxera in the 1880s. It never quite went away. Science played a prominent role in debates about what specifically constituted wine in the years preceding passage of tsarist Russia's wine purity law in 1914, in ramping up production after Stalin's famous embrace of champagne as part of the socialist good life in 1936, and in late-Soviet efforts to curtail the consumption of vodka and fortified wine. Consequently, like the American winemakers whom French connoisseurs disparaged as 'chemists' at the Exposition Universelle in Paris in 1900, Russian winemaking—especially its more commercial aspects—was more often than not a scientific endeavour.[6]

The latter was partly a result of chronology—the science of viniculture and oenology dated to the late nineteenth century, precisely when Russian winemaking began to grow rapidly. As a result, Russia was never much beholden to the idea that winemaking was artisanal, guided by traditions passed down over many generations (although as the next chapter will show, Russian winemakers understood that presenting themselves in this way was often lucrative). The prominence of science in Russian and Soviet winemaking also reflected the peculiar imperial dynamics along the Black Sea. Nathanial Knight has noted that Russia, by offering an 'awkward triptych: the west, Russia, the east', often confounds the 'stark dichotomy' between Orient and Occident upon which the analyses of Edward Said and others hinge.[7] The story of Russian winemaking further complicates these divisions by adding a second category in-between East and West—European or Europeanized subjects of the empire. The presence of the latter in the vinicultural

---

[5] W. Bruce Lincoln, *In the Vanguard of Reform: Russia's Enlightened Bureaucrats, 1825–1861* (De Kalb, IL, 1986). On the distinction between natural philosophy and science, see Mark Harrison, 'Science and the British Empire', *Isis* 96, no. 1 (March 2005): 56.

[6] Van Troi Tran, 'Grapes on Trial: Wine at the Paris World's Fairs of 1889 and 1900', *Food and Foodways: Explorations in the History and Culture of Human Nourishment* 21, no. 4 (2013): 268.

[7] Nathaniel Knight, 'Grigor'ev in Orenburg, 1851–1862: Russian Orientalism in the Service of the Empire?', *Slavic Review* 59, no. 1 (Spring 2000): 77.

territories was the by-product of the idea, which had existed in Russia since the time of Peter the Great, that wine production and consumption were European characteristics, important parts of the etiquette and consumption patterns that comprised Norbert Elias's 'civilizing process'. The non-Russian peoples of the Black Sea, with their long-standing and deeply entrenched wine traditions, thus had a claim on one aspect of European-ness that the core of the empire lacked. In this context, the science of viniculture and oenology, which was more often than not of European origin, was compensatory; it re-established imperial hierarchies that had been turned on their head by wine's strange ideological baggage at the periphery of Europe. Science too was European. It was an expression both of Russia's enlightened imperial policies, and of Russian membership in the concert of Europe.[8]

The marriage of science and state power was especially evident in Russia's response to phylloxera. Few pests have caused more economic destruction. Spread from its North American home via the global trade in live plants in the mid-nineteenth century, phylloxera was thought to be present in two-thirds of the world's vineyards, about six-million hectares total, by the early twentieth. After the means of transmission was identified in the late 1860s, scientists traced the trade in American vines—coveted by Victorian-era gardeners—to Bordeaux, England, Ireland, Alsace, Germany, and Portugal. No country suffered more than France, where wine constituted the largest export after textiles and provided the government with one-sixth of its total revenues. Between 1875 and 1890, total annual wine production in France (not including Algeria) fell from more than 80 million hectolitres to less than 25 million. By the time phylloxera was brought under control in the early twentieth century, total costs exceeded 11 billion French francs, more than double the indemnity of the Franco-Prussian War.[9]

By comparison, the costs of the phylloxera epidemic in Russia were small, as was the size of Russia's wine industry.[10] Yet Russia's encounter with phylloxera was deeply revealing, because for many years authorities persisted with radical measures despite news from the Midi of a more effective approach. This stubbornness was largely the affair of Aleksandr Kovalevskii, a pioneering natural

[8] The literature on science as an agent of imperialism is broad. See, for instance, Lewis Pyenson, *Cultural Imperialism and the Exact Sciences: German Expansion Overseas, 1900-1930* (New York, 1985); Michael Adas, *Machines as the Measure of Men: Science, Technology, and the Ideologies of Western Dominance* (Ithaca, 1989); Megan Vaughan, *Curing Their Ills: Colonial Power and African Illness* (Cambridge, 1991); Paolo Pallodino and Michael Worboys, 'Science and Imperialism', *Isis* 84, no. 1 (March 1993): 103–108; Lewis Pyenson, 'Cultural Imperialism and the Exact Sciences', *Isis* 84, no. 1 (March 1993): 91–102; Francine Hirsch, *Empire of Nations: Ethnographic Knowledge and the Making of the Soviet Union* (Ithaca and London, 2005).

[9] Richard Smart, 'Phylloxera', in *The Oxford Companion to Wine*, ed. Jancis Robinson (Oxford, 3rd ed., 2006), 521–2; Harry W. Paul, *Science, Vine, and Wine in Modern France* (Cambridge, 1996), 10; Leo A. Loubère, *The Red and the White: A History of Wine in France and Italy in the Nineteenth Century* (Albany, 1978), 157.

[10] 'Filoksera v Rossi i bor'ba s neiu', *Vestnik vinodeliia* no. 1 (1894): 40–44.

scientist and the chairman of the Bessarabian Phylloxera Commission. Born in 1840 in Vitebsk guberniya, Kovalevskii embodied the characteristics associated with Bazarov, Ivan Turgenev's nihilistic antihero of the 1860s generation: a hard-headed, unsentimental, and often inflexible commitment to science as a panacea for society's ailments. Although he was said to be on friendly terms with Mikhail Bakunin, Kovalevskii's correspondence betrayed little patience for politics beyond the universities where he worked. Instead, as his equally famous sister-in-law, the mathematician Sofia Kovalevskaia noted, Kovalevskii was a 'towering nihilist' solely for his dedication to laboratory and fieldwork.[11] As a young man, Kovalevskii spent two years in Heidelberg and Tübingen, where he studied zoology with Heinrich Bronn, a palaeontologist who helped create the field of biostratigraphy (dating fossils by the rock layers in which they are embedded), and who was the German translator of Charles Darwin's *On the Origin of Species*. In 1862, Kovalevskii returned to St Petersburg to begin his graduate work in embryology. There he devoted himself to the lancelet, a rod-shaped, translucent sea creature thought to be a vertebrate. Kovalevskii showed instead that the lancelet was a transitional (of the highest order) invertebrate, and that its embryonic development paralleled that of vertebrates. Kovalevskii followed with similar studies on phoronids (horse worms) and ascidians (sea squirts) that showed the essential morpho-logical similarities between vertebrates and invertebrates. The latter research caught the eye of Darwin, who credited Kovalevskii's comparative embryology in *The Descent of Man*. Along with his younger brother Vladimir, an evolutionary palaeontologist who was famous for his studies of ungulate fossils, Kovalevskii became one of the most influential advocates of Darwin's ideas in Russia.[12]

Kovalevskii was named chairman of the Bessarabian Phylloxera Commission in 1880, six years after he took a position at Novorossiysk University in Odessa. Until he left for a position at St Petersburg University in 1890, Kovalevskii was the chief 'ideologue' for the radical measures to combat phylloxera—incineration, subsoil fumigation with pesticide, and quarantine.[13] Even after moving to St Petersburg, Kovalevskii remained the nominal head of the commission until its emasculation in 1895, leading a joint Russian-French phylloxera expedition to the Caucasus in 1893.[14] Consequently, more than any other individual Kovalevskii was blamed for Russia's disastrous response to phylloxera. Landowners and peasants

---

[11] S. V. Kovalevskaia, *Vospominaniia i pis'ma*, ed. S. Ia. Shtraikh (Moscow, 1961), 230, quoted in Alexander Vucinich, *Science in Russian Culture, 1861–1917* (Stanford, 1970), 108.

[12] O. Ia. Pilipchuk, *Aleksandr Onufrievich Kovalevskii, 1840–1901* (Moscow, 2003); V. A. Dogel', *A. O. Kovalevskii* (Moscow, 1945); Alexander Vucinich, *Darwin in Russian Thought* (Berkeley and Los Angeles, 1988), 34–39; Vucinich, *Science in Russian Culture*, 108–19.

[13] Pilipchuk, *Aleksandr Onufrievich Kovalevskii*, 124.

[14] V. D. Sevast'ianov, 'Uchastie akad. A. O. Kovalevskogo v rabote obshchestva sel'skogo khoziaistva iuzhnoi Rossii', in *Odesskaia oblastnaia nauchnaia konferentsiia posviashchennaia 150-letiiu so dnia rozh-deniia A. O. Kovalevskogo. 10–12 maia 1990 g. Tezisy dokladov* (Odessa, 1990), 46–8; R. O. Faitel'berg, E. A. Kameneva, L. M. Smychok, and V. D. Novik, 'Razvitie idei i rabot A. O. Kovalevskogo v bor'be s vinogradnoi fillokseroi' in *Odesskaia oblastnaia nauchnaia konferentsiia*, 55–6.

perceived him as insensitive to the social and economic costs of radical measures. And critics in the scholarly world and beyond alleged that the state's financial generosity had corrupted good judgment. The latter charge was spurious, but there is little doubt that Kovalevskii's defence of radical measures was premised on a scientific misunderstanding.

What follows is a transnational genealogy of failure: how an idea that was born in the laboratories and the field stations of Provence, that was fine-tuned in the vineyards of Swiss Ticino and Valais, and that was then exported to the Russian south via a friendship between Kovalevskii and a French museum director, found fertile soil in the vineyards of Bessarabia, despite mounting evidence of its futility. For more than a decade after it had been discredited as a cure in Western Europe, the use of pesticide, the central component of radical measures, endured in Russia. For many educated laymen and scientists, the use of pesticide was under-girded by faith that modern science held the cure for society's ills. As Daniel Beer has argued about late-tsarist Russia, science, in contrast to the obscurantist state, embodied the possibility of reform 'in accordance with the secular pre-scriptions of empiricism and rationality'.[15] More important for Kovalevskii, radical measures were necessitated by an unusual Russian reading of Charles Darwin's theory of biological speciation, which saw the 'struggle for existence' occurring on the inter- rather than intra-specific level.[16] The phylloxera epidemic thus became a case study, albeit one that was playing out in accelerated fashion, of the struggle between *Vitis vinifera* (Common grape), the species to which all European wine varietals belonged, and *Vitis labrusca* (Fox grape) and *riparia* (River Bank grape) the American vines that conveyed phylloxera to Europe and were immune to its ravages.

In the latter respect, this chapter contributes to a body of scholarship that illu-minates the 'local-ness or particularity' of Russian science.[17] As the geographer David N. Livingstone has pointed out, scientific knowledge is thought to possess 'ubiquitous qualities', yet it is also 'the product of specific spaces' that are highly variegated by site, cultural arena, and chronology.[18] In the fight against phyllox-era, these variegations were evident in the realm of speciation theory, where

[15] Daniel Beer, *Renovating Russia: The Human Sciences and the Fate of Liberal Modernity, 1880–1930* (Ithaca, 2008), 2.

[16] For discussion of the Russian discomfort with the 'struggle for existence' in Darwinian theory, see Daniel P. Todes, *Darwin without Malthus: The Struggle for Existence in Russian Evolutionary Thought* (Oxford, 1989); Alfred I. Tauber and Leon Chernyak, *Metchnikoff and the Origins of Immunology: From Metaphor to Theory* (Oxford, 1991), 68–100.

[17] Susan Gross Solomon, 'Circulation of Knowledge and the Russian Locale', *Kritika: Explorations in Russian and Eurasian History* 9, no. 1 (Winter 2008), 14.

[18] David N. Livingstone, *Putting Science in Its Place: Geographies of Scientific Knowledge* (Chicago, 2003), xi, 86. On national styles of scientific thought, see Jonathan Harwood, *Styles of Scientific Thought: The German Genetics Community, 1900–1933* (Chicago, 1993); Paul Forman, 'Weimar Culture, Causality, and Quantum Theory, 1918–1927: Adaptation by German Physicists and Mathematicians to a Hostile Environment', *Historical Studies in the Physical Sciences* 3 (1971), 1–115.

Russian scientists such as Kovalevskii were more prone than their counterparts in the West to emphasize intra-specific cooperation in response to resource scarcity. At the Bessarabian Phylloxera Commission, Kovalevskii's unorthodox take on Darwinist theory intersected with governmental power and economic exigency to rule out experiments in alternate treatments. For aggrieved growers, who saw their vineyards uprooted and incinerated for the commonweal, this was the crux of the problem: state power was enlightened by science, thus making it infallible. However, faith in modern science was still faith—it existed outside the realm of reason and, in the case of radical measures, contrary to a growing body of evidence that suggested their uselessness.

This chapter is also an exercise in 'crossed history', *histoire croisée*, in that it seeks to illuminate the 'process of intercrossing in practical as well as intellectual terms' of Odessan politics and Bessarabian vineyards, on the one hand, and laboratories in Marseilles and Villefranche-sur-Mer, where the first experiments with insecticide occurred, on the other. Chief among the assumptions of the *histoire croisée* approach is that transnational historical phenomena are characterized by specific intersections between national contexts, and 'that something occurs within the crossing process' at these intersections that historians should strive to elaborate.[19] Part of the broader Russian borrowing of French language, culture, and ideas that had been underway since the early eighteenth century, the specific intersection between the Russian south and French Midi in the fight against phylloxera was the professional and personal relationship between Antoine-Fortuné Marion, the director of the Museum of Natural History in Marseilles, and Kovalevskii. As the use of pesticide, the central component of radical measures, crossed into Russia, it was transformed from a poorly working palliative measure for sick vines in France, to an utterly non-working cure for the epidemic as a whole in Bessarabia. This suggests that the root cause of Russia's calamitous response to phylloxera was not so much what Russia borrowed—a technology of questionable utility—but how, specifically, that technology came to Russia. The chief conduit for the transference of radical measures from Marseilles to Odessa turned out to be a person who was uniquely ill-equipped to abandon that approach, even when faced with its myriad failures.

*   *   *   *   *

Phylloxera was identified as the cause of vineyard blight in 1868, when Félix Sahut pulled a dying vine from the ground in the heavily infected Rhône valley,

---

[19] Michael Werner and Bénédicte Zimmerman, 'Beyond Comparison: *Histoire croisée* and the Challenge of Reflexivity', *History and Theory* 45 (February 2006), 30–50, 31, 38. *Histoire croisée*, in Werner and Zimmerman's usage, builds upon and includes 'connected', 'shared', and 'entangled' transnational approaches. As Michael David-Fox has recently argued, the history of Russian and Soviet science has long been open to explicitly transnational approaches, even though neither tsarist Russia nor the Soviet Union were nation-states: see Michael David-Fox, 'The Implications of Transnationalism', *Kritika: Explorations in Russian and Eurasian History* 12, no. 4 (Fall 2011), 888–93.

not far from Saint-Rémy, and saw tiny yellow aphids on the roots. Jules-Émile Planchon, a professor of botany at the University of Montpellier, confirmed the link between insect and disease in his laboratory. Because of the centrality of wine to the national economy, the French government courted potential cures with a prize of 300,000 francs. In 1875, the High Phylloxera Commission recommended the application of liquid carbon disulphide (CS_2), an insecticide distinguished by high flammability and low auto-ignition temperature, through subsoil injectors over a number of other treatments. The use of an insecticide had several perceived advantages. Vines that were already sick could be palliated. It was less expensive and more scalable than competing proposals. And it was consonant with the positivistic spirit of an age in which modern chemistry had already eliminated some of the uncertainty of agriculture. In the 1840s and 1850s, copper sulphate, the active ingredient in a preparation called *bouillie bordelais*, had been success-fully used against another vine pest indigenous to North America, the fungus powdery mildew, whose presence was confirmed in Crimea in 1865.[20]

By the early 1880s, however, the use of carbon disulphide had faded in France, as growers discovered that it could not permanently cure vines of infection, and that claims about its palliative effects were dubious at best. Other techniques, such as hybridization (crossbreeding vines of different species), vineyard flooding during dormancy, and even electroshock also proved ineffective or impossible to scale. Yet one technique, which was endorsed by a conference of growers and pro-ducers in Bordeaux in 1881, had proven effective. Planchon noticed early on that North American vines appeared resistant to the diseases they conveyed. In 1873, Planchon spent several months in the United States collecting and categorizing vine samples with Charles Riley, the Missouri state entomologist who was the first to recognize that the French and American vine aphids were identical. Indigenous American grapevines tend to produce 'foxy' wines, a deeply opprobrious descrip-tion among connoisseurs that is meant to conjure tastes and scents that are unc-tuous and animalistic, rather than the desirable fruity, nutty, and herbal qualities of *Vitis vinifera*. Planchon showed that it was possible to fission the resistance of American vines from their inferior wine qualities by grafting European scions onto American rootstock.[21] This had one chief advantage over carbon disulphide— it worked. It had several disadvantages as well. As Planchon's early experiments revealed, not all American vines could survive in the soils of France, nor were they all immune to phylloxera. Moreover, because grafting required the import-ation of millions of American vines and was ill-suited to mechanization, it was exceedingly expensive. Finally, despite the triumphant rhetoric of the so-called

---

[20] Paul, *Science, Vine, and Wine*, 9–25; Kolleen M. Guy, *When Champagne Became French: Wine and the Making of a National Identity* (Baltimore, 2003), 86–117; Anon., *Otchet o deistviiakh Imperatorskago obshchestva sel'skago khoziaistva iuzhnoi Rossii v 1866 godu* (Odessa, 1866), 19–20.

[21] Jules-Émile Planchon, *Les vignes américaines: leur culture, leur résistance au phylloxera et leur avenir en Europe* (Montpellier and Paris, 1875).

Americanists who advocated it, grafting was not a cure for sick vines. Instead, as French vineyards slowly and inevitably perished, peasants and estate owners would replace them with grafted vines that were resistant to phylloxera. Above all else, the failure of alternate treatments encouraged the conversion of French vine-yards to grafted vines.

Word of the French epidemic arrived in the Russian south in the fall of 1869, when the Russian ambassador in Paris forwarded a letter from the president of the Scientific Society of the South in Marseilles to the governor of Kherson guberniya.[22] As the scale of French devastation became clear, Alexander II banned the import of grape vines and cuttings in 1873, thus making it all but impossible for Russian viniculturalists to conduct the sort of experiments that were underway in Montpellier.[23] Eight years later, Alexander III approved prohib-itions against the import of all live plants, compost, potting soil, grape stamens (used in the cross-pollination of varietals such as Cabernet Sauvignon and Petite Syrah) and leaves into the Caucasus, which accounted for more than 60 per cent of the empire's wine production.[24] In April 1882, delegates at a vinicultural con-gress in Sevastopol, by then aware that previous legislation had failed to keep phylloxera out of Crimea and the Caucasus, recommended that the live-plant ban be widened to all of Russia. Because such a law would likely have put Russia in violation of the Treaty of Berne (1874), they required that all live plants be routed through ten customs stations on the western and southern frontiers, where they could be closely inspected. They also asked foreign consuls in St Petersburg to provide lists of reputable nurseries in their home countries that could sell plants certified free of phylloxera.[25]

The latter compromise was codified in Russia's 1885 law on phylloxera, which limited the import of live plants to specified customs stations, and allowed the Ministry of Finance and the Ministry of State Domains to prohibit even veget-ables from entering Russia should their presence threaten the safety of vineyards. Prohibitions on external trade were accompanied by a series of escalating internal rules—drawn up initially by provincial authorities in the south—that sought to regulate the movement of vinicultural items between infected and uninfected areas.[26] The 1885 law, which tried to systematize the hodgepodge of local restric-tions, limited internal trade to one-year-old, un-trellised cuttings. Commerce in older cuttings and in all rooted and un-rooted vines was punishable by a fine of up to 300 roubles or three months in prison.[27]

---

[22] DAOO, f. 22, 0. 1, d. 610, ll. 1–3.
[23] *Polnoe sobranie zakonov Rossiiskoi imperii* [hereafter PSZ], ser. 2, vol. 46 (St Petersburg, 1876), 447.
[24] PSZ, ser. 3, vol. 1 (1885), 26.
[25] DAOO, f. 22, o. 1, d. 612, ll. 130–132ob., 135. Delegates to a vinicultural congress in Tiflis made similar recommendations in 1885. See DAOO, f. 22, o. 1, d. 617, l. 21.
[26] DAOO, f. 5, o. 1, d. 1521, ll. 96–96ob.
[27] PSZ, series 3, vol. 5 (1887), 38.

The situation in Russia was thus similar to that in Burgundy, where the import of American vines was banned from 1874 to 1887, because of fears that their presence would accelerate the rate of infection. Like in Burgundy, none of Russia's internal or external restrictions were a failsafe way of preventing phylloxera from spreading. Vineyard inspectors often came across vines that were imported from abroad despite the prohibitions. These included not only the first vines to fall sick on Kristi's estate near Teleshov, which came from Germany at least two years after the 1873 decree, but also plantings from nurseries in Hungary and Reutlingen that had escaped official notice. Finally, the usefulness of vinicultural inspections—a central component of internal restrictions—was dubious because vines could be infected for many years before they became visibly sick. The only foolproof way to detect whether a vine was free of phylloxera was to uproot it, which was analogous to using autopsy as a means of determining human life expectancy. In a July 1886 report to the Minister of Internal Affairs, Khristofor Roop, the governor-general of Odessa, admitted that the vines on Kristi's estate had been infected for at least eight years before the disease became evident; another batch of dying vines may have been infected for as long as fifteen years.[28] After phylloxera was confirmed to be in Bessarabia, vineyard inspectors discovered that the K. I. Ber nursery in Kremenchug had unwittingly spread disease by selling seemingly healthy vines from its popular garden-supply catalogue. The Nikitskii Botanical Garden in Yalta, one of the pinnacles of horticultural expertise in Russia, appears to have done the same.[29]

Facing the likelihood of vineyard destruction at the hands of a foreign pest, the Russian government's initial inclination was to make its western border impermeable to infection. The realization that international quarantine had failed was the backdrop for the Committee for the Study of Bessarabian Vineyards, which was formed in 1880 as the predecessor to the Bessarabian Phylloxera Commission (1885). Located in Odessa, Russia's main wine entrepôt because of its limestone catacombs and modern transportation facilities, and attached to the Imperial Society for Agriculture in Southern Russia, the committee was charged with both Bessarabia and the less intensively cultivated Kherson guberniya, and later, Kiev and Podol'sk guberniyas.[30] Its members included Kovalevskii, the zoologists Ignatii Vidgal'm and Vladimir Zalenskii, the botanist L. V. Reingard, provincial representatives of the Ministry of State Domains, and several prominent growers. It also worked closely with the Odessa Entomological Commission, where the

---

[28] DAOO, f. 5, o. 1, d. 1521, ll. 16ob–17ob.

[29] DAOO, f. 22, o. 1, d. 612, ll. 17–17ob; d. 614, ll. 138–39.

[30] For figures on Odessa as a centre of the Russian wine trade, see K. Shul'tsa, 'Neskol'sko slov o vinogradarstva v Odesskom uezde' in *Trudy komiteta vinogradarstva*, vyp. 1 (1901), 161–4; Ruben Guliev, Robert Guliev, Aleksandr Prilipko, and Valentin Stremiabin, *Vino, vlast' i obshchestvo* (Kyiv, 2006).

biologist and future Nobel Laureate Il'ia Mechnikov was active.[31] Similar bodies were set up in Simferopol and Tbilisi, albeit with less eminent scientific representation, and in Rostov-on-Don under the auspices of the Free Economic Society. Although there was no specified hierarchy, these latter bodies deferred to Odessa on questions of science.[32]

Kovalevskii was named chairman of the Bessarabian Phylloxera Commission because he was one of a very small number of natural scientists in Russia already familiar with the aphid. He first encountered phylloxera during research at the Russian Zoological Station in Villefranche-sur-Mer, which he visited on three lengthy occasions in 1874–5, 1878–9, and 1881–2.[33] There Kovalevskii befriended and collaborated with the director of the Natural History Museum in Marseilles, Antoine-Fortuné Marion, whose subsoil fumigation technique led to an appointment on France's High Phylloxera Commission. With funding from the Compagnie des chemins de fer de Paris (PLM), which stood to profit from the transportation of insecticide to infected vineyards, Marion conducted the first large-scale tests of carbon disulphide in Provence in the 1870s.[34] He was also a proponent of Charles Naudin's secondary-effect hypothesis, which held that phylloxera was not the root cause of vineyard destruction, but a symptom of an underlying malady that made vines vulnerable to plant lice. Although Kovalevskii briefly mentioned Marion's views about secondary effect in a letter to Il'ia Mechnikov in March 1879, he did not embrace the hypothesis himself. Instead, with Mechnikov's encouragement, he devoted himself to potential biological treatments for phylloxera, a line of research pioneered by Louis Pasteur at the behest of the French state. However, according to Kovalevskii, Marion thought that Pasteur 'didn't really look, despite all the financial support…but everything was covered up by the glory of his immunological work'.[35]

Kovalevskii proposed to work with two types of fungi: *Isaria*, a genus of entomopathogenic mould that had previously proven effective against the larvae of grain weevils; and *Botrytis bassiana*, a species of powdery fungus that had nearly destroyed the silkworm industry in the early part of the nineteenth century. The former appeared to be most promising. During his return trip to Villefranche

[31] On Mechnikov's activities, see E. V. Zverezomb-Zubovskii, 'I. I. Mechnikov i A. O. Kovalevskii v zashchite rastenii', *Zashchite rastenii ot vreditelei i boleznei* no. 11 (November 1961): 59–61.

[32] On the formation of the Crimean committee, see Mikhail Ballas, *Vinodelie v Rossii: istoriko-statisticheskii ocherk*, vol. 1 (St Petersburg, 1895), 105–108.

[33] Data on Kovalevskii's travels are culled from Dogel', *Kovalevskii*, 139–41; Pilipchuk, *Aleksandr Onufrievich Kovalevskii*, 142. On the zoological station, see Sergei I. Fokin, 'Russian Biologists at Villafranca', *Proceedings of the California Academy of Sciences* 59, ser. 4, supplement 1, no. 11 (30 September 2008): 169–92.

[34] Paul, *Science, Vine, and Wine*, 37.

[35] A. O. Kovalevskii, *Pis'ma A. O. Kovalevskogo k I. I. Mechnikovu (1866–1900)*, ed. Iu. I. Polianskii (Moscow and Leningrad, 1955), 121; Aleksandr Kovalevskii, 'O bor'be s filokseroiu', in *Otchet i trudy Odesskago otdela Imperatorskogo Rossiiskago obshchestva sadovodstva za 1886 god* (Odessa, 1887), 72–82.

in 1881, Kovalevskii placed a single phylloxera aphid with *Isaria* spores in a damp glass chamber. The aphid soon died and was quickly covered with mould. Under a microscope, the aphid appeared to have been so thoroughly consumed that only the mould's filaments were visible. In December 1881, Kovalevskii wrote to Mechnikov that he was continuing these experiments by carrying *Isaria* spores and phylloxera together in his pocket, hoping the spores would penetrate the aphid's trachea.[36]

Of course, no biological treatment against phylloxera proved effective, and Kovalevskii eventually abandoned his experiments with *Isaria*. He did not return to France until 1892, and to the Russian Zoological Station in Villefranche until 1895. But he did leave convinced that the cure for phylloxera ultimately lay in Marion's experiments with carbon disulphide. Home in Odessa, Kovalevskii was not naïve about the chances of preventing infection. In an August 1884 report to the Imperial Society for Agriculture in Southern Russia, he noted that the main task of the committee was to determine 'the first moment' vines became symptomatic, so the subsequent spread could be minimized as much as possible. Because it was widely assumed that vineyard blight would enter Bessarabia from neighbouring Romania, Kovalevskii focused resources on a 30-kilometre-wide corridor along the border, from Khotinsk uyezd in the north to the mouth of the Danube. From 9 August to 10 October 1884, with a two-week reprieve for rainy weather, one of the Kovalevskii's colleagues at Novorossiysk University explored the corridor. His summary report was pessimistic, because Bessarabia's southernmost uyezd, Izmail, which had been lost to the Romanian principalities as a result of the Crimean War, was re-annexed by Russia after the Russo-Turkish War.[37] The areas along the lower Danube and Prut thus fell beyond the reach of the empire's initial quarantine laws. Although Kovalevskii's colleague found no sign of active infection on either side of the border (indeed, the nearest Romanian outbreak, in the Prahova region, was more than 160 kilometres to the south-west), there was good reason to believe that phylloxera was already present. Near the city of Kantemir on the lower Prut, the inspector discovered a large concentration of vines imported fifteen years earlier from nurseries in Romania and Champagne. The Commission maintained its focus on Romania in 1885, when Vidgal'm led a summer expedition to Romania's wine regions to gauge the threat of cross-border infection.[38]

Kovalevskii's focus on the western border stemmed from his fear that Romanian growers were too overwhelmed by phylloxera to halt its spread northeast. Their supposed helplessness in the face of phylloxera contrasted with Russia's preventive mobilization. The focus on the border also reflected the less admirable

---

[36] Kovalevskii, *Pis'ma*, 117, 121–2.
[37] On territorial shifts, see Charles King, *The Moldovans: Romania, Russia, and the Politics of Culture* (Stanford, 2000), 22–3.
[38] DAOO, f. 22, o. 1, d. 617, ll. 5–5ob., 38; d. 614, ll. 147, 151–2.

fact that limited financial resources necessitated a selective defence. In 1884, the Committee for the Study of Bessarabian Vineyards was able to support the salaries of only two vineyard inspectors, who were charged with all of Kherson and Bessarabia guberniyas. In 1885, it was able to employ three inspectors. Consequently, requests for money were one of the most ubiquitous forms of interaction between the committee and higher authorities.[39]

In the absence of concrete data about the effectiveness of carbon disulphide in Bessarabian vineyards, there were powerful forces lining up behind Kovalevskii at home. In June 1884 the Imperial Society for Agriculture in Southern Russia hosted a talk by the Crimean landowner A. N. Iznar, who had just returned from France. Iznar did not mince words: the French situation was 'hopeless'. The 'radical destruction' of phylloxera by chemical means—disinfecting the soil with carbon disulphide—was less costly than grafting, but still onerously expensive. Moreover, because it was impossible to inject the insecticide on a vine-by-vine basis, ostensibly healthy plants often perished as a result of treatment. Nonetheless, Iznar claimed that carbon disulphide was the best tool French growers had at their disposal to slow phylloxera, because grafting onto American rootstock was an 'impractical chimera' that would 'ruin grape growers...for dubious results that will take at least a century to realize'.[40] At the Sixth Provincial Entomological Congress in Odessa in 1886, M. V. Neruchev, the former editor of the defunct journal *Russkoe sel'skoe khoziaistvo* [Russian Agriculture], seasoned his own report on a trip to France with a similarly dim view of 'Americanization': 'They promoted the American vine, exulting its glory as the single means of defeating phylloxera. It is difficult for us to agree with that.'[41]

There were two reasons for scepticism about grafting among Russian growers. First, the Russian wine industry had struggled for many years to counteract the perception among domestic consumers that Russian wines were less desirable than imports. Even though Planchon demonstrated that European scions could be grown on American rootstock, fears persisted for many decades in Russia and elsewhere that the resulting production would suffer. Rejecting Americanization was thus an affirmation of the purity of Russian wine relative to its foreign competition.[42] Second, the costs of grafting were difficult to justify given the economic realities of viniculture in the Russian Empire. With the exception of a few high-profile crown estates, such as Abrau-Diurso, growing operations tended to be minor affairs: small landowners with small production levels and exceedingly tight margins. In 1882, municipal officials in Sevastopol, hoping to encourage greater investment in viniculture in the hills surrounding the naval port, tallied

---

[39]   DAOO, f. 22, o. 1, d. 617, ll. 25, 33; f. 5, o. 1, d. 1521, l. 152.
[40]   DAOO, f. 22, o. 1, d. 612, ll. 56–60.   [41]   DAOO, f. 5, o. 1., d. 1376, l. 31.
[42]   DAOO, f. 22, o. 1, d. 612, l. 65ob. On the similar resistance of wine *négociants* in Champagne to grafting, see Guy, *When Champagne Became French*, 86–9.

the start-up costs that aspiring growers faced. They found that by the time a vineyard produced a viable harvest in its fourth season, the grower had exhausted 1,959 roubles per desyatin (roughly 1.1 hectares). That figure included 1,200 roubles to purchase vines, and assumed no finance costs. A start-up loan, at 5 per cent interest, raised total costs after year four to 2,451 roubles per desyatin. At that point, the first harvest could be expected to yield 983 litres (80 *vedra*) of un-aged, barrelled wine per desyatin, which would fetch 240 roubles total (at the relatively optimistic price of 3 roubles/*vedro*). After four years, the total return on viniculture in Sevastopol was an unenviable 10 per cent.[43] Three years later, another estimate put the total costs, after year four, of planting a new vineyard on the southern shore of Crimea at 4,442 roubles per desyatin.[44]

In his talk at the Entomological Congress in 1886, Neruchev indicated that Bessarabian vintners, whose wines traded at a steep discount to Crimean labels, were able to eke out a small profit or break even only by ignoring costly, modern cultivation methods. Pruning during dormancy, removal of ancillary blooms during spring, cross-pollination, and elaborate frost protection could raise the costs of production beyond the revenues. Every desyatin of mature Bessarabian vines produced, on average, just over 5,000 litres of wine, which might fetch 75 roubles from a wine merchant. The costs of modern cultivation could be more than double that sum.[45] While Neruchev's figures were skewed by the marginal soil paradox that is common to winemaking (wines from the least productive regions, such as the Akkerman uyezd at the mouth of the Dniester, often fetched double the price per volume as wines from more fertile areas), wholesale conversion to grafted vines was economically unfeasible for most growers.

Kovalevskii was aware of the economic hurdles to replanting on American rootstock, as well as the fears among growers about a decline in quality. Yet the principal reasons for his resistance to grafting lay elsewhere. After returning from Villefranche-sur-Mer in 1882, Kovalevskii's role in the fight against phylloxera was primarily administrative and ambassadorial. At least once a month, he presided over commission meetings, where he orchestrated the radical measures that would make him unpopular among growers. He shared news from the anti-phylloxera campaign with the lay press in Odessa, Kishinev, and elsewhere, sometimes penning the articles himself. And he often spent the summer months traveling wine regions at home and abroad, visiting zemstvos and other local institutions to meet with landowners and peasants whose livelihoods were at stake. One trip in

---

[43] *Doklad komissii*, 2–3. On the economic challenges of viniculture in Bessarabia, see A. Kipen, 'Vinodel'cheskii krizis v srednei Bessarabii', in *Trudy s"ezda vinogradarei i vinodelov (10–20 fevralia 1902 g.* (Moscow, 1902), 1–10. On the costs of planting grapevines in Tsinandali, see STA, f. 354, o. 3, d. 1, l. 41.

[44] Iakov Bank, *O primenenii novogo sposoba razvedeniia vinogradnikov v razstilku (en chaintres) k mestnym usloviiam iuzhnogo berega Kryma* (Moscow, 1885), 4.

[45] DAOO, f. 5, o. 1, d. 1376, l. 30ob.

1887 took him first to Kishinev, then to Ploiesti, the capital of the Prahova region in Romania, then to an ampelography school in Budapest, where American vines were the objects of study, and finally to a nursery for American vines in Klosterneuburg, outside of Vienna.[46]

The result was incongruous. Even though Kovalevskii's work with the Bessarabian Phylloxera Commission had ceased to be scientific, his promotion of radical measures and hostility to grafting were premised both on his identity as a scientist and the positivistic worldview that it entailed, and on the research in comparative embryology for which he was famous. The former took shape as a cultural bias against grafting, what James Scott has identified, in a different context, as an '*unscientific* scorn for practical knowledge'.[47] Like other members of the Bessarabian Phylloxera Commission, Kovalevskii often couched Planchon's grafting as the 'traditional' cure. His characterization was not entirely unfair. The Romans had perfected vinicultural grafting at least two millennia earlier, in the second century BCE, when Cato described it in *De agri cultura* [On Agriculture].[48] This contrasted with carbon disulphide, which was undisputedly novel. It was produced in France in a modern factory, and was dispensed by machine, the subsoil injector. For Kovalevskii and many others, carbon disulphide exemplified a new age in agriculture, when modern chemistry would remedy the ancient problems of soil infertility and pestilence.

Even more important was Kovalevskii's understanding of phylloxera in light of Darwinist selection theory and his research in comparative embryology. In May 1891, after being criticized in the press for the failures of radical measures, Kovalevskii wrote to Mechnikov to explain his resistance to Planchon's 'traditional' cure—the success of which was being trumpeted in France. 'It seems to me that the phylloxera issue, the [downy] mildew issue, and even the old [powdery mildew] issue', in short, all the vine diseases indigenous to America, 'are united in one general question about the struggle for existence between the European species—*Vitis vinifera*—and the American species of grapes, which are now squeezing out the European species'. According to Kovalevskii, this struggle began when European settlers tried to cultivate the European grape on American soil. Their efforts were always undone by blight they could not explain. The struggle then continued in the 1830s and the 1840s, when 'amateurs' brought the Isabella varietal (*Vitis labrusca*) to Europe, and with it, powdery mildew. Because Isabella was immune to the disease it transmitted, it soon supplanted the European grape in regions afflicted by mildew, such as the eastern Black Sea coast. In time, as more growers replaced their mildewed vineyards, phylloxera also appeared.

---

[46] Kovalevskii, *Pis'ma*, 136.
[47] James C. Scott, *Seeing Like a State: How Certain Schemes to Improve the Human Condition Have Failed* (New Haven, 1999), 305; emphasis in original.
[48] Tim Unwin, 'Grafting', in *Oxford Companion to Wine*, 320.

Moreover, Kovalevskii feared that phylloxera was not the end of the onslaught. He likely had in mind the highly destructive fungal disease black rot, which in the mid-1880s was unwittingly imported into France from the eastern United States on phylloxera-resistant rootstock. Thus, disease was the 'enabler' of the American grape; it 'cleared the soil for the American grape, and after the initial panic, forced the French to make peace with the American vine', to grant it 'the right of citizenship'.

> We, the different phylloxera institutions, the Americanists and the radicalists, are taking sides in this struggle over plant types, either as allies of the American vine and phylloxera in its campaign against the European vine, or as defenders of the latter. It is still not clear who will gain victory, but *Vitis vinifera* is in perilous danger…Just as the Europeans are poisoning savage tribes with smallpox and alcohol, so too are American varietals poisoning *Vitis vinifera* with their diseases, thus clearing a path for themselves.[49]

Kovalevskii's linking of phylloxera with the 'struggle for existence' between European and American grapes reflected a distinctively Russian variation on selection theory: the conflict that drove biological change occurred on an inter- rather than intra-specific level. As Peter Bowler has shown, while there was wide scientific consensus in *fin-de-siècle* Europe that life had evolved over many aeons, there was hardly any on the exact mechanism of biological change. Darwin's view that natural selection was the cause of adaptation and speciation was not widely accepted until it was synthesized with Mendel's laws of heredity in the early part of the twentieth century.[50] Moreover, there was great scepticism about Darwin's selection theory among Russian natural scientists, in particular, because of its apparent Malthusianism.[51] Darwin's repudiation of the harmonious and balanced view of nature, in favour of the essentialness of population pressure and intra-specific competition over scarce resources, struck many Russian observers as an expression of British economic liberalism rather than natural law. As Daniel Todes has argued, such views were contrary to deep-seated features of Russian culture, which privileged cooperation and collaboration in light of resource scarcity. Kovalevskii's inter-specific revisionism almost certainly reflected the influence of his friend and collaborator, Il'ia Mechnikov, who was concerned with inter-specific conflict throughout his career, in large part because he rejected the Malthusian notion that overpopulation drove the struggle for existence. In 1879, Mechnikov showed that 'directed' inter-specific conflict (infection with a

---

[49] Kovalevskii, *Pis'ma*, 173–4.
[50] Peter J. Bowler, *Evolution: The History of An Idea* (Berkeley and Los Angeles, 2009), 224.
[51] Todes, *Darwin without Malthus*. See also James Allen Rogers, 'Russian Opposition to Darwinism in the Nineteenth Century', *Isis* 65, no. 4 (December 1974): 487–505.

parasite) was an effective means of controlling beet weevils in the Russian south. The success of that treatment underlay his encouragement that Kovalevskii investigate similar possibilities for infecting phylloxera with *Isaria*.[52]

Kovalevskii would therefore have resisted the free-market appropriation of Darwin's 'struggle for existence' that was common in Western Europe, even as his casual conflation of race and species would have been familiar to advocates of a different form of social Darwinism—one that was racially tinged and that underlay the rise of eugenics.[53] However, because Kovalevskii's emphasis was on the symbiotic relationship between American vines and phylloxera, the significance of his word choice lies elsewhere. Kolleen Guy has argued that the French battle with phylloxera intersected broader European concerns about America's sudden ascendance, because grafting raised 'specific questions about grape origins and the role of terroir' in the production of wine, and thus potentially undermined French claims to mastery in the field.[54] For many European consumers, the Americanization of what lay below the soil in French vineyards was the functional equivalent of the Americanization of what lay above, not to mention the wine that resulted from such compromised vines. In this light, Kovalevskii's resistance to grafting bore some resemblance to long-standing tropes in Russian culture and politics, particularly Filofei's sixteenth-century conception of Moscow as the third Rome, which presented Muscovy as the last bastion of uncorrupted Christianity, and which enjoyed great cultural currency in the nineteenth century to explain Russia's manifest destiny as imperial power.[55] In a world where French grapes were increasingly grown on American rootstock, Russian wine, made from varietals perfected in Burgundy and Loire, became more authentically French than the wines of France.

Darwinist theory aside, there was much about phylloxera that Kovalevskii did not grasp. Most important, the chief threat that phylloxera posed was economic not existential. Because vines could be infected for many years before perishing, phylloxera did not interfere with propagation, which in commercial vineyards occurred via cuttings rather than sexual reproduction to assure varietal homogeneity. And vineyards in sandy soils enjoyed almost complete immunity to phylloxera, a factor that all but guaranteed the survival of un-grafted *Vitis vinifera* in at least some parts of the world.[56]

---

[52]   Todes, *Darwin without Malthus*, 91–3.

[53]   On the different forms of social Darwinism, see Diane Paul, *The Politics of Heredity: Essays on Eugenics, Biomedicine, and the Nature-Nurture Debate* (Albany, 1998); Mike Hawkins, *Social Darwinism in European and American Thought, 1860–1945: Nature as Model and Nature as Threat* (Cambridge, 1997).

[54]   Guy, *When Champagne Became French*, 99.

[55]   Marshall Poe, 'Moscow, the Third Rome: The Origins and Transformation of a "Pivotal Moment,"' *Jahrbücher für Geschichte Osteuropas* 49, no. 3 (2001), 412–42. For a discussion of the salience of this trope in the Soviet period, see Katerina Clark, *Moscow, the Fourth Rome: Stalinism, Cosmopolitanism, and the Evolution of Soviet Culture, 1931–41* (Cambridge, MA, 2011), 1–41.

[56]   The immunity that sandy soil provided was known in Russia: see Gosudarstvennyi arkhiv v Avtomnoi respubliki Krym [State Archive of the Autonomous Republic of Crimea, hereafter GAARK], f. 156. o. 1, d. 16, l. 106.

At stake was the commercial viability of vineyards. Paradoxically, Kovalevskii's policies served to aggravate the already cruel economics confronting growers in the Russian south. Unlike the French chemists, Kovalevskii never intended carbon disulphide to be used as a palliative treatment. Instead, in what became the chief bone of contention, Kovalevskii ordered diseased vines, as well as healthy vines within a ten to twenty vine radius, to be uprooted and incinerated, and carbon disulphide injected into the soil to a depth of one meter to kill any remaining aphids. The latter was the so-called Swiss method of using carbon disulphide, because it had been devised in the vineyards of Valais and Ticino. Unfortunately for Kovalevskii, the Swiss method proved decidedly less popular in Russia than Swiss chocolate and watches. Opposition quickly developed among peasant growers and estate owners, who were angered at the perceived tyranny of the Bessarabian Phylloxera Commission, and among critics in Moscow, St Petersburg, and elsewhere, who saw in the mounting failures of the Swiss method the corrupting influence of the state's financial generosity and even an indictment of Darwin's selection theory.

The first brand of opposition stemmed from heavy-handedness. The Ministries of State Domains, Internal Affairs, and Finance, which were charged with implementing the 1885 phylloxera law, excelled mainly at angering the persons most impacted by blight. Once an infected vineyard was identified, landowners and peasants were forbidden, without special permission, from performing any vineyard work between 1 April and 1 October, when the leaf form of phylloxera might be present. This meant that the economic consequences of diagnosis were often immediate, since a final crop could not be salvaged. More than any other factor, the destruction of seemingly healthy vines, often pregnant with grapes, set growers against officials. At a meeting of the Bessarabian Phylloxera Commission in October 1887, Kristi expressed astonishment at the commission's inflexibility: it had long been known, he argued, that vines could produce viable harvests for many years after infection.[57] To prevent scofflaws from concealing phylloxera, growers were obligated under threat of financial penalty to report all symptoms of blight, and barred from treating infected vines themselves. Moreover, because Russia's wine belt was situated close to international borders, the most plentiful supply of excess labour for the anti-phylloxera campaign came from local military garrisons. In November 1886, Khristofor Roop assigned 240 soldiers to the destruction of vineyards in the Orgeev uyezd. He later lent 400 soldiers to the Crimean Phylloxera Commission for similar work. The military's role helped underscore the perception that growers were under assault. In at least one instance, a peasant shot at intruders from the phylloxera commission. Similar reports of violence and threats against vineyard inspectors came from the Gori

---

[57] DAOO, f. 5, o. 1, d. 1776, l. 147.

region of Georgia.[58] There were also widespread rumours that hordes of vinicultural dilettantes in uniform were unintentionally spreading phylloxera while traipsing through the countryside, and conversely, that inspectors were paid by the number of sick vines they identified, and thus had a disincentive to eradicate blight. Aware of the latter rumour, P. E. Leonard, a grower in the Bender uyezd south-east of Kishinev and chairman of the Bessarabian Agricultural Society, refused to let an inspector bring unknown vineyard workers onto his land because of his suspicion that the sudden appearance of similar workers a month earlier had caused his vines to fall sick.[59]

By the fall of 1887, only a year after the discovery of phylloxera, Bessarabian growers were in such turmoil over the actions of the phylloxera commission that the local press had caught on. 'The point is that no one believes', wrote one journalist, 'not in the danger borne by owners of vineyards, which have not yet been diagnosed, nor in the reassignment of vineyard workers, who are temporarily placed under the control of inspectors'.[60] Even the *Daily News* (UK) correspondent in Odessa heard about the growing unhappiness. He wrote, in stilted English, to the Imperial Society for Agriculture in Southern Russia to request information on the measures that were being undertaken against 'this serious and yearly extending insect plague'.[61] Although much of the domestic press coverage gently ridiculed the popular belief that local vineyards enjoyed some sort of immunity to phylloxera—that 'Bessarabian plants are not afraid', as one writer put it—there was no way to minimize the scale of opposition to the commission's slash-and-burn policies. Growers simply did not like radical measures, regardless of their effectiveness, because of the apparent injustice of a triage system that put the welfare of healthy vineyards ahead of those that were already sick.[62]

These were the circumstances that Karl Lindeman encountered during his visit to Bessarabia in September and October 1887. A professor of zoology at the Petrovskaia Agricultural Academy on the outskirts of Moscow, Lindeman had made a name for himself as an expert on grain pests. Although he later became a prominent figure in the Octobrist party, Lindeman's sudden role in the phylloxera debate appears to have been motivated more by imprudence than politics. At a meeting of the Bessarabian Agricultural Society in Kishinev at the end of September, Lindeman shared his views about Kovalevskii's anti-phylloxera campaign from the podium. 'Nothing justifies radical measures in the struggle with phylloxera', Lindeman told conference attendees, 'except the desire among members of the commission, who have received thousands of rubles from the

---

[58] STA, f. 243, o. 7, d. 184, ll. 9–12 of pamphlet 'Soveshchanie po delu o bor'be s fillokseroiu v Rossii', which lacks separate archival page numbers.

[59] DAOO, f. 5, o. 1, d. 1521, ll. 96ob, 110ob., 120; d. 1776, ll. 64–64ob, 72.

[60] 'Boiatsia li Bessarabskie kusty filoksery ili net?' *Odesskii vestnik* (21 September 1887). This article is available at DAOO, f. 5, o. 1, d. 1521, l. 179.

[61] DAOO, f. 5, o. 1, d. 1521, l. 248.   [62] DAOO, f. 5, o. 1, d. 1521, l. 79; d. 1776, l. 72.

government, to divide the sum among themselves, and in such a manner, to supplement their temporary salaries with huge travel allowances'.[63] Lindeman was subsequently invited to air his concerns about radical measures at a meeting of the Bessarabian Phylloxera Commission. On 26 October 1887, in front of an audience that included Mikhail Raevskii, then the chairman of the Crimean Phylloxera Commission and president of the Imperial Horticultural Society, and formerly the director of the Department of Agriculture in the Ministry of State Domains, Lindeman argued that radical measures had proven completely ineffective, that there was no scientific evidence that indicated the results should have been different, and that import restrictions had been futile. Six years after French growers shifted their attention from pesticide to grafting in Bordeaux, Russian scientific consensus on phylloxera had finally collapsed.

Yet the parameters of the debate in Russia differed significantly from the French experience. First, no one argued that grafting was the solution to vineyard blight. To the contrary, Lindeman's target was always the perceived tyranny of the phylloxera commission. He argued that growers should be allowed to fight or ignore vineyard blight as they saw fit, regardless of whether that entailed grafting or carbon disulphide. According to Leonard, who summarized Lindeman's position at the meeting's sixth session on 31 October, phylloxera was 'not such a terrible enemy that necessitated . . . heroic measures'. In his belief that a *modus vivendi* between grower and insect was possible, Lindeman's views bore some resemblance to Charles Naudin's secondary-effect hypothesis, even though he never questioned the primacy of phylloxera to blight.[64] Similarly, Kristi and Leonard, whose bête noire was the commission's policy of destroying infected vineyards before a final harvest, asked that all inspections cease while vineyard workers picked grapes. Leonard also took umbrage at Kovalevskii's assertion that the unhappiness among landowners was 'unimportant', because it reflected their unwillingness to see beyond their private interests.[65] While Kovalevskii's word choice was unfortunate, failure to account for the tension between the interests of landowners whose vineyards were infected and those whose vineyards were not, haunted the anti-phylloxera campaign. It was one of the major impetuses behind an early twentieth-century revision of the empire's phylloxera law, which offered compensation to landowners who sacrificed vineyards for the greater good.[66]

Second, even though no one argued for grafting onto American rootstock, it had become simply impossible, in light of the spread of phylloxera in Bessarabian vineyards, to do the opposite, to argue for the efficacy of radical measures. Simply put, the blight was spreading faster than infected vineyards could be

[63] DAOO, f. 5, o. 1, d. 1521, l. 220ob.   [64] DAOO, f. 5, o. 1, d. 1776, ll. 144–5.
[65] DAOO, f. 5, o. 1, d. 1776, ll. 33ob, 52, 147, 152, 172.   [66] STA, f. 243, o. 7, d. 416, l. 26.

uprooted, incinerated, and fumigated.[67] Instead, Kovalevskii's allies emphasized the reasonableness of radical measures given the Russian context. According to Raevskii, phylloxera was 'the most dangerous enemy that our agricultural production has encountered', but the efforts to halt its spread were hampered by the fact that 'our government could not spare the means to study this problem and immediately place the struggle on a correct path'. Despite the material constraints, experts had twice vetted Russia's anti-phylloxera policies at nationwide congresses in Sevastopol (1882) and Tbilisi (1885). Raevskii also alleged that Lindeman mistook radical measures' myriad problems for their futility. While quarantine had failed to stop the spread of phylloxera in Bessarabia and Georgia, it had worked elsewhere, such as Algeria and Crimea. The sudden reappearance of phylloxera near the Crimean village of Petrovo-Solovovo in the early 1880s, several years after it was thought to have been vanquished from the peninsula, was thought to have been linked with an old, undiscovered infection, not the permeable barriers of quarantine.[68]

After several days of debate and assurances from Kovalevskii that he would be more attentive to the concerns of landowners, commission members voted. Sixteen persons supported a continuation of radical measures and the Swiss method; four supported the French model of palliative treatment. The commission also unanimously rejected two competing proposals—one that would authorize the distribution of American vines to willing growers, and one that would further tighten the import restrictions on American vines. Instead, by a twelve-to-eight margin, the commission decided to create a field station to investigate which American vines were most suitable for the Russian south.[69]

The Lindeman controversy in 1887 was the last moment that radical measures were publicly vetted in Bessarabia, and perhaps the last moment that they retained sufficient support within the commission to continue. Because of the hazards of transporting carbon disulphide, its costs were large, but not large enough to warrant building a domestic production facility for a chemical that had only one identified use.[70] By 1887, more than two million roubles had been spent, which worked out to almost 2,000 roubles per hectare of treated vineyard. By one estimate, the cost of destroying and disinfecting an existing vineyard by radical measures was roughly the same as the cost of planting and cultivating a new vineyard, albeit on un-grafted vines, for four years until its first viable harvest.[71] Before the blight began to wane in Bessarabia in the early twentieth century, more than 180,000 hectares (1,800 square kilometres) of vineyards had perished, many for the second time. The fact that many of these second-round casualties could have been prevented,

---

[67] This was the retrospective conclusion of the head of the Department of Land Affairs in the Caucasus in 1898. See STA, f. 243, o. 7, d. 263, l. 259.

[68] DAOO, f. 5, o. 1, d. 1776, ll. 25ob–26, 28.   [69] DAOO, f. 5, o. 1, d. 1776, ll. 159, 177.

[70] STA, f. 243, o. 7, d. 184, l. 2.   [71] *Doklad komissii*, 2–3.

at the marginal cost increase of unavoidable investments in nurseries for American vines, made the failures of radical measures even more stark.

In 1890 Kovalevskii took a position at St Petersburg University and stepped away from the day-to-day affairs of the Bessarabian Phylloxera Commission. By then, his public notoriety had spread beyond the grape growers of Bessarabia to the intellectual circles of the north. In the late 1880s and early 1890s, Lazar Popov, who wrote a science column under the pseudonym El'pe for Aleksei Suvorin's conservative *Novoe vremia* [New Times], turned his attention to the fight against phylloxera.[72] Best known as a sceptic of selection theory, Popov was likely motivated by Kovalevskii's association with Darwin, not the failures of radical measures, but his criticism cut deep. In May 1893, while traveling to Kishinev, where he was scheduled to meet Marion before embarking on a joint Russian-French scientific expedition to the Caucasus, Kovalevskii wrote to Mechnikov that the criticism was taking an emotional toll.

> I don't know how things will turn out [with the expedition], but you already saw how our friends in *Novoe vremia* have ruined the first impression. I will try one more time to explain it, and then I will give up phylloxera for good.[73]

Despite Kovalevskii's departure, radical measures remained official policy until 1895, when the Russian government, in accordance with the recommendations of a nationwide vinicultural conference in St Petersburg, submitted to the inevitable destruction of un-grafted vines, and reconfigured the roles of the phylloxera commissions in Odessa, Simferopol, Rostov-on-Don, and Tbilisi to emphasize grafting, nursery development, and the oversight of a mandatory vineyard insurance scheme to pay for replanting. By then, opposition to radical measures was so broad that many of Kovalevskii's initial critics—such as Kristi, on whose estate phylloxera's presence was first confirmed in Bessarabia in 1886—had won election to a nationwide phylloxera commission.[74] As a result, subsequent legislation on phylloxera included many of the protections for which growers had long lobbied, such as an appeal mechanism for persons whose vineyards were found to be infected.[75] By 1895, it had become evident that radical measures were a boondoggle, a 'false path', as one critic put it.[76] 'Everyone knows that planting grape vines that

---

[72] See, for instance, El'pe [L. K. Popov], 'Po povodu filoksernogo voprosa', *Novoe vremia* no. 5449 (2 May 1891). El'pe published a similar series of articles on 27 March, 7 and 21 April, and 5 May 1888 under the title 'Nauchnye pis'ma: filoksernyi vopros'. These articles can be found in full at DAOO, f. 5, o. 1, d. 1803, ll. 64–7. On El'pe's view of Darwin, see Vucinich, *Darwin in Russian Thought*, 88–9, 129.

[73] Kovalevskii, *Pis'ma*, 200. On the preparations to receive the expedition in the Caucasus, see STA, f. 351, o. 1, d. 2, ll. 76–76ob.

[74] STA, f. 243, o. 7, d. 184, ll. 1–12 of pamphlet 'Soveshchanie po delu o bor'be s filokseroiu v Rossii'.

[75] STA, f. 243, o. 7, d. 667, ll. 7–9ob.

[76] Belen-de-Balliu, untitled essay, 108. See also V. E. Tairov, 'Frantsuzy o prof. Marione', *Vestnik vinodeliia*, no. 2 (1894), 67–70.

are not grafted onto American varietals makes no sense', wrote one member of the Ekaterinoslav and Tauride Guberniya Committee on Viniculture and Winemaking in 1915, 'because the vines will die completely from phylloxera within four to five years'.[77] While carbon disulphide continued to be used in the Caucasus and elsewhere against highly isolated outbreaks of phylloxera, it was never again couched as anything more than a means of forestalling the spread of phylloxera, and even the evidence for that was dubious.[78] In places like Kutaisi, where nearly every vine was infected, carbon disulphide was understood to be a pointless expense.[79] With the exception of the Stalin period, when quarantine policies were resurrected in southern Ukraine and the Caucasus because of a shortage of American vines, no one seriously questioned the wisdom of grafting onto American rootstock after 1895. There was simply no other way to guarantee vineyard longevity.

Despite their failures, the historical verdict on Kovalevskii's radical measures turned out to be largely positive. Soviet historians praised Kovalevskii's attempts to reconcile Darwinist theory with the practicalities of phylloxera prevention, even as they glossed over the details about how this was done. They attributed the failure of radical measures to popular resistance, which they saw as a symptom of capitalist individualism, greed, and unwillingness to band together to fight a common foe.[80] Soviet historians' unease with Kovalevskii's scientific justification for radical measures reflected the realities of the Stalin and Khrushchev periods. Starting in the 1930s, any discussion of Kovalevskii's views on inter-specific competition and the limits they imposed on his understanding of phylloxera, was bound to raise potentially dangerous questions about intra-specific competition, genetics, and the modern evolutionary synthesis then underway in Western biology.[81]

Paradoxically, Soviet historians denied Kovalevskii his most important identity—that of scientist—when explaining his role in the fight against phylloxera. They missed the fact that the failure of radical measures was, at its core, scientific, and that the roots of this failure stretched far beyond Russia's borders to Kovalevskii's friendship with Marion, and their experiments in Marseilles with carbon disulphide. In the phylloxera epidemic, Kovalevskii saw the outlines of Darwin's 'struggle for existence'. Pitting the European grape against its American counterpart, this struggle was always uneven because of the latter's evolutionary advantage. Thus Planchon's grafting, which Kovalevskii was prone to dismiss publicly as the 'traditional' cure, and which he often juxtaposed in an uncomplimentary

---

[77] GAARK, f. 156, o. 1, d. 16, l. 106.   [78] STA, f. 243, o. 7, d. 263, l. 260.
[79] STA, f. 243, o. 7, d. 184, l. 3.
[80] See, for instance, Peliakh, *Istoriia vinogradarstva*, 115; Zverezomb-Zubovskii, 'I. I. Mechnikov i A. O. Kovalevskii v zashchite rastenii', 60–61; Dogel', *Kovalevskii*, 107. The Ukrainian writer Mikhailo Kotsiubyn'skyi first put forth the view, in his short story 'Dlia obshchego blago', that the popular resistance to radical measures was a symptom of capitalism.
[81] On the plight of Soviet genetics under Stalin, see Ethan Pollock, *Stalin and the Soviet Science Wars* (Princeton, 2006), 63–8; David Joravsky, *The Lysenko Affair* (Chicago, 1970), 202–17; Nikolai Krementsov, *Stalinist Science* (Princeton, 1997), 54–83.

way with the promise of modern chemistry—was never a viable option, because it amounted to a conscious decision to forsake the imperilled European grape. It was not unexpected that Kovalevskii would espouse radical measures in the early 1880s—after all, many scientists in France and Switzerland held out similar hope for carbon disulphide, albeit as a palliative measure, before their optimism began to flag after the Bordeaux conference in 1881. Unusual were the reasons why Kovalevskii embraced radical measures as a cure, and why he continued to defend them in the late 1880s amid overwhelming evidence of their futility. There was simply no other way forward, he believed, if *Vitis vinifera* was to be spared extinction. In this manner, the chief conduit for the transference of radical measures from Marseilles to Odessa transformed a palliative measure for sick vines in France, which had dubious results at best, into a cure for the epidemic as a whole in Russia, which, as it turned out, did not work at all. In this transnational genealogy of failure, the act of crossing saw not merely the transference of a technology to Russia, but the transformation of that technology as well.

Of course, for reasons that Kovalevskii could not grasp—and that no scientist would fully understand for several more decades—his justification of radical measures was flawed, and more than a decade of anti-phylloxera work would come to naught. Questions of Darwinism aside, it may be the case that Russian scientists such as Kovalevskii, who enjoyed tremendous popular esteem, and who were often juxtaposed with an obscurantist state and a popular discourse of backwardness, were predisposed to this sort of protracted mistake, confusing futility for necessity out of conviction that modern science held the key. In the case of phylloxera, that conviction proved to be a very heavy burden for Kovalevskii.

✳   ✳   ✳   ✳   ✳

There is a strange coda to Russia's encounter with phylloxera. The aphid remained a substantial menace in the Soviet Union through the 1960s and 1970s, when the Crimean quarantine finally and fully faltered nearly a century after it had been instituted. Between 1962 and 1976, 19,000 hectares of vineyards in Crimea died of phylloxera, and another 25,000 were known to be infected.[82] This was still minor by nineteenth-century Bessarabian standards, but Crimea—with its prestigious former crown-estate vineyards such as Massandra and Novyi svet—had never been as intensively cultivated as the Caucasus or the Dniester river valley. Vinicultural agronomists continued to counsel the use of carbon disulphide to slow the spread of infection, and advocated new compounds such as hexachlorobutadiene (C_4Cl_6), the potency of which as a pesticide was unfortunately matched by its potency as a herbicide. But there would be no more replacing dead vineyards with un-grafted vines. Everyone knew that was a fool's errand.

[82] TsDAVO Ukraïny, f. 5201, o. 1, d. 593, l. 21; d. 597, l. 44.

In 1973, the Main Administration for Winemaking in Ukraine began receiving letters from an agronomist named V. M. Poichenko. Poichenko had made a name for himself as an expert on phylloxera, co-authoring the Soviet Union's authoritative guidebook to prevention and treatment.[83] Poichenko claimed to have found the Holy Grail—a means of preventing the infection of un-grafted vines. Poichenko wrote that he wrapped the roots of seedlings and cuttings in a 'protective, multi-layered, durable shell' composed of fiberglass, and that he injected a compound of fiberglass and organic pulp into vineyard soil around the roots of already established vines. This, Poichenko wrote, 'blocked phylloxera's path to the roots'. Poichenko presented his findings at scientific meetings in Simferopol and Yalta in 1974, where his colleagues deemed it such a hare-brained scheme that it did 'not require any verification'. Not willing to admit defeat, Poichenko reached out to a number of higher-ranking institutions and officials, claiming that his scientific findings were being suppressed and that his rights as inventor (as guaranteed by articles 40 and 47 of the Soviet constitution) were being violated. The persons to whom Poichenko addressed his complaints often forwarded them to others, so that by 1978 the Kiev Scientific-Research Institute for Hygiene, the State Inspectorate for the Protection and Rational Use of Land, the Ukrainian Committee on Nature Protection, the All-Union Academy for Agricultural Sciences, the Soviet Ministry of Food Production, and even the First Secretary of the Central Committee of the Communist Party of Ukraine, Vladimir Shcherbitskii, had all weighed in on Poichenko's findings. Their opinions were uniformly negative, for reasons that ranged from fears about food safety and soil pollution to bad science. Some were even annoyed by Poichenko's persistence. Summarizing the consensus, the Main Administration for Winemaking saw 'no reason to spend money for research on a problem that has no prospects for production'.[84]

Poichenko's quixotic campaign to convince his superiors of success in an endeavour that had confounded so many other scientists in Russia and abroad persisted until 1981, when the Ukrainian Central Committee instructed its agricultural department to refuse Poichenko's request to be named director of a yet-to-be-formed laboratory dedicated to phylloxera.[85] Eighty-six years after tsarist authorities admitted they had made a mistake by embracing the recommendations of one of Russia's most influential and respected natural scientists, the Soviet government saw, if not a crackpot in Poichenko, then a naïve scientific idealist. Science offered no silver bullet for phylloxera, which meant the cure would remain nearly as old as European viniculture itself. Poichenko's findings remained untested.

[83] I. A. Kazas, A. S. Gorkavenko, and V. M. Poichenko, *Filloksera i mery bor'by s nei* (Simferopol, 1960).
[84] TsDAVO Ukraïny, f. 5201, o. 1, d. 691, ll. 22–24.
[85] TsDAVO Ukraïny, f. 5201, o. 1, d. 1000, ll. 8–9.

3

Authenticity

Wine and the Ambivalence of Modernity

On 10 February 1902, at the invitation of the Moscow Committee on Viniculture and Winemaking, two hundred of the most prominent persons in the Russian wine industry gathered in Moscow for the Congress of Viniculturists and Vintners. On their agenda was a so-called 'crisis in winemaking' that had been unfolding for many years. The crisis, of course, included the force majeure of phylloxera, which required the slow-motion abandonment of vineyards that represented many years of investment. In wealthy France, estate owners and peasants were saddled with the costs of phylloxera for many decades; in poor Russia, with its small and economically precarious wine industry, the costs of phylloxera raised questions about the industry's future viability and strained the positivism that had infused commercial Russian winemaking since its inception a century earlier.

Yet congress delegates also lamented a crisis of human cause: steadily falling prices for domestic wines, which made it difficult for all but the hardiest producers to turn a profit; the industry's struggles to navigate a government monopoly on alcohol sales that mostly outlawed direct sales to consumers, even in vinicultural regions; inadequate rail infrastructure for transporting wine north without spoilage; onerous rail fees that discriminated between wine in glass bottles (which was expensive to transport), and wine in wooden barrels (which was cheap); insufficient cellar and warehouse space in Bessarabia, southern Ukraine, and the big cities of the north; the growing complexity, opacity, and anonymity of supply chains that linked grower, winemaker, and consumer; the glut of 'falsified' wines—mixtures of genuine wine, fruit juice, grain alcohol, sugar, and worse—that merchants produced at the end of those supply chains; and most important, troubling evidence that the burgeoning Russian middle class, contrary to the aristocracy, did not much care for wine made in the European fashion. Many Russian vintners had become very skilled at producing wine of good quality. Most Russian consumers appeared to prefer something different—the sweet, strong, and inexpensive concoctions that merchants blended and sold. Contrary to the Austro-Hungarian and German worlds, where the embrace of 'natural' wine was explicitly linked with the so-called *Judenfrage* via the prominence of Jews in agricultural commerce and long-standing, anti-Semitic tropes of inauthenticity and deception, Russian wine merchants were mainly guilty of giving Russian consumers what

Whites and Reds: A History of Wine in the Lands of Tsar and Commissar. Stephen V. Bittner, Oxford University Press (2021).
© Stephen V. Bittner. DOI: 10.1093/oso/9780198784821.003.0004

they wanted.[1] According to one estimate at the turn of the century, Russian consumers annually purchased more than five million *vedra* (61.5 million litres) of ersatz wine. After a century of tortured progress—of rising cultivation levels, improving wine quality, and even a number of successes in international tasting competitions, all punctuated by many lost fortunes and dashed dreams—Russian winemaking was foundering on the shoals of misguided policy and popular taste.[2]

Among the participants at the Moscow Congress was Aleksandr Kipen, who reported on the dimensions of the crisis in central Bessarabia. Born in 1870 into a Jewish family in Melitopol, Kipen would later achieve modest fame beyond the world of wine as a short-story writer, drawing comparisons to Turgenev. Kipen's entry in the *Brockhaus and Efron Jewish Encyclopedia* notes that, like Turgenev, he 'showed great familiarity with European life'. The latter came from a degree earned at the École Nationale Supérieure Agronomique in Montpellier, where Kipen became an expert on vinicultural grafting not far from where Planchon first devised the method as a weapon against phylloxera. After leaving Montpellier, Kipen found work in Kutaisi (western Georgia) and Bessarabia, overseeing the conversion of phylloxera-infested vineyards. He published a short story, 'Meteorological Station', in 1903, the first of many that chronicled the provincial intersection between aristocratic life, the liberal intelligentsia, national discontent, and popular rage at the beginning of Russia's revolutionary epoch. Despite first-hand familiarity with the 1905 pogrom in Odessa, Kipen was not a Zionist, seeing in the so-called Jewish question a broader question about the future of authoritarian Russia.[3]

In the published version of his report that circulated after the congress, Kipen drew an unexpected, and because it was included in a footnote, almost hidden linkage between the French experience with phylloxera, and the falsified wines that were then plaguing Russian vintners. In the mid-1880s, he noted, the use of sugar in winemaking was legalized in France, in order to ensure that harvested grapes produced adequate levels of alcohol to protect against spoilage, and to increase the quality of finished wine that was too high in acidity. The latter was achieved through a process derived by a Burgundy winemaker, Abel Petiot de Chamirey, in the mid-nineteenth century, where a solution of sugar and water was mixed with the grape pomace that collected at the bottom of fermentation tanks. The result, after a second fermentation, was similar enough in composition to the original wine that the two solutions could be mixed to mitigate high acidity

[1]   Kevin D. Goldberg, 'Reaping the *Judenfrage*: Jewish Wine Merchants in Central Europe before World War I', *Agricultural History* 87, no. 2 (Spring 2013): 224–45.
[2]   STA, f. 243, o. 7, d. 355, l. 27 and pamphlet after l. 50. On wine falsification, see V. E. Tairov, 'Postavshchiki fal'sifikatorov', *Vestnik vinodeliia*, no. 1 (1894): 1–6.
[3]   The Brokhaus and Efron entry on Kipen is available at https://ru.wikisource.org/wiki/ЕЭБЕ/Кипен,_Александр_Абрамович.

and low sugar levels in the latter.[4] However, as French growers struggled to fine-tune their grafted vines to French soils and climates, more crude forms of adulteration became common, such as adding sugar to finished wine. This stoked fears that traditional ways of winemaking in France had died alongside vines infected with phylloxera. In Vouvray and Rochecorbon, such fears were the impetus for local campaigns against wine adulteration. In 1900, the French Ministry of Internal Affairs outlawed entirely the use of sugar in winemaking.[5]

Kipen's story illustrates the dilemma that Russian winemakers faced as they tried to find their way out of crisis. The Petiot method was an early landmark in the science of oenology. Although it promised to make good wine more abundant, it also appeared to represent the falsification of an important component of the French cultural patrimony—fine wine. The latter was not an unusual concern in the last decades before the First World War, as European food cultures began to diverge from the economies and methods of food production. Belief in the existence of distinct national cuisines became part of Europe's burgeoning nationalist discourses. From French champagne to Hungarian paprika, foodways were evidence of the singularity of the nation among others, and of deep social and cultural cohesion.[6] Yet food and drink were increasingly standardized commodities. They were creatures of modern, scientifically informed modes of production and distribution, and subject to chemical tests for purity, uniformity, and safety.[7] Like the cosmopolitan and polyglot German Romantic thinkers who celebrated the authenticity of traditional peasant ways amid transformational change, these developments were seemingly incongruous, but not unrelated: the veneration of national cuisine was a reaction to advancements that threatened its particularism.

---

[4] This process is explained in John A. Mooney, 'Vinum de Vite: The Wine of the Mass', *American Ecclesiastical Review* 22 (April 1900): 360.

[5] A. Kipen, 'Vinodel'cheskii krizis v srednei Bessarabii', in *Trudy s"ezda vinogradarei i vinodelov (10–20 fevralia 1902 g.)* (Moscow, 1902), 10; James Simpson, *Creating Wine: The Emergence of a World Industry, 1840–1914* (Princeton, 2011), 59–63.

[6] See, for example, Kolleen M. Guy, *When Champagne Became French: Wine and the Making of a National Identity* (Baltimore, 2003); Leslie Chamberlain, 'Ideology and the Growth of a Russian School of Cooking', in *National and Regional Styles of Cooking*, ed. Alan Davidson (London, 1981), 140–47; Thomas M. Wilson, 'Food, Drink, and Identity in Europe: Consumption and the Construction of Local, National and Cosmopolitan Culture', in *European Studies* vol. 22, *Food, Drink, and Identity in Europe* (Amsterdam and New York, 2006), 11–30; Menno Spiering, 'Food, Phagophobia, and English National Identity', in *European Studies* vol. 22, *Food, Drink, and Identity in Europe*, 31–48; Tara Moore, 'National Identity and Victorian Christmas Food', in *Consuming Culture in the Long Nineteenth Century: Narratives of Consumption, 1700–1900*, ed. Tamara S. Wagner and Narin Hassan (Lanham, MD, 2007), 141–54; and the collection of essays in Peter Scholliers, ed., *Food, Drink, and Identity: Cooking, Eating, and Drinking in Europe since the Middle Ages* (London, 2001).

[7] See, for example, Adele Wessell, 'Between Alimentary Products and the Art of Cooking: The Industrialisation of Eating at the World Fairs: 1888/1893', in Wagner and Hassan, *Consuming Culture*, 107–24; Alessandro Stanziani, 'Municipal Laboratories and the Analysis of Foodstuffs in France under the Third Republic: A Case Study of the Paris Municipal Laboratory, 1878–1907', in *Food and City in Europe since 1800*, ed. Peter J. Atkins, Peter Lummel, and Derek Oddy (Aldershot, 2007), 105–15; Vera Hierholzer, 'The "War Against Food Adulteration": Municipal Food Monitoring and Citizen Self-Help Associations in Germany, 1870s–1880s', in Atkins et al., *Food and City in Europe since 1800*, 117–28.

Late-tsarist Russia was not immune to these developments. The idea of Russian cuisine as something valuably distinct from the French cookery ascendant among the aristocracy, began to gain currency among the intelligentsia during the first half of the nineteenth century.[8] Yet contrary to Europe, the particularistic culture of Russian food was mitigated by anxieties about Russia's civilizational identity. Russian foodways, in short, had to be recognizably European, at the same time that they were distinctively Russian. This was especially true of Russian winemaking, which seemed to rebut—in a small way, at least—an official and popular discourse on Russian backwardness vis-à-vis Europe.[9] Since the Black Sea territorial annexations of the late eighteenth and early nineteenth centuries, which brought indigenous wine cultures into the Russian Empire, winemaking stood as evidence of Russia's cultural refinement, the civilizing ethos of its imperial policies, and most important, its growing European-ness. Thus Crimea, which was home to the empire's most prestigious vineyards, stood to become the new Languedoc, and New Russia, which comprised the southern Ukrainian steppe, a European version of California, where Russians had tried to cultivate wine grapes at the Russian-America Company's Fort Ross encampment.[10] Of course, Russian elites spoke and wrote in these ways because they more often feared the opposite was true: New Russia was definitely not California, and Russia, despite its growing wine industry, differed from Western Europe in myriad worrisome ways.

Because of this ideological baggage, Russian winemaking was fertile ground for science. The previous chapter showed that vinicultural science was often compensatory in effect, as it righted imperial hierarchies that had been turned on their head by the wine economies and cultures that Russians encountered along the Black Sea. This chapter shows that oenology, the science of winemaking, came to be understood as a powerful leveller between Russia and the established wine economies of Europe, and later within Russia itself, between the prestigious estate vineyards on the southern shore of Crimea and impoverished peasant proprietors elsewhere. During the last decades of the nineteenth century, the widespread application of scientific methods, which were of European origin, transformed viniculture and winemaking in ways that would have bewildered earlier generations of growers and vintners. Trellised vineyards, which maximized the amount of foliage that came into contact with sunlight, gradually replaced vines that grew around trees, a common practice in Georgia, and sticks planted upright in the ground, common in Bessarabia and southern Russia (see Figure 3.1). Genetic

[8]   Alison K. Smith, *Recipes for Russia: Food and Nationhood under the Tsars* (DeKalb, IL, 2008).

[9]   On Russian backwardness, see Yanni Kotsonis, *Making Peasants Backward: Agricultural Cooperatives and the Agrarian Question in Russia, 1861–1914* (New York, 1999).

[10]   Andreas Schönle, 'Garden of the Empire: Catherine's Appropriation of Crimea', *Slavic Review* 60, no. 1 (Spring 2001): 1–23; L. A. Orekhova, ' "Krym skoro zastavit zabyt', chto est' Shampan' i Bordo": stranitsy istorii krymskogo vinodeliia', in *Dionis-Vakkh-Bakhus v kul'ture narodov mira*, vyp. 2, ed. V. P. Kazarin (Simferopol, 2005), 16–34; Ruben Guliev, Robert Guliev, Aleksandr Prilipko, and Valentin Stremiabin, *Vino, vlast' i obshchestvo* (Kyiv, 2006), 12.

Figure 3.1. Trellised vineyard in southern Russia, ca. 1905–1915. 'Vineyards and Gazebo', Prokudin-Gorskii Collection, Prints and Photographs Division, Library of Congress.

diversity began its century-long decline, as nursery managers in Russia and abroad sought to preserve and standardize desirable varietal characteristics by using cuttings rather than sexual reproduction to propagate new vines. Instruments such as the hydrometer came into use to manage the interplay of temperature, alcohol, and sugar after wine grapes were crushed. Elaborate chemical analyses sought to disaggregate the impact of climate, *terroir*, and varietal on grape composition. Climate-controlled storage and transportation facilities reduced the prevalence of spoilage before wine could be brought to market. Decades of painstakingly compiled meteorological data became the basis for new investments in viniculture, where the multiyear gap between financial outlay and viable harvest did not make it a business for the faint of heart. Even the vines themselves were altered by grafting to protect them from the scourge of phylloxera.

These changes did not occur all at once. Old ways coexisted with the new, even beyond the 1917 caesura when viniculturists in the Soviet Union found themselves subject to the same political forces that sought to modernize and regulate the grain economy of the north. Yet there is little doubt that Russian winemaking, especially its more commercial facets, became less hidebound in the late-tsarist decades, despite an outward veneration of tradition, longevity, and age that Russian vintners borrowed from their Western counterparts. As a result, Russian winemaking became more standardized, both in terms of the scientifically informed practices that yielded grapes and wine, and in terms of the wine itself, which became more uniform across vintage, varietal, and producer.[11]

Mark Steinberg has recently argued that during the final tsarist decades residents of St Petersburg were aware that they inhabited an age characterized by progress. Yet they were less certain that progress was a good thing, much less something that increased aggregate human happiness.[12] St Petersburg offered unmatched opportunities for individual freedom and diversion; it was also characterized by anomie, social confusion, widespread criminality, and moral decay— the afflictions of modernity, many persons thought. A similar ambivalence was present in controversies surrounding oenology. By the first years of the twentieth century, it had become common in Russia for commercial vintners to remediate flawed must with sulphurous acid, which helps stabilize wine as it ages by prohibiting the growth of acetic acid and wine's transformation into vinegar, and more commonly with sugar, which is fuel for the fermentation process. These technologies promised to democratize a previously rare luxury item—good domestic wine—by making it more abundant and less expensive for consumers. They also promised greater affluence for growers and vintners in regions far from the prestigious estate vineyards on the southern shore of Crimea, where less than perfect climates and soils resulted in less than perfect wine.

To oenology's critics, however, these practices undermined the very purpose of winemaking, which was to produce something artisanal, with age-old varietals on vines that were perfectly acclimated to their microclimates and soils, using techniques honed over many generations. Similar to the French wine *négociants* who wondered whether it was possible to produce authentically French wine with phylloxera-resistant vines grafted onto American rootstock, Russian critics of oenology worried that science had transformed the very nature of wine.[13]

---

[11]   While parallel developments occurred in France in the context of phylloxera (see Harry W. Paul, *Science, Vine, and Wine in Modern France* (Cambridge, 1996)), commercial winemaking in the new world—in California, Argentina, and Australia, in particular—tilted toward science, mechanization, and big-business economies of scale from inception. This reflected chronological overlap—the advent of commercial viniculture in these places coincided with the advent of oenology, for instance—as well as the sense that science and industry were the tools of the upstart (see Simpson, *Creating Wine*, chs 9–11). But just as important was the comparative absence of elitist notions of winemaking as an artisanal endeavour. As Paul Manning has argued about California, such notions were generated retrospectively: see Paul Manning, *The Semiotics of Drink and Drinking* (London, 2012), 23.

[12]   Mark D. Steinberg, *Petersburg Fin de Siècle* (New Haven and London, 2011), 3–6.

[13]   Guy, *When Champagne Became French*, 99.

Oenology may have been progress, but had something valuable and distinctively European been lost along the way? If producing fine wine in the European fashion conveyed status, what was the point of taking scientific shortcuts?

In the years before world war, revolution, and civil war nearly destroyed Russian viniculture entirely, these were the questions at the forefront of the Russian wine industry. They underscored the ambivalence that proponents of the particularistic culture of wine felt about the standardizing impulses of oenology, and challenged facile equivalencies between the meanings of Europe, progress, and refinement in late-tsarist Russia. In a country where wine had always been understood as much more than something to drink, the characteristics that made wine authentically European were far from insignificant.

*   *   *   *   *

On the western shore of the Dniester estuary, south of the old Turkish fortress at Akkerman, lies the vinicultural community Shabo (Chabag). Settled initially in the 1820s by colonists from Vaud and blessed like Champagne-Ardenne with soils high in sand and chalk, Shabo became renowned over the course of the nineteenth century for producing wine of good quality, which could sell for five times the price of wines from neighbouring Russian and Ukrainian peasant communities. Shabo's vinicultural expertise, which was transmitted across several nineteenth-century generations, and which was combined with tax incentives, conscription exemptions, and unique patterns of heritable landholding, produced many of the trappings of small-town affluence: a local physician, a bank, a post office, and even a number of local wine magnates who surrounded themselves with the comforts of domesticity. As Carol Stevens has shown, however, the premium commanded by Shabo wines likely declined to a few kopecks per *vedro* (12.3 litres) by the end of the nineteenth century, as Shabo winemakers ran up against the reality of wine in the empire of vodka: a small domestic market, stiff competition from abroad, and inadequate domestic transportation infrastructure from the vineyards of the rural south to the wine consumers of the urban north.[14]

Indeed, the initial success of Shabo aside, winemaking in the Russian Empire had always been a precarious economic venture. For wealthy estate owners on the southern shore of Crimea and elsewhere, it was less a business than a labour of love and marker of identity. The latter were balms for the inevitable late-spring freeze, harvest-time rain, bout of pestilence, and the financial disaster that ensued. For poorer proprietors in Bessarabia, southern Ukraine, and the Caucasus, commercial viniculture (as opposed to production for home consumption) was precarious because it was subject to economic and natural forces far beyond the grower's control. Moreover, making wine was no easy thing: the bounty of a

---

[14] Carol B. Stevens, 'Shabo: Wine and Prosperity on the Russian Steppe', *Kritika: Explorations in Russian and Eurasian History* 19, no. 2 (Spring 2018): 292–8.

successful harvest could easily be ruined by mistakes in production that were as mystifying as they were common: exposure to extraneous bacteria, too much oxygen in the barrels, fermentation or storage at the wrong temperature—the list of potential problems was almost endless. Proponents of the vinicultural economy often noted that wine grapes were among the empire's most lucrative crops— a hectare of vineyards, for instance, produced far more income each year than a hectare of wheat. Yet vineyards also had start-up and maintenance costs commensurate with their high returns. Few fortunes were made in the wine business, and many were lost.

There was also the problem of weather. At best, the Russian Empire's vinicultural territories were liminal to the northern hemisphere's ten-degree Celsius isotherm, south of which large-scale viniculture was possible. In 1877, the tsarist government's statisticians published sixteen years of weather data to underscore for potential vintners the salubrious southern Crimean climate. Simferopol recorded an average annual temperature of 9.6 degrees Celsius, Sevastopol 11.6, Karabakh (Alushta) 12.6, and Yalta 13.6. While these locales experienced only one October (1861) and two April (1861 and 1875) freezes, Simferopol recorded an absolute low of –28.7 degrees, and Sevastopol –26.2 degrees, cold enough to kill even dormant vines.[15] Similarly wide fluctuations characterized vinicultural territories less advantageously positioned vis-à-vis the isotherm. The Odessa region, long the undeclared capital of the tsarist and Soviet vinicultural establishment, was seemingly ideal for viniculture because it had an annual heat summation (the annual sum of daily high temperatures) in excess of 3,400 degrees Celsius. Nonetheless, in the winter of 1836 and 1892/3, Odessa's vineyards perished from temperatures as low as –30 Celsius.[16]

The profound difficulties of viniculture in Russia's continental climate were the unspoken subtext for much of the debate on phylloxera in the previous chapter. Even Aleksandr Kovalevskii, an embodiment of the era's scientific optimism, told Bessarabian growers in 1887 that the costs of replanting vineyards raised unavoidable questions about the economic viability of their operations. Bessarabia, after all, did not have Bordeaux's perfectly suited climate.[17] During the Soviet period, vinicultural agronomists trained vines to be flexible in regions prone to extreme cold, so vines could be buried under the earth before the first snow and then excavated in the spring. During the tsarist period, protections against extreme cold, like the science of predictive meteorology, were extremely limited. Even

---

[15] I. Bok and G. Ershov, eds., *Vinogradarstvo i vinodelie v Rossii v 1870–73 godakh*, Statisticheskii vremmenik Rossiiskoi imperii, seriia II, vyp.15 (St Petersburg, 1877), 75–6.

[16] Guliev et al., *Vino, vlast' i obshchestvo*, 6, 50. The Soviet method of calculating heat summation differed from the so-called Winkler index, which was devised by A. J. Winkler and Maynard Amerine at the University of California, Davis in the mid-twentieth century, and which is now the standard. That scale counts only the daily high temperatures of the growing season, 1 April to 31 October.

[17] DAOO, f. 5, o. 1, d. 1776, l. 187.

after harvest, Russia's extreme weather confounded efforts to bring wine to market. Merchants in Moscow and elsewhere complained repeatedly about broken barrels, popped corks, and spoiled wine—in short, wine shipments from the south that were ruined by winter ice and summer heat.[18]

By the mid-1890s, however, it had become clear to many persons in the Russian wine industry that government policy was exacerbating the difficulties posed by nature. Critics principally had in mind the state monopoly on alcohol sales, which Sergei Witte, who was inspired by a similar scheme in Germany, introduced in stages beginning in 1894. The monopoly replaced a system of excise taxation that had existed for distilled alcohol, beer, and mead since 1863. To ensure the widest possible payment of alcohol taxes, the monopoly did away with the elaborate system of excise tax verification and oversight that had evolved after 1863, and limited the sale of alcohol, including conventional wine, to state-owned stores (so-called *kazenki*) and accredited merchants. In Tauride guberniya, which included Crimea and a large swathe of mainland Ukraine south of Dnieper River, the monopoly actually increased the number of retail outlets that sold wine, from fifteen in 1895 to thirty-three in 1900. Yet other types of establishments that sold wine went into steep decline: the number of Russian wine cellars fell from 233 to 219; public eating houses from 955 to 235; and foreign wine (so-called Rhine) cellars from 393 to 97.[19]

The idea of a monopoly on alcohol sales was not new to Russia. Beginning in the sixteenth century, state monopolies had alternated with *otkup*, a tax farming arrangement where private individuals or groups purchased the right to collect alcohol taxes.[20] For viniculturalists and winemakers, the monopoly was nothing short of a disaster, because it put them at the mercy of a small number of commercial middlemen and curtailed a long-standing right to sell directly to consumers. Even though the monopoly was cloaked in the language of temperance and public health, winemakers accused it of aggravating the glut of falsified wines in the Russian marketplace—wines that were strengthened with alcohol and sweetened with sugar after production, typically by merchants. Under the jurisdiction of the monopoly, Russian wine producers had lost control of the object of their labour. Indeed, given the frequency of wine falsification at the hands of merchants, Russian winemakers had lost control of the production process itself, of determining when a wine was finished. In Marxist terms, winemakers had become alienated.[21]

[18] STA, f. 354, o. 3, d. 33, l. 3.
[19] G. I. Gogol'-Ianovskii, 'O vozmozhnosti vvedeniia monopolii v Zakavkaze', in *Trudy s"ezda*, 2; 'Po povodu predstoiashchago naloga na vino', *Vestnik vinodeliia*, no. 6 (1894): 323–8; 'K proektu naloga na vino', *Vestnik vinodeliia*, no. 11 (1894): 643–54.
[20] Mark Lawrence Schrad, *Vodka Politics: Alcohol, Autocracy, and the Secret History of the Russian State* (Oxford, 2014), 94–5.
[21] N. A. Lobun'ko, *Vinogradarsto i vinodelie Stavropolia: stranitsy istorii* (Stavropol', 2004), 456–69; K. A. Kolokol'nikov, *Razvitie vinnoi monopolii v Tomskoi gubernii s Semipalatinskoi oblast'iu, v sviazi s istoriei vinnoi monopolii v Sibiri* (Tomsk, 1914).

Not surprisingly, viniculturalists and winemakers were almost uniformly grim in their view of the monopoly: it had created 'difficult circumstances' and 'abnormal local conditions', wrote one Bessarabian winemaker in 1901. Even Shabo, once the paragon of vinicultural wealth, had fallen on hard times after Bessarabia was moved under the jurisdiction of the monopoly in 1896. 'Our village, formerly a Swiss colony, arose on account of the Russian government's desire to develop and improve the viniculture of Bessarabia', one city official wrote in 1901.

> Our fathers, who left their native land and settled here for that purpose, worked in the most unfavorable conditions, and fully met the hopes of the government; the Shabo region became famous, and not only in all of Russia, for its grapes and wine.

However, because it curtailed demand for wine by restricting the locations where and even times when it could be sold, the monopoly made it difficult for winemakers to find buyers willing to pay fair price. Often winemakers gave their wine away for free, the city official wrote. The latter allegation was more than hyperbole. Because producing wine with sufficient alcohol was a long-standing difficulty in areas liminal to the ten-degree Celsius isotherm, Shabo's winemakers often found themselves in possession of items of declining value, because wines with less than 11 per cent alcohol were prone to spoilage unless properly stored. Even in good years, Bessarabian winemakers struggled to produce wine with alcohol contents above 9 per cent. This put accredited wine merchants in distant cities at a distinct advantage in negotiation over wholesale prices. 'All that remains', wrote Aleksandr Kipen, 'is to wait for a buyer, while sitting at home, writing letters to wine merchants'. Shabo lobbied for the right to sell its wine by commission through licensed merchants, in order to exert greater control over price, and petitioned repeatedly for permission to open new warehouse and cellar facilities, knowing that the ability to preserve wine for long periods would assist in negotiations with merchants. But the petitions were always denied 'without explanation of the reasons, creating in the south several monopolists of the wine trade, at whose mercy we reside, and who threaten us hourly with a syndicate'. As Kipen put it in 1902, it was 'no secret' among merchants that Bessarabian producers lacked adequate storage space for their wines.[22]

In Kipen's telling, the principal victims of the wine monopoly were peasant proprietors, whose wines sold for wholesale prices that correlated inversely with the tax. This reflected the peculiarity of peasant production in Bessarabia, where a significant proportion of wine went to distilleries, where it was turned into grape vodka, brandy, or something approaching grappa. In 1885, when the excise tax

---

[22] Kipen, 'Vinodel'cheskii krizis', 3; DAOO, f. 22, o. 1, d. 626, ll. 7, 49–49ob.

was 4 kopecks per percentage point of alcohol, Bessarabian peasants sold 1.5 million *vedra* (18.4 million litres) of wine to distilleries; by 1892, when the excise tax rose to 6 kopecks, this figure had fallen by two-thirds. In economic terms, demand for Bessarabian peasant wine was highly elastic: producers paid for the bulk of the excise tax in the form of reduced demand or reduced wholesale prices. Very little of the tax was borne by consumers or merchants. In its original iteration, the wine monopoly included several loopholes meant to protect peasant proprietors from elastic demand. Peasants, for instance, had the right to sell wine freely, without going through *kazenki* or accredited merchants, at seasonal bazaars and fairs. Consequently, in the first years of the monopoly, large amounts of Bessarabian peasant wine were exported to neighbouring Kherson, Podolsk, and Kiev guberniyas. However, these loopholes were slowly tightened. By 1902, Bessarabian peasants had the right of trade at bazaars and fairs only within Bessarabia proper. Moreover, there were rumours that this right would soon be limited to only those producers who owned five desyatins (5.5 hectares) or more of land. In the final year before the institution of the wine monopoly in Bessarabia, producers and merchants sold 1,300 barrels of wine (640,000 litres) at the Tiraspol bazaar; within a few years, the volume of wine trade at the bazaar had fallen by 87 per cent.[23]

Despite its disproportional impact on peasants, wealthy producers were not spared the reduced demand and downward pressure on wholesale prices that the monopoly engendered. In Bessarabia, Kipen wrote, large proprietors, who tended to cultivate French varietals, found that even cognac production had become unprofitable, because their costs of cultivation were comparatively high. Similarly, a 1901 survey of viniculture on the southern shore of Crimea, found that estate owners were suffering from the monopoly's distancing of producer and consumer. Because Crimean producers could no longer sell directly to consumers, wine drinkers often had no idea where their wines originated, much less who made them. This was especially disastrous for the southern shore, where high land and labour prices made it difficult for producers to compete on price with their counterparts in the Caucasus and Bessarabia. In the 1890s, Crimean producers—inspired by the vagaries of wine production in Bordeaux, where wine from a famous château might sell for ten times the price of wines from neighbouring villages—began to speak about the price premium of *terroir* as a way of compensating for their high production costs (see Figure 3.2). They now found that the wine monopoly had introduced a degree of anonymity into the sales chain that made *terroir* more opaque than ever.[24]

---

[23] Kipen, 'Vinodel'cheskii krizis', 1–2; STA, f. 243, o. 7, d. 355, l. 50/6.

[24] A. Volzhenikov, *Sovremennoe polozhenie vinodel'cheskogo khoziaistva na IuBK* (Simferopol, 1901), 1, 4, 15.

Figure 3.2. Wine and cognac display case owned by the trading house Vladimir Vishniakov at the Agricultural, Handicraft, and Industrial Exhibition in Borovichi in 1894. Vishniakov produced wine and cognac at an estate on the southern shore of Crimea, near Alushta, and sold directly to consumers in Moscow and St Petersburg prior to the alcohol monopoly. Slavic and East European Collections, The New York Public Library, *Al'bom Borovicheskoi oblastnoi sel'sko-khoziaistvennoi, kustarnoi, i promyshlennoi vystavki* (n.p., 1894).

Around the turn of the century, the idea of convening a national congress to resolve the crisis began to appear in local vinicultural records, particularly in Bessarabia and Georgia, which bore the brunt of the unfolding catastrophe. There were ample precedents for such an endeavour. As Joseph Bradley has noted, the final fifty years of tsarist rule witnessed more than 1,000 association congresses, despite the fact that Russia was 'hardly known for its associational impulse or its public assemblies'.[25] Moreover, similar congresses on the condition of national and regional winemaking had occurred in Sevastopol (1882), Tbilisi (1885),

---

[25] Joseph Bradley, *Voluntary Associations in Tsarist Russia: Science, Patriotism, and Civil Society* (Cambridge, MA, 2009), 211.

Kishinev (1892), and Novorossiysk (1899 and 1900). Russian winemakers, to the surprise of no one, had proven very adept over the years at talking about wine in official settings. As one of the principals of the 1902 Moscow Congress admitted from the dais, 'when the topic is winemaking, I can speak without break for twelve hours'.[26]

Planning for the congress coalesced around two figures—Prince Lev Golitsyn, Russia's most acclaimed vintner, and Vasilii Tairov, the editor of *Vestnik vinodeliia* (Winemaking Bulletin), and a long-time figure in the world of Bessarabian wine. Though widely known to be enemies, a fact that the congress would put in sharp relief, Golitsyn and Tairov were the only persons with the reputations and political connections to chaperone a solution to the unfolding crisis through government channels. It is difficult to imagine a more different pair. Born in 1845 in tsarist Poland, Golitsyn knew all the advantages of aristocratic birth and extravagant wealth, with an estate childhood and polyglot homeschooling that resembled something Adam Mickiewicz might have described in *Pan Tadeusz*. After earning a degree from the University of Paris, Golitsyn had careers in the Ministry of Foreign Affairs, the Russian bar, and provincial politics. In 1878, he bought 230 hectares of land in the hills outside of Sudak, which he named Novyi svet, and began to grow grapes and make wine. Golitsyn did the latter with such élan that in 1891 Alexander III named him chief vintner for the southern crown estates—Abrau-Diurso, Massandra, Livadiia, Ai-Danil', and Sudak. By the turn of the century, Golitsyn's sparkling wines from Abrau-Diurso and Novyi svet, which included a special 'coronation' cuvée, were nearly as coveted among knowledge-able Russian consumers as more famous labels from France, Italy, and Spain. Among Novyi svet's many accolades was a grand-prix (best-in-show) medal from a competition in Bordeaux that coincided with the Exposition Universelle in Paris in 1900. The winning bottle was a sparkling wine from the 1899 harvest, which bested numerous grand crus from famous châteaux. More than a century later, Golitsyn's success remains the unquestioned acme of Russian and Soviet winemaking, proof of a vinicultural potential along the northern Black Sea coast that remains mostly unrealized.[27]

Golitsyn embodied a strand of winemaking that grew out of the Russian variant of what Norbert Elias has termed the 'civilizing process'.[28] While Russia's first encounter with winemaking likely occurred in the seventeenth century, when Persian merchants planted *Vitis vinifera* near Astrakhan, the wider consumption, and later, production of wine were part of Russia's post-Petrine embrace of

[26] N. K. Laman and A. N. Borisova, *Kniaz' Lev Sergeevich Golitsyn: vydaiushchiisia russkii vinodel* (Moscow, 2000), 299.
[27] Laman and Borisova, *Kniaz' Lev Sergeevich Golitsyn*, 161; Ballas, *Vinodelie v Rossii*, vol. 6 (St Petersburg, 1903), 283–8.
[28] Norbert Elias, *The Civilizing Process*, vol. 1: *The History of Manners*, trans. E. Jephcott (Oxford, 1978).

European cultures and values.[29] By the latter half of the nineteenth century, Russia imported vast quantities of wine each year from France, Italy, Spain, Portugal, and Hungary. Russian demand for foreign sparkling wine was so great (at nearly a million bottles per year, between 1896 and 1900) that the French producer Henri Roederer opened a production facility in the Langeron neighborhood of Odessa, and brought his *chef de cave* from Rheims to oversee production from base wine that originated with Roederer's traditional growers.[30] The consumption of European wine thus became a marker of social status and identity in late-tsarist Russia, as it had been in seventeenth-century England and Scotland, where it was associated with aristocratic and royal power.[31] The ubiquity of foreign wines on elite Russian tables in the late nineteenth century fostered a culture of connoisseurship and, in the case of Golitsyn, a determination to raise the level of domestic winemaking and domestic wine palates, particularly among the burgeoning middle class, to European standards. Even though Golitsyn was blessed with one of the oldest and most famous aristocratic names in Russia, he reputedly told friends that the title he prized above all others was 'Russian vintner'.[32]

Whereas Golitsyn represented the elitist, civilizing aspects of Russian winemaking, Tairov traced his roots to a more egalitarian, indigenous, and provincial strand. Born in a village in Armenia in 1859, Tairov spent his formative years in Yerevan and Tiflis (Tbilisi), where wine was embedded in indigenous economies and cultures many millennia before the Russian annexation. With degrees from the Petrovskaia Agricultural and Forestry Academy (later the Timiriazev Agricultural Academy) in Moscow and an oenological institute in Klosterneuburg (lower Austria), Tairov worked in Wiesbaden and Montpellier before founding *Vestnik vinodeliia*, the most important source for news about Russia's fledgling wine industry and for disseminating foreign expertise among growers and vintners. Tairov came to fame during the phylloxera debates of the 1880s and 1890s, which he followed from his native Transcaucasia, as a rare advocate for grafting in a country where confidence in the efficacy of pesticide persisted long after it had been discredited in France. After the principal French proponent of using pesticide against phylloxera, Antoine-Fortuné Marion, visited the Caucasus in 1893, Tairov launched a broadside against Marion in the pages of *Vestnik vinodeliia*,

[29] V. V. Vlasov, *100 let dorogoiu V. E. Tairova* (Odessa, 2005), 6.
[30] M. V. Nerucheva, 'Vvoza v Rossiu inostrannykh vin i polozhenie ikh na rynke', *Trudy s'ezda vinogradarei i vinodelov v Odesse (s 9 po 15 fevralia 1903 g.)* vol. 2 (Odessa, 1903), no pag.; *Materialy po peresmotru torgovykh dogovorov* (St Petersburg, 1913), 19–31; A. M. Mikhailenko and T. E. Dontsova, *Put' k priznaniiu: stranitsy istorii Odesskogo zavoda shampanskogo vin (XIX–XXI vv.)* (Odessa, 2007), 9–14; *Ustav iuzhno-russkago obshchestva Genrikh Rederer v Odese* (Odessa, 1896); Arcadius Kahan, *The Plow, the Hammer, and the Knout: An Economic History of Eighteenth-Century Russia*, ed. Richard Hellie (Chicago, 1985), 197.
[31] Charles C. Ludington, 'Drinking for Approval: Wine and the British Court from George III to Victoria and Albert', in *Royal Taste: Food, Power and Status at the European Courts after 1789* (Farnham, 2011), 59.
[32] Laman and Borisova, *Kniaz' Lev Sergeevich Golitsyn*, 6.

accusing him of wilfully ignoring the success of grafted vines in France. As a bureaucrat in the Ministry of Agriculture and Land Management, Tairov oversaw viniculture in Izmail (on the Russian side of the Danube delta) and Bessarabia. At the same Exposition Universelle where Golitsyn's sparkling wine won the grand-prix medal, Tairov was awarded a gold medal for his contributions to the science of winemaking and was later elected a member of the Paris-based International Vinicultural Commission. In 1902, Tairov planted an experimental vineyard in Odessa that would become one of the Soviet Union's foremost centres for vinicultural studies, despite early Soviet scepticism about his loyalty and class background.[33]

Despite their differences, Tairov and Golitsyn appeared to agree, at the outset, that the monopoly had exacerbated the 'crisis in winemaking', but was not its root cause. Their agreement likely stemmed from recognition that the monopoly was a lucrative tax scheme, which their complaints, however valid, were unlikely to dislodge. Instead, Tairov and Golitsyn seized on the language of public health and temperance, which had surrounded the monopoly at its inception, and argued that the chief cause of the crisis was the ubiquity of so-called 'falsified wines' that the monopoly had inadvertently fostered, and the deleterious effects of consuming falsified wines. Indeed, when it came to public health it was far from clear that the monopoly had its promised effect. The Moscow Committee on Viniculture and Winemaking disseminated materials suggesting that the monopoly had actually increased rates of drunkenness in vinicultural territories. Denied the right to sell their own production, peasant proprietors were more likely to drink what they produced. Moreover, as consumers discovered that the sale of alcohol was restricted by time and location, they were more likely to purchase vodka and fortified wine than conventional wine.[34]

Falsified wines were so ubiquitous in the monopoly marketplace that there were widely disseminated recipes for them. Some bore more than a passing resemblance to Venedikt Erofeev's famously drunken directions, a century later, for concocting 'Canaan Balsam' and 'Tear of a Komsomol Girl'. An 1885 guidebook to winemaking and distilling described, without irony or shame, how to create various 'Russian wine 'treasures', including a sherry that bore no compositional resemblance to anything that was made in Jerez, and a Málaga Alicante that comprised a mixture of communion wine, rum, a cypress-flavoured liquor, prunes, Chinese cinnamon, and the seeds of the marshmallow plant, among other things. Some recipes offered merchants a way to increase the volume of expensive imported wines, presumably without alerting customers to the fact that they were being scammed. The recipe for 'Santorini' called for white Kizliar chikhir, which

[33] V. E. Tairov, 'Frantsuzy o prof. Marione', *Vestnik vinodeliia*, no. 2 (1894): 67–70; Vlasov, *100 let*, 9–11; M. Peliakh, *Istoriia vinogradarstva i vinodeliia Moldavii* (Kishinev, 1970), 120–21.
[34] STA, f. 243, o. 7, d. 355, l. 50/8.

was a low-quality, homemade wine from the Caucasus, yeast, roasted bitter almonds, minced vanilla beans, and genuine Santorini wine. There were even recipes for falsifying domestic wines. Mixing ten *vedra* of red chikhir (or any 'second rate' red wine) with a pound of dried raspberries, an eighth of a pound of flower tea, and half a bottle of 160-proof alcohol reputedly produced, after filtration, a decent imitation of a Kakhetian red. These were only the most reputable falsifications; they were not the wines they purported to be, but they were not unsafe or inappropriate for consumption. The same could not be said for all falsified wines. Glycerin, which can have a powerful laxative effect, was sometimes used by wine merchants as a thickening agent because it is water soluble. As the author of the summary report from the 1902 Moscow Congress noted, the interests of public health might better be served by encouraging vintners to falsify their own wines, rather than allowing merchants to do it for them.[35]

Health concerns aside, there was a large constituency for reform. In the absence of a national wine-purity law, the city of Ekaterinoslav (Dnipro) took matters into its own hands. In 1896, the city's duma forbade the sale of wine adulterated with dyes and essences, boric acid, sodium borate (borax), lead, and 'other things harmful to health'. The city also required truth in advertising: henceforth, wine labelled as 'pure' (*tsel'noe*) and 'natural' had to be free of artificial additives.[36] Moreover, commercial vintners were almost unanimous in their view that falsified wines were a plague on an industry that increasingly produced at European standards. Falsified wines preyed on the popular taste for drink that was both strong and sweet, a near impossible combination for vintners to create via conventional means because sugar is consumed by yeast in the chemical reaction that produces alcohol. Falsified wines capitalized on the indeterminacy of the Russian word *vino*, which was often a byword for vodka in literary and popular usage, and on regulations that specified that anything sold as wine could have an alcohol content up to 22 per cent, more than twice what most vintners could achieve by fermenting grape must.[37] Despite the occasional concoction of fruit juice and grain alcohol that passed as wine, most falsified wines began their lives in the same production facilities as authentic wines. Between 1887 and 1890, the city of Moscow received 450,000 *pudy* (7,371,000 kilograms) of wine shipments from the south. Yet Moscow merchants sold nearly twice that amount of domestic wine to consumers. Between 1890 and 1899, the gap between imports and sales grew to nearly two million *pudy* (32.6 million kilograms). Similar discrepancies between input and output characterized St Petersburg, Nizhnyi Novgorod, and other cities

---

[35] Lobun'ko, *Vinogradarstvo i vinodelie Stavropolia*, 477.   [36] GAARK, f. 156, o. 1, d. 16, l. 20.

[37] A. Salomona, 'Sostoianie nashei vino-torgovli i znachenie g. Odessy k vinnago rynke', *Trudy komiteta vinogradarstva Imperatorskogo obshchestva sel'skogo khoziaistva iuzhnoi Rossii*, vyp. 1 (Odessa, 1901), 157–8; Iu. V. Orlitskii, 'Vodka-seledka: Alkogol'naia leksika v russkoi rifme', in *Literaturnyi tekst: problemy i metody issledovaniia, 8. Motiv vina v literature*, ed. I. V. Fomenko (Tver, 2002), 4; STA, f. 243, o. 7, d. 355, l. 50/4.

of the north. While some discerning merchants cellared wines they deemed immature or undervalued in present market conditions (thus creating the possibility of years where the amount of wine they sold exceeded the amount they bought), many more merchants sought to 'improve' the bottles they sold at retail by adding sugar, alcohol, and liquid to the barrels they bought at wholesale.[38] More than any other factor, the latter practice was the cause of the discrepancy between wholesale and retail volume.

As Kipen argued from the dais of the Moscow Congress, it was impossible to disaggregate the monopoly from wine falsification: the former, for reasons that were not entirely clear, had increased the frequency of the latter. Kipen surmised that the linkage stemmed from the arrogance of the large wine-trading firms, the principal beneficiaries of the monopoly, who thought they better understood what the drinking public wanted than winemakers themselves. Like wine *négociants* in France, Russia's wine-trading firms claimed to be engaged in *coupage*— blending finished wines together to improve their characteristics, or with Petiot wine to lower acidity and raise sugar levels. These were not 'natural wines', Kipen wrote, but nor were they 'falsified'. Similar production methods were common at even the most famous châteaux in Bordeaux. Yet merchants were also engaged in other sorts of blending that clearly departed from the French experience, such as adding sugar, grain alcohol, calcium carbonate (*mramornyi poroshok*)—which lowers the Ph of wines too acidic for consumers' tastes—or worse. No one knew for certain how widespread such practices were, because wine merchants rarely admitted to engaging in them. However, as the data in the previous paragraph suggest, such practices were likely ubiquitous. In Bessarabia, sugar shipments to the Strasheny rail station north of Kishinev, where many wine-trading firms had their facilities, nearly quintupled between 1896 and 1902. Only the wine-trading firms could explain why.[39]

Concerns about the prevalence of falsified wines were by no means unique to Russia. They reflected foodways that were increasingly industrialized and populated by anonymous commercial middlemen, concerns about brand protection and the rights of producers vis-à-vis merchants in complex economies where the two were increasingly distant, well-publicized scandals about food purity in Europe and North America, the advent of chemical agriculture both as practice and health concern, and fears that there was very little truth in the new medium of advertising.[40] While Russian advocates of a ban on wine falsification frequently

---

[38] Vlasov, *100 let*, 12; V. E. Tairov, 'Postavshchiki fal'sifikatorov', *Vestnik vinodeliia* no. 1 (1894): 1–6; Lobun'ko, *Vinogradarstvo i vinodelie Stavropolia*, 479.

[39] Kipen, 'Vinodel'cheskii krizis', 4–5.

[40] See, for instance, Stanziani, 'Municipal Laboratories', and Hierholzer, 'The "War Against Food Adulteration."' As Sally West has argued, concern about truth in advertising encouraged Russian merchants to seek government endorsements for their products, typically in the form of a state seal that could be used in advertising: see Sally West, *I Shop in Moscow: Advertising and the Creation of Consumer Culture in Late-Tsarist Russia* (DeKalb, IL, 2011), 70–71.

cited, as model, a French prohibition in existence since the fourteenth century, there were closer analogues elsewhere in Europe: the 1890s saw bans on wine adulteration come into force in Germany, Austria, Hungary, Romania, Spain, Italy, and Switzerland.[41]

On the surface, the shift in focus from monopoly to purity appeared to favour Golitsyn, who often spoke of his wines as being 'natural'. Yet it also allowed Tairov to make a case for the science of oenology by drawing a distinction between the falsification of wine by merchants, and the application of the latest oenological methods by producers. This became the question confronting delegates at the Moscow Congress, and the question that split Golitsyn and Tairov most completely: whether the oenological remediation of flawed must was the functional equivalent of falsification. The debate between Tairov and Golitsyn makes for compelling reading because of its acrimony, which had very deep roots. As early as the 1880s, Golitsyn and Tairov had argued in the pages of vinicultural publications and from the podia of various wine-industry meetings about the appropriate role of foreign methods and expertise in Russian vineyards. In the years preceding and following the Moscow Congress, this mutated into an argument about the generally poor quality of Bessarabian wine, which Golitsyn, who looked more favourably on the wholesale adoption of French methods of vineyard cultivation, blamed on rudimentary techniques.[42] At the 1902 congress, where the subject was wine falsification, there was again no shortage of real and feigned offence. Writing about the congress in retrospect, Tairov noted that the experience reminded him of the Latin maxim, *homo homini lupus*; delegates' enthusiastic response to Golitsyn's keynote address resembled a scene from Gogol's 'Inspector General'.[43]

Yet the chief significance of Golitsyn and Tairov's debate lies not in its rancorous tone, but in the way it cuts at odd, unexpected angles across so many of the axes that historians use to make sense of late-tsarist Russia, dividing European from modern and science from progress, and blurring a long-standing conceptual divide between Russia and Europe. Originating in the works of the eighteenth-century historians Nikolai Karamzin and Mikhail Shcherbatov, the idea of Russian civilization as something distinct from and superior to the West blossomed in the 1840s under the umbrella of Slavophilism, and later came to form the basis of Russian nationalist ideology. In recent years, scholarship on Slavophilism has undergone sharp revision, as historians such as Susanna Rabow-Edling and Katherine Pickering Antonova have rejected 'stark oppositions' in favour of investigations that emphasize similarities between Enlightenment and Romantic thought, and that reveal how self-identified Slavophiles, far from rejecting

[41] Vlasov, *100 let*, 12.   [42] Guliev et al., *Vino, vlast' i obshchestvo*, 46.
[43] Vasilii Tairov, 'Moskovskii s"ezd vinogradarei i vinodelov', *Vestnik vinodeliia* no. 5 (1902): 264. I located this issue of *Vestnik vinodeliia* in STA, f. 243, o. 7, d. 355, pamphlet after page l. 50.

outright European rationalism and culture, drew from both canons of thought in seemingly contradictory ways.[44]

In a similar fashion, the controversy over oenology jumbled and juxtaposed the seemingly fixed and synonymous categories of European, modern, science, and progress. For instance, Golitsyn, who was a Francophile in his private and professional life, accepted the standard French connoisseur's definition of what made a wine great—a sense of *terroir*, a capacity for improvement over time, and balance between acidity, alcohol, and fruit. The greatest achievement of French winemaking, in Golitsyn's view, was the pairing of grape with soil and climate. 'Every region [in France] has its own distinct character', he told delegates at the Moscow Congress.

Every region has its own varietals: in the north, where there is little sun, Pinot is planted, which ripens early. This is the varietal that made Champagne and Burgundy great. It grows in chalky-sandy soils. In the south you see different varietals: the wonderful vineyards of Hermitage [an *Appellation d'origine con- trolee* in the northern Rhône], with its shale soil, is made for Syrah. In Bordeaux's gravelly soil, there is Cabernet.

This was not science, Golitsyn argued, but the result of 'more than a thousand years' of experience, of trial and error, of monks who painstakingly crossed grapes to create varietals suited to local climate and soils, all the time hoping that their wines would grace the tables of royals. 'And what are we doing in Russia?' Golitsyn asked. 'Nothing. With the exception of the Caucasus and part of the Black Sea region, we hardly know what to plant.'[45]

In Golitsyn's view, Russian growers and vintners had learned nothing from the French, focusing instead on 'how to add sugar to wine', which to Golitsyn's great disappointment had become 'the stirring question of our congress!' Russian vint- ners did not hesitate to use foreign, geographically specific names to describe their wines—*kheres* (Jerez, meaning sherry), Madeira, Bordeaux, and Sauternes. They struggled to create a knock-off Château Lafite that was cheaper than the real thing, a Château d'Yquem from different varietals entirely, and a 'one-ruble port that is not, in fact, a port'. Nomenclature and label mattered more to them than substance; oenological shortcuts and outright misrepresentation took the place of measured experience. Golitsyn argued that Russian attempts to copy European

[44] Susanna Rabow-Edling, *Slavophile Thought and the Politics of Cultural Nationalism* (Albany, 2006), 5–7; Katherine Pickering Antonova, *An Ordinary Marriage: The World of a Gentry Family in Provincial Russia* (Oxford, 2013), 207–208. Rabow-Edling and Antonova are writing in response to an older view of Slavophiles as romantic utopians. See, for instance, Andrezj Walicki, *The Slavophile Controversy: History of a Conservative Utopia in Nineteenth-Century Russian Thought*, trans. Hilda Andrews-Rusiecka (Oxford, 1975); Nicholas Riasanovsky, *Russia and the West in the Teaching of the Slavophiles: A Study of Romantic Ideology* (Gloucester, MA, 1965).
[45] Laman and Borisova, *Kniaz' Lev Sergeevich Golitsyn*, 297–8.

wines were also a form of falsification. Echoing Peter Chaadaev's famous assertion that Russia contributed nothing to human progress, and that it distorted what it borrowed, Golitsyn told congress delegates that Russian winemakers were not even knowledgeable about the wines they were trying to copy: 'even while imitating, we cannot explain to ourselves what we are doing.'[46]

Golitsyn, however, was hardly Chaadaev in his views of Russia and the West. To the contrary, Golitsyn insisted that wine was a Russian institution long before vineyards appeared in Bordeaux and Burgundy. He argued that Russia's first vintner was Noah, who as a very old man (in his 400s) planted grapes on the slopes of what was believed to be Mount Ararat. (Golitsyn failed to mention, however, that Noah's adventure in winemaking proved to be ill-advised, according to Genesis 9. It precipitated the 'curse of Canaan', when Ham took sexual advantage, in unspecified ways, of his father's drunkenness.) Golitsyn pointed out that the Russian Empire comprised territories suitable for viniculture that were at least ten times the size of all of France. Unwittingly anticipating the Soviet Union's sizeable investments in ampelography, he argued that Russian viniculturists had to develop new varietals that were suited to Russia's soil and climate and to Russians' distinctive palate with its preference for strong and sweet wines, despite the fact that 'the very best varietals', in his view, invariably meant European grapes. (Golitsyn's sparkling wines were made from the same varietals planted in Champagne, Alsace, and Burgundy: Chardonnay, Pinot, Riesling, and Aligoté.) Likewise, Golitsyn used his speech at the congress to commemorate the contributions of Russia's greatest Westernizer, Peter the Great, who 'enlisted the best craftsmen of grapes and vines', and of Peter's successors to the throne. Yet he specifically exempted from his history of benevolent royal patronage Anna Ivanovna (Anna of Courland), Peter's niece who occupied the throne from 1730 to 1740. Popularly remembered for her obsequiousness in the face of all things German, Anna Ivanovna offended Golitsyn's public persona as Russian patriot, and contradicted his nativist narrative of Russian winemaking.[47]

Just as Golitsyn combined a Francophile's respect for the wines of Burgundy and Bordeaux with a nationalist's angry conviction that Russians had their own illustrious and forgotten history of winemaking, Tairov's views were also seemingly contradictory. He accepted the leading role of Western oenologists and ampelographers in the science of winemaking and vineyard management. In fact, much of *Vestnik vinodeliia* was devoted to disseminating and expanding this knowledge, thereby underscoring, if only implicitly, that Russia too was contributing to the betterment of humankind through the science of winemaking. These

[46] Laman and Borisova, *Kniaz' Lev Sergeevich Golitsyn*, 299; STA, f. 243, o. 7, d. 355, l. 50/5; and Peter Yakovlevich Chaadayev, *Philosophical Letters and Apology of a Madman*, trans. Mary-Barbara Zeldin (Knoxville, TN, 1969), 39–51.

[47] Laman and Borisova, *Kniaz' Lev Sergeevich Golitsyn*, 289.

were concrete signs of Russia's involvement in the concert of Europe. At the same time, Tairov denied that there was anything, to borrow a term that Golitsyn and his allies were prone to use, 'natural' about fine French winemaking, from which Russians vintners needed to learn. 'Wine', Tairov argued 'is the result of the technical treatment of grape juice by introducing, as necessary, small quantities of temporary substances (such as sulphurous acid)'. Consequently, adding sugar to wine after fermentation, which was the sort of falsification that Moscow wine merchants were prone to perpetrate, was not the same as adding sugar to wine before primary or secondary fermentation. The former merely sweetened an already finished wine; the latter was fuel for the fermentation of a wine that was still in embryonic form.[48] Put another way, French wine was made great not only by ancestral techniques, not only by varietals that were adapted over many centuries to local soil and climatic conditions, and not only by an ineffable sense of *terroir*. French wine was also made great by oenology.

Tairov's denial that there was any such thing as 'natural' wine was emblematic of his polemical style. He took delight in tormenting the older Golitsyn with humour, common sense, and an ingratiating, old-fashioned deference to Golitsyn's social position and storied family history. In his post-congress comments, which were published in *Vestnik vinodeliia*, Tairov wrote that Golitsyn was surely trying to be humorous in his keynote address. After all, Golitsyn had failed to mention Noah's son Ham, whose curse did not suggest that Russia had a glorious vinicultural past. Nor did Golitsyn mention the apocryphal story that orthodoxy's acceptance of alcohol figured prominently among the reasons for Grand Prince Vladimir's conversion of Kievan Rus in the tenth century, which would have underscored the strong headwinds that wine faced in a place long accustomed to stronger forms of drink. And Tairov was humorously obsequious even in disagreement: 'fairness demands an acknowledgement that the honorable prince, on this festive occasion, spiced up his speech with the assertion that the "winemaking literature" encourages the falsification of wine, by allowing the use of sugar and grain alcohol.' This was just slander directed at *Vestnik vinodeliia*, Tairov wrote, and far from the truth.[49]

*　*　*　*　*

Because so much of the controversy in Moscow concerned the remediation of grape must with sugar, sympathies in the debate between Tairov and Golitsyn broke down largely on regional and economic lines. As wine varietals ripen, acid content falls as sugar content rises, in some cases to the point that cluster stems become hard and woody, indicating that fruit development has ceased. Because sugar is necessary to produce alcohol, sufficient sugar content at harvest helps

---

[48] Tairov, 'Moskovskii s"ezd', 270.   [49] Tairov, 'Moskovskii s"ezd', 261.

protect wine against spoilage. It is also the basis for residual sweetness. Thus, regions with long growing seasons, such as the southern shore of Crimea, enjoyed distinct advantages over regions where night-time frosts in late summer and early autumn often forced premature harvests, such as Bessarabia and the mountain valleys of the Caucasus. This interplay between weather and sugar was the subtext for the controversy in Moscow, as Tairov couched oenology as a way to compensate for the climatic deficiencies of less blessed growing regions. More than 200 delegates participated in the congress, 60 per cent of whom were from the southern shore of Crimea, where only about 3 per cent of the Empire's wine production originated. All of Tauride guberniya, which included the southern shore, accounted for only about 10 per cent of the Empire's wine production in 1888. Ten delegates came from Kizliar in Dagestan (roughly 12 per cent of the Empire's wine production), five from Bessarabia (19 per cent), three from Georgia (41 per cent), and one from Astrakhan (0.01 per cent). Some vinicultural regions, including Podolia and Ekaterinoslav (in western Ukraine and New Russia, respectively), lacked any representation. Yet as Aleksandr Steven, the Minister of Agriculture and State Domains pointed out, despite his own deep ties to Crimea, the purpose of the Congress was to make it 'easier to turn away from [vintners'] narrow local interests and discuss the objective needs of Russian viniculture in its aggregate'.[50]

For Tairov, the imbalance in geographical representation was emblematic of everything wrong with viniculture in the Russian Empire. 'The congress was not "all-Russian"', he alleged, because the Moscow Committee simply invited wealthy producers, principally from Crimea, to participate. Despite the fact that Bessarabia and the Caucasus accounted for the majority of wine produced each year in the Russian Empire by volume, the mostly peasant proprietors of these regions did not have enough wealth or influence to travel to Moscow. Most were probably unaware that the congress was occurring. Yet there was an element of disingenuousness in Tairov's concern. For instance, the Caucasus region (which included lands on both sides of the ridgeline) accounted for roughly 60 per cent of the empire's wine production. According to Tairov's logic, this should have resulted in a clear majority of delegates at the Moscow Congress. Yet only about 10 per cent of the production in the Caucasus was destined for external markets in the north or abroad. The remaining 90 per cent was consumed locally, where wine had long been a central component of indigenous diets and cultures. Consequently, producers in the Caucasus were much less vulnerable to wine falsification than their counterparts in Bessarabia and elsewhere, despite the immense volume of wine that they produced.[51]

---

[50] Tairov, 'Moskovskii s'ezd', 262. Wine production percentages can be found in F. R. Ungern-Shternberg, 'O vinodelii na Iuzhnom beregu Kryma', in *Istoriia vinodeliia Kryma: Sbornik*, vyp. 2, ed. V. V. Mitiaev (Massandra, 2001), 218.

[51] STA, f. 243, o. 7, d. 355, l. 50/8; Tairov, 'Moskovskii s'ezd', 260.

Yet there was no mistaking the financial condition of Bessarabian growers, which was near catastrophic. The region had been deeply affected by phylloxera during the 1880s and 1890s, with total vineyard losses exceeding 180,000 hectares (1,800 square kilometres). Yet even growers who had converted to grafted vines (and usually, in the process, to European varietals) struggled to eke out a profit, partly because of the absence of adequate cellar space, and partly because their wine, with comparatively low alcohol levels, was more prone to spoilage. Thus, in Tairov's view, the resistance to the oenological remediation of flawed must was little more than a naked attempt among wealthy Crimean estate owners—whom he referred to as the 'silk-tongued southern shore Demosthenes [plural in the Russian]'—to entrench their market advantage and superior incomes relative to producers in Bessarabia and elsewhere. Despite the fact that *Vestnik vinodeliia* had been publicizing the deleterious effects of wine falsification for more than a decade, it had become, in the view of wealthy Crimean producers, the principal proponent of falsification because it advocated for the science of oenology. Adding sugar or Petiot wine to must prior to fermentation had become no different than adding sugar to sweeten a finished wine.[52]

Tairov's allusion to the ulterior motives of the Crimean delegates at the Moscow Congress was almost certainly the catalyst for a rumour, widespread in late 1902 and 1903, about an impending tsarist decree authorizing the destruction of Bessarabian vineyards. In the view of many Crimean growers, the solution to vineyards that produced crush with inadequate sugar was not the addition of sugar before fermentation, but the destruction of those vineyards altogether. At a vinicultural congress in Odessa in February 1903, a year after Moscow, fears of misguided state intervention remained paramount. Kipen mentioned that several speakers in Moscow had encouraged Bessarabian growers to replace their vines with those more suitable for the region's climate. This elicited in Moscow suggestions to 'uproot all unprofitable vines'. Golitsyn, who was also present at the Odessa congress, then made matters worse: 'I said [in Moscow], plant grapes in places where they will flourish, but where frogs hop about, do not plant grapes. It would be better to plant corn there.'[53]

Superior sugar levels aside, however, it was not clear that Crimean vineyards were any more lucrative than vineyards elsewhere. At a Crimean vinicultural congress in Simferopol in November 1901, delegates complained about many of the same problems that Tairov would attribute to production in Bessarabia and the Caucasus in 1902: low wholesale prices, overcrowded wine cellars, excess supply, and the ubiquity of wine falsification. In one writer's estimation, the financial condition of producers on the southern shore of Crimea was actually worse than in Bessarabia and the Caucasus, where viniculturists had spent the previous

[52] Tairov, 'Moskovskii s"ezd', 262–4.   [53] Guliev et al., *Vino, vlast' i obshchestvo*, 46.

decade converting to grafted vines, and thus benefitted from young, bountiful vineyards. Crimean vines, to the contrary, remained mostly un-grafted, because of a strict vinicultural quarantine that kept phylloxera at bay on the peninsula until the mid-twentieth century. The 'facts', wrote one advocate for Crimean growers, showed that the southern shore, by virtue of its unique climate and soil, produced 'not a very large amount of grapes'. Yet on the southern shore especially, land and labour prices were comparatively high, and Russian consumers had not yet shown a willingness to pay a premium for Crimean 'terroir'. In the years after its international acme in Paris in 1900, even Golitsyn's Novyi svet faced persistent financial difficulties, in large part because of Golitsyn's expensive insistence on tending vineyards and making wine in the French manner. Fearing that his life's work would soon vanish, Golitsyn asked Nicholas II to accept more than half of Novyi svet as a gift, which amounted to a peculiar form of bankruptcy. In the spring of 1912, Nicholas visited Sudak and accepted a key to Novyi svet's wine cellar. The gift transformed Novyi svet into a crown estate, like Massandra and Abrau-Diurso, and freed Golitsyn from much of his tax obligation. Photographs show Golitsyn strolling on the beach at Sudak with his new neighbours, the royal family.[54]

For their part, Golitsyn and his allies at the Moscow Congress asserted that they merely had the interests of Russian consumers at heart. While nearly everyone at the Moscow Congress agreed that wine falsification needed to be outlawed entirely, Golitsyn wanted to extend protections to consumers of remediated wines by requiring that bottles be labelled as 'artificial', 'beet root' (because of the use of beet sugar), 'fortified', 'sugared', and so on. Golitsyn's sparkling wines, which benefitted from Crimea's sub-tropical sun and long growing season and needed little in the way of remediation, would simply be labelled 'natural'. As Kevin Goldberg has argued about late-nineteenth-century Germany, 'victual categories' such as 'natural' were often socially and political constructed in ways that reaffirmed existing hierarchies: 'In response to the industrializing forces of German viniculture, landed elites began defining their wines as "natural," buttressed by the suspect premise that their products had been provided by nature, unaltered by man.'[55] Eighty years before Eric Hobsbawm and Terence Ranger popularized the concept of 'invented tradition', Tairov recognized Golitsyn's 'natural' wine as exactly that—an invented tradition; moreover, the label 'natural' suggested, in Tairov's view, an element of 'scientific exactitude' (nauchnost') that was entirely unjustified. Natural wine could be produced only by letting grapes rot in an open container; all other wines, including all that were desirable enough to drink,

---

[54] Volzhenikov, *Sovremennoe polozhenie*, 1–4. On the start-up costs of viniculture in Crimea, see *Doklad komissii po razvitiiu vinodeliia v okrestnostiiakh Sevastopolia* (Sevastopol, 1882), 2–3. On the fate of Novyi svet, see Laman and Borisova, *Kniaz' Lev Sergeevich Golitsyn*, 164–85, 343.

[55] Kevin D. Goldberg, 'Acidity and Power: The Politics of Natural Wine in Nineteenth-Century Germany', *Food and Foodways* 19, no. 4 (2011): 296.

required myriad forms of unnatural, human intervention: from the ways varietals were created (sometimes through the laborious crossing of vines such as Petite Verdot and Syrah), to the strains of cultivated yeast that were used to supplement the wild yeasts on the skins of the grape that produced alcohol, to the choice of vessels where fermentation occurred. Allowing vintners in less blessed growing regions to add cane and beet sugar before fermentation or sulphurous acid after fermentation to preserve wine was simply common sense.[56]

Tairov did not miss the irony that the chief advocate for truth in labelling—for 'scientific exactitude', as he put it—was also oenology's greatest critic. Both Tairov and Golitsyn carelessly tossed about caricatures of the other. Tairov, in Golitsyn's view, was a bullying man of science, and Golitsyn, vice versa, was a benighted snob. Yet there were elements of truth in both. In reality, Golitsyn tended to be selective in his endorsement of science: modern vineyard management techniques, typically of French origin, were beneficial; oenology was less so. But he sometimes articulated a scepticism, which was widespread among some producers, about the utility of science and modern modes of production for winemaking. As one writer noted, in Bordeaux and Burgundy wine had become an industry characterized by modern factories

> with all the technical improvements: mechanized engines, lifting machines, refrigeration and heating, which facilitate the correct approach to production where the human hand hardly touches the grape clusters. The result is hardly wine of a high quality, but it is cheap to buy.[57]

Echoing Golitsyn's view, the most important question facing growers and producers, according to this critic, and the most important determinant whether a wine was good or bad, was the type of vines to plant given local conditions. For this task, wisdom gained from experience and practical knowledge—in short, what the anthropologist James Scott called, in a different context, 'mētis'—was far more useful than science and technology.[58]

*   *   *   *   *

After more than a decade of additional discussion, refinement, and rising pressure from domestic vintners, Nicholas II signed a 'Law on Grape Wine'. The site of the signing was auspicious: the Romanovs' Livadiia Palace in Crimea, a few kilometres from the crown estate vineyards at Massandra and Ai-Danil'. The date was not: 24 April 1914, three months before Russia blundered into the First World War and prohibition became the law of the land, and three years before the

---

[56] Tairov, 'Moskovskii s'ezd', 275.   [57] Volzhenikov, *Sovremennoe polozhenie*, 9.
[58] James C. Scott, *Seeing Like a State: How Certain Schemes to Improve the Human Condition Have Failed* (New Haven, 1999), 309–41.

autocracy itself crumbled. Despite his relationship with Golitsyn, Nicholas II approved a law that largely paralleled Tairov's views. This was less a betrayal of friendship than an acknowledgement that the types of oenological remediation that Tairov had advocated in 1902, amid so much controversy, had become routine in the decade that followed. The law allowed for the use of limited amounts of sulphurous acid (200 milligrams per litre) as a preservative. The law allowed vintners to add cane or beet sugar to must before or during fermentation, but only to bring the resulting wine up to 10 per cent alcohol by volume. The law allowed for the strengthening of finished table wines, but only with distilled alcohol derived from grapes, only by 4 percentage points, and only so that the resulting wine did not exceed 10 per cent alcohol by volume. So-called 'fortified wines', such as Port, could not have an alcohol content exceeding 25 per cent. The law accommodated technologies that post-dated the Moscow Congress, such as the use of the clarifying compound isinglass, a collagen collected from the dried swim bladders of fish. Finally, the law drew clear distinctions between the roles of producers and merchants, in effect outlawing the post-production falsification that had plagued domestic vintners for nearly two decades by clearly specifying what ingredients could be added to wine. Merchants could engage in *coupage*, the blending of finished wines, and they could strengthen wines that were so low in alcohol that spoilage was a concern. Yet they could do so only within the parameters of the wine purity law. The addition of sugar to wine was forbidden to them entirely; this was the prerogative of the winemaker. Golitsyn's views carried the day in one regard: the blending of Russian and foreign wines was prohibited, and any Russian wine that bore a foreign name on its label had to clearly indicate that it was of Russian origin. There would be no more Sauternes from Crimea, no more Bordeaux from Kakheti. Russian wine would henceforth exist without the crutch of misrepresentation.[59]

Nearly two decades in the making, Tairov's legislative victory proved to be short-lived. No sooner had local authorities drawn up plans to enforce the wine purity law than Russia's vinicultural economy began to contract in response to war. In January 1915, agricultural officials in Simferopol warned that a mounting shortage of copper sulphate, which was used to treat outbreaks of the vine fungus downy mildew, threatened the entire Crimean grape harvest. Manufactured in France and England, its supply lines had been disrupted by hostilities. By August, one year into the war, officials in Tiflis warned that the grape harvest in all of Georgia's vinicultural regions would be 'less than average', citing shortages of copper sulphate and uncertainty about whether the tsarist government planned to implement new restrictions on the sale of wine.[60] The latter referred to a poorly

---

[59] Commentary on and a copy of the wine purity law are available in Lobun'ko, *Vinogradarstvo i vinodelie Stavropolia*, 596–610.

[60] GAARK, f. 156, o. 1, d. 16, ll. 7 (copper sulphate), 81 (enforcement), 205–205ob (enforcement).

articulated and seemingly arbitrary wartime prohibition that Nicholas endorsed. In August 1914, the governor general of Odessa restricted wine sales to the hours of 11 a.m. to 2 p.m., inspiring similar ordinances in Melitopol, Feodosia, and Simferopol. By the summer of 1915, restrictions had become more encompassing, albeit in ways that suggested there was no clear understanding about whether wine was actually subject to prohibition. In June, the city of Yalta moved to restrict speculation in wine by forbidding winemakers from selling to commercial middlemen who did not own or represent stores. In August, the city of Simferopol banned the sale of wine entirely. Winemakers responded by petitioning local authorities, sometimes successfully, for the right to sell their wine directly to consumers, thus reinstating the status quo prior to the establishment of the alcohol monopoly.[61] Amid so much chaos, few had any use for 'natural' wines or debates on wine purity.

Questions about Russian wine's authenticity, which were so poignant in the first years of the twentieth century, never fully went away. In the mid-1920s, after the wartime prohibition on wine was lifted and the old tsarist monopoly formally abolished, proponents of the Soviet wine industry found themselves battling a similar scourge of sweetened and strengthened wine. In the wake of Russia's passage through Armageddon, however, the villains wore red—Soviet administrators of the wine trade who responded to the market demand of NEP by offering consumers what they wanted, despite the new Soviet government's commitment to acculturation and enlightenment. By the 1960s and 1970s, nearly all wine produced in the Soviet Union violated the 1914 wine purity law. It was strengthened with grain alcohol and sweetened after fermentation with sugar. The recipes were less elaborate—Soviet vintners never tried to concoct a Château d'Yquem or a Châteauneuf du Pape, as tsarist merchants had done. Yet the scale of Soviet production was many times greater. For all intents and purposes, Soviet wine was falsified wine. For the heirs of Tairov and Golitsyn, wine cosmopolitans who never disappeared from the Soviet Union, the situation was no less scandalous than it had been during the tsarist period, even as their perceptions of victimhood shifted from impoverished growers and winemakers in Bessarabia and southern Ukraine to consumers who were denied proper wine. As the Soviet Union battled a growing epidemic of alcoholism, it was hard to ignore the fact that the Soviet wine industry—which often produced wine with alcohol contents approaching 20 per cent, in short, half-strength vodka—was partly complicit. The tastes of the drinking public proved to be far more intractable than either Tairov or Golitsyn cared to admit.

Among the historians who have focused on the passage of Russia's short-lived wine purity law, emphasis invariably falls on the manner it came into existence.

---

[61] GAARK, f. 156, o. 1, d. 16, l. 208ob (Simferopol ban); d. 23, ll. 1–1ob (escalating municipal restrictions), 13ob (petitions). On the origins of prohibition, see Schrad, *Vodka Politics*, 169–97.

It was drafted by a non-state employee, Tairov, who solicited the advice of merchants, growers, and vintners in the pages of his journal. It was vetted by the Moscow Congress of Viniculturists and Vintners in 1902 and by similar gatherings in earlier and later years; and it was submitted numerous times to regional vinicultural committees for revision and comment.[62] Unnoticed are the unusual schisms that the debate about wine remediation opened: between notions of European and modern, science and status, progress and refinement. Both Tairov and Golitsyn understood the production and consumption of wine to be a European trait. They were palpable evidence of Russia's essential Western-ness—from the times of Noah on, in Golitsyn's view. But there the affinities ended. According to Golitsyn, the significance of wine lay in the status it conveyed, both for producer and consumer. The best producers aspired to create fine wines by methods honed through the ages, by trial and error and local expertise; knowledgeable consumers with refined palates aspired to drink these wines. The modern science of winemaking would destroy this aspirational culture, by reducing the premium consumers were willing to pay for 'natural' wines that were indistinguishable in taste from remediated wines, and it would diminish the status that the production and consumption of 'natural' wines conveyed. Golitsyn and Tairov diverged most completely on the question of progress. For Tairov, modern oenology meant greater wealth for producers in Bessarabia and the Caucasus, and better, more plentiful wine for consumers. For Golitsyn, modern oenology threatened not only the financial well-being of Novyi svet, but an entire culture of wine.

The debate about oenology in Russia paralleled the divergence in Europe between the particularistic culture of food, and its growing standardization as a result of modern modes of production and distribution. Yet these tendencies were jumbled in ways that reflected both the peculiarity of late-tsarist Russia, and the ideological baggage of Russian winemaking, which was always about more than grapes and wine. The upstart from a modest background in provincial Armenia, who tirelessly advocated for the less fortunate and non-Russian growers of Bessarabia, was a man of science; the Europeanized aristocrat whose wines were compared with the best of France, embraced out of nationalist conviction and self-interest local knowledge and the wisdom of experience.

At its core, the controversy about wine that erupted in Moscow in 1902 reflected two very different notions about the location of European-ness in late-tsarist society: did it reside in the rational and scientific ethos of the Enlightenment and its bearers, or in the sensuous and elitist values of the aristocracy? It may be the case that Tairov, by trying to democratize a luxury item with the tools of

---

[62] On public vetting in the legislative process, see Lobun'ko, *Vinogradarstvo i vinodelie Stavropolia*, 470–85; Vlasov, *100 let*, 13; B. Bertenson, 'Trudy soveshchaniia po vinodeliiu', in *Trudy komiteta vinogradarstva Imperatorskogo obshchestva sel'skago khoziaistva iuzhnoi Rossii*, vyp. 3 (1902–7) (Odessa, 1908), 124–37; STA, f. 243, o. 7, d. 387, ll. 8–15.

science sought European-ness in both locations. Yet for Golitsyn, there was no question that the advent of oenology and its application to Russian winemaking were deeply ambivalent developments, as they spelt the destruction not of fine Russian wine—in fact, oenology promised to do the opposite—but of the exclusivist and aspirational culture that surrounded it. In Golitsyn's view, fine Russian wine was civilizing precisely because vintners did not take oenological shortcuts. Only in a country where wine represented so much more than something to drink, could it carry such importance. Wine's authenticity was nothing less than proof of Russia's place in the concert of Europe.

4

Commerce

Selling Wine in the Age of Revolution

In 1922, Mikhail Shlapakov, who identified himself as a 'contractual counterparty' (*kontragent*), wrote a letter to the new State Vinicultural and Winemaking Syndicate in Moscow. Ostensibly about the efforts of the Crimean section of the Commissariat of Agriculture to fulfil an order for 10,000 *vedra* of wine, the equivalent of more than 130,000 litres, the letter included a promise of loyalty to the new Soviet state.

> I understand the idea of Soviet politics. I know there will be no return to the past. Based on the conditions expressed by Lenin, 'for a long time and in earnest', I am certain that those businessmen, who have willfully remained in Russia, and who have proposed to work in Russia, must accept all that is new that Soviet power dictates to us, adapting ourselves to the new circumstances. From this it is a direct conclusion that if in the past I was a contractual counterparty for large Russian and foreign companies, then in the present, by virtue of objective circumstances, I should become a contractual counterparty for the Council of People's Commissars and large cooperative organizations.

Despite botching the order of Lenin's encomium to the Tenth Party Conference in May 1921 (which Lenin, in turn, had borrowed from Valerian Osinskii), about how party members must commit themselves to NEP, Shlapakov's letter encapsulated the strange Zeitgeist of NEP: the new Soviet state sought the assistance of self-styled capitalists and businessmen who were motivated by profit. Criticizing the 'unwieldiness' and 'lethargy' of the Commissariat of Agriculture, Shlapakov proposed the creation of a new agency to oversee all wine production and sales. Such a move would create 'profitable conditions' both for the Commissariat of Agriculture and, Shlapakov boldly predicted, for himself. Indeed, profit and business acumen were core to Shlapakov's understanding of bureaucratic efficiency. He argued that a new agency constituted from 'people with commercial backgrounds', such as himself, 'and based on personal interest, will undoubtedly surpass apparats formed from Soviet experts'.[1]

---

[1] Gosudarstvennyi arkhiv Rossiiskoi federatsii [State Archive of the Russian Federation, hereafter GARF], f. R130, o. 6, d. 448, ll. 4–4ob.

Whites and Reds: A History of Wine in the Lands of Tsar and Commissar. Stephen V. Bittner, Oxford University Press (2021). © Stephen V. Bittner. DOI: 10.1093/oso/9780198784821.003.0005

Shlapakov's letter was also emblematic of the paradoxical politics of wine in the early Soviet state. Eight years earlier, the passage of tsarist Russia's short-lived wine purity law underscored the growing clout of producers, and the political acceptance of the idea that vintners, rather than commercial middlemen who better understood what consumers desired, had final say over the composition of wine. Wine, in other words, was important enough to regulate, not with the intention of limiting its consumption or ensuring good health (as late-Soviet-era anti-alcoholism campaigns attempted), but of promoting what in the 1930s was called *kul'turnost'*. As Steve Smith and Catriona Kelly have argued, the predilections and preferences of the urban 'boulevard' were the cause of a great deal of highbrow consternation in the final tsarist decades. 'It was hard', they write, 'for the trad-itional Russian intellectual...to accept that tastes in pleasure varied according to changing norms for personal fulfillment'.[2] This was the problem that commercial vintners faced: the popular preference for wine that was fortified with grain alcohol and sweetened with sugar did not correspond to vintners' perceptions about what constituted wine in general, much less fine wine. In 1914, the government of Nicholas II embraced the Europeanized palates of producers over the allegedly vulgar and banal tastes of consumers. This privileged a definition of wine that was unmistakably European, and it made wine an official tool of acculturation long before *kul'turnost'* ever became part of the political lexicon.

In the latter regard, the history of wine suggests the sort of subtle continuity across the revolutionary caesura, between the modernization of the late-Imperial period and the civilizing process of Stalinism, that in recent years has engendered a great deal of scholarly interest.[3] This chapter, however, seeks to explore some-thing different: an unexpected disjuncture in Russia's age of revolution. In the final tsarist decades, the market for wine became increasingly regulated. Its pro-duction and sale were constrained not only by the wine purity law, but by Sergei Witte's state monopoly on alcohol sales, which was enacted in stages beginning in 1894 amid popular concern for temperance, and sustained through the end of the tsarist period by the huge sums of money it drew into state coffers.[4] Modelled on a scheme that Bismarck enacted in 1886, the monopoly brought wine sales under state supervision, and effectively ended the seventy-year-old practice of

---

[2] Steve Smith and Catriona Kelly, 'Commercial Culture and Consumerism', in *Constructing Russian Culture in the Age of Revolution*, ed. Catriona Kelly and David Shepherd (Oxford, 1998), 121.

[3] See, in particular, Catriona Kelly and Vadim Volkov, 'Directed Desires: *Kul'turnost'* and Consumption', in *Constructing Russian Culture*, 291–313; Yanni Kotsonis, 'Introduction: A Modern Paradox—Subject and Citizen in Nineteenth- and Twentieth-Century Russia', in *Russian Modernity: Politics, Knowledge, Practices*, ed. David L. Hoffmann and Yanni Kotsonis (New York, 2000), 1–18.

[4] See, for instance, Kate Transchel, *Under the Influence: Working Class Drinking, Temperance, and Cultural Revolution in Russia, 1895–1932* (Pittsburgh, 2006), 31; Irina R. Takala, *Veselie Rusi: Istoriia alkogol'noi problem v Rossii* (St Petersburg, 2002), 100–103; Francis W. Wcislo, *Tales of Imperial Russia: The Life and Times of Sergei Witte, 1849–1915* (Oxford, 2011), 166; N. A. Lobun'ko, *Vinogradarsto i vinodelie Stavropolia: stranitsy istorii* (Stavropol', 2004), 456–69.

producers selling directly to consumers.[5] Because it put winemakers at the mercy of licensed merchants, who had a monopoly on retail sales, critics often cited the monopoly as the principal cause of the 'crisis in winemaking', which beset the industry at the turn of the century. Yet the monopoly was also reflective of an industry that had become too large, too lucrative, and too important, for reasons that transcended economics, to escape the regulatory gaze of the state.

In the wine industry, the new Bolshevik government thus inherited a model of state regulation that advanced societal refinement and acculturation, and that was financially advantageous to the broader state goals of industrialization and modernization. Yet the Russian Revolution did not immediately result in socialism in the wine industry, nor even sustain the previous level of state involvement. Instead, by erasing a vast canon of tsarist law that regulated everything from phylloxera prevention to wine falsification, the revolution created a mostly unfettered, unregulated market for wine that lasted through the 1920s.[6] In the view of many persons in the wine industry, Soviet power had succeeded, above all, in creating chaos—in short, the sort of free market that had not existed at the end of tsarist rule.

The latter evaluation is perhaps not so unusual. In the 1920s, many Soviet communists, hardened by careers in the underground, pre-revolutionary party and by military service in the Civil War, saw the 'snout of the Philistine', as Vladimir Mayakovsky put it, lurking in the recesses of Lenin's New Economic Policy. Intended principally as a retreat to the market to allow the recovery of agriculture and retail commerce after seven years of war and revolution, NEP could never be mistaken for communism. It was temporary, strategic, and combined with a ban of factionalism within the party to ensure that its proponents never mistook it as permanent, and its opponents as betrayal. Unusual was the constituency that offered such grim estimations of NEP's freewheeling ethos. The wine industry was hardly a bastion of communist sympathy. During the late-tsarist years, it was dominated by aristocrats and foreigners. It was notable for its disparagement of popular tastes, and its genuflection to Western expertise and achievement. To use the terminology of the age, these were 'bourgeois specialists', 'fellow-travellers', 'Nepmen', and worse. Yet like the Communist Party's Left Opposition, many of these persons advocated a muscular role for the state to restore order amid the chaos of the market. Wine, in their view, was just too important to leave alone.

This chapter uses the politics of wine commerce during the NEP years to present an unusual, and in many ways counter-intuitive history of that first Soviet decade. Historians have often characterized NEP as a period of revolutionary

---

[5] Fedot Fedotovich Ivankin, *Alkogol': dorevoliutsionnye aktsii, pai, obligatsii i vremennye svidetel'stva Rossiiskoi imperii. Katalog* (Moscow, 2010).

[6] T. B. Zabozlaeva has cataloged this canon of law: see T. B. Zabozlaeva, *Shampanskoe v russkoi kul'ture* (St Petersburg, 2007), 341–95.

modesty, where the need to rebuild after seven years of war and revolution took precedence over the Marxist dream of destroying private capital and capitalists. The fundamental political debates of NEP—the well-chronicled party factionalism that flourished despite Lenin's injunction at the Tenth Party Congress—hinged principally upon some party members' unease with the policies of accommodation toward class enemies, and other party members' defence of those policies. Looking at the 1920s through the prism of wine, however, communist and class enemy appear to be far less salient identities than producer (grower and/or vintner) and seller. In fact, both segments of the wine economy—production and sales—were similar in that they combined a thin gloss of communist administration at the top, with broad ranks of non-communists and outright opponents of Bolshevism at the middle and bottom. Of course, deep ran communist scepticism about the commercial sector and the people who worked in it—middlemen and merchants such as Shlapakov, who proposed to profit from an arbitrage scheme between the vineyards of the south and the stores of the north. As Amy Randall noted in her study of Soviet retail trade under Stalin, many communists in the 1920s assumed that commerce was 'un-Soviet' by nature.[7] Yet in the wine industry in particular, producers had scant better claim on the sympathy of the new Soviet government. The vast majority were small-scale growers and private landowners. They were likely to be non-Russian. Some were the descendants of colonists from abroad. Prior to 1914, their vineyards and production facilities were important sources of employment for local populations. Likewise, commercial vintners were often children of privilege with extensive ties to the tsarist government. Nonetheless, because of the perceived importance of wine as a hallmark of *kul'turnost'*, and because of a deep-seated and often irrational fear that commercial middlemen were inordinately and unjustly profiting from the sale of wine, the Soviet government sought to protect persons who almost certainly would have been labelled speculators, exploiters, or worse had they been planting rye near Riazan rather than tending vineyards near Kherson. The fact that in the early years of NEP the principal commercial villain, in the eyes of many, was an agency subordinate to the Supreme Council of the National Economy (Vesenkha), the Central Wine Trade Administration (Vintorg), which coordinated wholesale and retail trade in wine, underscored the irony of the moment.

While the deregulation of wine production and sales in the 1920s represented an unexpected departure from the experience of the late-tsarist period, concern about the deleterious impact of commercial middlemen, particularly on producers, had direct precedent in the fin-de-siècle, as it was the principal motive behind the 1914 wine purity law. The story of wine across the revolutionary divide thus blurs the categories that historians often use to make sense of the different groups and

---

[7] Amy E. Randall, *The Soviet Dream World of Retail Trade and Consumption in the 1930s* (New York, 2008), 11.

interests that collided in 1917. Like the ostensibly bourgeois newspapers that engaged in 'anti-bourgeois' propaganda in the spring and summer of 1917, and the new Soviet leaders who found a useful model of a fully mobilized and militarized state in tsarist Russia's experience in the First World War, wine raises questions about what specifically it meant to be communist and non-communist in Russia's age of revolution, about the differences between the late-Imperial and early Soviet periods, and about where and why Soviet policies originated.[8]

David Engerman has noted that many Western observers of the Soviet Union in its first decades were entranced by what George F. Kennan called the 'romance of economic development'. Regardless of their political sympathies, Western observers shared with their Soviet counterparts a belief in rapid economic development and the unavoidability of its costs, which produced a blindness to Stalinist atrocity.[9] This chapter argues for the existence of a similar, unexpected commonality among groups whose political differences are usually understood as paramount. Because of wine producers' struggles to eke out a profit in the tsarist period, and because of widespread and well-justified fears about what kind of wine consumers really desired, the principal figures in the early-Soviet wine industry were deeply sceptical about the comparatively free market that NEP had created. They shared with the communist administrators to whom they ultimately answered a deep-seated belief that the state was the most rational and benevolent tool for ordering the wine business, for ensuring that quality remained a paramount concern, and for guaranteeing that the great project of Westernization— which wine had represented from that first moment in the seventeenth century when foreign merchants planted *Vitis vinifera* near Astrakhan—continued without interruption. Like the subjects of Engerman's study, such beliefs engendered their own forms of blindness about the intentions of Soviet power.

*   *   *   *   *

One of the most striking features in histories of viniculture and winemaking in the Russian Empire and the Soviet Union, especially those published after 1917, is the absence of prosaic disaster: late-spring frosts, rain before harvest, mildew on the grapes, too much acetic acid in the bottles. In short, the blessings and

---

[8] Boris I. Kolonitskii, 'Antibourgeois Propaganda and Anti-"Burzhui" Consciousness in 1917', *Russian Review* 53, no. 2 (April 1994): 183–96; Peter Holquist, 'What's So Revolutionary about the Russian Revolution? State Practices and New-Style Politics, 1914–1921', in Hoffmann and Kotsonis, *Russian Modernity*, 87–111.

[9] David C. Engerman, 'Modernization from the Other Shore: American Observers and the Costs of Soviet Economic Development', *American Historical Review* 105, no. 2 (April 2000): 383. Catriona Kelly has noted the existence of similar unexpected political affinities in the realm of architectural preservation. The Petrograd activist Konstantin Romanov, for instance, saw the early Soviet state as a potentially useful tool for preserving church architecture. See Catriona Kelly, *Socialist Churches: Radical Secularization and the Preservation of the Past in Petrograd and Leningrad, 1918–1988* (DeKalb, IL, 2016), 43–4, 54–5.

blunders that distinguish great wines from the pedestrian are absent in accounts of Russian and Soviet winemaking, even though fragmentary archival evidence suggests that such things were constantly on the minds of growers and producers.[10] Contrary to histories of more renowned wine-producing regions such as Bordeaux and Tuscany, Soviet vintners seemed to produce no memorable vintages, when all the factors beyond human control aligned with the skills of growers and vintners to produce unmistakably great wine; nor did Soviet vintners suffer any terrible vintages that were mainly suitable for conversion to vinegar (which happened on occasion). Instead, according to published accounts, there was an ever-rising line of production, consumption, and success, suggesting that the Russian Empire, and later the Soviet Union was becoming a wine power in its own right.

Of course, beyond the pages of these histories, Russian producers were all too familiar with disaster, perhaps more so than their counterparts in France and Italy. Over the course of a century, they survived four catastrophes of human cause or exacerbation: the slow-motion devastation of phylloxera, which came ashore in Crimea sometime before the late 1870s, when it was discovered, and the tsarist government's botched response to it; Russia's 'continuum of crisis' during the First World War and the years of revolution and Civil War; the German and Romanian occupation and plundering of southern Ukraine, southern Russia, and Crimea in the Second World War; and the conflation of wine with vodka in late-Soviet anti-alcoholism policy.[11] Among these catastrophes, the period of war and revolution was most devastating. Entire swathes of the wine belt were shorn from the Soviet Union at the end of the First World War. Bessarabia, the site of roughly 20 per cent of the tsarist empire's vinicultural production, was annexed by the Kingdom of Romania, a loss that would not be avenged until the Red Army occupied the region according to the secret protocols of the Molotov-Ribbentrop pact in 1940. Odessa, which had been Russia's chief wine entrepôt for more than a century, was occupied by French forces in 1919.[12] Shifting battle lines in Crimea and the Ukrainian south made wine cellars a tempting target for both sides in the Civil War.[13] Even Transcaucasia slipped away from the Bolsheviks, albeit only temporarily.

---

[10] See, for instance, the 1923 annual report for the Kotsiuvinshchina vine nursery, which records activities in its vineyards on nearly a day-by-day basis, and the 1924–5 'operation plan' for the Aleshkovskii vine nursery: TsDAVO Ukraïny, f. 4182, o. 1, d. 1l. 1–7; d. 2, ll. 1–9ob., respectively. A significant exception to the prosaic-disaster lacuna in Russian wine histories is Mikhail Ballas's magisterial six-volume set, *Vinodelie v Rossii* (St Petersburg, 1895–1903). Ballas describes in exacting detail the impact that late-spring freezes, rainy summers, and early-fall snowstorms had on various vintages in the wine producing regions of the empire.

[11] Peter Holquist, *Making War, Forging Revolution: Russia's Continuum of Crisis, 1914–1921* (Cambridge, MA, 2002).

[12] Peter Kenez, *Civil War in South Russia, 1919–1920* (Berkeley, Los Angeles, and London, 1977), 180–91.

[13] V. V. Vlasov, *100 let dorogoiu V. E. Tairova* (Odessa, 2005), 17.

Overarching it all was a prohibition on the retail sale of alcohol, which the tsarist government enacted in 1914 for the sake of wartime sobriety, and which the Bolshevik government left in place, in the case of wine, until 1920. In truth, the prohibition on the sale of wine was never absolute. In the months preceding September 1914, when Nicholas II announced that he had abolished the sale of vodka entirely, provincial authorities in the south—perhaps sensing the winds of temperance—carved out a number of exemptions to prohibition that more or less survived the war years. In August 1914, authorities in Odessa restricted the retail sale of wine to the hours of 11 a.m. to 2 p.m., a scheme that their counterparts in Simferopol, Feodosia, and Melitopol copied. In September 1915, wine producers in Crimea, many of whom had considerable political influence, were given the right to sell finished wine directly to consumers, as long as they secured the approval of provincial tax authorities beforehand. Because this exemption failed to account for Crimean Tatars, who commonly sold unfinished grape must to wine producers, the exemption was later widened to wine at any stage of production. Worse than prohibition, for commercial growers and vintners, were the general wartime conditions. The war disrupted the supply of copper sulphate, which was manufactured in England and France, and which was commonly used as a vineyard fungicide. In the fall of 1915, authorities in Tiflis indicated that insufficient supplies of copper sulphate was one reason the Transcaucasian harvest was smaller than average. By 1916 and 1917, amid the general economic crisis of the terminal phase of tsarism, even domestic distribution networks began to crumble.[14]

By 1920, officials in Glavspirt, the Main Administration for Liquor and Alcohol Production, estimated that total commercial vineyard plantings, under comparatively modern forms of cultivation, had fallen from 232,000 desyatins (2,529 square kilometres) in 1914 to 71,000 (774 square kilometres) in 1920, principally because of territorial losses in Bessarabia and Transcaucasia. Total pre-war production had been 66.1 million *vedra* (buckets), the old Russian measurement for volume that was the equivalent of nearly 870 million litres of wine. By 1920, that figure had fallen by 90 per cent.[15] A second vineyard census that circulated within Sovnarkom after the reincorporation of Transcaucasia in 1922, and that appears to have been written at the behest of Nikolai Zhidelev, an Old Bolshevik and founding member of the Cheka who oversaw wine production and sales in Sovnarkom's Administrative Department (*upravlenie delami*), found that 150,000 desyatins (1,638 square kilometres) of commercial vineyards, the equivalent of 60 per cent of pre-war plantings, were lost to the Soviet Union in Bessarabia or perished during these years. Those vines that remained survived in 'semi-wild conditions'

---

[14] GAARK, f. 156, o. 1, d. 16, l. 205; d. 23, ll. 4–4ob., 13ob., and 17.
[15] RGAE, f. 738, o. 1, d. 10, l. 18.

and were only half as fecund as they had once been, due to many years without pruning and maintenance.[16]

For growers and vintners, the years of war, revolution, and prohibition resulted above all in poverty and predation. The former crown estate at Abrau-Diurso, located 20 kilometres west of Novorossiysk on the Black Sea, and once the personal property of the Romanov family, was reorganized as a *sovkhoz* at the advent of Soviet power, but its pre-war grandeur had been destroyed. 'It is possible to call the condition [of Abrau-Diurso] catastrophic', one official wrote to the Central Executive Committee in Moscow in 1922. 'The same is true of its food and money [supplies], bandits reign over the area, workers are hungry and in tatters, but they nonetheless preserve significant supplies of valuable wine in the hope that the center will bring help.' The latter was more than hyperbole. In 1919, Anton Frolov-Bagreev, the chief vintner at Abrau-Diurso and later the so-called father of Soviet Champagne, was held captive by armed workers demanding the keys to Abrau-Diurso's cellars. When Frolov-Bagreev refused, he was ordered to be shot, a fate he avoided only when his subordinates hid him among wine barrels and petitioned for his clemency. Help arrived in Abrau-Diurso in 1921, through the offices of the Commissariat of Foreign Trade in Novorossiysk, but the accompanying terms were so onerous and exploitative that *sovkhoz* workers refused to accept them. The commissariat proposed to trade 500 *pudy* of American flour, likely obtained from Red Cross famine relief supplies, at the rate of 1 *pud* flour (16.38 kilograms, worth about 7 million roubles) for every 1.5 *vedra* (19.68 litres, worth 39 million roubles) of wine.[17]

In Crimea, which in 1920 became General Wrangel's last stronghold after defeat in the North Caucasus, the situation was equally dire, as shifting battle lines and the imminence of White defeat turned wine cellars into precious family heirlooms that needed to be evacuated, and objects of looting if they were not. There the anti-Bolshevik military government of southern Russia found itself besieged by requests to authorize the evacuation of aristocratic wine cellars, which were neither small nor easy to transport. The Golitsyn family, the heirs to Russia's most famous vintner, sought permission to ship under international flag 20,000 bottles, principally bearing labels from Novyi svet and Abrau-Diurso, from the family's cellar via the port at Feodosia. Because shipping space was at a premium in the waning days of the Civil War, many persons took matters into their own hands. On 5 April, port agents in Yalta raided the Greek steamship Constantine, which sailed under the flag of the League of Nations. They discovered in its hold 1,000 bottles of thirty-year-old wine from Massandra, which a

---

[16] GARF, f. R130, o. 6, d. 442, l. 27.

[17] GARF, f. R130, o. 6, d. 442, ll. 8ob–9. On Frolov-Bagreev, see Konstantin Bogdanov, 'Soviet Champagne: A Festive History', trans. Rosie Tweddle, *Forum for Anthropology and Culture*, no. 9 (2013): 235. These prices are denominated in the first Soviet rouble, in circulation from 1917 to 1921.

former tsarist minister of agriculture was trying to send to a member of the Crimean government who had already fled Russia. Because it was not clear whether the wine had been legally procured from Massandra, or plundered, the shipment was held pending investigation. For its part, Wrangel's military government saw in the Massandra cellars an asset that could be sold to support resettlement abroad and continued struggle at home. In the summer of 1920, the military government's Agricultural Administration ordered its representatives in Europe to arrange the export and sale of 40,000 to 100,000 *vedra* of Massandra wine. It was the equivalent of 524,800 to 1,312,000 litres.[18]

In the context of retreat and evacuation, it was often hard to distinguish government initiative and legitimate business ventures from looting. In the months before Mikhail Frunze's forces conquered Crimea, the firm Iurovet (an acronym for the Southern Russian Society for Foreign Trade) tried to capitalize one last time on foreign fascination with wines from the southern shore, which had achieved significant renown in the final tsarist decades. In May 1920, a Iurovet delegation arrived in London to conduct a tasting of samples from 250 barrels of red table wine (1915 vintage), 232 barrels of white table wine (1913), 250 barrels of port (1912), and 25 barrels of Muscat (1912), all Crimean by origin, and all shipped from Crimea via Istanbul under conditions meant to ensure their quality. Invited were 'famous wine specialists' and 'tasters' from London trading companies. 'The reviews of these specialists exceeded our most optimistic expectations', one member of the Iurovet expedition reported, 'especially if we take into consideration that the wine delivered to London was not from the crown estate vineyards, and in no way approximated the best samples of the corresponding Crimean estate wine varietal'. The London critics found that the red and white table wines were of 'superior quality', and would 'absolutely find sales on the market'. The port was 'exceptional and comparable to the best ports from Portugal'. And the Crimean Muscat was far better than the Spanish Muscat commonly sold in Britain. After a contract had been finalized, the secretary of the purchasing firm confided that the wine Iurovet offered was of far better quality than 300 barrels of Crimean wine the firm had previously purchased from a private seller. That wine, apparently, had been looted and spirited to London in less auspicious conditions.[19]

Even after the advent of Soviet power in Crimea, wine remained an object of convenient profit for a government that had scant funds to spare, and for a population that lived in desperate poverty. Throughout 1921, Crimean *sovkhoz* workers destroyed stockpiles of 'old highly valuable wines' from the former crown estates by individual looting and consumption, simple neglect, and unauthorized sale. They had an unexpected incentive to do so. The Commissariat of Agriculture, which according to early Soviet law had the sole right to purchase wine from

---

[18] GARF, f. R356, o. 2, d. 71, ll. 1–9.   [19] RGAE, f. 738, o. 1, d. 10, l. 42.

sovkhozy, attached to it such low prices that wine appeared to be 'without value' in the eyes of the Soviet state. 'From time to time we sell [illegally] a *vedro* of table wine for 1,000,000 rubles, and a *vedro* of fortified wine for 1,800,000 rubles, or for one *pud* of flour', a correspondent from a *sovkhoz* outside of Yalta wrote to Sovnarkom in Moscow. 'At these rates, it is possible for us to sell enough wine in Yalta to pay for necessary winter work in the vineyards.' Yet at the same time, from its offices in Simferopol, the Commissariat of Agriculture purchased wine for significantly lower prices—240,000 roubles for a *vedro* of table wine from Masssandra, and 760,000 roubles for fortified wine—and even demanded the right to cellar space at Massandra and the use of increasingly rare bottles for wine bought in barrels. The grain exchanges that the Commissariat of Agriculture orchestrated were also less advantageous for the *sovkhoz*, valuing wine at between 20 and 25 per cent of what the *sovkhoz* could arrange on its own. Soviet power 'is carrying out a wine operation that is clearly destructive and even criminal', wrote a Sovnarkom official, O. N. Klinkova, after visiting the southern shore of Crimea in the fall of 1921. Speaking with *sovkhoz* workers 'whose truth cannot be verified but who inspire confidence', Klinkova wrote that there were no supplies or money to pay for vineyard upkeep. The illegal sale of wine was occurring with 'good intentions', and was 'no more criminal than the sales of Narkomzem [the Commissariat of Agriculture] itself'.[20]

In truth, the problems plaguing Crimean production ran deeper than the crises caused by war and revolution. As the prices commanded by Crimean wines soared in the late-tsarist years amid a string of successes in international competitions, savvy merchants began to buy up Crimean production in order to blend with less expensive wines from Bessarabia and Turkestan. While the resulting concoctions could be labelled Crimean by origin, according to tsarist law, the result was a 'de-personalization' of Crimean wine for the sake of profit. Similarly, in the early years of NEP, the Commissariat of Agriculture was prone to add water to the stocks of fortified Crimean wine it sold, so the total volume of wine it had on hand after sale did not diminish. 'Even now among wine merchants', Klinkova wrote,

> the conviction reigns that they should not release into the marketplace pure Crimean wine, so that it exists only as an additive for wine from the Caucasus, Turkestan, and other places, in order to give those wines a Crimean identity and artificially raise their prices.

The latter tendency was evident as late as 1924, when the Commissariat of Agriculture's Concessionary Affairs section considered a fanciful proposal, apparently of internal provenance, to export wine from the southern shore of Crimea

---

[20] GARF, f. R130, o. 6, d. 442, ll. 8ob., 27–8. Prices are denominated in the first Soviet rouble, in circulation from 1917 to 1921.

to France. The authors of the plan, who were plainly ignorant about the elaborate hierarchies of *terroir* that governed French wine, and about the renown that wines from the prestigious crown estate vineyards on the southern shore had achieved in the final tsarist decades, hoped to entice French producers with the idea of blending Crimean and French wine to bolster the alcohol content of the latter. To officials in the Crimean office of the Winemaking Administration, whose input the Commissariat of Agriculture sought, this was a ridiculous idea for several reasons, but principally because it treated Crimean wine as an interchangeable commodity, reducible in the end to its alcohol content. This was the logic of vodka, not *terroir*. Given the fact that nothing like this arrangement had ever existed in the tsarist period, Crimean officials thought it highly unlikely that French producers would compromise the *terroir* of their wines in this manner. Moreover, the problem in Crimea was not that the quality and quantity of production had fallen so precipitously that such desperate measures were warranted. In fact, Crimean production levels had begun to rebound in 1923, when 689 desyatins (753 hectares) of vineyards in wine *sovkhozy* produced 97,000 *vedra* (1,192,130 litres) of wine, up from 40,000 *vedra* (491,600 litres) two years earlier. However, domestic demand and distribution networks had collapsed to the point that many *sovkhoz* workers were experiencing starvation, despite substantial stockpiles of wine in their cellars.[21]

It was an article of faith among the principals of the early Soviet wine industry that Soviet power was uniquely suited to solve these problems, by encouraging the consumption of wine, by regulating its production and sale, and by rationally pairing varietal and region. In some places, wine had proven commercially viable in the past only if blended with Crimean production. Attention to viability would help Soviet vintners effect 'regionalization', in short, a sort of proto-*terroir*, where each vinicultural region, on the basis of 'natural selection', would produce only those wines for which it was best suited.[22] Contrary to France, where the idea of *terroir* as something ineffable and essential to great wine emerged in response to the standardizing impulses of modern production, in the Soviet Union *terroir* was principally a problem for science: pairing the right grapes with the right soil and the right climate.[23] Because vineyard productivity in Crimea was one-fifth what it was in the Caucasus, it made little sense to grow the same varietals in both places. Crimea was ideal for dessert wines and varietals that commanded a premium among consumers; the Caucasus, Turkestan, and southern Ukraine were best suited for table wines.

Despite the grim appraisals about the state of domestic viniculture at the beginning of NEP, optimism about the Soviet Union's potential as a wine power emerged undiminished from seven years of war and revolution. 'By virtue of its

---

[21] GARF, f. R8350, o. 1, d. 2473, ll. 1–2.   [22] GARF, f. R130, o. 6, d. 442, l. 25.
[23] Kolleen M. Guy, *When Champagne Became French: Wine and the Making of a National Identity* (Baltimore, 2003), 41–4.

natural conditions', wrote the same Sovnarkom official who bemoaned Soviet efforts in viniculture and winemaking in 1922, 'Russia might become a leading winemaking country, developing a zone of industrial viniculture', meaning viniculture characterized by modern modes of production, 'to the extent of its natural boundaries, that is, with an area of 2 million desyatins'. The latter figure, nearly 22,000 square kilometres of vineyards, was nine times the area that was thought to be under modern cultivation at the end of the tsarist period. It was the equivalent of the total modern vinicultural area of France, Italy, Portugal, Spain, Germany, and Austria put together. While it was de rigueur to note that the tsarist government had squandered this natural potential, letting upstarts like Australia and South America surpass Russia in vineyard area, only the most cynical communist could deny the successes of the former crown estate vineyards, Massandra, Ai-Danil', Abrau-Diurso, and Novyi svet, which had few rivals outside of France. Even in the Caucasus, where many of the most promising vinicultural areas in Kakheti and elsewhere were incorporated into crown estates after conquest in the nineteenth century, and where tasting successes had been modest, the marginal soil paradox common to viniculture meant that harvests were bountiful—often seven to nine times greater per desyatin than vineyards in Crimea. While the resulting wine was 'cruder' (*grubee*) than its Crimean counterparts, because the vines had not struggled to produce grapes, it was 'characteristic', meaning varietals tasted as they should. To the most sanguine proponents of Soviet viniculture in Sovnarkom and elsewhere, realizing the Soviet Union's full wine potential meant nothing less than ending the scourge of alcoholism. 'Tempered over the course of centuries by rotgut (*sivukha*), the Russian organism will finally break the habit of drunkenness.'[24]

*   *   *   *   *

Soviet attempts to bolster viniculture and winemaking began in the waning months of the Civil War, as large sections of the Black Sea wine belt were reincorporated into territories administered from Moscow. Vineyards and production facilities on the crown estates were transferred directly to the Commissariat of Agriculture's Sovkhoz Administration. Although this included many of the Russian Empire's most prestigious wineries, such as Abrau-Diurso and Ai-Danil', total vineyard area was small: 300 desyatins (327 hectares) in Crimea, 500 in the North Caucuses, 100 in that part of Bessarabia that remained in the Soviet Union, and 500 in Transcaucasia. Production on the former crown estates was 450,000 *vedra* (5,535,000 litres) in 1921, less than 10 per cent of all post-war production.[25] With the exception of a handful of foreign specialists who were employed on crown estates prior to 1914, and whose fates after 1917 remain uncertain,

[24] GARF, f. R130, o. 6, d. 442, ll. 23–4.   [25] RGAE, f. 738, o. 1, d. 10, l. 18.

nationalization did not amount to many practical changes in daily routines. Nor did it quickly ameliorate post-war deprivation.

Small-scale growers, responsible for the vast majority of vineyard acreage, posed more pressing problems. Because serfdom had not existed to a significant extent in the south, most viniculturalists tended to be homesteaders and private landowners.[26] During tsarist times, they were also the principle source of wine that was subject, after sale to middlemen, to adulteration. On 8 April 1920, Sovnarkom authorized viniculturalists to make wine. In truth, this was more encouragement than authorization, since prohibition was by no means the only reason in 1920 to let grapes rot on the vines. Yet it did draw a legal distinction between wine and vodka, which remained an object of prohibition until 1925, and it anticipated the decree of 26 August 1920, in which Sovnarkom overturned a ban on the retail sale of wine (with less than 20 per cent alcohol content), which had been in place since the beginning of the First World War. In order to stimulate production, the Commissariat of Agriculture was given a monopoly on wholesale wine purchases, thus creating a single government wine reserve for new production. An agency subordinate to the commissariat, the Winemaking Administration, was charged with promoting best practices among growers and vintners and supervising the wine reserve.[27]

Six years after the state monopoly was abolished as part of the wartime ban on the retail sale of alcohol, and three years after the Bolsheviks came to power, the Soviet Union created a monopoly on wholesale wine commerce that very much resembled Witte's scheme.[28] Like Witte's scheme, it was impossible to disaggregate entirely the monopoly from the revenue, particularly via exports, that its proponents hoped it would generate. Yet as the proposal to export Crimean wines to France indicated, the ambitiousness of export schemes often correlated inversely with the wine knowledge of the schemers. In 1920, K. M. Frenkel, a member of the collegium of Glavspirt, and for a short time the director of Vintorg, encouraged his colleagues to be realistic about export plans. The 'high quality of Russian wine of certain varietals and types provides a basis to suggest the possibility of selling these wines on the foreign market', Frenkel wrote. Yet he also noted that the Western market was crowded with wines from France, Spain, Portugal, Italy, and Algeria, and that it had proven very difficult for even the best Russian wines of the tsarist period—from the crown estates at Novyi svet, Abrau-Diurso, and elsewhere—to compete on price with Western competitors. Given the fact that Russian wines had been entirely absent during the years of war and blockade and the costs of advertising, Frenkel thought there were good reasons to

[26] Willard Sunderland, *Taming the Wild Field: Colonization and Empire on the Russian Steppe* (Ithaca and London, 2004), 108.

[27] RGAE, f. 738, o. 1, d. 10, l. 32.

[28] On wartime sobriety efforts, see Mark Lawrence Schrad, *Vodka Politics: Alcohol, Autocracy, and the Secret History of the Russian State* (Oxford, 2014), 178–81.

be sceptical about export success.[29] According to an addendum that was attached to a report that circulated within Glavspirt on the introduction of the wine monopoly, and that appears to have been authored by Frenkel, vinicultural regions like Turkestan, which emerged from the years of war and revolution comparatively unscathed, stood to benefit in the short term from the export of wine abroad, even though such activities would come at the expense of raisin production. Indeed, Turkestan had recently turned over 50,000 *vedra* of wine to the Commissariat for Foreign Trade for sale abroad. Yet Frenkel argued domestic demand for wine would soon catch up and surpass the production levels of the vinicultural regions, thus meaning that any wine exported abroad would have to be replaced by 'foreign surrogates'.[30]

The latter was the problem that the wine monopoly sought to remedy, by replacing a consumer-driven demand that was highly atrophied and fickle as a result of tsarist wartime policy and the general collapse of the economy, with a state-driven demand that was, in theory, infinite, or at least far in excess of productive capacity. In this respect, the wine monopoly diverged from other policies associated with War Communism, such as grain requisitions, the nationalization of industry, and rationing, which had an 'expressed anti-bourgeois character', and which were supply-driven, meaning they were about ensuring adequate supplies of food and matériel in a context where demand far outstripped supply.[31] Nonetheless, such distinctions were lost once the shift to NEP occurred. On 9 August 1921, as part of the Soviet state's general retreat from the agricultural and retail sectors of the economy, the Soviet wine monopoly was abolished, less than three weeks before its first birthday, and according to many critics in the wine industry, long before it had served its purpose. 'Permitting free trade in wine', warned one unknown official from the Commissariat of Agriculture, 'which until this time has been a product monopolized by the state, restricted from general consumption, exposes wine to the conditions of the market, with all the economic consequences that arise from that'.[32]

These 'economic consequences' had several interlocking dimensions. Most important, there were good reasons to fear that consumer demand for wine, at least for the sort that the Soviet wine industry produced, was weak, even in the absence of vodka. The latter remained under full prohibition until 1924, when 54 proof vodka (so-called 'Rykovka') was permitted, and in partial effect until the following year, when 80 proof vodka appeared on store shelves for the first time since 1914. Demand for wine adulterated with grain alcohol and sugar—in short,

---

[29] RGAE, f. 738, o. 1, d. 10, ll. 32–2ob.   [30] RGAE, f. 738, o. 1, d. 10, l. 28.

[31] Nataliia Lebina, *Sovetskaia povsednevnost': normy i anomalii ot voennogo kommunizma k bol'shomu stiliu* (Moscow, 2016), 23. See also Mary McAuley, 'Bread without the Bourgeoisie', in *Party, State, and Society in the Russian Civil War: Explorations in Social History*, ed. Diane P. Koenker, William G. Rosenberg, and Ronald Grigor Suny (Bloomington, 1989), 158–79.

[32] RGAE, f. 738, o. 1, d. 10, l. 3.

falsified wine—was a different matter. In the pre-war period, de facto wine consumption was thought to be at least two times larger than official consumption figures suggested, mostly because of the prevalence of falsified wines in the marketplace. This was a problem that the defunct wine purity law had remedied, albeit only briefly, and that prohibition and the Soviet wine monopoly had prevented from recurring. With the latter going the way of the wine purity law in 1920 and 1921, however, there were no longer any legal restraints on, nor mechanism for preventing the adulteration of wine up to 20 per cent alcohol.

The abolition of the wine monopoly also created a great deal of confusion about the specific roles of and the relationship between the Winemaking Administration, Glavspirt, and Vintorg. The Winemaking Administration was left without much of a portfolio in the absence of a single government wine reserve, much less a source of income. Yet it was supposed to serve as the liaison between *sovkhoz* and private growers, on the one hand, and state power on the other, helping rebuild viniculture in the process. The administration found itself in such dire financial straits in 1921 that it took out a loan from the State Bank, without any ability to repay. For all intents and purposes, Klinkova wrote in a report to Zhidelev in 1922, the Winemaking Administration had become an 'insolvent debtor'. It was 'powerless to perform practical work'. It engaged 'only in assaults on Vintorg'. It succeeded mainly in 'holding meetings and writing reports'. And it had not a single bottle of wine in its Moscow cellar that it could sell to support vineyard upkeep. The end of the wine monopoly similarly removed Glavspirt from the wine economy, albeit with less disastrous results. Because their chief job was regulating, in light of prohibition, vodka that was in immense demand, many persons in Glavspirt thought they were well-positioned to tackle wine adulteration. Thus, its collegium members initially opposed the repeal of the wine monopoly, and then in the aftermath of repeal advocated for a greater institutional role for Glavspirt. 'It is necessary to focus on one, undeniable fact', a Glavspirt official wrote:

the full indeterminacy and chaos of current conditions in this important industry. At present, it has all the attributes of atrophy and paralysis...There is a single correct path forward: transfer the entire winemaking economy (wineries, wine caves, warehouses, and cellars) to Glavspirt, and carefully examine the fate of small-scale, 'working' viniculture and winemaking that is of artisanal character.[33]

It is tempting to see the latter as an early call for the collectivization of viniculture and winemaking. Yet it was a peculiar sort of call, since it was devoid of the ideological overtones that so often accompanied discussions of the grain economy.

---

[33] RGAE, f. 738, o. 1, d. 10, ll. 17, 28.

Small-scale viniculturalists were never couched as inveterate speculators, intent on sabotaging Soviet power. Instead, they were victims of an unregulated market, where the real money lay in commerce. In 1921 and 1922, this was the domain of Vintorg, which was flush in comparison with the Winemaking Administration. Vintorg had at its disposal all the wine that had been confiscated from individual and commercial cellars during the Civil War. Its inventory included 89,000 *vedra* of wine from the best Crimean *sovkhozy*, the former crown estates, and it occasionally acquired wine that made its way to Moscow by informal means.

In the early months of NEP, there were several creative schemes put forth to alleviate the bureaucratic inequity between commerce and production, from the creation of a publicly owned shareholding company, in which the key players of the wine industry would contribute funds to support growers and vintners in return for a proportional share of their production, to the creation of a centralized wine syndicate, which would coordinate all aspects of wine production and sales, to public–private ventures, which would entice foreign capital with the promise of export revenue. Yet nothing progressed beyond paper, because Frenkel, the head of Vintorg, was 'categorically opposed' to any arrangement that lessened the sway of his agency by giving the newly emasculated Winemaking Administration a role in commerce. In Frenkel's view, the chief problem plaguing wine production was insufficient demand, which only Vintorg could solve. Until Soviet citizens began to purchase wine in greater amounts, efforts to bolster production, the charge of the Winemaking Administration, would prove counterproductive.[34]

It is easy to fathom why so many persons outside of Vintorg were uncomfortable with this status quo. The parallels with the late-tsarist period were too evident to ignore. Soviet power had succeeded in recreating, in bureaucratic form, the status quo prior to the enactment of the wine purity law in 1914. Given the last-minute timing of the latter, this should not be surprising. As Lewis Siegelbaum has noted, the Soviet administrative state, meaning those agencies that were subordinate to the commissariats and ultimately Sovnarkom, functioned much as their tsarist predecessors had, under a different nomenclature to be sure, but with many of the same personnel.[35] Before 1914, for a variety of reasons, producers were at a competitive disadvantage to merchants, who frequently adulterated wine with sugar and alcohol to cater to popular tastes. By 1921, wine had again slipped beyond the benevolent gaze of government regulation, with many of the same deleterious results. In 1921 and 1922, Vintorg even ordered the adulteration of wine in its stockpiles with grain alcohol, thus creating something that was not necessarily wine, but definitely in demand. It was 'criminal falsification', Klinkova

---

[34] GARF, f. R130, o. 6, d. 442, ll. 29–30.
[35] Lewis H. Siegelbaum, *Soviet State and Society between Revolutions, 1918–1929* (Cambridge, 1992), 17.

wrote, ignoring the fact that the tsarist wine purity law went the way of tsarism in 1917, and that all wine below 20 per cent alcohol was legal. Such concoctions were 'intended, it seems, to serve up the old tsarist monopoly under a new sauce', this time with Vintorg as chef. To be sure, the parallel with the tsarist period was imperfect. Because of prohibition, some cases of falsification, namely those where the final products had alcohol contents exceeding 20 per cent, were prosecutable as 'bootlegging' (*shinkarstvo*), and thus tended to be the affair of enterprising individuals and private stores rather than government institutions.[36] Moreover, until late 1922 Vintorg lacked a network of state stores, the so-called *kazenki* of the late-tsarist period, which were authorized to sell alcohol. Instead, it sold 'half-strength' vodka (in reality, wine fortified with alcohol to 20 per cent) to cooperatives and privately owned stores. Nonetheless, by responding to consumers' demand for adulterated wine, Vintorg showed that its policies were 'determined by trade, and that the wine trade has been transferred to an agency that has nothing in common with viniculture and winemaking'.[37] The idea of wine as a vessel of *kul'turnost'* had been forsaken entirely.

The official concern about Vintorg's activities suggests how flexible and ambiguous NEP could be to the bureaucrats tasked with implementing it, and how rife with paradox were those months in 1921 and 1922 when they were doing so. In the view of the Sovnarkom official, O. N. Klinkova, who investigated the wine economy at the behest of Nikolai Zhidelev, wine producers—among whom, of course, the crown estates-turned-wine *sovkhozy*, and much greater numbers of private vineyard owners—were being exploited by an arm of the Soviet government, Vintorg, which realized an unfair proportion of the revenue generated from their production. 'The merchant has not one vine of vineyard', Klinkova wrote. Yet proceeds from the sale of wine 'serve to strengthen the commercial apparat, which strangles producers'. In the Soviet state especially, growers and vintners must have the right 'to sell the fruit of their own labor'. Vintorg erred in other ways as well. It offered consumers an adulterated product, thus forsaking the civilizing properties of wine and resurrecting the worst part of the tsarist wine monopoly. It engaged in unfair competition with the Winemaking Administration, acting like a monopolist even though the Soviet wine monopoly had been abolished. Why are the 'methods of a purely capitalist order, that is...competition between two organizations', being tolerated at all, an official in the Commissariat of Agriculture asked about Vintorg.[38]

The inequity between wine producers and sellers was sufficiently glaring that it caught Lenin's attention. In February 1922, he wrote to Ivan Miroshnikov, an aide in Sovnarkom's Administrative Department, to ask whether wine prices were denominated in gold roubles, whether they were higher than pre-war prices, who

[36]   GARF, f. R393, o. 65, d. 29, l. 1. (Consulted at the Hoover Institution, Stanford University.)
[37]   GARF, f. R130, o. 6, d. 442, l. 33.   [38]   GARF, f. R4085, o. 21, d. 3706, ll. 25, 31.

specifically profited from the sale of wine, and 'who follows and answers for these affairs in toto'. After several weeks, Zhidelev responded, explaining that the wine economy was overseen by two institutions, Vintorg and the Winemaking Administration. He wrote that wine was sold both by government enterprises, such as GUM and Mostorg, where prices were low, and by private individuals on a commission basis, where prices were significantly higher. This made it difficult to ascertain the true cost of wine (*sebestoimost'*), but any profits that were realized were supposed to go to the development of the vinicultural and winemaking industry.[39] As Lenin's query indicated, there were powerful interests lining up behind the idea that the unequal division between Vintorg and the Winemaking Administration was unjustifiable and unsustainable, and that the Soviet Union needed a single person or institution to answer for the wine industry in toto. Until the end, Frenkel argued that such an idea was a 'hopeless mess', and that the status quo, where wine was manufactured under the supervision of an agency subordinate to the Commissariat of Agriculture, deposited in the cellars of Vintorg, and then sold via government and private stores, was no different from buying the wine directly from the producer. Displaying wilful ignorance about the impact of a retail monopoly on wholesale prices, Frenkel argued that the present arrangement meant only that producers had one customer to sell to rather than many. 'You will produce it, and I will sell it', he supposedly said.

In truth, Frenkel was not the only one distrustful of centralization. Because vineyards were predominantly located in the non-Russian south, the wine economy was always understood to be key to the so-called 'Eastern question', which was shorthand for Soviet efforts to build support among non-Russian peoples in Crimea, the Caucasus, and Turkestan. Here the goal was to avoid measures that would stifle local initiative and control. It would be 'wholly unjust', a Sovnarkom official wrote, 'if we denied [local growers and producers] free command of their product, which would at the same time create for us political enemies'.[40] For these reasons, several of the proposals to reorganize viniculture and winemaking in the early years of NEP originated not in the agencies empowered in these affairs, Vintorg and the Winemaking Administration, but among officials charged with administering the Soviet Union's ethnic diversity. In 1922, the Russian Republic's Commissariat of Nationalities put forth proposals to create an excise tax on wine, to ban wine adulteration and falsification, and to create a tariff that would fund the return of barrels from the big cities of the north to the winemaking regions of the south. In that same year, Dagestani representatives to the Commissariat drew up a plan to create regional-level wine trusts. While the inner-workings of these trusts were not elucidated, similar proposals that circulated in the early 1920s

[39] V. I. Lenin, *Pol'noe sobranie sochinenii*, vol. 54 (Moscow, 1975), 182–3, 618.
[40] GARF, f. R130, o. 6. d. 442, l. 30.

hinged on the idea that regional trusts were bulwarks against the encroachment of the centre.[41]

Frenkel was in no position, however, to argue that the status quo he defended benefitted producers more than the untested proposals that circulated in the Commissariat of Nationalities and elsewhere. On 22 April 1922, despite his opposition and at the urging of the Workers' and Peasants' Inspectorate, the All-Russian Central Executive Committee approved the creation of a new institution, the State Vinicultural and Winemaking Syndicate, as an arm of the Commissariat of Agriculture. The wine industries in the Russian Federation's constituent republics were organized into republic-level trusts, thus offering a degree of local autonomy. Subordinate to the new syndicate were both the Central Winemaking Administration and Vintorg. The latter was reorganized as a for-profit business, one of the 160-odd joint-stock companies that were chartered during NEP to harness private and foreign capital to achieve state goals, in this case, rebuilding the wine industry.[42] Its charge was the

> production, processing, and sale of wine and wine materials, the standardization and sorting of wine, the control of cellars and bottling, the production of cognac, grappa, other spirits, and fruit wines, and the wholesale and retail trade of these things.

Vintorg had to manage all of this while making money for the Commissariat of Agriculture, Vesenkha, and private individuals who contributed 1,000 gold roubles per share for some portion of the 1,750 remaining shares that represented a one-third ownership stake.[43] To prevent an arm of the early Soviet state from acting as a monopolist that engaged in unfair competition in the wine trade, and that impoverished producers, Soviet leaders rechartered it as a for-profit business venture.

*   *   *   *   *

Behind the unusual bureaucratic politics of the early NEP years was an awkward relationship between Soviet power and the remnants of the tsarist wine industry. The problem lay not just with the Shlapakovs—self-styled business persons and salesmen who were keen to prove that they were flexible enough to be useful to the Soviet state. In fact, Shlapakov is fairly unusual in the archival record because he was on the sales side of the wine industry. It is much easier to trace his

---

[41] GARF, f. R1318, o. 7, d. 161, ll. 15, 155.

[42] Alan M. Ball, *Russia's Last Capitalists: The Nepmen, 1921–1929* (Berkeley and Los Angeles, 1990), 154–5; Alan M. Ball, 'Private Trade and Traders during NEP', in *Russian in the Era of NEP: Explorations in Soviet Society and Culture*, ed. Sheila Fitzpatrick, Alexander Rabinowitch, and Richard Stites (Bloomington, 1991), 89–105.

[43] GARF, f. A442, o. 1, d. 8, ll. 3, 20–20ob; f. R1318, o. 7, d. 161, ll. 40, 203; f. R1726, o. 1, d. 40, l. 5.

counterparts on the production side, where almost every high-ranking person presented an awkward resumé by virtue of the wealth that the industry attracted in the late-tsarist period. Ambitious commercial vintners cut their teeth on crown estates and trained abroad. Many were children of privilege, university graduates, scientists, and agronomists. At the hostile extreme in the early 1920s were former aristocrats and tsarist officials, many of whom chose emigration over the likelihood of persecution in the Soviet Union. Golitsyn's heirs, bearers of one of the oldest aristocratic names in Russia and loyal military servitors of the tsar, left for France in the early 1920s, and for good reason. Friends and colleagues who remained in Crimea after it fell to the Bolsheviks were quickly ordered to appear in Sudak for 'registration'. Among the casualties of that initial roundup was the son-in-law of the former crown estate vinicultural inspector and chamberlain to the royal family. He was shot. His son perished at sea while trying to escape to Istanbul.[44] André Tchelistcheff (Andrei Chelishchev, b. 1901), whose father was chief justice of the Russian Imperial Court, nearly died in battle against the Bolsheviks in Crimea in 1921. In emigration in California in the 1930s, Tchelistcheff would become one of the principal architects of Napa Valley Cabernet Sauvignon, which over the course of a generation would replace Petite Verdot as the valley's characteristic varietal.[45]

More common were persons who were antipathetic to Bolshevism, but who stayed on, with varying degrees of success, in hopes of finding a *modus vivendi* with Soviet power. Vasilii Tairov, late-tsarist Russia's preeminent vinicultural scientist and the long-time editor of *Vestnik vinodeliia* (Winemaking Bulletin), was of modest origins in rural Armenia, a fact that helped him survive the revolution, despite numerous personal connections to high levels of the tsarist government in St Petersburg and Odessa. In 1922, the experimental vineyard station outside of Odessa that Tairov had founded nearly two decades earlier on the basis of funds collected from growers and vintners was named for him. Yet it proved to be a short-lived honour: in 1926, Tairov was fired, and in 1927 the station was renamed for Kliment Timiriazev, who cut a more revolutionary figure in Bolshevik eyes. Anton Frolov-Bagreev (b. 1877), the 'father of Soviet Champagne', had better revolutionary credentials: he temporarily lost his job at the Abrau-Diurso crown estate in 1905 when he spoke at a revolutionary meeting. Yet Frolov-Bagreev was also the son of a high-ranking tsarist bureaucrat, the chief representative of the Ministry of State Property in Tobolsk Province, whose wealth allowed Frolov-Bagreev to train in Bordeaux and Madeira as a young man. Georgii Gogol'-Ianovskii

---

[44] N. K. Laman and A. N. Borisova, *Kniaz' Lev Sergeevich Golitsyn: vydaiushchiisia russkii vinodel* (Moscow, 2000), 224–49.
[45] L. A. Mnukhin, Avril Marie, and Véronique Lossky, eds., *Rossiiskoe zarubezh'e v Frantsii, 1919–2000: biograficheskii slovar'* (Moscow, 2008), 472–3. The elder Chelishchev wrote a memoir about the life his family abandoned in emigration: V. N. Chelishchev, *Vospominaniia o zhizni v Kaluzhskoi gubernii: byt i nravy rossiiskoi provintsii kontsa XIX—nachala XX vv.* (Kaluga, 2009).

(b. 1868), the author of the first Soviet-era guidebooks to viniculture and winemaking and a prominent participant in discussions at Vintorg after it was rechartered as a joint-stock company, worked on the crown estate in Tsinandali in the decades prior to the revolution. Professional success in the 1920s—an academic posting at the Timiriazev Agricultural Academy and administrative positions in the Commissariat of Agriculture—could not save Gogol'-Ianovskii from arrest in 1930 or 1931. Not zealous enough in his embrace of Ivan Michurin, he was an early victim of Trofim Lysenko. Aleksandr Keller (b. 1865), the influential Massandra vintner, had been a close confidant of Prince Lev Golitsyn prior to the latter's death in 1916, and had worked on the crown estates at Massandra, Livadiia, Ai-Danil', and Abrau-Diurso, even becoming director of the latter in 1906. Keller retired in 1917, perhaps sensing that his future career prospects were limited, and then came out of retirement in the 1920s to work on several Crimean *sovkhozy*. From 1926 to 1928, Keller was chief winemaker for the Azerbaijani Wine Syndicate. Sergei Okhremenko (b. 1860), the chief vintner at the Magarach Institute in Yalta from 1890 to 1925, trained in Montpellier with Jules Émile Planchon, the biologist who devised vine grafting as an effective anti-phylloxera method. Okhremenko was married to a foreigner who spoke several different languages and served as Okhremenko's window onto Western scholarship about viniculture. Sergei Bogdanov (b. 1888), Frenkel's chief antagonist at the Winemaking Administration before the creation of the State Vinicultural and Winemaking Syndicate in 1922, came out of *zemstvo* politics, which were known more for gentry liberalism than proletarian radicalism.[46]

To be sure, at least in its initial incarnation, Soviet power was capacious enough to accommodate persons with less than perfect resumes. Indeed, Bogdanov established his Bolshevik credentials by serving as chairman of a revolutionary committee in Turkestan, and then as a political officer (commissar) in the Caucasus during the Civil War. Other persons in the early Soviet wine industry had to show that their opposition to tsarism, which had often come at great personal cost prior to 1917, was consonant with Bolshevism. Nikolai Prostoserdov's (b. 1873) long career as a Soviet oenological scientist began when he was sent by the Commissariat of Agriculture to survey the state of Crimean viniculture after Wrangel's evacuation. Prostoserdov had good revolutionary credentials, even if they were not of the Bolshevik sort: he was sentenced to prison in 1905 and twice had his term extended for involvement in the Union of Struggle for the Emancipation of the Working Class. Though founded by Lenin in 1895, the union had become associated with a reformist brand of Marxism that was closer in

---

[46] N. S. Okhremenko, ed., *Russkie vinodely* (Simferopol, 1965), 62–9 (Frolov-Bagreev); 139–41 (Keller). On Gogol'-Ianovskii, see G. I. Gogol'-Ianovskii, *Rukovodstvo po vinogradarstvu* (Moscow, 1928); G. I. Gogol'-Ianovskii, *Rukovodstvo po vinodeliiu* (Moscow, 1932); David Joravsky, 'Terror', *Voprosy filosofii* no. 7 (1993): 140–46. On Bodganov, see 'Nikolai Sergeevich Bogdanov', *Vinodelie i vinogradarstvo SSSR* no. 4 (1975): 62. On Tairov, see Vlasov, *100 let*, 17–20.

orientation to Menshevism. While on reconnaissance in Crimea in 1920, Prostoserdov met Mikhail Khovrenko (b. 1860), a specialist on Port, Madeira, and Cahors production. Armed with a degree from the Higher Moscow Technical School, Khovrenko studied viniculture at the Magarach Institute under the supervision of Aleksandr Salomon (b. 1842), one of the founding fathers of tsarist viniculture. After working abroad, which was de rigueur for ambitious Russian vintners in the final tsarist decades, Khovrenko was briefly detained by the tsarist police in 1906 for revolutionary activity. In the mid-1920s, Khovrenko found professional success as chief winemaker at Glavvino, the State Winemaking Syndicate in Moscow, before being demoted to a similar position in Uzbekistan in 1927. Mikhail Shcherbakov (b. 1866), who at the time of the revolution was the director of the Nikitskii Botanical Garden, an important centre for ampelographic research outside of Yalta, did not have much of a revolutionary resume prior to 1917, except a general interest in 'progressive ideas', and more significantly, a university friendship with Aleksandr Ulianov, Lenin's ill-fated older brother. According to a story that Shcherbakov's colleagues often told about him, the tsarist general in charge of Yalta, Ivan Dumbadze, once visited the botanical garden and noticed a photo of Ulianov in an album lying on a side table in Shcherbakov's office. 'And who do you have here?' Dumbadze asked. Without hesitating, Shcherbakov answered, 'That is my university comrade, Aleksandr Ulianov. But I have an even better photo of you, General!' Shcherbakov stayed on at the Nikitskii Botanical Garden until 1922, when he took a university post in Simferopol. Later in his career, he was assigned to work in the Kuban and then in the 1930s, to an oenological laboratory in Moscow. Some holdovers from the tsarist period got along with Soviet power simply because their pre-revolutionary resumés were so vague or bland as to be entirely non-threatening. The official Soviet biography for Mikhail Gerasimov (b. 1888), whose illustrious career in Soviet vinicultural and oenological science resulted in a Lenin Prize and election to the Italian Academy of Viniculture and Winemaking in 1961, contains no details about his life prior to 1917.[47] Even the Bolshevik administrators who oversaw the wine industry had significant peccadillos. Aleksandr Neizhmak (b. 1886), Frenkel's successor who ran the Vintorg after it was reorganized as a joint-stock company, joined the party in 1915, cut his teeth in Ukrainian union politics, and was a delegate to the Tenth Party Congress in 1921. Yet Neizhmak's posting at the administration may have been a form of ironic punishment for involvement in the Workers' Opposition in

---

[47] Okhremenko, *Russkie vinodely*, 69–75 (Shcherbakov), 75–82 (Prostoserdov), 82–9 (Gerasimov). On Prostoserdov and Khovrenko, see http://sortov.net/lyudi, which contains brief biographies of many prominent persons in the tsarist and Soviet wine industries (accessed 15 October 2017). On Gerasimov, see N. Oreshkin, 'Predislovie', in *Izbrannye raboty po vinodeliiu 1925–1955 gg.*, ed. M. A. Gerasimov (Moscow, 1955), 3–4.

1920 and 1921. Neizhmak was shot in April 1938 as part of a broader culling of former Vesenkha employees.[48]

As Neizhmak and Gogol'-Ianovskii's fates indicate, many of these persons would prove to be fatally compromised by the subsequent standards of Stalinism. Even by the more flexible and pragmatic yardstick of NEP, it was hard to ignore the fact that the luminaries of the early-Soviet wine industry were, for the most part, the luminaries of the late-tsarist wine industry, which makes Sovnarkom's concern about Vintorg's predatory policies all the more paradoxical. Yet it is also clear that this cohort possessed valuable wine knowledge for the NEP context, as practical abilities in viniculture and oenology were in short supply, a result of the industry's general collapse and emigration abroad. Equally important was a dearth of what might be called wine cosmopolitanism—that is, people who were familiar with European cultures and economies of winemaking. As Michael David-Fox has noted, throughout the 1920s and 1930s, 'the west continued to play an extraordinary dual role as capitalist enemy and exemplar of civilized modernity'.[49] The latter part of David-Fox's observation is especially apt for the early Soviet wine industry, which accepted not only Western predominance in the field, but Western standards of excellence. This became evident at the beginning of 1923, when the Soviet government began to liquidate the stockpiles of foreign wine it had seized from private hands after the revolution. In Moscow, the biggest bounty came from the cellar of the commercial firm Levet (*Leve*) on Stoleshnikov Alley. To ensure that Vintorg would not part with any rare treasures from the Levet cellar without adequate remuneration, it organized an eight-person Commission for the Establishment of Prices on Foreign Wines to conduct four blind 'tastings' (*degustatsii*). Included on the commission were both Gogol'-Ianovskii and Khovrenko. An enviable task confronted them: hundreds of bottles from Mosel, Saint-Estèphe, and Châteaux d'Yquem (1884), Haut-Brion (1896), Latour (1890), Margaux (1911), Fourreau (1911), Lafite Rothschild (1904), and many others, had to be scored on a five-point scale, so that the nearly 375,000 bottles in the Levet cellars, as well as smaller stashes in municipal bottle and barrel cellars, could be assigned prices for the NEP marketplace. In short, the commission devised the Soviet Union's first *preiskurant* (price-list) for foreign wines. Reflecting the Russian palate for fortified and sweet wines, at the top of the *preiskurant* were a Superior Old Port for 170 roubles, two vintages from Château d'Yquem, a Premier Cru Supérieur wine known for its sweetness from the Sauternes region in Bordeaux, for 160 and 149 roubles, and a late-harvest Riesling from Schloss

---

[48] Neizhmak's fate is documented at https://ru.openlist.wiki/Нейжмак_Александр_Никифович_ (1886), which is part of the *Otkrytyi spisok* database of victims of Soviet repression (accessed 15 October 2017). His presence at the Tenth Party Congress can be confirmed in *Desiatyi s'ezd RKP(b). Mart 1921 goda. Stenograficheskii otchet*, vol. 10 (Moscow, 1921), 770.

[49] Michael David-Fox, 'Stalinist Westernizer? Aleksandr Arosev's Literary and Political Depictions of Europe', *Slavic Review* 62, no. 4 (Winter 2003): 734.

Johannisberg in Rheingau for 93 roubles. (All prices on the *preiskurant* were denominated in the so-called third Soviet rouble, which was the equivalent of 100 second Soviet roubles, in circulation in 1922, and 1,000,000 revolutionary roubles, in circulation from 1917 to 1921.) Red vintages from Châteaux Haut-Brion and Lafite Rothschild, principally Merlot and Cabernet Sauvignon blends with small amounts of Cabernet Franc and Petit Verdot, were comparatively inexpensive at 30 and 51 roubles, respectively.[50]

The Levet tasting said a great deal about the way Soviet authorities viewed both wine and wine experts in the 1920s. Contrary to the proposal that emanated from the Commissariat of Agriculture in 1924 to export Crimean wine to France, the tasting commission did not treat wine as an interchangeable commodity, reducible in value to its alcohol content or volume. The tasting commission tended the idea that wine was a vessel of *kul'turnost'*, and as such, a linkage between European cultural norms and Soviet aspirations. The commission thought it reasonable for Soviet consumers to pay more for a good bottle than a mediocre bottle. Indeed, differentiating between the sublime and the pedestrian was the principal reason the commission was formed. Contrary to the Stalin period, when luxury goods were presented as symbols of future mass abundance even as they were distributed in ways that were hardly egalitarian, there was no attempt to gloss over the commission's chief beneficiaries: high-end consumers, for whom adequate pricing meant the absence of shortage; and the state, for whom adequate pricing meant a maximum return on assets.[51] The commission, in other words, served as an economic arbiter of good taste. The latter could be quantified in ways that transcended the reputations of producers by averaging the scores of eight judges on a five-point scale, and that generally (but not always) correlated with price. The commission's top-scoring wines were unsurprising: a 1904 Château Lafite Rothschild and an 1884 Château d'Yquem both earned above 4 in the final tally, the only two wines to do so. Yet its members assigned the former a lower price than lower-scoring Rieslings from Nierstein (Rheinhessen), Johannisberg (Rheingau), Zeltinger (Mosel), and elsewhere in Germany, perhaps reflecting the fact that Soviet consumers did not covet great Bordeaux in the same way that wealthy British consumers did.

Throughout the 1920s, the carry-overs from the tsarist period continued to press for interaction with their foreign counterparts, in part because Soviet producers remained dependent on their foreign counterparts for mundane items like corks (which were imported from Germany), and in part because of their confidence that the Soviet Union would one day become a great exporter of wine.

---

[50] RGAE, f. 738, o. 1, d. 7, ll. 3–17.
[51] Julie Hessler, 'Cultured Trade: The Stalinist Turn toward Consumerism', in *Stalinism: New Directions*, ed. Sheila Fitzpatrick (London and New York, 2000), 184–5; Sheila Fitzpatrick, *The Cultural Front: Power and Culture in Revolutionary Russia* (Ithaca, 1992), 216–37.

Of course, there were limits on the extent of foreign interaction, but in the 1920s these were more often financial than ideological. Business travel abroad, typically to advertise Soviet wines to foreign consumers, was always subject to dispassionate cost–benefit analysis. In April 1927, the chief Soviet trade representative in Paris notified Vintorg that it was not advisable to participate in an upcoming culinary exhibition in Paris, because not all wines it wished to display could arrive in time, and because the trade representative had not received a special allocation to support Vintorg. The trade representative thought it more important for Vintorg to participate in the Foire de Paris, an international trade fair held annually since 1904, where Soviet food producers had recent success. During the previous year, *Maslotsentr*, the agency that oversaw butter production, won a medal for the quality of its display at the Foire. Because the costs of outfitting the exhibition space were steep (estimated at 150,000 French francs, or 12,500 Soviet roubles per 100 square meters of space), Soviet participants would have to share exhibition space. Nonetheless, 'given the active presence of our comestibles on the French market and the success of individual goods', the trade representative wrote, 'we consider it necessary and advisable to participate in this exhibition, for which we are already actively preparing'. Yet even with an official invitation and encouragement from Soviet authorities, Vintorg declined, proposing instead an appearance at an exhibition in Reval (Tallinn) that would be less expensive.[52]

There were other tasks, too, for which skillsets honed before 1917 were valuable. Because Vintorg's charge was to turn a profit, which could be used to rebuild production infrastructure, cost was an omnipresent concern. After the initial wave of private-cellar expropriations during the Civil War, foreign wines became a diminishing resource because of insufficient funds for purchases abroad. Between October 1926 and March 1927, foreign bottles accounted for only 1 per cent of sales in Vintorg's stores, a figure exceeded by Abrau-Diurso alone, which competed for a similar segment of the marketplace. Yet the Soviet wine industry did its best to compensate for the comparative poverty of the era. In the 1920s, Crimean producers often concluded sale agreements for wine 'of the Château d'Yquem varietal'. This meant not bottles of the highly prized Sauternes, which were increasingly rare, but late-harvest white wines that cost a fraction of their French inspiration. Vintorg was also merciless in assessing the profitability of stores in its network and the competitiveness of its pricing. In March 1927, it ordered the closure of the stores in its Leningrad network that consistently lost money. In November 1925, in response to competition from an Armenian firm, it cut its wine prices in Leningrad by up to 33 per cent, 'offering big advantages to customers in terms of value, in terms of credit, and in terms of markdowns'. At other moments, it raised prices to take advantage of an unusually good vintage, increased consumer demand, dwindling supplies, or rising supply costs. Purchase agreements with producers in the south, most often the regional wine trusts established by the bureaucratic reshuffling in 1922, were concluded only after fierce negotiating about price and quality. This was the professional milieu of Shlapakov.[53]

Yet it would be wrong to assume that Vintorg competed within a free market. Profit mattered, in other words, but the competition was never meant to be fair. Vintorg frequently used to its advantage its bureaucratic clout, a product of an ownership structure that gave a two-thirds stake to the Commissariat of Agriculture and Vesenkha. Almost immediately after its chartering, the Vintorg board instructed Aleksandr Neizhmak to take steps to liquidate 'petty wholesale and retail stores that might cause harm to Vintorg'. Indeed, competition of any sort was a persistent thorn in the side of Vintorg, a reminder perhaps that it had once enjoyed the perquisites of a monopolist, and that competitors often sought advantage by adulterating wine. As the NEP economy began to seize up in 1928, Vintorg's Commercial Section indicated that 'consumer demand and the health of the [wine] market' as a whole were contingent on 'eliminating unhealthy methods of competition'—a reference to the downward pressure on retail prices that competition caused, and to the persistence of falsified wine. Vintorg's powerful institutional backers were helpful in other regards as well. In December 1926, the Council of People's Commissars decreed that the pre-revolutionary customs stamps found on bottles of foreign champagne would become void on 1 March of the following year, and that all bottles without a Soviet stamp would be declared contraband, as they lacked proof of lawful importation. This was an easy problem for Vintorg to solve with its powerful benefactors: on 12 February, the Commissariat of Finance ordered the Main Customs Administration to work with Vintorg to re-stamp bottles of foreign champagne in its possession. It was a nearly impossible hurdle for many of Vintorg's private, independent competitors.[54]

On one level, the reorganization of Vintorg in 1922 worked as intended. Throughout the 1920s, it struck wholesale agreements with regional wine syndicates in Crimea, Turkmenistan, Georgia, the North Caucasus, and elsewhere. Yet it competed on price with other retail organizations that did the same, such as the Moscow Oblast Union of Consumer Societies. In fact, when Vintorg was abolished in 1930 (effective 1 January 1931), a development that was indicative of broader shifts in the economy during Stalin's 'Great Break', the explicit reason was the absence of a dedicated supply line. The regional wine syndicates developed their own retail arms, produced for export, and grew less reliant on wholesale purchasers, bottlers, and resellers such as Vintorg. In 1930, Vintorg's bottling

---

[53] GARF, f. A442, o. 1, d. 3, ll. 9, 20; d. 2, l. 24; d. 1, l. 12.
[54] GARF, f. A442, o. 1, d. 8, l. 7; d. 13, l. 27; d. 16, ll. 39–39ob.

facilities operated at 15 per cent capacity. Like its erstwhile competitor, the Central Winemaking Administration, it had few bottles in its cellar at the end.[55]

While the absence of a monopoly on wholesale wine purchases may have lessened downward pressure on prices, the purpose of the 1922 bureaucratic reshuffling was greater: to generate a surplus that could be used for rebuilding battered vineyards and production facilities. This linkage is much more difficult to prove. It may the case that administrators in Sovnarkom, such as O. N. Klinkova, the author of the 1922 report to Zhidelev that helped precipitate reorganization, cared more about eliminating the odious parallel with the late-tsarist period, where wine merchants appeared to profit at the expense of wine producers, than about the impoverishment of producers to which the odious parallel was so often linked as cause. In truth, by the mid-1920s, producers and sellers faced a common enemy in vodka, which became fully legal in 1925. In mid-1926, Vintorg officials in Leningrad noted four consecutive quarters of declining wine sales, which they attributed to a 'general lull in the market and a general financial depression'. A year later, it had become clear among their Moscow counterparts that rising demand for the newly legal vodka was the chief culprit, and the principal reason that Vintorg had missed its target for the eight months from October 1926 to May 1927 by 28 per cent. 'In its activities, joint-stock company Vintorg periodically experiences financial difficulties', a Vintorg official wrote in an undated letter that was likely from 1927. 'Financial difficulties' here was a euphemism not being able to pay the bills.[56] Vodka quickly became the wealthy king of the late-NEP marketplace for alcohol, wine an impoverished pretender to the throne.

This was the crux of the problem. Early Soviet demand for unadulterated wine was weak, in part because the late-tsarist market for wine—aristocrats and the urban middle class—had been decimated by revolution and civil war, and in part because demand for conventional wine had always been weak in comparison with vodka. There were, of course, exceptions. In the Caucasus, which accounted for more than half of all wine production at the turn of the century, wine was deeply embedded in local economies and cultures of consumption. There demand emerged from war and revolution intact. Yet because the vast majority of local production in the Caucasus was consumed locally (often by its producers), it existed outside the commercial networks that brought wine from the vineyards and production facilities of the south to the stores of the north. Georgian peasants, in short, were in no position to keep Ai-Danil' and Abrau-Diurso in the black.

This is perhaps why the constituency for NEP was so thin in the world of Soviet wine: without government support, the wine industry could not exist, at least in

---

[55] GARF, f. A442, o. 1, d. 43, l. 51.   [56] GARF, f. A442, o. 1, d. 3, l. 66; d. 6, l. 2; d. 10, l. 14.

the shape that its principals, the vast majority of whom were holdovers from the tsarist period, wanted. Despite the fact that the Soviet state inherited a regulatory model that promoted assimilation to Western modes of consumption while generating tax revenue, it moved in its initial decade to deregulate wine. In 1920, Sovnarkom lifted the prohibition on the sale of wine that had been in place since the beginning of World War I. This was a good thing, for sure, since it allowed producers to re-enter the marketplace and raise funds for rebuilding vineyards and production facilities. Yet Sovnarkom then abolished a government monopoly on wine sales that substituted the infinite demand of the state for the atrophied and fickle demand of consumers. In 1921, the state's principal commercial arm for wine, Vintorg, began offering consumers the adulterated product they desired, driving home the fact that the ideal of wine purity had disappeared alongside tsarism. When faced with complaints about Vintorg's policies vis-à-vis producers, the Soviet state rechartered Vintorg as a joint-stock company, forcing it to compete for profit in the NEP marketplace.

Paradoxically, the Soviet state's retreat in the 1920s from the regulation of wine coexisted with the idea that wine was important in ways that transcended economics. Like in the late-tsarist period, wine was a vessel of *kul'turnost'*, a tool of acculturation, and a palpable linkage between Soviet aspirations and Western reality—even if those aspirations were naively optimistic, such as the prediction that the total area of modern vineyard cultivation in the Soviet Union would soon surpass that of Western Europe. To be sure, these ideas about wine existed on the side of a Soviet state, which was struggling to balance a vision of the communist future with the pragmatism of the present. They could be found among the former crown-estate vintners, such as Anton Frolov-Bagreev and Aleksandr Keller, holdovers from the tsarist period who struggled to adapt to life and work on newly formed *sovkhozy*. They survived in Vintorg's Commission for the Establishment of Prices on Foreign Wines, whose membership included famous wine cosmopolitans such as Georgii Gogol'-Ianovskii and Mikhail Khovrenko. Even in the corridors of Sovnarkom, staff members such as O. N. Klinkova continued in the face of deregulation to press for policies that resembled those of the late-tsarist period: wine purity was important enough to regulate, and merchants should not profit inordinately or unfairly from the labour of growers and vintners. Indeed, these were the principal reasons that producers presented such a sympathetic case in the early 1920s, and that a Soviet agency was criticized for its predatory commercial policies. It is unlikely that the bearers of these ideas about wine were the foundation for Stalinism's more beneficent approach to wine. That existed elsewhere—in the backgrounds of Stalin and his cohort in Transcaucasia, in the great 'civilizing process' that Stalinism entailed, and in the desire to match the West in a realm where its supremacy and mastery had long been unquestioned. Yet it is easy to see how the bearers of these ideas would have seen something in Stalinism worth supporting, even as Stalinism spelt the destruction of so many of them. 'Champagne is an important sign of material well-being, of the good life', the *Book of Delicious and Healthy Food* quoted Stalin as saying in 1936. The holdovers from the tsarist wine industry would have heartily agreed. The politics of wine made for strange alliances built on unexpected affinity, but also blindness.[57]

[57] On Stalin's proclamation about champagne, see Jukka Gronow, *Caviar with Champagne: Common Luxury and the Ideals of the Good Life in Stalin's Russia* (Oxford, 2003), 17.

5

Hospitality

Soviet Winemakers and the Stalinist Gift Economy

More than six decades after Stalin's death, the American wine writer Alice Feiring, a prominent champion of 'natural wine' and traditional Georgian varietals and winemaking methods, met in Tbilisi one of Stalin's preferred vintners, Givi Chagelishvili. An old man at the time of the encounter, Chagelishvili recalled that he was first approached by the secret police after graduating with a degree in oenology in 1950. Chagelishvili was chosen because he 'had the most innocent history', meaning no relatives who opposed Soviet power. What followed were three years overseeing a Stalin-only production line that used corks from Portugal and bottles from Romania to prepare a small amount of wine each week for inclusion among a shipment of Georgian delicacies that Stalin liked, such as lamb from Imereti. Chagelishvili knew that his wine comprised only a small proportion of what crossed Stalin's table, because other wineries had similar arrangements. Chagelishvili made Chinuri, a white varietal grown in the Kartli region that surrounded Stalin's native Gori, and Tavkveri, a red varietal that is unusual because it is female in gender and must be planted alongside male or intersexed vines for pollination. In both cases, Chagelishvili told Feiring, Stalin preferred wines that were fermented and aged in kvevris, clay vessels that are lined with bee's wax and buried in the ground, rather than in the steel or concrete fermentation tanks and oaken barrels used in modern production facilities.[1]

Feiring's account nicely encapsulates the importance of wine during the Stalin period. It shows that wine producers enjoyed the support of powerful patrons in Moscow, particularly Stalin, but also Anastas Mikoyan, who was part of a cohort of communists from Transcaucasia who rode Stalin's coattails to positions of great influence. Wine was thus part of the northward advance of Georgian culinary ways among a new Soviet elite keen to try 'a taste of the dining practices of Stalin's Kremlin'.[2] In the 1930s, Mikoyan oversaw the food industry and the drafting of the influential cookbook, *The Book of Delicious and Healthy Food*—topics that

---

[1] Alice Feiring, *For the Love of Wine: My Odyssey through the World's Most Ancient Wine Culture* (Lincoln, NE, 2016), 56–9.

[2] Erik R. Scott, *Familiar Strangers: The Georgian Diaspora and the Evolution of the Soviet Empire* (Oxford, 2016), 99–100. See also Paul Manning, *The Semiotics of Drink and Drinking* (London, 2012), 148.

Whites and Reds: A History of Wine in the Lands of Tsar and Commissar. Stephen V. Bittner, Oxford University Press (2021).
© Stephen V. Bittner. DOI: 10.1093/oso/9780198784821.003.0006

have received a significant amount of scholarly attention in recent years.[3] The latter text was especially important for the wine industry, despite the fact that it devoted only a small number of its columns to wine, because it was the source of Stalin's oft-cited 1936 assertion that champagne was part of the good life of socialism. The latter endorsement appears to have derived from Stalin's more famous bon mot from 1935: 'life is getting better, comrades, life is becoming more joyous.'[4] As Jukka Gronow has argued, over the course of the 1930s, the good life of socialism came to resemble the good life of capitalism, even though most Soviet citizens were offered only occasional samples of future abundance, such as ice cream, champagne, and German-style *wurst*. 'The Party optimistically promised every Soviet citizen the best that both the old and the new world had to offer', Gronow writes, 'and at a moderate price.'[5]

Feiring's account also speaks to the unusual combination of tradition and modernity that characterized Soviet winemaking: the wine that Stalin preferred was produced in the ancient way, in kvevris, which are thought to have come to Georgia in the distant past from the Fertile Crescent.[6] Although Feiring counts kvevris as a near casualty of Soviet power, and is generally prone to extol all ways traditional as superior to modern modes of production, kvevris remained common throughout the Soviet period in Georgian household production, where as late as the 1970s about half of all Georgian wine was made and grapes were grown.[7] Kvevri wines lack the wood tones that come from barrel ageing, and white kvevri wines are left in contact with grape skins after fermentation, which produces a deep amber colour, similar to whisky. Colloquially, they are referred to as orange wines in reference to their colour. Stalin's tastes for the traditional

---

[3] See, for instance, Irina Glushchenko, *Obshchepit: Mikoian i sovetskaia kukhnaia* (Moscow, 2010); Edward Geist, 'Cooking Bolshevik: Anastas Mikoian and the Making of the *Book about Delicious and Healthy Food*', *Russian Review* 71, no. 2 (2012): 295–313; Gian Pierro Piretto, 'Tasty and Healthy: Soviet Happiness in One Book', in *Petrified Utopia: Happiness Soviet Style*, ed. Marina Balina and Evgeny Dobrenko (New York, 2009), 79–96; Jukka Gronow and Sergey Zhuravlev, 'The *Book of Tasty and Healthy Food*: The Establishment of Soviet Haute Cuisine', in *Educated Tastes: Food, Drink, and Connoisseur Culture*, ed. Jeremy Strong (Lincoln, NE, 2011), 24–57; Ronald D. LeBlanc, 'The Mikoyan Mini-Hamburger, or How the Socialist Realist Novel about the Soviet Meat Industry Was Created', *Gastronomica: The Journal of Critical Food Studies* 16, no. 2 (Summer 2016): 31–44; Evgenii Dobrenko, 'Grastronomicheskii kommunizm: vkusnoe vs. zdorovoe', *Neprikosnovennyi zapas* no. 2 (2009): 155–73.

[4] Konstantin Bogdanov, 'Soviet Champagne: A Festive History', trans. Rosie Tweddle, *Forum for Anthropology and Culture*, no. 9 (2013): 236.

[5] Jukka Gronow, *Caviar with Champagne: Common Luxury and the Ideals of the Good Life in Stalin's Russia* (Oxford, 2003), 8, 18. The role of the authoritarian state in promoting wine production and consumption was not a uniquely Soviet phenomenon. Brian J. Griffith argues that the 'centralization, standardization, and collective marketing campaigns' of the inter-war years in fascist Italy, rather than an ancient, ineffable cultural connection, made wine a fixture on the tables of Italy's 'respectable classes': see Brian J. Griffith, 'Bringing Bacchus to the People: Winemaking and "Making Italians" in Fascist Italy, 1919–1939' (PhD diss., University of California, Santa Barbara, 2020), 2.

[6] On the ancient history of winemaking in the Black Sea region, see N. I. Vinokurov, *Vinogradarstvo i vinodelie antichnykh gosudarstv severnogo prichernomor'ia* (Simferopol and Kerch, 2007).

[7] Open Society Archive [hereafter OSA] 300-80-1, Box 898, File: Sel'skoe khoziaistvo: vinogradarstvo, 1960–93, Elizabeth Fuller, 'Kulaks to Blame for Georgia's Disastrous Grape Harvest', 2.

Georgian wines aside, however, the characteristic winemaking achievement of the Stalin period was technological: Anton Frolov-Bagreev's 'continuous method' of sparkling wine production, where linked fermentation tanks under five atmospheres of pressure, roughly what is found inside a bottle of champagne, produce sparkling wine over the course of a few weeks. Frolov-Bagreev's method differs from the so-called *méthode traditionnelle*, in which sugar and yeast are added to a finished wine prior to bottling to produce champagne's characteristic effervescence. The continuous method is less laborious because dead yeast cells are consumed by triggering autolysis through the addition of wood chips, which produces wine clarity, rather than through the lengthy process of bottle riddling and sediment disgorgement. For this invention, which in future decades would be widely embraced by wine-producing upstarts outside the Soviet Union, Frolov-Bagreev received the Order of Lenin and the Stalin Prize in 1942. These were not Frolov-Bagreev's first commendations for winemaking: Nicholas II had previously awarded him the Orders of Saints Anna and Stanislav.

It is no surprise that tradition and modernity coexisted in the world of Soviet wine. Since the 'great wine blight' of the late nineteenth century, European viniculture and winemaking had become increasingly scientific and industrial endeavours, even as winemakers embraced the language of tradition, continuity, and artisanship. The latter was a by-product of the former, a sort of cognitive unrecognition that was often useful and lucrative. As Robert Ulin has argued about Bordeaux, even the prized *grand cru* designation, which was formalized in the eighteenth and nineteenth centuries to refer to vineyards that produced wine of consistently high quality, was an invented tradition. It was devised in response to the arrival of high-quality, less expensive wines from Portugal and Italy, competition from small-scale peasant proprietors, and the reality that many châteaux were no longer owned by aristocratic families with centuries of vinicultural experience.[8]

This chapter explores a similar, unexpected relationship between tradition and modernity, albeit one that ranged far beyond the ways Soviet wine was produced. It traces the Stalinist-era politics of one of the Soviet Union's most prestigious wineries, the former crown estate Massandra, which was founded in 1894 in Yalta, and of its neighbour, the Magarach Institute, which comprised both a wine production facility and a research centre dedicated to the science of viniculture and winemaking. Magarach traced its roots to 1828, when Mikhail Vorontsov, the governor of New Russia and one of the most important early patrons of the Russian wine industry, championed its creation as part of the Nikitskii Botanical Garden. In the years following the Second World War, Massandra shared its campus with Magarach. This chapter also considers post-war events at Abrau-Diurso,

[8] Robert C. Ulin, '*Terroir* and Locality: An Anthropological Perspective', in *Wine and Culture: Vineyard to Glass*, ed. Rachel E. Black and Robert C. Ulin (London, 2013), 75.

which was founded in 1870 west of Novorossiysk. Separated by about 200 kilometres of coastline and the Straits of Kerch, and on nearly the same latitude, Massandra and Abrau-Diurso had a shared history that dated to the 1890s, when Lev Golitsyn was put in charge of the crown vinicultural estates in Crimea and the Caucasus. Together, Abrau-Diurso, Massandra, Magarach, and their numerous *sovkhozy*, field stations, and production facilities, stood as the pinnacles of Soviet winemaking: they produced the Soviet Union's most coveted wines; they employed the Soviet Union's most accomplished winemakers.

In the years after the Second World War, several prominent employees at Massandra were fired and two were arrested following a lengthy investigation into the misuse of wine. A similar investigation occurred at Abrau-Diurso, although it did not result in arrests or firings; and similar questionable activities were evident at the Magarach Institute, although they did not attract the attention of investigators. In all three locales, administrators had become accustomed to getting things done in unusual ways, and at Massandra in particular, to using the wine as a social currency that was consumed jointly in gratis tastings with visiting dignitaries and employees on important holidays. Their behaviour was fostered in part by the de-routinization of Soviet life during the war years, when the old ways of doing things fractured in the face of evacuation and retreat. In anthropological terms, wine administrators were participants in a 'gift economy', a system of transactions where reciprocity took forms that were not clearly material. Writing about Marcel Mauss's comparative and diachronic study of gifts, Marshall Sahlins argues that 'the gift is the primitive way of achieving the peace...a form of political contract'. Sahlins' insight about gifts' 'coefficient of sociability' is apt for the inner workings of Stalinism, where political power was often realized by paternalistically distributing items in short supply. According to Katherine Verdery,

> the whole point [of socialism] was *not* to sell things. The center wanted to keep as much as possible under its control, because that was how it had redistributive power; and it wanted to give away the rest, because that was how it confirmed its legitimacy.[9]

Amid the Soviet Union's general scarcity, comestibles were among the most important gifts, 'not merely an expression of wealth...[but] a general form of wealth'.[10] As James Heinzen has observed, the Soviet alcohol industry in general was a 'leading—and natural—location for entrenched networks of high-level gift giving', and one of the principle reasons laws were passed in the post-war years

---

[9] Marshall Sahlins, *Stone Age Economics* (Chicago and New York, 1972), 169, 183; Marcel Mauss, *The Gift: Forms and Functions of Exchange in Archaic Societies*, trans. Ian Cunnison (New York, 1967); Katherine Verdery, *What Was Socialism, and What Comes Next?* (Princeton, 1996), 26.

[10] Manning, *Semiotics of Drink and Drinking*, 156.

prohibiting the employees of economic ministries and subordinate organizations from giving gifts to the local party elites who were supposed to oversee them.[11] Even in the comparatively flush 1960s, the informal and illegal trade in alcohol from places of production was a common enough occurrence that Otar Iosseliani depicted it in his 1966 film about Georgian winemaking, *Falling Leaves*.[12] Administrators at Massandra, Magarach, and Abrau-Diurso thus walked a precarious path between hospitality and instrumentality when they shared wine with important visitors. Yet they appear to have succeeded, because investigators from Moscow never couched their behaviours as tacit forms of bribery, nor as bribery masquerading as gift giving. Instead, winemakers were accused of misusing (*zloupotreblenie*) wine that belonged to the state. In other words, they were too generous giving things that were not theirs to give.

In the context of post-war Stalinism, as Moscow tried to curtail the centrifugal forces and regional autonomies that had flourished during the war years, these activities became the proximal cause of the downfall of Nikolai Sobolev, the director of the Massandra Wine Complex. Although it is not the purpose of this chapter to detail the chain of events that led to that proximal cause, the cause or causes of first instance were likely in a broader campaign against corruption in the alcohol industry in the post-war years, and in a mounting case in Leningrad against a number of local party and state officials who were accused of using the All-Russian Trade Fair, which Leningrad hosted in January 1949, to promote local over national interests, and even secession from the Soviet Union. While never officially acknowledged at the time, the so-called Leningrad Affair resulted in the arrest and trial of more than two hundred persons, of whom twenty-three were subject to the newly reinstated death penalty, including one of the party's rising intellectual stars, Nikolai Voznesenskii. It was linked to events in Crimea through the person of Nikolai Solov'ev, who had served as secretary of the Leningrad Oblast Party Committee before taking over the Crimean Oblast Party Committee in 1946. Solov'ev was executed alongside Voznesenskii in 1950.[13]

The fact that the Soviet wine industry experienced repression is not unexpected. As the previous chapter shows, industry officials and prominent vintners began to run afoul of Soviet power almost as soon as Soviet power came into existence. Yet even as the formal charges against growers and vintners remained

---

[11] James Heinzen, *The Art of the Bribe: Corruption under Stalin, 1943–1953* (New Haven, 2016), 55.

[12] *Giorgobistve*, dir. Iotar Iosseliani, 1966.

[13] On corruption in the alcohol industry, see Heinzen, *The Art of the Bribe*, 55–6, 84–5; on the Leningrad Affair, see David Brandenberger, 'Stalin, the Leningrad Affair, and the Limits of Postwar Soviet Russocentrism', *Russian Review* 63, no. 2 (2004): 241–55; David Brandenburger, Alisa Amosova, and Nikita Pivovarov, 'The Rise and Fall of a Crimean Party Boss: Nikolai Vasil'evich Solov'ev and the Leningrad Affair', *Europe-Asia Studies* 71, no. 6 (July 2019): 951–71; Benjamin Tromly, 'The Leningrad Affair and Soviet Patronage Politics, 1949–1950', *Europe-Asia Studies* 56, no. 5 (July 2004): 707–29; Catriona Kelly, '"The Leningrad Affair": Remembering the "Communist Alternative" in the Second Capital', *Slavonica* 17, no. 2 (2011): 103–22; V. F. Mikheev and G. F. Mikheev, '"Leningradskoe delo" (po materialam sledstvennykh del)', *Noveishaia istoriia Rossii* no. 1 (2013): 178–98.

largely uniform across the decades—espionage, sabotage, and always vague counter-revolutionary activities—the targets of repression changed—from persons with problematic backgrounds, as defined by class, religion, or ethnicity, to persons who were products of the Soviet system and who had achieved a good deal of success as Soviet winemakers. Once vulnerable for whom it employed, the Soviet wine industry had become, in the post-war years, vulnerable for what it made—items that were commonly given by winemakers as tokens of hospitality and gratitude, whose 'coefficient of sociability' lay partly in the fact that they were consumed collectively, shared among old partners and new allies in tasting rooms. As officials at Massandra and elsewhere probed the boundary between generosity and instrumentality in opening the wine they produced for guests, they raised questions about who in Soviet society had the power to bestow gifts of state property. When the Ministry of State Control took an interest in the alleged misappropriation of wine, Sobolev and a handful of others discovered that such prerogatives were ultimately reserved for persons with far more power and influence than they.

∗   ∗   ∗   ∗   ∗

In December 1935, Mikhail Chernov, the Soviet Commissar of Agriculture, wrote to Jānis Rudzutaks (Rudzutak), deputy chairman of the Council of People's Commissars, seeking approval to send Soviet vinicultural delegations to the International Congress of Viniculture, which was scheduled to meet in Tunis and Lisbon in 1936 and 1937, and to the Exhibition on Viniculture and Winemaking, which was scheduled for Paris in 1937. Chernov's request was consonant with the spirit of the age. After languishing during the early 1930s, when all eyes were on the collectivization of the grain economy, Soviet viniculture would soon be identified by Stalin as an important component of the agricultural sector, and an important contributor to the general good. Moreover, the late 1930s, a period that corresponded with the Popular Front in Western Europe and growing Soviet confidence at home, was one of the high points for Soviet involvement in international exhibitions—most famously, the Exposition Internationale in Paris in 1937 and the World's Fair in New York in 1939, where the Soviet Union constructed elaborate pavilions to advertise the achievements of socialism. Even at home, the All-Union Agricultural Exhibition opened in Moscow's Ostankino district to great fanfare in 1939. After receiving a supporting letter from the Commissariat of Finance, Chernov's request made its way to the desk of Valerii Mezhlauk, who was head of Gosplan and deputy director of the Administrative Department of the Council of People's Commissars. Mezhlauk wrote that he considered it 'inexpedient' to participate in international vinicultural exhibitions at such a time. Chernov's request was denied.[14]

---

[14] GARF, f. R5446, o. 18, d. 707, ll. 2–8.

Chernov's letter and its accompanying documentation, which number less than a dozen archival pages, survive as more than a vestige of a naïve, ill-fated endeavour. Within three years, every person associated with the request—Chernov, Rudzutaks, and Mezhlauk—had perished in the Great Purges on charges that included espionage and treason. Chernov proposed that Soviet industry officials would benefit from contact with their foreign counterparts, yet such contact had become exceedingly dangerous in the context of Stalinism. For the Soviet wine industry, the denied junkets to Western Europe and North Africa exemplified the political constraints of the era. In the late 1920s, Vintorg officials had declined opportunities to participate in international exhibitions in Paris, proposing to go to Tallinn instead, because it was less expensive. A decade later, opportunities for foreign travel had disappeared entirely, even as the wine industry found itself the beneficiary of government largesse and patronage it could scarcely have imagined during the 1920s.

Industry officials were frank about their unexpected financial blessings and the omnipresent dangers that came with them. At the end of 1938, the Magarach Institute in Yalta filed its annual report with the Ministry of Food Production in Moscow. The report briefly described the institute's illustrious history. Founded in 1828 on the grounds of the Nikitskii Botanical Garden, the institute had grown from a modest nursery for European vines, to a vocational school for vineyard workers, and by the end of the tsarist period, to an institute of higher education whose graduates in viniculture and oenology could be found in wine-producing regions across the Russian Empire. Yet the early Stalinist years were a difficult period, a fact that the author of the annual report acknowledged, and that contrasted with the heroic narrative often told about the so-called 'Great Break'. In 1931, the institute lost its all-union designation as part of the Nikitskii Botanical Garden. It was subordinated instead to the Crimean and then the Russian Commissariats of Agriculture as the Crimean Zonal Station for Viniculture and Winemaking.

> During these years when the foundations of socialism were built, the attention of the party and government was on heavy industry, defense, and raising up the grain and animal-husbandry economies. At that time, Magarach received very meager allocations, and was not able to develop in the necessary manner its work, which is required for strengthening the economy of Crimea.[15]

As late as 1936, the year that witnessed its sudden elevation, the Magarach Institute noted that its chief concern was the 'organic connection between the quality and quantity of grape production and specific varietals of grapes'. This corresponded with a broader emphasis on quality that characterized Soviet

---

[15] RGAE, f. 8543, o. 2, d. 38, l. 13.

consumption politics in the latter part of the 1930s.[16] But it was also code for not doing anything that required a lot of money, such as planting new vineyards or investing in new production equipment. Thus, the institute's plan of work for the year—its list of scientific studies it intended to undertake—included a very unscientific exploration of the 'single, socialist, planned economy' that was Soviet viniculture, where the production of each separate republic and region comprised an 'organic whole'. This holistic ideal, which the institute called *uvolgiia* (from the Latin word for grape, *uva*), distinguished Soviet viniculture from its capitalist adversaries. 'These regional economies do not compete against each other but complement each other; they do not pursue short-term competitive advantage but insist on the goal of harmonious development in the interests of working people.'[17]

The latter was undoubtedly consonant with official theories about the Soviet economy. But it also bore some resemblance to debates that split the field of Soviet architecture in the late 1920s about the specific characteristics that made a building socialist. These debates were brought to a halt in the early 1930s, largely out of official frustration with architects' famous penchant for sectarianism: henceforth, Soviet architecture was socialist by location, not by any intrinsic characteristics.[18] For the Magarach Institute, the situation changed suddenly in July of 1936, when Mikoyan designated the institute the All-Union Scientific-Research Station for the Wine Industry, and made it subordinate to the federal Ministry of Food Production. The reasons for the institute's good fortune were not initially clear, least of all to its employees. Yet the author of the 1938 annual report was quick to see in the institute's promotion something greater:

> With the increase in general welfare, the question arose about provisioning working people with fresh grape juice and grape wine, and from that, the question about increasing the harvest from existing vineyards, widening the area of new vineyards, and reconstructing the wine industry.[19]

Consequently, in the late 1930s, Soviet winemakers found themselves under pressure not to produce wine in ways qualitatively different from their capitalist counterparts, but to produce many times more of it. The promised abundance of a luxury item would be the distinguishing characteristic of Soviet viniculture, not any holistic ideal about different wine-producing regions working in cooperation rather than competition. In July 1936, for instance, Valerii Mezhlauk presented Stalin with a proposal for the development of Georgian viniculture. Mezhlauk envisioned nearly doubling the total vineyard area in Georgia by 1940, from

[16] RGAE, f. 8543, d. 39, l. 2; Gronow, *Caviar with Champagne*, 3.

[17] RGAE, f. 8543, o. 2, d. 39, l. 3.

[18] Hugh D. Hudson, *Blueprints and Blood: The Stalinization of Soviet Architecture, 1917–1937* (Princeton, 1994).

[19] RGAE, f. 8543, o. 2, d. 38, l. 13.

32,000 to 60,000 hectares (600 square kilometres), with extra money allocated for tractor purchases, the importation of phylloxera-resistant American rootstock, and the construction of vine nurseries and wine cellars. Special emphasis was placed on planting varietals for champagne, one of the previously rare luxuries that Soviet leaders were confident they could make widely available on short order: Rkatsiteli, Saperavi, Pinot noir, and Aligoté. Finally, Mezhlauk proposed the development of 'regionalization' (*raionirovanie*), a sort of proto-*terroir* that was common in discussions of the future of Soviet viniculture, and perhaps an acknowledgement that the earlier discussions about regional cooperation could be repackaged into something useful. According to Mezhlauk, Kakheti was ideal for Saperavi, Mtsvane, and Rkatsiteli; Imereti for Tsitska; Racha for Usakhelauri; and Mingrelia for Odzhaleshi.[20]

While the Georgian wine industry had enviable patrons in Stalin, Mezhlauk, and others, it did not have a monopoly on the Kremlin's support. Chagelishvili noted, for instance, that Stalin also took a liking to Moldovan wine in the postwar years, perhaps because its availability was a reminder that the Soviet Union had righted a historical wrong in the Second World War by reincorporating a territory it had lost at the end of the First World War. Moreover, Jukka Gronow has shown that many other wine regions in the Soviet Union received substantial production investments after Stalin's 1936 proclamation about champagne. At the Magarach Institute in Yalta, for instance, planning began almost immediately for the huge production increases that Stalin's endorsement required. According to statistics circulated by the Main Administration for Winemaking, the Soviet Union was on track to produce 12 million bottles of champagne in 1942, up from 600,000 in 1937; conventional wine production was expected to grow at a slower but still substantial rate, from just over 9 million decalitres to 13.3 million decalitres during the same period. The Magarach Institute revised its research agenda, which had traditionally emphasized basic, scientific concerns, to fit the new mandates. Its five-year plan for 1938 to 1942 included projects on scaling up Frolov-Bagreev's continuous method of champagne production, so it would become the industry norm; increasing the selection of grape varietals available to producers; devising standard protocols for blending wines; and creating national and republic-level wine reserves for ageing and preserving wine. Seeing these projects through to completion would take money and support from important persons in Moscow, which the institute suddenly had in relative abundance.[21]

---

[20] GARF, f. R5446, o. 29, d. 32, ll. 1–7.

[21] RGAE, f. 8543, o. 2, d. 91, ll. 8, 18, 24. In addition to Mezhlauk's plan to double the size of Georgian vinicultural production, the Magarach Institute found official authorization for its ambitious agenda in three other decrees that emanated from Moscow: a joint Sovnarkom and Central Committee decree, 'On the production of Soviet champagne, *marochnoe* [vintage] dessert, and table wines of Massandra' (28 July 1936); a Sovnarkom decree 'On widening the material base for the production of Soviet champagne and high-quality dessert wine in RSFSR collective farms' (2 May 1937);

Increased government largesse coincided with new risks. In February 1938, Ivan Burov (b. 1895) was arrested on charges of being a German intelligence officer; in October, he was executed in Krasnodar. The general director of the Abrau-Diurso Wine Complex, which had a long-standing collaborative relationship with the Magarach Institute that dated from the tsarist period, Burov was one of the highest-profile victims of repression in the wine industry in the 1930s. His arrest, which came after a lengthy public shaming campaign about deficiencies in champagne production, may have been precipitated by the denunciation of a subordinate, Vasilii Kholodov, who worked as a dispatcher at Abrau-Diurso. Kholodov was arrested a day earlier than Burov and was sentenced to five years in a corrective labour camp for spreading counter-revolutionary slander. Massandra lost three employees in 1938, including the director of its brand store in Simferopol, Iakub Abliakimov (b. 1908), and a vineyard agronomist, Zeims Bizer (b. 1901). According to *Otkrytyi spisok*, there were at least thirty-three persons arrested during the Stalin years who listed their primary profession as 'winemaker', or who were studying to become winemakers, seventeen in 1937 and 1938 alone. Among this latter group, the ethnic diversity and elite roots of the wine industry were on full display. Among the victims was Eduard Schitt (b. 1888), a German by nationality who served as an officer in the tsarist army. Arrested first in 1919, and then again in 1933, Schitt worked briefly as the 'chief winemaker' at a Ministry of Food Production factory in Kursk prior to his final arrest in April 1937. Schitt was executed in December. Other German victims in 1937 included Emil' Andris (b. 1890), a winemaker at a *sovkhoz* in Azerbaijan. He was sentenced to eight years in a corrective labour camp, and then released in April 1940 on appeal. Konstantin Frank (b. 1899), a German by nationality, may have avoided a worse fate. While working toward the equivalent of a PhD in viniculture, Frank oversaw several vineyards and vinicultural laboratories near Odessa and in Georgia in the 1930s. Remaining in Odessa as a privileged *Volksdeutscher* during the German and Romanian occupation, Frank was named director of an agricultural institute that administered the vineyards where he had previously worked. As the Red Army advanced on Odessa in 1944, Frank arranged rail passage for his family to Austria. In subsequent decades, as a scientist at Cornell University's Geneva Research Station, Frank played a seminal role in introducing *Vitis vinifera*, the European wine grape, to growers in New York's Finger Lakes region. Spiridon Popov (b. 1895), a Greek by nationality, was arrested in October 1937 and sentenced to ten years corrective labour. Popov was the 'master-winemaker' at the Trofimov wine factory outside of Odessa. Semen Khundadze (b. 1873), a Georgian by nationality and an aristocrat by social origin, was executed in September 1937 in Tbilisi. Among the charges against the former winemaker at

and the decree of Sovnarkom's Economic Soviet, 'On the procurement prices for industry grapes' (28 June 1938).

Tbilisi's Samtrest wine factory was active participation in an 'espionage-terrorist, subversive-sabotage organization' that sought to create 'confusion in the selection and shipment of wine for blending, thanks to which the quality of wine fell, and wines were produced that did not correspond to their label markings'. Khundadze's boss at Samtrest, Aleksandr Tushmalishvili, met a similar fate, as did the director of Tbilisi's Wine Factory no. 1, Georgii Nioradze (b. 1908), and the winemaker at the Tsinandali *sovkhoz*, Nikolai Mshvenieradze (b. 1903), the latter because he had engaged in 'counter-revolutionary sabotage work' that cost his *sovkhoz* 300,000 roubles.[22]

There were similar, albeit smaller concentrations of winemaker arrests in the wake of the Shakhty trial of German engineers in 1928, and around the assassination of Sergei Kirov in 1934. Similar to the impact of the Great Terror on the wine industry, the casualties of these earlier repressions tended not to be Russian. One victim was Fridrikh-Genrikh Shteiman. Born in the Mennonite settlement of Gnadenfeld in Kabardino-Balkaria in 1883, Shteiman was expelled from the Soviet Union in 1935 for counter-revolutionary activity. In addition, there were seventeen persons arrested during the Stalin years who identified their primary profession as grape grower (*vinogradar'*); ten were German by nationality, and two were Greek. These casualty lists are obviously incomplete, as they are limited to persons whose expertise—growing grapes and making wine—were industry specific. *Otkrytyi spisok* indicates that there were many dozens more arrests of persons who worked in the industry in other capacities—as pipe fitters, workers, machine operators, and so on. Given the imprecise meaning of *vinzavod* and *vinkombinat*, acronyms which sometimes refer to a winery, but more often mean a distillery (from the word *vinokurennyi*), an exact count is impossible. Some wine factories made wine; many more made vodka.[23]

The usual caveats about source representativeness and categories aside, these figures underscore how narrow the slice of vinicultural and winemaking expertise was in the Soviet Union. The wine industry, despite its historical linkages with the old aristocracy and crown estates, did not present a huge number of targets for

---

[22] These arrest records are available at https://ru.openlist.wiki/ with the following names after the final black slash: Буров_Иван_Никотович_(1895); Холодов_Василий_Григорьевич_(1904); Аблякимов_Якуб_Халилович_(1908); Бизер_Зеймс_Ильич_1901; Шитт_Эдуард_Васильевич_(1888); Андрис_Эмиль_Фридрихович_(1890); Попов_Спиридон_Петрович_(1895); Хундадзе_Семен_Фомич_(1873); Ниорадзе_Георгий_Трофимович_(1908); Мшвениерадзе_Николай_Константинович_(1903). The number of winemakers arrested during the Stalin years can be ascertained by searching for винодел at https://ru.openlist.wiki/Открытый_список:Заглавная_страница. On Tushmalishvili, see L. I. Shleiger, *Polveka s vinom: vspominaniia vinodela 'Massandry'* (Simferopol, 2001), 20. Jukka Gronow describes the public shaming campaign against Burov (misidentified as Vurov) in *Caviar with Champagne*, 17–21. On Frank, Tom Russ, *Finger Lakes Wine and the Legacy of Dr Konstantin Frank* (Charleston, SC, 2015), 24–35.

[23] Shteiman's arrest record is available at https://ru.openlist.wiki/Штейман_Фридрих-Генрих_Фридрихович_(1883). The number of grape growers arrested during the Stalin years can be ascertained by searching for виноградарь at https://ru.openlist.wiki/Открытый_список:Заглавная_страница.

arrest. As Sheila Fitzpatrick has argued about an early phase of Stalinist terror, that surrounding the so-called Cultural Revolution (1928–31), terror's motives may be evident in terror's results, often the promotion of a cohort of loyal Soviet experts into positions of power.[24] Yet the Soviet Union, first out of simple neglect and then because of more pressing priorities elsewhere, had thus far failed to produce its own cohort of vinicultural and winemaking experts. Until the post-war years, it remained reliant on persons who received professional training during the tsarist period. As Khundadze and Schitt's fates indicate, some tsarist-era lives were impossible to forgive, but it was not easy to dispose of persons with their skill sets, particularly after Stalin's embrace of the industry in 1936.

These observations are borne out by German Valuiko, who joined the Magarach Institute in 1955. In an autobiography first published in the 1990s, and then revised a decade later 'as new facts appeared', Valuiko attempted to catalogue the casualties of Soviet power who came from the wine industry. One of the giants of Soviet oenology and viniculture, Valuiko played a prominent role in transforming the Magarach Institute into a respected, socialist-world alternative to the famous vinicultural programmes at the University of Bordeaux and the University of California, Davis. Born in 1924 in Tbilisi, Valuiko was trained by many of the famous names of late-tsarist viniculture who, despite less than perfect resumés, found a *modus vivendi* with Soviet power—Mikhail Khovrenko, Mikhail Shcherbakov, and Anton Frolov-Bagreev. By the time Valuiko arrived at the institute as a graduate student, he had fought his way with the Red Army to Germany and had earned a degree from the Academy of the Ministry of Food Production in Moscow. He was thus emblematic of what he called the 'middle generation' of Magarach scholars: trained by persons who cut their professional teeth during the late-tsarist decades, and the trainer of persons who would lead the institute into the post-Soviet decades. According to Valuiko, Soviet winemakers in general were exceptional for their long lives. Valuiko attributed this both to the health benefits of wine, and to winemakers' skills in navigating the dangerous politics of the Stalin era. Aleksandr Egorov (b. 1874), for instance, a central figure in Georgian winemaking, lived to be ninety-five; Nikolai Prostoserdov (b. 1873) died at eighty-eight. Thus, at the Magarach Institute, the casualties of repression in the 1930s tended to be peripheral. Nikolai Sokolov, whom Valuiko knew through Sokolov's daughter, Elena Datunashvili (b. 1923), an expert in the bio-chemistry of wine, was twice arrested in the 1930s and 1940s. 'He was a wonderful engineer', Valuiko wrote, 'the most intelligent and honest person, a great lecturer on agricultural technology. Students loved his classes.' In the early 1930s, Sokolov travelled to the United States to familiarize himself with American agricultural technology. Upon his return, Sokolov was accused of espionage, and

---

[24] Sheila Fitzpatrick, *The Cultural Front: Power and Culture in Revolutionary Russia* (Ithaca, 1992), 149–82.

sentenced to ten years corrective labour, part of which he spent working on the
Volga-Baltic Canal. Upon his release, Sokolov found work at an agricultural institute in the Kuban.

> While telling students about domestic and American machines, he approached
> an American plough, knocked on it with his pointer, and there rang out a thin
> 'ding'. 'This is the American plough.' Then he approached our plough, hit it with
> his pointer, and there rang a deafening 'boom'. 'And this', he said, 'is our plough.'

Amid the anti-Western xenophobia of the post-war years, Sokolov's pedagogy,
with its implied criticism of the quality of Soviet machinery, was the basis for an
accusation of cosmopolitanism. Sokolov again disappeared into the camps, this
time for good.[25]

The Magarach Institute's internal documents from these years underscore the
extent of transformation it underwent: from a scientific research station, where
production was a secondary or even tertiary concern, to an experimental winery.
The institute's year-end report for 1938 noted that it had 'experienced a series of
organizational quarrels' that 'negatively affected' the implementation of its
research plan. 'One of the serious and negative moments' occurred at the end of
1937, when the institute's senior management was removed as part of its elevation
from regional-level field station to national-level research institute.[26] For four
months, until April 1938, the institute operated under temporary leadership,
many from the newly reorganized Massandra Wine Complex. The institute's temporary leadership immediately set about 'reconstructing the work of the station,
so that there existed the minimal conditions necessary for fulfilling its plan'. Given
the substantial time lag between vineyard investment and viable harvest, this was
easier said than done. The institute's vineyards were suitable for field and ampelographic research, but not for producing large amounts of wine. The institute
needed to be 'completely re-equipped', the author of the 1938 report noted, as its
winemaking facilities lagged its modern Soviet counterparts by ten years or more.
The institute's champagne specialists were reassigned to Inkerman factory outside
of Sevastopol, where they might have a greater impact on production.[27] In 1936,
the institute was organized into two sectors: a vinicultural sector, with departments
of agro-technology, selection, ampelography, agro-chemistry and soil science,
agro-meteorology, and economics and labour, all of which coordinated with
experimental vineyards at Balaclava, Sudak, Anapa, and on the northern Crimean
steppe; and a processing sector, with departments of winemaking, chemistry, and

---

[25] G. G. Valuiko, *Magarach: liudi, sud'by, vina* (2nd edn, Yalta, 1998). A scanned copy of this text,
albeit without page numbers, is available at http://eurowine.com.ua/?q=node/17026. The previous
passages, about the long lives of winemakers and Sokolov's fate, come from the chapters titled 'Moi
uchitelia' and 'Srednee pokolenie uchenykh "Magaracha"'.

[26] RGAE, f. 8543, o. 2, d. 156, l. 3.   [27] RGAE, f. 8543, o. 2, d. 156, ll. 4 (quote), 9.

microbiology. By 1941, as the institute's mandate turned toward production, its organizational chart shifted as well: departments of selection, agro-technology, fortified and dessert wines, champagne, economics, microbiology and biochemistry, and vine protection.[28]

While insiders privately bemoaned the new emphasis on production over research, there were bright spots. For instance, the new agenda likely helped protect the institute from Lysenkoism, which reverberated through the vinicultural community in the post-war years. The chief victim of Lysenko among vinicultural scientists was the director of Odessa's Tairov Institute and its selection department, N. P. Naumenko. In 1950, Naumenko was fired and exiled to work as an agronomist on a kolkhoz, after it was discovered that Naumenko's candidate's dissertation conflicted with the ideas of Lysenko.[29] Moreover, Mikhail Gerasimov, who had been named Chief Winemaker at the Ministry of Food Production after nearly a decade in Georgia, returned to the institute in 1938. The director of the institute's biochemistry laboratory from 1928 to 1931, Gerasimov had become one of the most respected names in Soviet viniculture. Though his superiors were in Moscow, Gerasimov maintained an office and laboratory in Yalta. Finally, in the wake of the reshuffling, Magarach employees with 'low qualifications, or even the absence of qualifications' were fired. The latter description applied to an engineer who led a research project on mechanization. He was 'absolutely unqualified in this area', the author of the 1938 year-end report noted, adding that 'he was a person who was accidentally identified at Magarach as a specialist in winemaking equipment'.[30]

Among the temporary leaders at the Magarach Institute at the beginning of 1938 was Nikolai Sobolev. Born in Kerch in 1904, and a party member since 1925, Sobolev was representative of the generation of Russian and Soviet winemakers that was notable for being mostly non-existent: persons who received their professional training between the advent of Soviet power in 1917 and Stalin's embrace of wine in 1936. By the standards of his industry peers, Sobolev had impeccable class credentials: his father was a railroad worker who died of tuberculosis in 1909, his mother a domestic servant who perished during the famine of the Civil War. Even Sobolev could claim some degree of class oppression: orphaned and fending for himself before Frunze's conquest of Crimea, Sobolev was briefly employed as a vineyard worker on an estate owned by the German baron and wine trader, F. O. Stahl. In 1922, Sobolev found work at an agronomy centre in Balaclava; in 1925, with Komsomol membership in hand, he was granted admission to a viniculture and winemaking school in Yalta. Upon graduation in

[28] RGAE, f. 8543, o. 2, d. 156, l. 5; L. B. Klimova-Donchuk, E. A. Bordunova, and L. P. Troshin, 'Istoricheskii fragment o sozdanii instituta vinograda i vina "Magarach" i shtrikhi ego nauchnoi deiatel'nosti', *Nauchnyi zhurnal KubGAU* 113, no. 9 (2015): 15–17.

[29] V. V. Vlasov, *100 let dorogoiu V. E. Tairova* (Odessa, 2005), 28.

[30] RGAE, f. 8543, o. 2, d. 156, l. 9.

1928, Sobolev was assigned to the Sofia Perovskaia *sovkhoz*, where he later became director.

Details about Sobolev's life come from a January 1945 autobiographical state-ment, the writing of which was a professional rite for Soviet citizens.[31] By then, Sobolev had participated in the defence of Sevastopol, which fell to German, Romanian, and Italian forces in 1942 after a six-month siege. He had been evacu-ated to the North Caucasus, where he was director of the Abrau-Diurso Wine Complex, and then Central Asia. Sobolev made no mention in his statement of his brief stint at Magarach, probably because his temporary oversight there was part of his job at nearby Massandra, which he directed from 1937 to 1950. He concluded with the most relevant information about a Soviet citizen who lived through the first Stalinist decade: 'I have never been on trial.' Perhaps in the heady, optimistic atmosphere of early 1945, with victory against Germany immi-nent, Sobolev could not see that he was tempting fate.[32]

*　*　*　*　*

Yalta was occupied by Axis forces for more than two-and-a-half years, from the autumn of 1941 to the spring of 1944. Though the vacation jewel of tsarist Russia and the site of the Allied conference in February 1945 between Stalin, Roosevelt, and Churchill, Yalta was a bit of a strategic backwater in Crimea, far less import-ant than the natural harbour and naval base at Sevastopol and the Straits of Kerch, which were sites of major fighting. Nonetheless, virtually every account of Massandra and Magarach emphasizes the wartime experience as one of the pin-nacles in institutional histories that stretched back, in the case of Magarach, to the early 1800s. This reflected, of course, the obligatory tropes of the post-war dec-ades, which saw the victory over Nazi Germany emerge as the Soviet Union's cen-tral myth and rallying point. But it also contained a kernel of truth. In October 1941, Massandra and Magarach were evacuated to Sochi on the Russian Black Sea coast. Many of Massandra's employees went on to Abrau-Diurso, which remained safely behind the lines for another year. Magarach settled in exile in Tashkent, where it went about the strange business of making wine and conducting research on wine while a war of annihilation was being fought to the west. Perhaps the institute's greatest wartime success came with the preservation of its wine cellar, the oldest contents of which dated to the early nineteenth century, and which were later couched as a national treasure, like the art in the Hermitage. The Magarach wine was loaded on a ship alongside the contents of Massandra's cellar. It survived several aerial bombardments at sea and spent the war years in safe

[31] Yuri Zaretskiy, 'Confessing to Leviathan: The Mass Practice of Writing Autobiographies in the USSR', *Slavic Review* 76, no. 4 (Winter 2018): 1027–47; Sheila Fitzpatrick, *Tear off the Masks! Identity and Imposture in Twentieth-Century Russia* (Princeton, 2005), 15–16.
[32] N. K. Sobolev, 'Avtobiografiia', in *Sobolev N. K.: Stat'i. Otchety. Prikazy*, ed. V. V. Mitiaev (Massandra, 2002), 9.

storage at the Ovchaly champagne factory outside of Tbilisi. Parts of Massandra's cellar, which comprised more recent wine, were sent to Moscow and Kuibyshev, where they helped bolster the confidence of a shattered Soviet government during that first dismal winter of 1941/2. On the very first day of fighting in Yalta, the Magarach Institute's emptied wine cellar was destroyed and its laboratories looted.[33]

The Magarach Institute's wartime documents make for incongruous reading. On the one hand, the institute diligently went about re-establishing a network of vinicultural research stations, similar to those it had lost in Crimea. By the end of 1942, it had vineyard affiliates in Kazakhstan, Kyrgyzstan, and Tajikistan, and a champagne factory in Tbilisi, with which it cooperated. On the other hand, the institute was glaringly impoverished in exile. For the entirety of 1942, it had less than 240,000 roubles in its budget, the vast majority of which it raised itself: 144,000 roubles from the sale of wine in Tuapse during evacuation, 20,000 from federal winemaking authorities, 10,000 from the Ministry of Food Production, and 65,000 that the director of the institute had personally carried out of Yalta, apparently in cash. Indeed, federal authorities were scarcely able to administer what remained of the pre-war wine industry, much less fund it. At the end of 1942, a date which corresponds with the Battle of Stalingrad and the easternmost extent of hostilities, the Main Administration for Winemaking had just seven facilities under its jurisdiction: champagne factories in Moscow, Gorky, Georgia, and Tashkent; wineries in Moscow and Sverdlov; and the exiled Magarach Institute in Tashkent. Much of the Soviet Union's vinicultural heartland—Moldova, southern Ukraine, southern Russia, and Crimea—was in occupied territory. Consequently, the institute's year-end ledger for 1942 is notable mainly for detailing efforts to collect even the most modest sums of money owed to it. During the evacuation from Yalta, 480 roubles had been given to an employee who was accompanying the contents of the wine cellar to Poti, so that whatever fees or bribes were necessary to save the wine could be paid along the way. The employee was conscripted before he could account for the money, which was deemed to be a loss. While there is no evidence that the funds were misused (or used at all), asking for a salary advance before conscription was a fairly common scam: at least two other employees did the same, absconding with smaller amounts of money. Another 625 roubles were written off after they were offered as temporary aid to the wife of one of the institute's professors. He died in Ashkhabad, while in transit to Tashkent; his wife died a short time later, in a hospital outside of Tashkent. No one knew where the money went.[34]

Among the heroes of these years was Aleksei Globa, who became director of the Institute after the 1938 interregnum. The conduit for the 65,000 roubles that were spirited out of Yalta in the fall of 1941, Globa was a savvy facilitator who

[33] Klimova-Donchuk et al., 'Istoricheskii fragment', 17.
[34] RGAE, f. 8543, o. 2, d. 718, l. 2; d. 813, ll. 2, 5–6.

knew the ways of the Soviet system. According to Vladimir Kosiura (b. 1938), who came to the institute in 1968 after winemaking stints in Moldova, Odessa, and Simferopol, and who wrote a lengthy defence of the institute and its history after Ukrainian authorities let it languish in the post-Soviet decades, Globa began planning for the institute's post-war resurrection even before he departed Yalta in 1941. He ensured the evacuation of barrels of recent Crimean wine, which he thought necessary to save as a blending agent—an 'ameliorator'—for wine from the first post-war harvests, which was likely to be of poor quality due to years of vineyard neglect. When the Magarach Institute was cleared to return to Yalta in June 1944, Globa arranged to have his employees accompany a train car of raisins from 'lower Magarach', as the institute's temporary home in Tashkent had become affectionately known. Once in Crimea, Globa sold the raisins, and used the proceeds to buy a fishing vessel. During the hungry post-war years, Magarach employees survived on regular catches of fish. When the Institute lost its premises on the Massandra campus, reputedly because Stalin wished to use it as a hunting lodge, Globa moved the institute into a tsarist-era gymnasium that had been built from donations made to Empress Maria Fedorovna, after the death of her husband Alexander III. Constructed with stone walls more than a metre thick, the gymnasium had survived Crimea's devastating 1927 earthquakes with minimal damage. When local party officials began to eye the institute's new home in the post-war years, amid complaints that there were not enough schools for Yalta's children, the institute used its own funds to construct a new school building in the centre of town. To re-equip the institute after it was plundered during the occupation, Globa petitioned Mikoyan to authorize a trip to the Soviet zone of Germany in the winter of 1946/7. Globa returned with a large quantity of chemistry utensils, appliances, equipment, even furniture. At best, Globa's booty was a small component of the 'vast project of imperial scavenging' that characterized the Soviet role in the socialist world in the post-war decades; at worst, it was a war reparation exacted from the institute's begrudging and frightened counterparts in Germany.[35]

Globa's skills in navigating the unusual circumstances of wartime evacuation and post-war reconstruction stand out because they so clearly resemble behaviours that in the late 1940s got his predecessor at the Magarach Institute, and later his counterpart at Massandra, Nikolai Sobolev, in trouble. There is very little evidence that Globa hewed closely to prescribed ways of doing things: he sold the institute's wine outside of normal channels; he got involved in the raisin and fish business; he spent a substantial portion of the institute's budget allocation on

[35] Vladimir Terent'evich Kosiura, 'Chtoby pomnili ili kto zashchitit istoriiu "Magaracha"?', *Slovo Sevastopolia*, 17 May 2012, http://slovo.sebastopol.ua/article171.html; Klimova-Donchuk et al., 'Istoricheskii fragment', 18–20. On the Soviet Union as an imperial scavenger, see Austin Jersild, 'The Soviet State as Imperial Scavenger: "Catch Up and Surpass" in the Transnational Socialist Bloc, 1950–1960', *American Historical Review* 116, no. 1 (February 2011): 109–32.

something that could not have been envisioned in Moscow, all in the hope of preserving a bit of the quiet life necessary for research and scholarly contemplation. Globa's skillset had been honed during the war, when the old ways of doing things crumbled amid the stresses of retreat and worries of defeat. Globa excelled at the ad hoc, at finding unusual solutions to pressing problems, aware all the time that some battles, such as saving the institute's pre-war building from becoming a Kremlin hunting lodge, could not be won.

It is clear, however, that Moscow tried to reassert some semblance of control over the wine industry in the months following the end of hostilities. In June and July 1945, the People's Commissariat of State Control, which operated as a sort of bureaucratic oversight and auditing organization, sent investigators to Massandra and Abrau-Diurso. Their findings were unsurprisingly bad. The vinicultural *sovkhozy* subordinate to Massandra, for instance, had missed their first post-liberation production targets by wide margins: the Gurzuf and Koktebel *sovkhozy* came in at 54 per cent of target; Ai-Danil' did better at 78 per cent. Crimean vineyards were unproductive because they had been mostly neglected during the two-and-a-half-year occupation. Occupation authorities appointed a loyal overseer for the Massandra estate—a member of the Nazi party named Hegel who had lived and worked in Georgia until 1929. Hegel compelled Massandra employees who remained in Crimea to work, and they succeeded in producing at least one vintage (1942). But vine maintenance—which improves longevity and long-term productivity—was mostly an afterthought. Hegel reportedly fled in 1944 as the Red Army massed in Gurzuf, and before his plan to dynamite Massandra's buildings could be carried out. Moreover, much of the winemaking and wine storage infrastructure at Massandra had been damaged during the war, and not always by combat. Buildings in the Gurzuf, Kastel', Ai-Danil', and Alupka *sovkhozy* were in active landslide zones, which were apparently the result of excessive precipitation. Kastel' was in danger of losing its cellar entirely, which was badly deformed by the shifting ground. Ai-Danil' had already demolished one building deemed unsafe.[36]

The *sovkhozy* subordinate to Abrau-Diurso, just west of Novorossiysk, were in equally bad shape. A significant portion of Abrau-Diurso's pre-war vineyards needed to be replanted entirely. Trellises were absent in nearly three-quarters of all vineyards. At the Molotov *sovkhoz*, plantings of Pinot noir, the principal grape in Abrau-Diurso's prized champagnes, had 'thinned' by 40 per cent. Like Globa, the leadership at Abrau-Diurso tried to arrange on its own the sale of wine and vodka (presumably made from grapes) to fund reconstruction. In 1944 and 1945, it sold 2,254 litres of wine to a fishing cooperative, 13,200 litres of wine to individual persons, 300 litres of vodka to a perfume factory, and another 1,957 litres of vodka to its own employees. Yet the Moscow investigators did not approve of

---

[36] GARF, f. R8300, o. 28, d. 1491, ll. 6, 13. On Hegel, see Shleiger, *Polveka s vinom*, 28.

Abrau-Diurso's self-sufficiency—its sale of wine was occurring in an 'uncontrolled' manner. Moreover, in 1945 when Abrau-Diurso received a state allocation to fund reconstruction work, it managed to spend only 15 per cent of the 460,000 roubles Moscow had offered by 1 May. Rebuilding trellises was a lot less pressing for most Abrau-Diurso employees than putting food on the table.[37]

Both Massandra and Abrau-Diurso responded in formal fashion to the commissariat's findings. 'Not a single industrial complex in the system of Main Administration for Winemaking or in the Krasnodar region suffered as seriously from the German occupiers as Abrau-Diurso and its subsidiaries', the director of Abrau-Diurso wrote.[38] The entire industrial complex—the wine factory, the *sovkhozy*, the laboratories—was destroyed. Much of Abrau-Diurso's pre-war workforce had been forced into German 'slavery', and had yet to reappear. Before the war, Abrau-Diurso had 1,850 employees; on 1 June 1945, only 775 remained. Stables that housed 410 horses in early 1941, now had twenty. Sixty per cent of employee housing had been destroyed. Seven tractors had disappeared. Vineyards were pocked with military fortifications and the residue of battle. Nearly 30 per cent of all vines had perished. In this context, the question was not about repairing Abrau-Diurso, the director wrote, but about building it anew.[39] Massandra made a similar case: two-and-a-half years of occupation, combat, and the isolation of Crimea from industrial and agricultural centres meant that reconstruction was painfully slow. 'If we are honest, the damage incurred by the Massandra Wine Complex during the German occupation can be estimated at two million rubles.'[40] In 1945, Massandra relied on the labour of 2,500 prisoners of war, but it was still missing sixty-four vinicultural and winemaking specialists. Following the expulsion of Tatars from Crimea in May 1944, Massandra annexed three former Tatar *sovkhozy*, which meant that its total vineyard area had actually increased during the war years, but the overall condition of vineyards was dire.

> As a result of poor maintenance, and in a number of cases, the complete absence of maintenance during the occupation of Crimea, all vineyard plantings are in terrible condition. They have lost the pruned shape of a vine. They have been crushed by tank tracks. They have for many years been clogged with damaging weeds. Vineyards have become cesspits of disease.[41]

It does not appear that there were any immediate repercussions to the commissariat's 1945 report. Even the Moscow investigators, who were typically inclined to see every target as attainable with sufficient effort, thought that the situation was mostly hopeless in the short term. Yet it did set the stage for the Ministry of

---

[37] GARF, f. R8300, o. 28, d. 1490, ll. 6–12, 17; d. 1491, ll. 6–7, 13.
[38] GARF, f. R8300, o. 28, d. 1490, l. 19   [39] GARF, f. R8300, o. 28, d. 1490, ll. 19, 29.
[40] GARF, f. R8300, o. 28, d. 1491, l. 21.   [41] GARF, f. R8300, o. 28, d. 1491, l. 36.

State Control (as the commissariat was renamed in 1946) to follow up with Massandra and Abrau-Diurso in 1949. It became immediately apparent that the stakes had risen. Investigators focused on a circular that the Ministry of Food Production sent to winemaking establishments on 26 July 1938, 'On the work of permanent tasting commissions'. The circular recognized that the act of tasting (*degustatsiia*) was the best way to determine the quality of wine. But it indicated that the composition of tasting commissions had to be limited to people with appropriate expertise, which typically meant people from the industry itself. In 1948, Massandra conducted at least sixty-two tastings that were plainly not in compliance with the 1938 circular, 'with different visitors, tourists, and other individuals who have no relation to the winemaking industry'. Beneficiaries included representatives from the Ministry of Finance, employees of the State Bank, members of the executive committee of the local soviet. They were served 'the best-reviewed vintage wines, champagne, and cognac not made by Massandra'. At Abrau-Diurso, the alleged corruption appears to have been more conventional: investigators from the Ministry of State Control found that 432,000 roubles had been embezzled or stolen since 1946, of which nearly half was in the form of wine, 'wine materials' (which typically meant grapes destined for wine), or distilled spirits.[42]

The investigations at Massandra and Abrau-Diurso were part of a broader crackdown on corruption in the liquor and wine industry in the post-war years. The highest profile victim was Vasilii Zotov, the federal Minister of Food Production, who was fired in 1949 for irregularities in alcohol production in one oblast. Mikoyan saved Zotov from criminal charges. As late as May 1953, more than a month after Stalin's death, twenty people were arrested in wineries in Uzbekistan, accused of embezzling more than three million roubles of wine and distilled alcohol, and bribing nearly everyone who might have taken notice. Their scheme including skimming distilled alcohol off the top of some fortified wines, thus lowering their alcohol content by 0.5 to 3 per cent from what was reported on their labels, and adding the alcohol to other fortified wines, which were then diluted with water at the point of sale to create wine that had no paper trail. Similar rackets were reported in Ukraine, Novosibirsk, Irkutsk, and elsewhere.[43] As Andrei Sushkov has argued, officials in Moscow were trying to rein in the unofficial networks and regional autonomies that wartime conditions had fostered. In distant Krasnoyarsk, the focus of Sushkov's study, the principal victim was Nikolai Maslov, the director of the local fruit and berry wine factory. According to eyewitnesses, Maslov frequently ordered his secretary to pull bottles from the production line to share with visiting dignitaries. He also sold liquor

---

[42] GARF, f. R8300, o. 28, d. 1572, l. 2; d. 1573, l. 3.
[43] GARF, f. R9415, o. 5, d. 127, ll. 17–19. My thanks to Jim Heinzen for sharing this document with me.

and wine to important persons at steeply discounted prices. Maslov's history of currying favour with the local elite proved valuable in 1948, when he was found guilty by a local court of falsifying his accounting and inventory to manipulate the currency reform. Initially sentenced to fifteen years of corrective labour, Maslov's sentence was commuted by a judge whom Maslov had generously provisioned in the past. 'As is well known, one favor deserves another (*dolg krasen platezhom*)', Sushkov writes.

> For the approaching May 1 holiday [1948], Maslov prepared a whole array of gifts for the local *nomenklatura* and delivered them to each apartment. To simplify things, he wrote a list—who got how many bottles. The selection of gifts directly correlated with the professional stature of the recipients. Thus, the chairman of the Krasnoyarsk krai executive committee, E. P. Kolushchinskii (officially, the second most powerful person in the krai) received three bottles of liquor, brandy, and fruit and berry wine, two bottles of distilled alcohol, and a container of sparkling water. Maslov gave the same selection, but without the distilled alcohol, to Kolushchinskii's deputy chairman, M. I. Gener.[44]

As word of Maslov's case reached Moscow, it threatened to tarnish Averkii Aristov, the powerful local party secretary who would later fall out of favour with Khrushchev. Consequently, the victory in court that Maslov celebrated with yet more corruption proved very short-lived. In Sushkov's view, the so-called 'Maslov affair' hinted at the difficulty the party would encounter in future decades while trying to curtail elite corruption through normal criminal channels rather than purges.

A similar motivation was almost certainly at play in Crimea and Novorossiysk, even though the corruption was far less stark than Maslov's cartoonish behavior. At Massandra, the initial response to charges of corruption came on 2 August 1949 from Ivan Okolelov (b. 1916), the director of Massandra's wine factory no. 1, and one of Sobolev's immediate subordinates. While not denying that wine tastings had occurred, Okolelov claimed that he had authorized them based on his understanding of a 1940 Ministry of Food Production decree, which limited tastings to employees 'directly connected to the manufacturing of wine'. In Okolelov's account, these were the circumstances surrounding the tastings that he supervised—they were for employees involved in the production of wine. Less than two months later, however, on 19 September, the Ministry of State Control notified Mikoyan that Sobolev had acknowledged the substance of the Ministry's findings:

---

[44] A. V. Sushkov, 'Vlast' i korruptsiia: rukovodstvo Krasnoiarskogo kraia i delo o khishcheniiakh produktsii na krasnoiarskom zavode plodovo-iagodnykh vin (1949 g.)', *Ural'skii istoricheskii vestnik* 32, no 3 (2011): 91. My thanks to David Brandenberger for sharing this article with me. See also Heinzen, *The Art of the Bribe*, 84–5.

on at least eighty-six occasions in 1948 and 1949, Sobolev and Okolelov had 'systematically used wine for the entertainment of different visitors, tourists, and other individuals', which included visiting vinicultural and winemaking students, specialists, and 'different workers who have no relation to tasting'. Okolelov had subsequently ordered his bookkeeper to 'write off' 41,381 litres of wine in order to hide the unauthorized use.[45]

The vast majority of this wine, the equivalent of about 60,000 bottles, appears to have been consumed internally, offered as gifts to employees, shared with visiting dignitaries, or ruined during the course of production, although investigators could ascertain the fate of only a small percentage of it. In 1948 and 1949, Sobolev and Okolelov gave away nearly 2,700 bottles of wine to Massandra employees, often on holidays. To mark Massandra's fiftieth anniversary in 1949, they opened 166 bottles, including eighty-one that were more than fifty years old. Fedor Okhrimenko, a winemaker known among Massandra employees as Batia, a term of endearment for an elderly man, disingenuously explained to investigators from the Ministry of State Control that the latter inventory debits were necessitated by a 'scientific-production celebratory tasting'. In 1948, the director of the Massandra's Alushta *sovkhoz* authorized the consumption of 50 litres of wine at a celebratory dinner for employees; in 1949, employees drank another 25 litres in celebration. Leonid Shleiger, who found work at Massandra in 1948 while pursuing a correspondence degree at the Odessa Technological Institute of the Food Industry, described in his memoirs the ubiquity of wine as a sign of hospitality in the professional life of Massandra. On a Sunday afternoon in the summer of 1951, Shleiger writes, Aleksandr Egorov (b. 1874), the main engineer-winemaker for the Massandra Complex, invited Mikhail Gerasimov, Nikolai Prostoserdov, Anton Frolov-Bagreev, and Nikolai Okhremenko—in short, the titans of Soviet winemaking—to taste wine from Massandra's cellar. It was the day before a conference at the Magarach Institute, and many of the industry's leading officials had congregated in Yalta.

> I took part in the opening [of the wine] and the presentation of the corks. A powerful group of people had gathered in the tasting hall and in the office...Everyone talked about the pride of making great wine. I served a Madeira from 1937, a red Livadiia Port wine from 1938, an Ai-Danil' Tokaji from the 1930s. The patriarchs remembered where and what they were doing during these years. Nikolai Prostoserdov read his poetry. The conversation touched on music...For a final drink, Aleksandr Egorov asked me to bring a French champagne, Moët et Chandon. Everyone commented on its very high

---

[45] GARF, f. R8300, o. 28, d. 1572, ll. 77–8; d. 1573, ll. 5–5ob., 22–3, 28–28ob.

quality. Less than a third remained in the bottle. I very carefully re-corked it, in order to share it with my work colleagues.[46]

Twenty years after Vintorg sold the Soviet Union's final stockpiles of foreign wine to raise capital for rebuilding the domestic wine industry, winemakers at Massandra uncorked a bottle from Épernay that was likely older than Soviet power. Its consumption was a token of hospitality and appreciation for the vini-cultural giants who had gathered in their tasting room, and in all likelihood, yet another misuse of state property.

As part of its investigation into Massandra, the Ministry of State Control focused on the Novyi svet champagne factory. Located sixty kilometres east of Yalta in Sudak, near the eastern end of the Crimean Range, and like Massandra, a former crown estate, Novyi svet had been affiliated with Massandra since the late-tsarist period, with the exception of a brief interlude in the 1930s when it was attached to Abrau-Diurso. Here the allegations of corruption were even less clear-cut than what was alleged to have occurred at Massandra's main facility, which had hardly risen to the level of 'Maslov affair'. The ministry reported to Mikoyan that the director of the factory, S. I. Belogubets, and his chief *shampanist*, Natalia Drboglav, had 'systematically written off wine to technological and manufactur-ing losses', in order to construct an 'off-the-books wine reserve'. This was an unusual allegation, but perhaps not so far-fetched. A wine reserve had clear prac-tical value in an economy where production was subject to many forces beyond human control, and where failure to meet production targets might be dangerous. A wine reserve could be used to cover a production deficit, as an alternative form of currency, and to grease important partners. In 1949, for instance, Massandra's Koktebel *sovkhoz* sent three barrels of wine, off the books, to Novyi svet, for reasons that were not entirely clear, but likely stemmed from their longstanding business relationship. Moreover, for reasons that were not peculiar to the Soviet system, a wine reserve had value. It facilitated *coupage*, the blending of different wines to enhance their characteristics. And large wine reserves, stretching over many years, were coveted by winemakers because they offered a way to gauge the impact over time of small changes in production—from the amount of sun and precipitation a vineyard received, to the date of harvest, to the use of oenological additives such as sugar and acid. The Magarach Institute evacuated just such a wine reserve to Poti in October 1941.[47]

Although not as substantial as the alleged fraud at Massandra, the inventory losses that Novyi svet recorded in 1948 were occurring at nearly every phase of production. Because Novyi svet had been built during the tsarist era, it produced champagne not by Anton Frolov-Bagreev's mechanized 'continuous method', but

---

[46] Shleiger, *Polveka s vinom*, 31.   [47] GARF, f. R8300, o. 28, d. 1573, ll. 47, 52.

by the same *méthode traditionnelle* that Prince Lev Golitsyn had employed. Thus, Novyi svet lost 500 litres of wine during *remuage* (which the Ministry of State Control investigators called *fil'tratsiia*, the process of manually turning bottles so sediment collects in bottle necks), 240 litres during labelling, 513 litres during transportation, and 5,781 bottles during disgorgement (the process where bottle necks are flash-frozen to remove the collected sediment). Some of these losses were undoubtedly legitimate: disgorgement, for instance, is a tricky process even in the best of circumstances. But the Ministry of State Control determined that most were not. Novyi svet was creating a paper trail of production losses to disguise the creation of a wine reserve.[48]

By the end of the year, Sobolev had received a 'strict reprimand' from the Ministry of State Control. He was ordered to repay Massandra 2,500 roubles in partial compensation for the wine that had been consumed without proper authorization. Okolelov was removed from his position as factory director, although he stayed on as the chief engineer-winemaker. The bookkeeper whom Okolelov had ordered to falsify the factory's inventory ledger was fined 500 roubles. At Novyi svet, Belogubets, Drboglav, and one subordinate were removed from their positions. And the director of Massandra's Koktebel *sovkhoz* was fired for transferring three barrels of wine to Novyi svet without the proper paperwork. Only Abrau-Diurso, whose director had been arrested and executed in 1937, emerged unscathed. The Ministry of State Control criticized the Abrau-Diurso managers for oversight so lax that employee theft was rife. But it found no official involvement in the theft of wine, nor in subsequent efforts to conceal the theft of wine. Ominously, the ministry forwarded all of its findings to the procuracy to evaluate whether criminal charges were merited.[49]

Here the archival record turns opaque, as do Soviet-era published accounts of Massandra and Magarach, which tend to locate the end of their Soviet formative histories alongside the liberation of Crimea and return from exile.[50] Yet for Massandra's winemakers, in particular, the final Stalinist years were clearly tumultuous. Despite the Ministry of State Control Investigation, Massandra received the Order of the Red Banner of Labour in 1949, in honour of its fiftieth anniversary and its wartime exploits. Many employees were also honoured, including Sobolev, who had been director of the Massandra Complex since 1937. He received his second Order of Lenin medal. In 1949, Stalin visited the winery with Walter Ulbricht, staying on the grounds of Massandra at the former palace of Alexander III. It was the same building that had once housed the Magarach Institute. The proximity of Kremlin elites, who were present not only at Stalin's vacation home, but at the nearby Yusupov Palace, which became a Central Committee residence after housing the Soviet delegation to the Yalta Conference

---

[48] GARF, f. R8300, o. 28, d. 1572, ll. 58–60.   [49] GARF, f. R8300, o. 28, d. 1573, ll. 28ob., 53.

[50] See, for instance, S. M. Mikhailov, Z. I. Levchenko, and S. N. Sukhanova, *Solnechnaia 'Massandra'* (Simferopol, 1975), 37–56.

in 1945, brought new risks. In 1950, Sobolev was transferred to Moldova, where he became director of the Bessarabian Wine Complex. This was almost certainly a demotion linked with the Ministry of State Control Investigation, and the for-warding of the case files to the procuracy for criminal review. According to one version of events, Sobolev was denounced by his chauffeur, who lived in an adja-cent apartment. The chauffeur overheard Sobolev complain about the promin-ence of Georgian officials in the Main Administration for Winemaking in Moscow, and about the apparent inequity in federal resources given to the Georgian and Crimean wine industries. This was easily conflated as criticism of Stalin himself. Already compromised by the Ministry of State Control investiga-tions, Sobolev and his wife were arrested. Sobolev was convicted of spying for the British and sentenced to a labour camp near Poltava. When his health began to fail, Sobolev's former colleagues at Massandra, at considerable risk to themselves, organized a shipment of medicine. Okolelov recalled in 1998 that one of Massandra's older mechanics, who was a 'vigilant communist', challenged him openly about the propriety of such assistance. Aleksandr Egorov wrote to Mikoyan, the food and wine industry's long-time patron, to press Sobolev's case. Egorov argued that the charges against Sobolev were clearly baseless, and that his personal opinion of Sobolev, which reflected years of close professional collabora-tion, could 'only be positive'. Egorov had no illusions about his own safety—his brother-in-law, also a winemaker, was shot during these years.[51]

Sobolev was not the only Massandra employee to experience repression in the final years before Stalin's death. In 1951, Pavel Novichkov, the chief winemaker at Massandra's wine factory no. 1, was arrested. Known for his refined wine nose, for making 'wines that were as elegant as himself', and for constructing his own wine barrels out of the belief that attention to small details yielded better wine, Novichkov remained in Crimea during the occupation, serving as a conduit for partisans who used wine as a currency to purchase food and medicine in the villages. In his memoir, Leonid Shleiger recalled seeing empty bottles from the 1942 harvest in nearby villages after the war, presumably the same bottles Novichkov had passed on to partisans. According to the logic of late-Stalinism, however, remaining voluntarily in occupied territory during the war was tantamount to treason. In the wake of Novichkov's arrest, his former colleagues gathered annually on his birthday to toast their friend with a concoction of his own making: a so-called 'Petrovskaia Vodka', which Novichkov made by soaking buds from a blackcurrant bush in alcohol, and after two weeks, mixing the extract with vodka.[52]

*   *   *   *   *

[51] I. N. Okolelov, 'Sobolev', in *Sobolev N. K.: Stat'i. Otchety. Prikazy*, ed. V. V. Mitiaev (Massandra, 2002), 140–41; A. A. Egorov, 'Otzyv o rabote Nikolaia Konstantinovicha Soboleva v vinkombinate "Massandra"', in Mitiaev, *Sobolev N. K.*, 8; Shleiger, *Polveka s vinom*, 21, 27, 30; Valuiko, *Magarach*, n. pag., chapter titled 'Opal'nye vinodely'.
[52] Shleiger, *Polveka s vinom*, 28–9.

Sobolev and Novichkov survived their brushes with repression. Sobolev was released from camp in 1953, when his case was reviewed as part of the first wave of post-Stalin amnesties. Formal rehabilitation soon followed, as did the restoration of Sobolev's party membership and awards. Work in the wine industry was harder to find. Sobolev returned to Crimea, hoping that his proximity to Massandra would lead to a job. Sobolev's successor, however, who had been appointed directly from Moscow, and who had benefitted from Sobolev's misfortune, was unwilling to take him on. An old friend in Rostov-on-Don, the director of the Don Wine Complex, invited Sobolev to join him there. In 1955, at Mikoyan's behest, Sobolev succeeded his friend as director, a position he held until his retirement in 1970. Novichkov remained in camp until 1954, when Kliment Voroshilov visited Massandra. After asking about the fate of the old winemaker whom he had met during the liberation of Yalta a decade earlier, Voroshilov arranged for Novichkov's release and return to Massandra. At Magarach, Aleksei Globa—the facilitator *par excellence*—stepped down as director in 1950, apparently of his own volition. German Valuiko noted in this memoir that Globa's successor, Tateos Katar'ian, formerly the chief scientific secretary of the Armenian Academy of Sciences, knew from events at neighbouring Massandra that he had to straighten out the institute's bookkeeping in short order. To that end, he recruited an accountant from the Institute of Subtropical Cultivation in Sukhumi with the promise of an apartment and ignored a reprimand from local party officials that there was something unseemly about offering a fringe benefit. Katari'ian remained director of the institute until his death in 1967, which occurred in the middle of a dispute with the chairman of the Main Winemaking Administration of Ukraine. Even in the absence of terror, the Soviet wine industry exacted a heavy toll on those who led it.

It is not clear what, if anything, Massandra leaders got in return for their generosity with important visitors and employees. The investigators from the Ministry of State Control never couched the misuse of wine as bribery, so it is unlikely there was any material reciprocity or explicit quid pro quo. It is clear, however, that many of the persons who were offered gratis tastings were potentially useful to Massandra—prominent winemakers, officials from the oblast soviet, and bureaucrats visiting from Moscow. Like the blat that was ubiquitous in the consumer economy, some favours might be returned in the distant future, and some never at all.[53] Most important was having a long bench of friends whom one could ask, which is perhaps what Sobolev and Okolelov, who were part of that first, mostly absent generation of authentically Soviet winemakers, tried to create. In the aftermath of a war in which so many Soviet routines crumbled, when even simple tasks became impossible, Sobolev would have understood the value of

---

[53] Alena V. Ledeneva, *Russia's Economy of Favors: Blat, Networking and Informal Exchange* (Cambridge, 1998).

such a network, and that using gifts of wine as a tool, however archaic, to create political allies was a small price to pay. In this regard, the wine industry lent itself to the gift economy in ways that were impossible to conceive in other sectors of the economy—there would be no giving visitors to metallurgical facilities free rolls of steel, for instance. Sobolev and Okolelov simply had the good sense to use the wine that Massandra produced in the same way that so many of their customers did—as a gift to express gratitude, hospitality, and friendship, and something that is best shared with old friends and new allies.

Yet the wine that Sobolev and Okolelov shared with visitors was ultimately not theirs to give, which was at the heart of the Ministry of State Control's case. While their behaviour did not constitute corruption on the scale of the Maslov affair in distant Krasnoyarsk, it was careless in the eyes of investigators, and that demanded retribution. Paradoxically, in the aftermath of the Massandra and Abrau-Diurso investigations, officials in the wine industry appear to have forgotten that they were explicitly protected by Soviet administrative law when it came to tastings— they were allowed to consume the wine that they produced to verify its quality. Formal tastings became relatively scarce in the 1950s, a fact that many persons in Valuiko's generation of winemakers would seek to correct as they worked to improve the quality of Soviet wine production in the face of growing fears about an epidemic of alcoholism (the subject of chapter 7). When prominent vintners were losing jobs and going to prison because of excessively generous tastings, many industry officials decided that it was best to err on the side of caution and end *degustatsii* altogether.

6

Taste

Soviet Wine and Western Connoisseurship

During the Khrushchev and Brezhnev years, Soviet wines began to appear in international tasting competitions. Absent from the European tasting circuit since the late-tsarist period, when wines from Crimea and Georgia won enough accolades abroad to generate demand from merchants in Paris and London, a handful of Soviet wines achieved critical success, at least within the socialist world. At the First All-World Wine Competition in Budapest in 1972, where nearly 1,400 wines from thirty-four countries were subject to blind tastings, and all but twenty-seven won some sort of commendation, Soviet producers received one high gold for a Magarach sherry made from Pedro Ximénez, eight gold, and twenty-four silver medals from the 102 bottles they entered. These were modest results. By comparison, Hungary, which entered sixty-six bottles, won sixteen high gold, twenty gold, and eighteen silver medals. Unremarkable were the entries from Spain, France, and Italy, the only countries in the world that produced a greater volume of wine than the Soviet Union, but no one there would mistake the competition in Budapest for critical tastings in London, Brussels, and Paris. Soviet results at the Second and Third International Wine Competitions in Bratislava in 1967 and 1971, which were managed by a different organization, were similar: the Soviet Union entered many bottles and won a few high distinctions.[1]

For a government concerned about contact with the outside world, wine tastings were an ideal form of cross-border interaction, since carefully curated bottles could be shipped to Budapest or Ljubljana unaccompanied. Compared to sport and ballet, other realms where the Soviet Union sought international distinction during the Cold War, the potential for embarrassing scandal was minimal.[2] There was also valuable wisdom to be gained from international juries. After Soviet white wines fared poorly at the Second International Wine and Cognac Competition in Yalta in 1970, 'lagging behind their best foreign counterparts', German Valuiko, one of the lead scientists at the Magarach Institute, urged Soviet vintners to

---

[1] *I. Borvilágverseny Budapest 1972* (Budapest, 1972), 132; *II. Medzinárodný konkurz vín. 14.–24. Augusta 1967* (Bratislava, 1967), 155–9; *III. Medzinárodný konkurz vín v Bratislave* (Bratislava, 1971), 155–6.

[2] David Caute, *The Dancer Defects: The Struggle for Cultural Supremacy during the Cold War* (Oxford, 2005).

Whites and Reds: A History of Wine in the Lands of Tsar and Commissar. Stephen V. Bittner, Oxford University Press (2021).
© Stephen V. Bittner. DOI: 10.1093/oso/9780198784821.003.0007

'carefully discuss and identify ways to eliminate deficiencies' that the jury described.[3] On occasion, international tastings offered opportunities for aggrandizement. No matter how modest the distinction, Soviet vintners sought to advertise their commendations to consumers. By the 1970s, the label for semi-sweet Soviet Champagne, which was made from Ukrainian grapes at the inelegantly named Moscow Champagne Factory (which before 1917 was the Smirnoff distillery), was adorned with gold medals from competitions in Budapest (1960 and 1964), Ljubljana (1964), Tbilisi (1969), Sofia (1969), and Yalta (1970), and silver medals from Moscow (1958) and Bucharest (1970). The label for the demi sec was only slightly less crowded. International medals could also be found on Armenian cognacs, Dagestani dessert wines, Crimean sherries and ports, and Moldovan Fetească Albăs, often many vintages removed from the award winners. The latter practice struck the few foreigners familiar with Soviet wine as odd at best and misleading at worst.

Coming after the hermetic freeze of late-Stalinism, when nearly all contact with the international wine community ceased, and when even the ritual of *degustatsiia* could be couched as the misuse of state property, the return of Soviet wines to tasting competitions reflected broader trends associated with the Khrushchev and Brezhnev years. During these decades, the Soviet Union shook off much of its insularity by opening its doors to foreign visitors and even to its own citizens, who, by necessity or privilege, had the opportunity to travel and work abroad. Nikita Khrushchev became the Soviet Union's international traveller-in-chief, embracing a public relations aspect of the Cold War in ways that had eluded his predecessor. Within a few years of Stalin's death, Moscow and Leningrad had become regular stops on the European cultural circuit. The Everyman Opera troupe visited in 1955–6, performing Gershwin's *Porgy and Bess*. Leonard Bernstein's New York Philharmonic followed in 1959. In 1956, a Picasso retrospective opened in Moscow, comprising works from Soviet museums and Picasso's personal holdings. It was organized at the lobbying of the writer Ilya Ehrenburg, who had known Picasso from his days in Paris before the revolution. Beginning in 1959, Moscow resurrected in biennial format an international film festival, which in future years would attract stars such as Yves Montand and award Frederico Fellini's *8 1/2* its grand prix. Moscow even hosted a Christian Dior fashion show and photo shoot in 1959. During the 1960s and 1970s, in the context of détente, interaction with the outside world broadened under a host of international organizations and arrangements that governed everything from sport and copyright to human rights and international air travel. Significant Soviet expatriate communities developed in Eastern Europe, the developing world, and to a lesser extent, the capitalist West: the families of Red Army officers and diplomats,

---

[3] G. G. Valuiko, 'II Mezhdunarodnyi konkurs vinogradnykh vin i kon'iakov', *Vinodelie i vinogradarstvo SSSR* no. 1 (1971): 13; RGAE, f. 468, o. 1, d. 2412, l. 2.

journalists, students, and specialists on Comecon exchanges. Soviet power was increasingly enmeshed in the structures of a world it had once shunned.[4]

While reflective of these broader trends, the return of the Soviet wine industry to international tasting competitions was also an unexpected development, as tasting competitions presented clear difficulties for Soviet producers, and not only because of their modest successes. Since the international expositions in Paris in 1889 and 1900, where fine wine was featured as a distinctively French accomplishment, wine competitions and expositions underscored the persistence of 'singularities' in an age of standardized commodity production. The competitive comparison of wine exemplified the 'great modernist and positivist ideals of universal order and classification', but it also underscored, at least in the case of France, the inimitable marriage of varietal, soil, and methods passed down over many generations. As V. T. Tran has noted, competitive wine tastings became common precisely at the moment that winemaking turned into a scientific endeavour. They juxtaposed the 'regional exceptionalism' of France, where wine was understood to be a monument to a distinct cultural heritage, with the 'chemical reductionism' of America, in particular, where wine was a recipe for science.[5]

Despite vinicultural histories in Bessarabia, Crimea, and Georgia that were many millennia old, the Soviet Union lacked a sense that its wines were monuments to a distinct cultural heritage, that they were 'singularities' in a world of bland copycats. This was because the Soviet wine industry, like its tsarist predecessor, was deeply imitative, both in the standards of excellence that it accepted, which were solidly French even at the expense of satisfying domestic consumers, and in the cultural meanings that were attached to wine, which were proof of the Soviet Union's civilizational pedigree. It also reflected the fact that the idea of *terroir*, as something essential to and ineffable in great wine was not much present in the Russian Empire and the Soviet Union.[6] Indeed, Soviet-era vintners often produced wine in ways that precluded the development of a finely tuned

---

[4] The literature on the Soviet Union's growing engagement with the outside world in the 1950s and beyond is large and growing. See, for instance, Anne Gorsuch, *All This Is Your World: Soviet Tourism at Home and Abroad after Stalin* (Oxford, 2011); Susan E. Reid, 'Picasso, the Thaw and the "New Realism" in Soviet Art', *Colloque Revoir Picasso*, March 26, 2015; Eleonory Gilburd, 'Picasso in Thaw Culture', *Cahier du Monde russe* 47, nos. 1–2 (2006): 65–108; Eleonory Gilburd, *To See Paris and Die: The Soviet Lives of Western Culture* (Cambridge, MA, 2018); Larissa Zakharova, 'Soviet Fashion in the 1950s–1960s: Regimentation, Western Influences, and Consumption Strategies', in *The Thaw: Soviet Society and Culture during the 1950s and 1960s*, ed. Denis Kozlov and Eleonory Gilburd (Toronto, 2013), 402–35; Oksana Bulgakowa, 'Cine-Weathers: Soviet Thaw Cinema in the International Context' in Kozlov and Gilburd, *The Thaw*, 436–81.

[5] Van Troi Tran, 'Grapes on Trial: Wine at the Paris World's Fairs of 1889 and 1900', *Food and Foodways: Explorations in the History and Culture of Human Nourishment* 21, no. 4 (2013): 268. Tran borrows the term 'singularity' from Lucien Karpik, *Valuing the Unique: The Economics of Singularities*, trans. Nora Scott (Princeton, 2010).

[6] On *terroir* see Heather Paxson, 'Locating Value in Artisan Cheese: Reverse Engineering *Terroir* for New-World Landscapes', *American Anthropologist* 112, no. 3 (September 2010): 444. As Kolleen M. Guy has argued, the development of a sense of *terroir* in nineteenth-century France was in response to a nation that was increasingly urban and industrial. *Terroir* reflected the persistence of a

sense of *terroir*—in centralized, state-owned factories that processed grapes from widely disparate vineyards (see Figure 6.1).[7]

There were other cultural deficits that hampered Soviet participation in international tasting competitions. In Western Europe and North America, the production and consumption of fine wine was cloaked in an elitist culture of wealth and connoisseurship. As Jarrett Rudy has argued about cigars, connoisseurs understand that consumption is organized hierarchically in ways that do not always correspond to price. Their knowledge about the stratification of taste distances them 'from the poor and nouveaux riches and... differentiate[s] the "civilized" from the "uncivilized" '.[8] The Soviet Union had always found ways to justify the existence of luxury and inequality at home, in part through the concept of *kul'turnost'*, which helped lend a socialist imprimatur to desires and practices previously seen as bourgeois.[9] Yet the Soviet Union had never tried to measure itself against foreign competitors in a realm so closely associated with elite pretentiousness. It had never sought to compete on a playing field so sharply tilted in its disfavour. This was prudent. Caviar and fur aside, the Soviet Union produced little that wealthy foreign consumers desired as markers of sophistication and taste, in the way that Italian fashion, Swiss watches, and French wines were a common currency among wealthy people around the world. Nor did the Soviet Union necessarily understand the world of elite connoisseurs, whose approval it sought, or even what it meant to be a connoisseur. In the early 1970s, one Moldovan winery disseminated promotional literature citing Roswell Garst's opinion that Soviet wines were the best in the world. A corn farmer and agronomist in Coon Rapids, Iowa, Garst became famous for hosting Khrushchev during his 1959 visit to the United States.[10] What Garst knew about wine, in particular, besides living in a country where wine connoisseurs were not so rare, was not elaborated. Similar encomiums from foreign visitors could be found in many other Soviet wineries. Wine tastings thus stood as a highly unusual interface between the Soviet Union and the outside world. By presenting wine for review, Soviet

'natural' France amid these changes. See Kolleen M. Guy, *When Champagne Became French: Wine and the Making of a National Identity* (Baltimore, 2003), 41–4.

[7] On Russian and Soviet *terroir*, see A. Volzhenikov, *Sovremennoe polozhenie vinodel'cheskogo khoziaistva na IuBK* (Simferopol, 1901), 1–4; Adam Walker and Paul Manning, 'Georgian Wine: The Transformation of Socialist Quantity into Postsocialist Quality', in *Wine and Culture: Vineyard to Glass*, ed. Rachel E. Black and Robert C. Ulin (London, 2013), 205; Paul Manning, *The Semiotics of Drink and Drinking* (London, 2012), 22–4.

[8] Jarrett Rudy, *Freedom to Smoke: Tobacco Consumption and Identity* (Montreal, 2005), 47. My thanks to Tricia Starks for referring me to the literature on tobacco connoisseurship.

[9] Sheila Fitzpatrick, *The Cultural Front: Power and Culture in Revolutionary Russia* (Ithaca, 1992), 218. On luxury in the Soviet Union, see Jukka Gronow, *Caviar with Champagne: Common Luxury and the Ideals of the Good Life in Stalin's Russia* (Oxford, 2003).

[10] On Garst, see Aaron Hale-Dorrell, 'The Soviet Union, the United States, and Industrial Agriculture', *Journal of World History* 26, no. 2 (June 2015): 295–324.

Figure 6.1. Soviet-era wine factory in Kahketi, 2013. Photograph by author.

vintners and officials invited judgment from foreign cultures of connoisseurship and sought critical approbation from persons whose values diverged sharply from their own.

This chapter traces the Soviet wine industry's opening to the outside world in the decades following Stalin's death. It shows that initial forays beyond Soviet borders were deeply practical—they involved patents, copyrights, scientific exchange, and even commerce, albeit of a highly limited sort. Yet they drew Soviet vintners and vinicultural scientists, particularly at the most prestigious wineries in Moscow, Crimea, and the Caucasus, into the culture of connoisseurship that surrounded the production and consumption of fine wine in the West. They led ultimately to an extraordinary encounter between Soviet vintners, industry officials, and scientists, on the one hand, and a prominent American connoisseur, on the other, who in the early 1970s sampled hundreds of Soviet wines as tourist, competition judge, and leader of a corporate delegation investigating the possibility of exporting Soviet wines to the United States. Their interaction suggests an opportunity in the early 1970s for Soviet vintners to reclaim some of the international renown that their tsarist counterparts had achieved nearly a century earlier. Similar disruptions, after all, were then underway in California, which was challenging long-standing hierarchies in the world of wine, as well as in South America and Australia. That this did not happen in the case of the Soviet Union is no surprise. The reason it did not happen was an influential connoisseur's overwhelmingly negative and often sarcastic appraisal of the taste of Soviet wine. Why and how that negative appraisal came about sheds light on the peculiarities of the Soviet economy, the limits of cross-cultural communication, the 'loss of confidence' that beset even loyal Soviet elites during the final socialist decades, and the way that perceptions of quality, taste, and place were intertwined and mutually reinforcing.[11] This chapter, in short, seeks to describe how Soviet wine tasted to someone who had basis for comparison.[12]

*   *   *   *   *

Soviet vintners participated in their first international tasting competition in 1955, when a handful of the Soviet Union's most prestigious wineries, mostly holdovers from the tsarist period, sent bottles to the First International Wine Competition in Ljubljana. Massandra won two gold and four silver medals; Magarach a silver medal, which was its first foreign commendation since a tasting in Turin in 1911. Industry officials deemed the results promising enough that they sent bottles again to Yugoslavia in 1957 and 1958, and to Hungary in 1958 and 1960 for review. What followed was a sort of golden age for Soviet vintners with a competitive streak: they participated in competitions in Yugoslavia in 1964;

---

[11] On the 'loss of confidence', see Stephen Kotkin, *Armageddon Averted: The Soviet Collapse, 1970–2000* (Oxford, 2001), 28. On the linkages between the perceived quality of food and place it originates, see Anne Meneley, 'Extra Virgin Olive Oil and Slow Food', *Anthropologica* 46, no. 2 (2004): 165–76.

[12] While food has long concerned scholars of Russian history and literature, historical studies of the taste of food and drink in Russia and the Soviet Union are comparatively rare and recent. See, for example, Alison K. Smith, 'Fermentation, Taste, and Identity', in *Russian History through the Senses: From 1700 to the Present*, ed. Matthew P. Romaniello and Tricia Starks (London, 2016), 45–66; Aaron B. Retish, 'The Taste of *Kumyshka* and the Debate over Udmurt Culture', in Romaniello and Starks, *Russian History*, 141–64.

Hungary in 1964, 1966, 1969, and 1972; Czechoslovakia in 1963, 1967, 1969; Bulgaria in 1966 and 1972; Romania in 1968; and East Germany in 1964, 1965, 1967, 1968, and 1970. In 1958, Soviet vintners crossed the ideological frontier and entered a competition at the Brussels World Fair. In time, Soviet vintners ceased being mere contestants in competition, and became judges and officers in the international organizations that supervised them. In 1965 and 1970, the socialist world's wine industries converged on Tbilisi and Yalta for the First and Second International Wine and Cognac Competitions.[13]

Tasting competitions were the public manifestation of an industry that was increasingly linked with its counterparts abroad, particularly in Eastern Europe, but also in France, Italy, West Germany, and the United States. (Soviet hostility to Franco precluded the establishment of similar ties with Spain—also a vinicultural superpower—until after 1977, when formal diplomatic relations opened.) Foreign ties were useful. Over the course of the 1960s, for instance, the wine industry's demand for glass bottles increased by 25 per cent, which produced a deficit of 10 million bottles per year by 1970, despite elaborate recycling schemes. Similar to modern bottling equipment that had to be purchased in France, because Soviet industry did not or was not able to produce anything similar, the bottle deficit was mitigated by imports from Eastern Europe. Likewise, in 1974 the Magarach Institute received permission to purchase from an American corporation an automated rotor machine that had the ability to sort grapes by colour.[14] Building upon technological and expertise exchanges that had existed since the late 1950s, Soviet wine authorities announced an agreement in 1975 providing ten years of 'scientific and technological cooperation' with Italy, which allowed Soviet vintners access to Italian equipment. Similar agreements were concluded the year before with Bulgaria, Romania, and Yugoslavia to provide Soviet growers with grafted (phylloxera-resistant) vines, another item in short supply. To be sure, there were constant reminders in these exchanges that the Soviet Union was not an international trade powerhouse. In 1983, plans to import 600,000 decalitres of grape must from Hungary were put on hold after it became clear that Uzhhorod, on the

[13] On the competition results, see S. M. Mikhailov, Z. I. Levchenko, and S. N. Sukhanova, *Solnechnaia 'Massandra'* (Simferopol, 1975), 137; G. G. Valuiko, *Magarach: liudi, sud'by, vina* (2nd edn, Yalta, 1998). A list of Magarach's foreign and domestic commendations can be found in Valuiko's first appendix, 'Nagrady, prisuzhdennye "Magarachu" na vystavkakh i konkursakh s 1869 po 2003 gody'; and in the following articles in *Vinodelie i vinogradarstvo SSSR*: V. P. Batrachenko and A. M. Safarian, 'Mezhdunarodnyi konkurs vin v Vengrii', *Vinodelie i vinogradarstvo SSSR* 3 (1970): 61–3; S. A. Gaspar'ian, 'Konkurs v Chekhoslovakii', *Vinodelie i vinogradarstvo SSSR* 4 (1970): 58–9; G. G. Valuiko, 'Vina, predstavlennye na II Mezhdunarodnyi konkurs vin i kon'iakov', *Vinodelie i vinogradarstvo SSSR* 2 (1971): 55–8 and 3 (1971): 55–7. On Soviet involvement in international vinicultural organizations, see Z. N. Kishkovskii, 'V Mezhdunarodnoi organizatsii vinogradarstva i vinodeliia', *Vinodelie i vinogradarstvo SSSR* 1 (1970): 59–61.

[14] RGAE, f. 468, o. 1, d. 443, l. 8 (France); d. 2412, l. 3 (bottle deficit); d. 3510, l. 69 (American corporation); and TsDAVO Ukraïny, f. 5201, o. 1, d. 1140, l. 73 (Hungary).

Soviet side of the border crossing with Hungary in south-western Ukraine, lacked the transportation infrastructure necessary to receive the must.[15]

Reliance on foreign bottling equipment and rotor machines underscored the technology gap that continued to plague Soviet winemaking. Yet it also indicated the industry's willingness to play by the rules of capitalism: foreign patents were inviolable. In fact, the Magarach Institute encouraged its winemakers and engineers to be as aggressive as possible in patenting its own technologies, in order to raise the profile of the institute abroad. The same was true at the Moldovan Scientific-Research Institute for Food Production, whose scientists and engineers registered ten international patents and received three copyright certificates in 1965. Among their inventions was a device that allowed for the 'uninterrupted' distillation of wine for cognac production, and a means of deriving food colouring for use in wine production. The Magarach Institute took out subscriptions for the patent bulletins of the United States, France, West Germany, Japan, and Great Britain so it could follow advances in winemaking technologies.[16]

Similar to their predecessors in the 1920s, industry officials hoped that investments in foreign equipment and vines would turn the Soviet Union into an export powerhouse. In 1970, the Magarach Institute estimated that only 0.06 per cent of total Soviet champagne, wine, and cognac production was exported abroad, although how it arrived at this figure is unclear. The market for imported wine in the Soviet Union was similarly tiny, between 1.5 to 1.7 per cent of all sales, the vast majority of which came from friendly countries such as Bulgaria and Algeria. In the view of Magarach scholars, the latter reflected the fact that 'per capita demand [for wine] in the USSR is significantly lower than in countries with advanced wine industries'.[17] Yet in the absence of significant domestic demand there were undeniable opportunities for exporting wine abroad in the 1970s and 1980s, particularly for an industry that had become one of the world's largest in the terms of volume of production. The Main Administration for Viniculture and Winemaking in Ukraine, for instance, planned to export 73,500 decalitres of wine (roughly a million bottles) in 1979, a 5 per cent increase from 1976 export levels. Recipients included friendly socialist countries such as East Germany, Czechoslovakia, Poland, Cuba, and Mongolia, but also Japan, which imported wine from Massandra. Ukrainian exports of an acid used in winemaking (likely tartaric) were also projected to double between 1976 and 1979, from 40 to 80 tonnes.[18] Yet the industry's export stallion was quickly becoming Soviet Champagne, whose popularity at

---

[15] TsDAVO Ukraïny, f. 5201, o. 1, d. 213, l. 65 (grafted vines); d. 332, l. 18 (Italy). On the winemaking exchanges of the late 1950s, see Jeremy Smith, 'Learning from the French: The Modernization of Soviet Winemaking, 1956–61', in *Reassessing Cold War Europe*, ed. Sari Autio-Sarasmo and Katalin Miklóssy (London and New York, 2011), 83–99.

[16] RGAE, f. 468, o. 1, d. 3510, l. 145 (Magarach); d. 106, l. 9 (Moldova).

[17] RGAE, f. 468, o. 1, d. 2807, l. 71.

[18] TsDAVO Ukraïny, f. 5201, o. 1, d. 779, l. 138 (wine and acid export levels); d. 1000, l. 59 (Japan).

home, success in international tasting competitions, and comparatively low prices generated demand in West Germany, Austria, Holland, Switzerland, and Italy. By the early 1980s, Ukrainian authorities had devised a two-tiered production system, where champagne bound for export came from the Novyi svet facility in Sudak and a factory in Artemovsk in eastern Ukraine. It was produced according to the *méthode traditionnelle*, in which sugar and yeast were added to finished wine prior to a second bottling to produce effervescence. Factories in Odessa and Kharkov made champagne for the Soviet marketplace according to Anton Frolov-Bagreev's mechanized and less costly 'continuous method'. In 1979, Ukraine exported 4.9 million bottles of Soviet Champagne, up nearly 50 per cent since 1976. By 1981, nearly 75 per cent of all Soviet Champagne manufactured in Ukraine was exported abroad.[19]

The chief upshot of tasting competitions and growing exports was a level of interaction with the foreign vinicultural community that was unimaginable before Stalin's death. By the mid-1960s, establishments such as the Magarach Institute were hosting numerous foreign delegations each year—fourteen in 1965, including groups from Finland, Japan, and Afghanistan; eleven in 1967, all from friendly countries in Eastern Europe; and twenty-three in 1969, from France, Austria, Lebanon, the United States, and Turkey, among other places.[20] By the 1970s, foreign visitors—who had once been so novel that their presence was invariably among the highlights in the institute's annual reports to the Ministry of Food Production in Moscow—were so frequent an occurrence and copious in number that they hardly merited an acknowledgement. Over time, opportunities for Soviet winemakers and vinicultural scientists to travel abroad widened as well, mostly to the people's democracies in Eastern Europe, where Soviet vintners advised and were advised under the auspices of Council for Mutual Economic Assistance (Comecon), but sometimes beyond the ideological frontier to Western Europe and North America. In 1966, Magarach sent scholars to Bulgaria, Warsaw, and Italy. In 1969, Pavel Golodriga represented the Soviet Union at the General Assembly of the International Organization of Vine and Wine in Paris. In 1972, Golodriga travelled to Budapest, where he served as a judge at the First All-World Wine Competition.[21] In 1974, the Main Administration for Viniculture and Winemaking in Ukraine sent employees on a two-week trip to the United States, where they familiarized themselves with the latest in American vineyard equipment, and to the Fourteenth Congress of Viniculture and Winemaking in Italy. By the early 1980s, as the Soviet Union sought to develop export markets for viniculture, Soviet winemakers often accompanied samples of their wines abroad, so

---

[19]   TsDAVO Ukraïny, f. 5201, o. 1, d. 1000, l. 59 (export destinations and 1981 figures); d. 1140, l. 63 (tiered production); d. 779, l. 138 (1976 and 1979 export figures).

[20]   RGAE, f. 468, o. 1, d. 104, l. 26 (1965); d. 829, l. 30 (1967); d. 1639, ll. 39–41 (1969).

[21]   RGAE, f. 468, o. 1, d. 444, l. 35 (1966); d. 1639, l. 28 (Golodriga in 1969); d. 2807, l. 40 (Golodriga in 1972).

they could speak knowledgably about them to wholesale buyers.[22] After Soviet vintners and vinicultural scientists returned home, they often wrote accounts of what they saw and learned for the industry's principal journal, *Vinodelie i vinogradarstvo SSSR* (Winemaking and Viniculture USSR). For Soviet vintners who regularly wined and dined with foreign visitors, and who occasionally travelled abroad, proof of their membership in a community of expertise and taste that transcended Soviet borders was not hard to find.[23]

In a post-Soviet memoir about his career at the Magarach Institute, German Valuiko noted that he visited 'practically all' of the Comecon countries in the course of his work, 'many several times'. Yet there were clear limits on Valuiko's foreign travel. Contrary to the experience of his Magarach colleague Pavel Golodriga, for instance, Valuiko was denied permission by the Crimean oblast party committee to travel to France and Yugoslavia. Even many years later, after Soviet power had collapsed, the blow hurt. 'Trips to advanced winemaking countries were good for synthesizing experience', Valuiko wrote. 'The absence of such trips lessened scholarly potential.' Denied a first-hand encounter with French winemaking, Valuiko came to understand the Comecon countries as technological middle grounds, where Soviet winemakers might see and use equipment manufactured in 'advanced capitalist countries'. But he also thought that the Soviet wine industry shared more than it received in its exchanges with Bulgaria, Romania, Hungary, Czechoslovakia, and 'especially Poland'. Valuiko's claim was almost certainly true in regard to Poland, which lost its vinicultural territories around Lviv in the annexations of 1945 and had only a small domestic wine industry. By emphasizing Soviet generosity with Bulgaria, Romania, and Hungary, however, Valuiko turned on its head a hierarchy of status in the socialist wine world that was reaffirmed many times over by the results of tasting competitions.[24]

Perhaps the most important upshot of the growing ease of travel across the Soviet border was the formation of collaborative professional relationships, correspondences, and friendships with winemakers and vinicultural scientists abroad. Valuiko, for instance, counted Dimitar Tsakov, the director of a winemaking institute in Sofia, and Ján Farkaš, a vinicultural scientist in Bratislava, among his friends and most respected colleagues. Farkaš helped Valuiko in experiments involving the use of 5-nitrofurylacrylic acid (5-NFA) as a wine preservative. Despite initial tests that suggested it was less noxious than sulphur dioxide, a common cause of flawed wine, Farkaš and Valuiko's experiments were curtailed when the Czechoslovakian and Soviet Ministries of Health banned 5-NFA out of

---

[22] TsDAVO Ukraïny, f. 5201, o. 1, d. 213, l. 51 (Italy and US); d. 1140 (wholesale tastings).

[23] See, for instance, the following articles in *Vinodelie i vinogradarstvo SSSR*: K. S. Pogosian and S. Ivano, 'Vinogradarstvo i vinodelie Iaponii', *Vinodelie i vinogradarstvo SSSR* 8 (1970): 30–33; A. Trofimchenko and K. Gvelesiani, 'Vinodelie i vinogradarstvo Respubliki Kipr', *Vinodelie i vinogradarstvo SSSR* (1971): 58–61.

[24] Valuiko, *Magarach*, no pag., in the chapter titled 'Sviaz' s zarubezhnymi uchenymi'.

fear that it was a carcinogen. Valuiko wrote in retrospect that the ministries had been successfully baited with health concerns by a prominent West German manufacturer of sorbic acid, a competing food preservative.

Among the foreigners who encountered the Soviet wine industry in the 1960s and 1970s was Maynard Amerine, the sole American on the eighteen-member tasting jury in Budapest in 1972. From his home in affluent St Helena, in California's Napa Valley, Amerine lived the life of a bon vivant and gourmand. Born in San Jose in 1911 and raised in modest circumstances on a fruit farm in the San Joaquin Valley, Amerine travelled widely through the world's wine regions in the 1960s and 1970s, collecting rare books on winemaking and noting in his journals the quality of food and drink he consumed on carefully regimented scales. Amerine often began his journeys with Mai-Tai fuelled bon-voyage parties, always among wealthy friends, at San Francisco's famous Polynesian bar, Trader Vic's. Amerine could complain about the absurdity of a twelve-dollar taxi fare to San Francisco Airport, 'which is surely the most expensive taxi drive in the world—and the driver looks like a low-paid peon'. Yet he did not hesitate to rearrange his travel itineraries to take in a new brasserie in Paris, or an up-and-coming winery in Mendoza. Amerine was not above occasional snobbery, scoffing in his journal at a TWA steward who 'questioned whether there *was* [such a thing as] a white Burgundy', after being asked to fetch a bottle of Meursault. But Amerine also had the ability to poke fun at himself, such as when he disparaged a fine Armenian cognac that he had unwittingly diluted with pungent mineral rather than neutral distilled water. It was a 'faux pas', he wrote dryly in his journal. A long-time member of the exclusive Bohemian Club in San Francisco, which hosted the annual Bohemian Grove conclave of politicians and industrial moguls in nearby Sonoma County, Amerine was on friendly terms with many of the founding figures of California's wine industry: Robert Mondavi; Ernest Gallo, who was a high school classmate and who reputedly helped bankroll Amerine's lavish travel itineraries; and André Tchelistcheff, the White Russian émigré who was chief vintner at Beaulieu Vineyards and the so-called father of Napa Valley Cabernet Sauvignon. Often seen in the company of his long-time companion and 'personal assistant' William Simms, Amerine's homosexuality was widely known yet rarely spoken about in an industry where conservative politics were predominant. Nor did it appear to affect his career in the military, where Amerine served for several decades after the Second World War as a reserve officer in the US Army Chemical Corps, eventually rising to a rank—full colonel—that required a top-secret security clearance.[25]

---

[25] Maynard A. Amerine Papers, Special Collections, UC Davis Library [hereafter UCD, Amerine Papers], box 12, folder 14, 'To Russia and Back, 1973', 1, 15; Molly O'Neill, 'Maynard Amerine, 87, California Wine Expert', *New York Times*, 13 March 1998. I am indebted to Axel Borg for much of the information I have collected on Amerine. When I first encountered the Amerine Papers in fall 2014, they were in the process of being inventoried and were missing many box and folder numbers. The

Amerine was also much more than a connoisseur of wine. As a professor in the agricultural school at the University of California, Davis, and the author of sixteen scholarly books and hundreds of articles, Amerine was one of the most influential vinicultural and oenological scientists of the twentieth century. He bore outsized responsibility both for the development of the California wine industry along European lines during the latter half of the twentieth century, and for turning Davis into a destination, like the University of Bordeaux, for aspiring vintners and growers from around the world. With scholarly interests that ranged from soil chemistry to the technologies of vermouth production, Amerine was most famous beyond the university for the Davis Scoring System (1959), which sought to systematize wine tasting by awarding points according to clearly defined criteria: appearance, colour, aroma and bouquet, volatile acidity, total acidity, sweetness, body, flavour, astringency, and general quality. Building on the work of the nineteenth-century French biologist, A. P. de Candolle, Amerine also helped devise the now standard method of heat summation (the seasonal sum of daily mean temperatures above 10 degrees Celsius) for evaluating climatic vinicultural potential. Later in his career, Amerine worked with a mathematician to develop methods for quantifying sensory perception. Because he often travelled with a basic inventory of scientific devices, Amerine (see Figure 6.2) had the unusual ability to determine both the quality of a wine—the prerogative of the connoisseur—and where, specifically, the winemaker had failed—in short, the skill of the scientist.

In 1962, 1971, and 1973, Amerine travelled through the Soviet Union's Black Sea wine belt—Moldova, southern Ukraine, Crimea, the Don, the northern Caucasus, Georgia, and Armenia—visiting wineries and tasting rooms, and meeting with growers, vintners, and scientists, some of whom—such as Valuiko and Golodriga—became friends and correspondents. Amerine recorded his impressions in lengthy handwritten journals, which he partly encoded lest they raise suspicion upon departure (an unfounded fear, as it turned out), and which he typed upon his return. Amerine also kept lengthy tasting notes, often on the *degustatsionnye listki* that his Soviet hosts provided. After sampling hundreds of wines, Amerine left the Soviet Union unimpressed. While in Tbilisi midway through his 1971 trip, he became so weary of local wines that he opened a bottle of Gallo Hearty Burgundy (which, paradoxically, was not a Burgundy, since it was blended from grapes that were not characteristic of the region, Petite Syrah, Zinfandel, and Carignan) that his travel companion, Ernest Gallo, carried as a gift for local vintners and officials. Before the 'Judgment of Paris' in 1976, when wines from Napa Valley's Stag's Leap and Château Montelena won top honours against several famous French producers, Hearty Burgundy was California's most famous wine, even gracing the cover of *Time* magazine in 1972. The bottle that Amerine

current citations, which I have updated to reflect the completion of the inventory, are accurate to the best of my knowledge.

Figure 6.2. Maynard Amerine, as photographed by Ansel Adams, at the University of California Experimental Vineyard, Oakville Station, Napa Valley, ca. 1964–1967. This photograph was part of the Fiat Lux project in commemoration of the University of California's centenary. Maynard A. Amerine Papers D-060, Special Collections, UC Davis Library.

opened in Tbilisi earned a '+' in his journal, and a note that 'it was certainly better than any Russian red we had'. Likewise, when he left the Soviet Union ten days later on a flight to Amsterdam, Amerine ordered a '*cold dry* double martini', which he deemed 'the most delicious drink of the trip so far'.[26]

Amerine was by no means the first Western intellectual to visit the Soviet Union on a fact-finding mission. Such trips were common in the 1920s and 1930s, as curiosity among Westerners about the 'great experiment' reached fever pitch. As Michael David-Fox has argued, these encounters with socialism in construction often challenged or reversed ideas of Western superiority. Doing so was the 'Holy Grail of Soviet cultural diplomacy', the primary reason why the Soviet Union opened its doors to outsiders during its first decades.[27] Yet Amerine may be the first foreign specialist who journeyed to the Soviet Union for explicitly epicurean reasons. He hoped to find great, undiscovered wine, which was the central preoccupation of all his journeys. Consequently, Amerine left for home with

[26] UCD, Amerine Papers, box 12, folder 3, 'To USSR, Holland, and Denmark', 35, 51. Emphasis is in the original.
[27] Michael David-Fox, *Showcasing the Great Experiment: Cultural Diplomacy and Western Visitors to the Soviet Union, 1921–41* (Oxford, 2012), 25. See also Michael David-Fox, 'The Fellow Travelers Revisited: The "Cultured West" through Soviet Eyes', *Journal of Modern History* 75, no. 2 (June 2003): 301.

hierarchies of status and accomplishment that were reaffirmed rather than challenged. The Soviet Union, in Amerine's judgment, was a bleak, unpromising landscape for wine. Its failings had less to do with flawed *terroir*, in his view, than with the comparative poverty and the peculiar incentives of socialism.

Here the story would surely have ended without note, if not for the fact that Amerine was a remarkably ungracious guest. He never hesitated to tell his hosts what he really thought about Soviet wine. He never tempered his criticism with an acknowledgement that his palate was subjective, a central contention from Kant to Lévi-Strauss in the scholarship on taste.[28] To the contrary, Amerine stood, perhaps unwittingly, as proof of Bourdieu's contention that taste corresponds with social position.[29] For their part, Soviet vintners and officials never challenged Amerine's sense of taste. They never argued that winemaking along the Black Sea had its own illustrious history, that Georgian and Crimean wines were singularities in a world where copying the French was so common that a California corporation made millions by selling a mislabelled concoction called Hearty Burgundy. To the contrary, Amerine's hosts embraced him as the very embodiment of expertise, and silently suffered his criticism. 'When their pride is hurt they react strongly (mainly by clamming up)', Amerine wrote in his 1973 journal, soon after telling his hosts that Soviet wines were so flawed as to be unsellable to consumers with knowledge and choice.[30]

*   *   *   *   *

Amerine first encountered the world of Soviet wine in 1959, when the experimental vineyard at Davis was included on the itinerary of a Soviet agricultural delegation. Among the dignitaries on that trip was Grigorii Kabluchko, director of the Moldovan Institute for Research on Horticulture, Viniculture, and Winemaking. Amerine organized for Kabluchko a tasting of wines from vineyards in the Napa and San Joaquin (Central) Valleys. Amerine then travelled to the Soviet Union for the first time in 1962, in part for the Tenth International Wine Congress, which opened in grand fashion at the grape and wine pavilion at the Exhibition of Achievements of the National Economy (VDNKh) in Moscow, and then moved on to Tbilisi for scientific discussions. Amerine remained in the Soviet Union for nearly a month, from 7 September to 4 October, visiting production facilities, vinicultural research institutes, and ampelographic stations in Moscow, Georgia, Crimea, Sochi, and Central Asia. The trip was part of an elaborate eight-month, round-the-world sabbatical that took Amerine first to Washington

---

[28]   For a survey of this literature, see Carolyn Korsmeyer, *Making Sense of Taste: Food and Philosophy* (Ithaca, 1999); Carolyn Korsmeyer, ed., *The Taste Culture Reader: Experiencing Food and Drink* (Oxford, 2005).

[29]   Pierre Bourdieu, *Distinction: A Social Critique of the Judgment of Taste*, trans. Richard Nice (Cambridge, MA, 1984).

[30]   UCD, Amerine Papers, box 12, folder 14, 'To Russia and Back, 1973', 27.

DC, where he had army obligations, and then to France, Spain, Portugal, Germany, Belgium (for the International Horticultural Congress), the Soviet Union, India, Thailand, and Japan. 'To escape administration, teaching, public relations, writing books, etc., was (and as I write is) the *raison d'être* of my *vacances de 1962* in Europe', Amerine wrote at the beginning of his travel diary.[31]

Amerine initially hoped to drive across Europe to Moscow and Georgia, as the Soviet Union had recently advertised the possibility of such excursions. He even made inquiries with the Mercedes-Benz and Volkswagen representatives in San Francisco about the cost of taking delivery of a new car in Frankfurt. When it became clear that the logistics of such a trip were impossible—in large part because the Soviet Union restricted the number of automobile corridors that were open to foreigners—Amerine arranged to travel by airplane, train, and ferry (from Sochi to Yalta). Amerine's dashed plans were the first in a litany of problems he encountered with Intourist: phantom hotel reservations, flights that were daily in principle but semi-daily in fact, missing airport transfers, and resistance to any activity that was not part of the original plan, such as a visit to a winery in Samarkand. When Amerine arrived in Leningrad on a connecting Aeroflot flight from Moscow, after a long day of travel from Brussels, he found that Intourist had no record he was supposed to be in the Soviet Union. 'Up late to the battle of Intourist', he wrote at the beginning of his diary entry for 28 September, after trying unsuccessfully to get permission to visit Kiev.[32]

Despite the difficulties with Intourist, Amerine found much that was admirable in the Soviet Union: the prominence of high culture in the public sphere, the treasures of the Hermitage ('full marks', he judged the rooms containing works by Matisse and Picasso), an ampelographic preserve in the hills above Yalta, and the Central Asian sky at sunset. Amerine was aware, of course, that his translator's job was to present the Soviet Union in the best light possible, but Amerine was not unwilling to be persuaded. He judged his translator's story about the 1,000 serfs who died of mercury poisoning while gilding the dome of St Isaac's Cathedral in St Petersburg 'a little anti-church propaganda, justified'. Amerine was also painfully aware that at least some Soviet propaganda about America was correct, such as *Izvestiia's* reporting on James Meredith, the first African-American student to enrol at the University of Mississippi. Upon returning to Moscow to work at the Lenin Library, after nearly three weeks in Georgia and Crimea, Amerine encountered an African delegation in the Hotel Ukraine.

How can they fail to be impressed with a 29-story hotel which probably costs them little?...What are we doing to counterbalance this? What can we do with the South hanging like a millstone around our necks?'[33]

---

[31] UCD, Amerine Papers, box 11, folder 19, 'The Escape of 1962', 1.
[32] UCD, Amerine Papers, box 11, folder 20, '1962 sabbatical: original 1st copy of typed notes', 26.
[33] UCD, Amerine Papers, box 11, folder 20, '1962 sabbatical: original 1st copy of typed notes', 2, 30, 40.

Yet Amerine's views of the Soviet Union were by no means uncritical. He had a preview of the strictures that his Soviet counterparts faced while at the horticultural congress in Brussels. There Amerine listened to a paper that a Soviet delegate read in English: 'The paper gave little or no data—simply said that by applying the principle of Mitchurin winter hardiness was obtained. Naturally no questions.' Mitchurin was Ivan Michurin, a respected horticulturalist whom Trofim Lysenko claimed to follow. Lysenko curried favour with Stalin and Khrushchev by insisting on the inheritability of acquired characteristics, a view that was supposedly more consonant with the immutable laws of Marxism-Leninism than the new science of genetics. After returning to California, Amerine noted in speeches to various civic and professional groups that the residue of Lysenkoism remained a powerful impediment to the development of Soviet vinicultural science.[34] Amerine also recorded several moments in his diary when he encountered flawed science, or when he felt his Soviet counterparts were less than truthful with him: the denial of the presence of vineyard disease when Amerine could plainly see the tell-tale signs of the leafroll virus; an assertion that Soviet wines high in sugar were stable because of the preservative effect of sugar, when they showed the taint of Lactobacillus, which converts sugar to lactic acid; the reassurance that an Azerbaijani cognac, which tasted 'hot' to Amerine, meaning its alcohol burned the palate, had only 45 per cent alcohol by volume, the normal amount, when in fact its label indicated it had 57 per cent. This was Soviet vinicultural science at its worst: image in the presence of a foreigner mattered more than truthful exchange.[35]

Nonetheless, Amerine met many scientists, winemakers, and agronomists whom he respected, who became friends and collaborators, and who helped him navigate his never-ending problems with Intourist: Mikhail Gerasimov, the chief vintner in the Main Administration for Winemaking; Aleksandr Egorov, who was then eighty-eight and the chief winemaker-engineer at Massandra; Tateos Katar'ian, the director of the Magarach Institute; Nikolai Okhremenko, the deputy scientific director of the Magarach Institute; Pavel Golodriga; and Mikhail Kaptsinel', an agronomist and official in the Ministry of Agriculture who spoke polished English, which was the by-product of six months spent at the University of California's Citrus Experiment Station in Riverside in 1947. Amerine often recorded the mailing addresses of his new friends in his journal. He left reminders for himself and for his secretary, who typed his diary upon his return to Davis, to send off-prints of scholarly articles and books, and to subscribe to the journal *Vinogradarstvo i sadovodstvo Kryma* (Crimean Viniculture and Horticulture).

---

[34] UCD, Amerine Papers, box 11, folder 19, 'The Escape of 1962', 54; box 35, folder 78, 'Vineyards and Wineries in the S.S.S.R.', speech to San Joaquin Aggie Alumni, Stockton, 21 February 1963, 2; and box 35, folder 81, 'Russian Vineyards and Wineries', speech to the Wine Institute, Fresno, 15 March 1963, 1.

[35] UCD, Amerine Papers, box 11, folder 20, '1962 sabbatical: original 1st copy of typed notes', 19, 25, 29.

After visiting a winery in Bukhara, Amerine wrote about the female vintner: 'We parted good friends, I hope.'[36]

Over the course of four weeks in the Soviet Union, Amerine developed a largely negative view of Soviet epicurean culture that subsequent trips failed to dislodge. At the heart of his emerging critique, which would not be fully formed until subsequent trips in 1971 and 1973, was Amerine's sense that taste was an afterthought and the customer unimportant. Amerine chafed against the slow service of Soviet restaurants, even losing his temper in Leningrad after waiting forty-five minutes for a cup of tea: 'Bad. Must not do', he chastised himself in his diary after returning to his hotel room. In Yalta, he managed to get a waitress to concede that the breakfast service was 'ploho' (*plokho*; bad). While in Tashkent, Amerine witnessed the 'terrible power of Russian waitresses', who moved two high-ranking military officers from one table to another in the middle of their meal. Bad restaurant service was usually the harbinger of bad food. Upon arriving at the Hotel Astoria in Leningrad, Amerine looked forward to dinner after the predictably poor fare on Aeroflot.

> *Quelle surprise!* It was, if possible, unbelievably bad (horrible): chicken noodle soup—oily and cold, beef stragoff (?) and potatoes (fried)—cold and stringy, and ice cream—o.k. The Shuguli [sic] beer cloudy and a lactic odor. Finally at midnight to bed. Dinner took two + hours because of the fantastically slow service.

Two days later, lunch at the Astoria—red caviar and sturgeon in the 'Russian style'—was better, but the accompanying white wine was of such poor quality that Amerine deemed it 'hard to get worse'. Even at the official receptions and site visits in Moscow that were linked with the wine congress, good wines were hard to find. Before departing for Tbilisi, international delegates were offered eight wines at a reception hosted by the minister of agriculture in the Metropol Hotel. Amerine's tasting notes were scathing: 'moldy apples, undrinkable', 'poor', 'no character except high SO_2', 'filter taste', 'bacteria?' Moreover, nearly every glass and bottle of wine that Amerine purchased on his own—in restaurants and stores—was flawed to the point of being undrinkable. One restaurant in Tbilisi served him a bottle of wine that had turned into vinegar.[37]

There were, of course, exceptions to the poor offerings. In general, the food and wine got better as Amerine travelled south, even if the restaurant service did not. He liked the salted cheeses and piquant stews of Georgia, and the vaguely Turkish fare, with its unusually spiced meats, in Central Asia. Lunch after the opening session of the wine congress in Tbilisi was accompanied by a 'fair' white wine,

---

[36] UCD, Amerine Papers, box 11, folder 20, '1962 sabbatical: original 1st copy of typed notes', 34.
[37] UCD, Amerine Papers, box 11, folder 20, '1962 sabbatical: original 1st copy of typed notes', 1, 3, 5, 7.

which made it one of the best wines of the trip so far. Even better was the afternoon tasting—sixteen wines, 'some quite good', Amerine wrote. Amerine was also impressed by wines served at the Georgian Agricultural Institute and the Samtrest Wine Factory in Tbilisi, and at the Magarach Institute in Yalta. At the Livadiia *sovkhoz*, a former crown estate near Yalta, the wines were a mixed lot, but the grapes that were served as dessert were excellent. A visit to a cognac factory in Samarkand produced a surprise in a '5-star cognac, meaning five years [old]. Good taste—halfway between California and [a French] cognac.' Yet the Soviet Union produced far more bad wine than good wine, Amerine thought. Moreover, the bad wines were bad in similar ways. They were oxidized, meaning they had begun to turn brown because of harmful exposure to oxygen, and had lost the fresh fruit and herbaceous flavours of the grape and vine. They were 'mousy', a deeply pejorative term for wine marred by Lactobacillus, which imparts an odour similar to that of mouse urine. And they were overly 'tannic', which refers to the polyphenols in the grape skins and seeds that cause red wine to taste dry. These were not problems that stemmed from deficient soil or inadequate climate, but a lack of winemaker expertise and care. Tannins, for instance, could be reduced by shortening the period grapes ferment 'on the skins'.[38]

Amerine's 1962 travel diary is mostly free of the moral conjecture that characterized his 1973 account. He understood the poor quality of Soviet wine as mainly symptomatic of the false starts and missteps of a nascent industry. Upon returning to Davis, Amerine often spoke about Soviet viniculture and wine production in familiar Cold-War terms—America was 'ahead' in wine production and vinicultural research, with Davis representing the apex of the latter; the 'Russians' were working very hard to catch up. Yet there were also inklings that Amerine was beginning to think about the problem of taste as unique to socialism. In March 1963, Amerine concluded a speech to the board of directors of the Wine Institute in Fresno by noting that the Soviet Union was investing such immense sums of money in wine production, success was inevitable.

If you push enough keys, you will eventually type the word success. Whatever else may go wrong in the Soviet Union they can hardly fail to come up with a rational wine industry producing quality wines—something that no other nation, including our own, has today. Only the problem of 'what do you mean by quality in socialist state' is an unsolved problem.[39]

---

[38] UCD, Amerine Papers, box 11, folder 20, '1962 sabbatical: original 1st copy of typed notes', 8, 13, 19, 38.

[39] UCD, Amerine Papers, box 35, folder 80, 'Russian Vineyards and Wineries', speech to the Wine Institute, Fresno, 15 March 1963, 2.

Amerine returned to the Soviet Union for a second time in the summer of 1971, with Ernest Gallo and other friends. Lacking the credentials that came from being a delegate to the International Wine Congress, Amerine found that Intourist was even less accommodating than before, and unwilling to arrange visits to wineries and research institutes that it did not consider normal fare for foreign tourists:

> The usual answers: 'no one is in, the person you wish is away, Mr. _____ can't see you until tomorrow...No such phone number, the phone doesn't answer, the phone answers but when one replies they hang up...No, we haven't been able to contact the Minister of Agriculture. They will be out today and tomorrow and the next day.'

Despite the passage of nine years between visits, Amerine found the same bad food at the Hotel Astoria in Leningrad, the same neglectful restaurant service in Moscow, the same inspiring museums and performances that he had previously awarded 'full marks', and even the same furniture and décor in the Hotel Oreanda in Yalta. 'Still as in 1962', he wrote in his journal.[40]

Intourist hurdles aside, Amerine visited the Ministry of Agriculture in Moscow, the Tairov Institute in Odessa, the Magarach Institute and Massandra in Yalta, the Armenian Scientific-Research Institute for Viniculture in Yerevan, and the Scientific-Research Institute for Fruit Farming and Viniculture in Alma-Ata. At Magarach, he renewed friendships with Golodriga and Valuiko, whom he had seen earlier in the year in Budapest. He collected books and pamphlets for the vinicultural library at Davis. He travelled to new places: Kiev (a destination that Intourist had refused him in 1962), Baku, Novgorod, and even the far-flung Bratsk hydroelectric dam in eastern Siberia. He discovered that Soviet vinicultural scientists had become more worldly in the intervening years, as they were generally aware what their counterparts in the West were doing, including at the University of California, Davis. And most surprising, Amerine found better wine, even in stores and restaurants, where one could purchase very good bottles from Hungary, Romania, and elsewhere, and respectable domestic bottles. (One of the best wines of the trip was a Hungarian Traminer.) To be sure, Amerine recognized that Soviet progress in winemaking had been modest and wildly uneven since his last visit—whites were better than reds, which remained almost uniformly bad, and sweet wines, such as Riesling, Madeira, and sherry, were better than dry wines. But there was some prescience in Amerine's 1963 prediction: Soviet investment in viniculture was beginning to yield successes. Amerine's own feelings about the Soviet Union, however, were hardening. 'One forgives and forgets poor accommodations and meals. These are not critical, however,

---

[40] UCD, Amerine Papers, box 12, folder 3, 'To USSR, Holland and Denmark', 7, 23.

annoying. What one can't forget is the sameness of cuisine and service…it seems a loss of human freedom is involved.'[41]

Amerine's final trip to the Soviet Union, in the summer of 1973, was devoted entirely to tasting wine. He travelled at the behest of Donald Kendall, the chairman of Pepsico, which had invested in a bottling facility in Novorossiysk.[42] In 1974, Pepsico projected production in the Soviet Union of 40 million bottles of Pepsi and was searching for ways to repatriate its rouble-denominated profits. While meeting in Moscow in April 1973 with Vladimir Lein, the Minister of Food Production, Kendall proposed that Pepsico export Soviet wine to the United States. It was not a far-fetched idea. Soviet Champagne, which had long been present in stores and restaurants in Eastern Europe, was already being exported to Western Europe. The purpose of Amerine's follow-up trip in July and August was to determine which wines were suitable for the American marketplace. Amerine initially proposed to Kendall that the latter include bottles cellared for many decades in Yalta and Tbilisi. 'For the snobs a little sediment is a guarantee of authenticity', he wrote about these wines, suggesting that American consumers might see them as prestigious. Yet Soviet authorities offered for sale only current and future production.[43]

Pepsico's investment was part of a broader commercial engagement between American companies and the Soviet Union that grew out of Richard Nixon's visit to Moscow in May 1972, and the signing of a bilateral trade agreement in October. While the Soviet Union refused in 1975 to implement fully the agreement, citing the punitive terms of the Jackson-Vanik Amendment restricting American trade with countries that did not honour freedom of emigration, American exports to the Soviet Union grew steadily, from $1.2 billion in 1973 to $2.3 billion in 1976. Exports typically comprised agricultural items, but licensing agreements—similar to the sort that Pepsico negotiated—were an important sidelight. Kendall, of course, benefitted from Soviet knowledge that Pepsi, which had been served at the American National Exhibition in Moscow in 1959, was an iconic American product. Other American companies struck similar agreements. Philip Morris manufactured 'Apollo-Soyuz' cigarettes from Virginia-grown tobacco at a factory in Krasnodar. Bendix, an engineering and manufacturing firm, negotiated a deal to manufacture spark plugs in the Soviet Union. Pan American Airlines, one of the earliest entrants into the Soviet market in 1968, shared with Aeroflot a route between Moscow and New York. In the words of one observer, American corporate executives gained 'important psychic rewards from flying into Moscow and

---

[41] UCD, Amerine Papers, box 12, folder 3, 'To USSR, Holland and Denmark', 52–3.

[42] 40 million is the figure reported to Soviet authorities. See RGAE, f. 468, o. 1, d. 3511, ll. 54, 65.

[43] UCD, Amerine Papers, box 6, folder 41, correspondence between Amerine and Kendall, 23 April 1973, and correspondence between Kendall and Lein, 27 April 1973. Evidence of Soviet wines in Eastern Europe can be found in the menu collection at the Wende Museum of the Cold War, Culver City, California.

playing the role of head of state'. In all cases, they found Soviet counterparts keen to secure sources of hard currency. It was a desire that was increasingly common across the socialist world, where revenue from the sale of bottled Bulgarian jams and Polish vegetables in Western markets helped disguise lagging economic performance.[44]

From the moment of his arrival, Amerine worried there was a misunderstanding about the purpose of his trip. Had a deal with Pepsico already been finalized, as Amerine's hosts indicated? Or was it contingent on a positive evaluation of Soviet wines, as Amerine himself understood? Upon arrival, Amerine asked that his itinerary, which had been arranged by the Ministry of Food Production and Intourist, remain focused on tastings, to avoid the stilted atmosphere of official receptions and the hard science of vinicultural field stations. Pepsico's representative in Moscow explained

> what our objectives were, how we would like to start work early and to work weekends and hence get back to Moscow early. The Deputy Minister agreed, but subsequent events...proved that the message had not been heard.

Indeed, perhaps out of a sense of hospitality, Amerine's Soviet hosts arranged a trip that was animated primarily by official receptions and site visits, first upon arrival in Moscow, when Amerine was greeted by four men from the Ministries of Agriculture and Food Production; then the following morning, when Amerine's Soviet travel companions made 'flowery allusions to my past visits and scientific reputation', and toasts to 'how good it was to have peace between our two nations'; and then during Amerine's first stop in Kishinev, where the itinerary included a visit to a vinicultural school where Anton Frolov-Bagreev, the father of Soviet Champagne, had once worked.

> At the end of dinner [I] complained about the lack of wines to taste. Only got a promise to taste them *after* a brandy tasting. Complained some more. Conclusion: they think they have the PepsiCola Co committed to take anything and that this trip is just to fill time.[45]

To Amerine, none of the itinerary, which also included reception-laden stops in Tiraspol, Yalta, Massandra, Tsinandali, Tbilisi, Yerevan, Krasnodar, and Abrau-Diurso, suggested that his Soviet hosts understood the purpose of his visit—to

---

[44] Daniel Yergin, 'Politics and Soviet-American Trade: The Three Questions', *Foreign Affairs* 55, no. 2 (April 1977): 517–18; Steven E. Harris, 'The World's Largest Airline: How Aeroflot Learned to Stop Worrying and Became a Corporation', unpublished manuscript; Tricia Starks, 'Marlboro REDS: Philip Morris, the Soviet Market, and Smoking in the USSR', unpublished manuscript. My thanks to Tricia Starks and Steven Harris for sharing these materials with me.

[45] UCD, Amerine Papers, box 12, folder 14, 'To Russia and Back, 1973', 1–2, 5.

select wines suitable for sale in the United States. An even worse sign was the quality of wine they served. Writing to Kendall upon his return to Davis, Amerine noted that

> We were shown primarily ordinary quality wines—some of very poor quality. The very fact that they would serve such mediocre wines to knowledgeable people…is significant…My critiques came as a distinct shock to them.[46]

Although Amerine did not acknowledge it, any confusion about the purpose of his journey stemmed from divergent understandings of the place of wine in the consumer economy. Amerine toured Soviet vineyards and wineries as connoisseur, scientific expert, and corporate ambassador. In the latter respect, he carried the concerns of Pepsico and a demand-driven economy: the success or failure of the wines he was examining was dependent on consumers' willingness to purchase them rather than competing bottles. Amerine's hosts, to the contrary, could not see beyond the horizon of their supply-driven economy, where the ability to produce at a specified level, regardless of demand, was of paramount concern. It was perhaps for this reason that Amerine's hosts devoted so much time showing him things he did not deem important: bottling lines, fermentation tanks, and production figures.

Despite the disappointment with his itinerary, Amerine managed to take notes on more than 140 bottles in formal tastings, and a few dozen more that he ordered to accompany meals. He recorded varietal, including percentages if wines were blended, and single or multiple vineyard, if not. He took note of vintage, which he could usually learn only by questioning the vintners, since Soviet wine labels often excluded the year of harvest to economize. Amerine recorded alcohol and sugar contents (percentages); total acidity, which is the sum of all fixed and volatile tartaric or sulfuric acids—but not both—expressed in grams per litre; and volatile acidity, which is the level of acetic acid introduced to grape must by external bacteria or yeast, thus beginning wine's transformation to vinegar. The latter measurements were taken by titration, a simple laboratory process that entailed adding small amounts of alkali to the distillate of wine. Finally, Amerine recorded the level of total and free sulphur dioxide, which was measured through a complex laboratory process called the Rippermethod. Used as a wine preservative since antiquity, sulphur dioxide reacts with oxygen to prevent oxidation. At high levels, its rotten-egg smell can be detected by nose and is a common cause of flawed wine.

For Amerine, these figures were little more than signposts. The ultimate quality of wine could be determined only by sense, and that is where his notes are most

---

[46] UCD, Amerine Papers, box 6, folder 41, correspondence between Amerine and Kendall, 28 August 1973.

illuminating. While in Moldova, for instance, Amerine found an Isabella (of the *Vitis labrusca* species indigenous to North America) that showed a 'foxy odor, like Mogen David, but [was] not sellable'. In Yalta, a Madeira made from Rkatsiteli that had aged four years in the sun was marred by an 'off odor...too sweet and hot'. The local sherry lacked the 'flor character' that comes from the ambient, indigenous yeasts of Jerez. The Crimean port was more promising: 'a raisin smell, has character, bitter aftertaste'. In Tsinandali, the eponymous red from 1970 was 'woody and acetic', while the 1971 vintage 'shows less [volatility], also woodiness not so noticeable'. At dinner in Tbilisi, a bottle of Gurjaani was 'too old, has volatility, sharp and woody. This may appeal to the Georgians, but it will not to the Americans'. The 1971 Cabernet from Abrau-Diurso was 'a big disappointment...with very bitter aftertaste', but only because an earlier vintage served the previous night was 'pleasant'. A sparkling rosé from Krasnodar produced lots of 'pink foam, [and was] young and fruity but too sweet'. Lunch at the Hotel Peking in Moscow was nearly ruined by 'Chinese dishes [that] were not Chinese', and then saved by a 'drinkable' Aligoté from Massandra.[47] In Amerine's tasting notes, wines could be thin, tannic, soft, volatile, sweet, tart, woody, spoiled, oxidized, not interesting, neutral, hazy, bitter, flat, caramelly, hot, fruity, awful, unbalanced, mousy, raisiny, young, clean, bacterial, with nice colour, able to dilute, acetic, pleasant, okay, yellow-green-amber, lacking nose, and (in the case of the Cabernet Sauvignon served on Amerine's departing Aeroflot flight), fair.

Amerine subjected everything he ate and drank in the Soviet Union to critical appraisal. He sometimes scored good wine (which was exceedingly rare) and good cheese (which was more common) on his 20-point Davis scale, but most often he relied on a simpler system, also of his own derivation: the designation ++ meant 'must have', + 'could have', o 'probably not', and – 'certainly not'. Amerine found only two 'must haves' in the Soviet Union. The first was a Moldovan Cabernet Franc (1969) from the Chumai *sovkhoz*, which his translator pompously called 'Château Chumy'. In his memoir, Amerine described the wine as 'not finished, but characteristic. Asked for further data, it comes from southern Ukraine'. In his finished tasting notes, which were typed upon returning to California, he gave it two plusses, the second added by pen, perhaps suggesting a change of heart, with the note 'nice Cabernet nose, young, possible'. The second 'must have' was a Muscat (1970) from the Magarach Institute in Yalta: it was 'typical from a south coast vineyard', Amerine wrote in his journal, '13 alcohol and 22 sugar. Very fine Livadia type. Has lots of Muscat aroma'. Finally, Amerine had found an unambiguously great wine. He scored it as a 17.5 on the Davis scale, indicative of a wine of outstanding characteristics having no defects. In addition, seven wines, three sherries, three dessert wines, and four brandies received plusses, 'could

---

[47]   UCD, Amerine Papers, box 12, folder 14, 'To Russia and Back, 1973', 3, 6, 14, 17, 24–5.

haves', according to Amerine's improvised scale, even though Amerine admitted afterward that 'some of these marks [were] overly generous'.[48]

However, most wines Amerine encountered were unremarkable or flawed in significant ways. Amerine scored sixty-two bottles with a minus sign—'certainly nots'—and six with an off-the-chart double minus, indicating revulsion. His comments, even on the terrible wines, were laconic. A 1971 Fetească Albă from the Trushenskii winery near Kishinev earned a double minus because it was 'oxidized'; a 1971 Tibaani red, which Amerine tasted in Tbilisi, was graded the same because it showed the 'usual spoiled character'. In general, the wines seemed to get worse the further east Amerine went, which may have reflected tasting fatigue and fraying patience, or the comparative advancement of winemaking in Moldova, where Western equipment purchased during the inter-war period was in use. By the time Amerine arrived in Georgia, even mediocre wines were rare, although a side excursion to Armenia to taste brandy helped relieve the tedium. After every tasting, Amerine spoke briefly about the recent history of winemaking in California and current vinicultural and oenological research at Davis, and shared his criticism of the day's fare with his hosts.[49] Although the specifics of those talks varied, Amerine often told his hosts that Soviet growers and winemakers were making many of the same mistakes. Soviet wines tended to have too much volatile acidity, meaning they were too close to vinegar for the palates of Western consumers and competition juries. Something was going haywire during production: either extraneous bacteria were contaminating the grape must, or wine was coming into contact with oxygen while in barrels or bottles, which allowed the bacteria to produce acetic acid. Too many Soviet wines were characterized by low alcohol, meaning they were prone to spoilage unless treated with excessive amounts of noxious sulphur dioxide. This suggested that Soviet grapes were being harvested before peak ripeness, or that the varietals in Soviet vineyards were not suitable given climatic conditions. Soviet wines exhibited woody flavours, meaning they were left for too long in barrels before bottling. And finally, Soviet wines lacked varietal distinctiveness: Pinots were indistinguishable from Cabernets, Aligotés tasted like Sauvignon blancs, and in Georgia, where regional labelling persisted, Kindzmaraulis tasted like Akhashenis. The latter was perhaps not surprising, given the fact that both were semi-sweet reds produced from Saperavi. But what specifically did the titular location confer, if not distinctive taste?[50]

---

[48] UCD, Amerine Papers, box 6, folder 41, 'Wines Tasted in the Soviet Union', 1, 5; and box 12, folder 14, 'To Russia and Back, 1973', 5, 13.

[49] See, for instance, UCD, Amerine Papers, box 12, folder 14, 'Lecture for Moscow Filial, Magarach', unnumbered pages 1–3.

[50] UCD, Amerine Papers, box 6, folder 41, 'Wines Tasted in the Soviet Union', 2, 7; box 12, folder 14, 'To Russia and Back, 1973', 26.

Over time, Amerine's unsparing honesty took a toll. While in Kishinev he wrote that 'all these wines were for local use so...perhaps should not be criticized. But they probably picked out the best – so?' Nonetheless, he explained to the editor of *Vinodelie i vinogradarstvo SSSR*, A. V. Trofimchenko, how fermenting Cabernet Sauvignon grapes for eight days 'on the skins' and not 'racking' (separating wine from its sediment) until day thirty caused excess malolactic fermentation, thus reducing total acidity and the ability of the wine to improve with age. That evening at dinner, Amerine was joined by only one of his Soviet counterparts. The same occurred the following evening, which Amerine understood as 'their way of saying Amerine asks too many embarrassing questions'. After a tasting in Yalta, Amerine asked German Valuiko, whom he knew from previous trips to the Soviet Union and Budapest, to give the summary critique, thus avoiding wounded egos. At the Cognac Factory in Yerevan, Amerine's only stop in Armenia, he prefaced his criticism by acknowledging that 'they make the best Armenian wines and brandies in the world'. This was complimentary on its surface, but hollow in substance, since nearly all Armenian brandies originated in the factory. In Krasnodar, Amerine told Trofimchenko that his journal would garner more respect outside the Soviet Union if it used proper scholarly citations.[51]

Beyond embarrassment, it is difficult to know for certain what Amerine's hosts, who were conditioned to be circumspect around foreigners, made of his unvarnished criticism. Amerine considered Pavel Golodriga and German Valuiko, both at the Magarach Institute, friends and gifted scientists, and there is some evidence that their views, which were tempered by first-hand familiarity with winemaking elsewhere in Europe, at least partly coincided with Amerine's. It was no coincidence that Amerine's favourite wine of the trip was a Muscat from Magarach. There, at least, vintners had succeeded in amplifying the regional and varietal distinctiveness of wine with sound production techniques. Yet Magarach, which represented the pinnacle of vinicultural and oenological expertise in the Soviet Union, was exceptional on Amerine's itinerary for the range of its international connections and arrangements. Between Amerine's 1971 and 1973 visits, for instance, Richard Nixon's famously cantankerous Secretary of Agriculture, Earl Butz, toured the Magarach facilities at the head of an official American delegation. In short, while Amerine's visit was momentous for the Soviet wine industry *in toto*, which sought export revenue, his presence at Magarach was not so unusual that it merited anything more than a laconic acknowledgement in the institute's annual report to Moscow.[52]

---

[51]   UCD, Amerine Papers, box 12, folder 14, 'To Russia and Back, 1973', 6, 8, 14, 24.
[52]   On Magarach's foreign connections, see RGAE, f. 468, o. 1, d. 3510, ll. 69, 145 (equipment and patents); d. 2413, ll. 33, 89–90; d. 2807, ll. 40, 44–45 (travel and visitors).

Despite wounded egos, it may be the case that Amerine's hosts succeeded in disabusing him of a common preconception about the Soviet Union. Amerine quickly discovered that wine constituted an unusually eclectic niche in a Soviet economy that was often characterized by the absence of consumer choice. While many of the obscure Georgian labels that Amerine tried in Tbilisi and Kakheti were difficult to find or comparatively expensive in the big cities of the north (wine pricing in the Soviet Union reflected production costs and 'zone' of sale— i.e., distance from the wine belt), the Inter-Republic Wine Factory in Moscow, which Amerine also visited, produced more than 200 different types of wine and brandy each year, from grapes emanating in Ukraine, Crimea, the north Caucasus, Georgia, Central Asia, and Moldova. Its eleven bottling lines, which were organized by vineyard region, were capable of producing 8,000 bottles per hour, nearly all for the Moscow market.[53] This sort of extreme—yet hyper-centralized—product diversity was clearly astonishing to Amerine. Quizzing his hosts about cuvée (tank) uniformity (see Figure 6.3), Amerine discovered that it was simply not a problem for Soviet vintners, because they accepted a priori that identically labelled bottles

Figure 6.3. Cuvée mark on fermentation tank, Soviet-era wine factory in Kahketi, 2013. Photograph by author.

---

[53] P. B. Azarashvili and V. P. Batrachenko, 'Moskovskii mezhrespublikanskii vinodel'cheskii zavod', *Vinodelie i vinogradarstvo SSSR* no. 2 (1971): 12–19.

from different cuvées would exhibit different sensory profiles. Paradoxically, Amerine encouraged his hosts to trim the number of wines they produced, and to standardize their output by paying more attention to cuvée uniformity, advice that Donald Kendall later repeated in a letter to Vladimir Lein. Amerine's judgment was less a scientifically informed variation on Lenin's 'better fewer, but better', than a reflection of his connoisseurship. While the diversity of the wine market-place in the Soviet Union might foster thoughtful connoisseurship, the way Soviet wine was produced confounded it, because finding good wine was left entirely to chance. There were few indicators available to Soviet consumers, least of all the labels themselves, whether a wine was good or bad. Amid so much product diver-sity, informed choice was impossible.

＊   ＊   ＊   ＊   ＊

By the end of Amerine's trip, officials in the Ministry of Food Production had heard of his overwhelmingly negative appraisal and understood that a deal with Pepsico was unlikely. When talks shifted to the question of price for the few wines Amerine deemed minimally acceptable, Nikolai Oreshkin, the deputy minister of food production, tried to steer discussion toward Soviet Champagne, which had a proven track record in Western markets, and indicated that Soviet authorities would not budge from the prices they demanded. If Pepsico did not acquiesce, other Western firms would, the deputy minister warned. Amerine left the Soviet Union recommending that Pepsico make no deal.[54]

   This was not the end of negotiations. In a strange coda to the already strange encounter between Amerine and the world of Soviet wine, Soviet authorities backed off their hardline on price and requested a second tasting. In February 1974, Nikolai Oreshkin led a Soviet vinicultural delegation to California. Among the delegation's luggage were several cases of wine, sherry, and cognac, which Oreshkin hoped would garner a more positive appraisal. Amerine tried to be a generous and attentive host in his native California, guilty of the same excessive hospitality and formality he had criticized while in the Soviet Union. He arranged a grand tour of wineries in Sonoma, Napa, Livermore, and Fresno. He reserved tables for his Soviet guests at Trader Vic's and the Bohemian Club in San Francisco and planned a dinner for them at the home he shared with William Simms in St Helena in the Napa Valley. Among the invitees for social events with 'the Russians', as Amerine called them, were many of the most prominent names in California winemaking: Rodney Strong, Ernest Gallo, Sam Sebastiani, Robert and Peter Mondavi, Louis Martini, and even André Tchelistcheff, who had nearly died on a Crimean battlefield fighting against the Bolsheviks in 1921. While a change in itinerary meant the Soviet delegation remained in California for only two days,

---

[54] UCD, Amerine Papers, box 12, folder 14, 'To Russia and Back, 1973', 26–27.

rather than the week it initially planned, thus confounding many of Amerine's plans, the Bohemian Club hosted the second tasting that Oreshkin had requested. The results were no different. In Amerine's view, Oreshkin's wines were too low in alcohol, too woody in flavour, insufficiently filtered, and lacking in varietal distinctiveness; the sherries, dessert wines, and cognacs were better, Amerine told Kendall, but American demand for these was weak. Nonetheless, largely at the insistence of Kendall, who championed closer economic ties with the Soviet Union, Pepsico began to import a Soviet champagne under the label Nazdorovya, through its subsidiary, Monsieur Henri Wines, Ltd. Produced in Krasnodar by Abrau-Diurso according to the *méthode champenoise*, where fermentation occurred in the bottle, rather than according to Anton Frolov-Bagreev's mechanized 'continuous method', Nazdorovya had limited success in the American market, in part because it was priced about the same as competing bottles from Moët et Chandon. Monsieur Henri had much greater success with Stolichnaya vodka, which became the principal way that Pepsico repatriated its profits from its bottling plant in Novorossiysk. There is no record that Amerine ever returned to the Soviet Union, probably because of the absence of great wines there. His travel journals suggest there were few better reasons to leave home.[55]

Upon leaving Moscow for Paris, Amerine borrowed a long-standing Soviet construction metaphor and told his hosts that they were building something significant. Now it was most important to choose the correct construction materials, an inventory of scientifically informed practices that could not guarantee great wine—the whims of nature prohibited certainty—but would substantially increase its likelihood. That Amerine found the vast majority of Soviet wine to be of poor quality was expected, since similar dichotomies of success in volume and failure in quality characterized other sectors of the Soviet economy. As Amerine wrote to Kendall before his 1973 trip, 'The Soviet wine industry has lived in a dream world ... There is very little effective feedback of consumer reaction or resistance.'[56] More surprising to Amerine was the fact that so many Soviet vintners appeared either perplexed by or oblivious to the problem of taste. Early in his trip, Amerine wondered why he was not offered more wines to taste; upon returning to California, he wondered why knowledgeable persons served him such terrible wine. While Amerine attributed both to his hosts' unjustified confidence that they had an export deal wrapped up, perhaps Moldovan winemakers knew their wines were lacking by Western standards and sought to conceal them; Georgian vintners did not, and blithely poured them.

---

[55] UCD, Amerine Papers, box 7, folder 12, correspondence between Amerine and Kendall, 12 February 1974; Frank J. Prial, 'Wine Talk', *New York Times* (4 June, 1975): 50; 'Annual Report for PepsiCo Inc., 1974', 19, https://www.industrydocuments.ucsf.edu/docs/npfw0229 (last accessed 15 December 2019). My thanks to Tricia Starks for referring me to the latter.
[56] UCD, Amerine Papers, box 6, folder 41, correspondence between Amerine and Kendall, 13 April 1973.

On 11 August, the evening prior to his departure from Moscow, Amerine acknowledged that Soviet citizens were conditioned to accept a great deal. 'Of course, people grow to like things they are accustomed to. Plain bathrooms, and the smells thereof, do not bother the Russians as much as it does us.'[57] Amerine's pre-departure observation paralleled something he wrote in 1962 about Soviet restaurant service: 'Of course, in matters of taste we should not impose our standards. The slowly (painfully slowly) served meal is normal here.'[58] It is not clear whether Amerine had wine as well as restaurant waitstaff and bathrooms in mind; if so, it was as close as he came to acknowledging the subjectivity of taste. Yet in many ways, Amerine's identity as connoisseur and scientist was predicated on the exact opposite sentiment: wine could be objectively identified as good or bad or mediocre. It could be scored with plus and minus signs or assigned numbers according to the criteria of the Davis Scoring System. This quantification of taste was the prerogative of the connoisseur; it reflected the skills and knowledge of growers and vintners, not a mystical *terroir* or artisanal secrets passed from generation to generation. Bad wine, in other words, was nothing more than a problem for science. In the latter respect, paradoxically, Amerine had much in common with his Soviet hosts, which is perhaps why they silently suffered his criticism. In their view, Amerine possessed an understanding of the technologies of winemaking and the characteristics that make wine great that was irreproachable. While Amerine's hosts often spoke proudly about Soviet production levels and advances in champagne technologies (namely Anton Frolov-Bagreev's 'continuous method', where secondary fermentation occurs in steel tanks rather than bottles), at no point did they ever challenge Amerine's palate. They never argued the obvious in response to Amerine's criticism—that taste is subjective. Instead, they accepted a priori Western superiority in the field of wine, as they did the judgement of a pretentious connoisseur from California. This was a loss of confidence.

Amerine too carried weighty preconceptions. As his pre-departure correspondence with Kendall indicates, Amerine placed his hopes principally on the old dusty bottles of Yalta and Tbilisi, on the contents of wine cellars that dated to the tsarist period. He warned Kendall that recent vintages, produced in a 'dream world' where supply was paramount and demand inconsequential, were not likely to be very good. Amerine's pessimism was undoubtedly shaped by his previous encounters with Soviet wine, as tourist and competition judge. Yet it also reflected his overarching impression of the Soviet Union. The incentives and feedback loops necessary for producing fine wine were simply not present. This did not rule out fine wine entirely, but it made it a matter of chance rather than routine. The anthropologist Anne Meneley has argued that elite food economies often exhibit a sort of radical 'reverse Orientalism', where positive perceptions of a given

---

[57]   UCD, Amerine Papers, box 12, folder 14, 'To Russia and Back, 1973', 28.
[58]   UCD, Amerine Papers, box 11, folder 20, '1962 sabbatical: original 1st copy of typed notes', 11.

place, such as Tuscany or the Mediterranean world broadly, reinforce positive perceptions about the quality and healthfulness of the comestibles that emanate from that place. Amerine's experience suggests the opposite: his 'negative imaginings' of the Soviet Union powerfully shaped and reinforced his negative judgment about the quality of Soviet wine.[59] Amerine's scientific optimism was always in conflict with his ideological pessimism.

It is important to ask why Soviet vintners sought to compete with their Western counterparts on such an unusual and seemingly uneven playing field. Perhaps it was because of their deep-seated confidence that science and technology would remedy the age-old problems of environment and comparative poverty. Perhaps it was because of an unspoken desire to dethrone the West in a realm where its mastery was all but unchallenged. Or perhaps it was because the Soviet wine industry, like its tsarist predecessor, was deeply imitative, as it was always linked with identities—European and cultured—that the consumption of wine embodied. As the following chapter will show, this especially true in the early 1970s, when the production and consumption of fine wine came to be understood as a way to stem a rising tide of vodka-fuelled alcoholism. The point was not to make wine that Soviet consumers would enjoy, but to make wine in the European fashion that was deserving of the approbation of even Western connoisseurs such as Maynard Amerine, and that would transform Soviet palates. In this way, wine simultaneously crystallized Soviet aspirations and failures.

[59]   Meneley, 'Extra Virgin Olive Oil and Slow Food', 166.

7

Quality

Wine and Alcoholism in the Age of Mature Socialism

In August 1965, employees at the Magarach Institute in Yalta, which had become the socialist world's alternative to the famous vinicultural and oenological programmes at the University of Bordeaux and the University of California, Davis, conducted a blind tasting of wines from Bulgaria and the different vinicultural zones of the Soviet Union—Armenia, Georgia, the Don, Central Asia, and elsewhere. The purpose of the tasting was to compare the white table varietal, Pearl of Csaba, which was cultivated in Hungary, Romania, Bulgaria, and the Soviet Union, with hybrids that Magarach scientists had developed at the Institute's Steppe Research Station north of Simferopol. Magarach tasters evaluated the wines on the basis of five criteria—0.5 points for transparency, 0.5 for colour, 3 for bouquet, 5 for taste, and 1 for varietal typicality—creating a 'composite mark' (*obshchii ball*) for each. The hybrid wines, which scored between 7.1 and 7.4 on the composite scale, fared better than the Pearl of Csaba benchmark (6.88), suggesting that 'some of the hybrids, in their characteristics and essences, are better than the world standard for Pearl of Csaba'.[1] This was the vinicultural jackpot. Soviet scientists had succeeded in creating new varietals of white wine that were superior to the old. Proof lay in the results of the blind tasting.

Because the Magarach tasting pitted a so-called old 'crossed' wine (meaning a wine made from a grape varietal that was initially created by hand pollinating the stigma of one varietal of *Vitis vinifera*, Madeleine Angevine, with the stamen of another, Muscat Courtillier) against new 'hybrid' wines (meaning they were made from grape varietals that were developed by the same process, but between vines of different species), it is tempting to dismiss the whole endeavour as a scientific lark. Yet just as important as the science of vine hybridization was the method of evaluation—the formal tasting, or *degustatsiia*—which was the characteristic event and venue of the late-Soviet wine industry. In the 1920s, tastings all but disappeared as the supply of foreign wine dwindled, and as the early Soviet wine industry struggled to produce anything deserving of critical appraisal. During the Stalin period, excessive tastings could be conflated with the theft or misuse of

---

[1] RGAE, f. 468, o. 1, d. 105, l. 7. On the 10-point Soviet tasting scale, see OSA, 300-80-1, Box 898, File: Sel'skoe khoziaistvo: vinogradarstvo, 1960–93, unnumbered page entitled 'USSR—Russians Raise a Toast to Château Moldavia'.

Whites and Reds: A History of Wine in the Lands of Tsar and Commissar. Stephen V. Bittner, Oxford University Press (2021). © Stephen V. Bittner. DOI: 10.1093/oso/9780198784821.003.0008

state property, a fact that was underscored by the arrests and firings at Massandra and Novyi svet in 1949. By the 1960s, however, critical tastings had become an almost ubiquitous feature of the Soviet wine industry, and the 'taster' (*degustator*) a holder of special skill and insight into what made wine good. A TASS report from 1964, for instance, announced the arrival of a 'welcome surprise for the best Soviet tasters': a slew of new Port wines from new vineyards in Kazakhstan in need of critical appraisal.[2] Likewise, in 1965 the Tasting Commission at the Moldovan Scientific-Research Institute for the Food Industry in Kishinev conducted a *degustatsiia* to determine whether ultrasound, which was used with bentonite to help clarify wine prior to bottling, impacted wine quality. The answer, which was arrived at only after a great deal of wine was sampled, was that it did not. Later in 1965, Magarach employees conducted a blind tasting of champagnes made from Pinot noir, Rkatsiteli, and Silvaner. According to the tasting notes, the top-scoring Pinot (8.46 on the composite) had a colour that was a 'tiny bit rosy', a bouquet that was 'strong, bright, lean, yeasty', and a taste that was 'clean, harmonious, full, expressive of acidity'. The top-scoring Rkatsiteli and the overall winner (8.65 on the composite scale) had a colour that was 'bright and hay-like', a bouquet that was 'characteristic of the varietal, lean, colorful, well-expressed', and a taste that was 'harmonious, clean, full, complemented by good acidity'.[3]

Similar tastings were common occurrences at wine factories and government agencies. Tasting commissions existed in the capital cities, often comprising the bureaucrats who administered wine production and various outside specialists; the most important of them, the Central Tasting Commission, was attached to the Ministry of Food Production in Moscow. Tastings could be acts of hospitality for visiting dignitaries and guests from abroad, who were provided with pre-printed *degustatsionnye listki* on which to record their thoughts, or deeply ponderous and competitive affairs, with results that were quantified and rank-ordered.

The sheer frequency of tastings in the Soviet Union during the 1960s and 1970s suggests that quality mattered, and that quality had a lot to do with taste. In fact, quality became something of a watchword for vintners in the final Soviet decades, as it had been in the late 1930s, present in nearly every discussion about the past and future of Soviet winemaking.[4] This was hardly expected. The NEP-era view of domestic wine—that it was an interchangeable commodity, reducible in value to its alcohol content and volume, devoid of *terroir*, and suitable for export to France as a blending agent—never entirely disappeared. In the mid-1960s, the vast majority of Soviet wine, 97 per cent, was sold in bulk, without vintages or varietals. It was red or white, fortified or ordinary, sweet or dry. Consumers might roughly

---

[2] OSA, 300-80-1, Box 898, File: Sel'skoe khoziaistvo: vinogradarstvo, 1960–93, unnumbered page titled 'Kazakhstanskie vina'.

[3] RGAE, f. 468, o. 1, d. 105, ll. 225–7.

[4] On the phrase 'for quality' (*za kachestvo*), see Jukka Gronow, *Caviar with Champagne: Common Luxury and the Ideals of the Good Life in Stalin's Russia* (Oxford, 2003), 6–7.

gather whence the wine came from the markings on the bottle, barrel, or cistern—
it was reasonable to conclude, for instance, that wine sold from a Donglavvino
(Main Administration for Winemaking in the Don) cistern was produced in the
Don region, but even that was no guarantee of the grapes' origins. Beyond this,
however, consumers were offered few details about provenance, taste, and appropriate food pairings. In its production of bulk wine, the Soviet Union was by no
means unique. Similar cultures of bulk wine existed in other socialist countries,
such as Bulgaria, where consumers drank copious amounts of wine, but allegedly
lacked a culture of wine, meaning a culture of connoisseurship.[5] In the United
States and Australia, bulk wine—often sold in jugs or boxes fitted with air-sealed
bladders—constituted an important component of the market, the everyday table
wine of the urban middle class.

Yet in the West, bulk wine coexisted with middle and highbrow wines that
fostered cultures of appreciation and connoisseurship. Despite its immense wine
output, the Soviet Union produced little self-conscious reflection on the way fine
wine was supposed to taste, or what distinguished good wine from bad. While it
had wine experts in great abundance—scientists, engineers, vinicultural agronomists; in short, the persons involved in the production of wine—it had no wine
critics who sought to enlighten consumers about what wines they should aspire
to drink, and barely a literature of connoisseurship.[6] Curious Soviet consumers
could turn to *The Book of Delicious and Healthy Food*, which included brief
descriptions of the Soviet Union's growing regions and characteristic wines, along
with advice on pairing and presentation for home cooks. But the cookbook had
little to say about how to discern independently wine quality, or what tastes
should be present in wine.[7] It was almost as if all Soviet wine was good enough

---

[5] See, for instance, Yuson Jung, 'Tasting and Judging the Unknown Terroir of the Bulgarian Wine:
The Political Economy of Sensory Experience', *Food and Foodways: Explorations in the History and
Culture of Human Nourishment* 22, nos 1–2 (2014): 44, n 7.

[6] Perhaps the closest the Soviet Union came to a literature of wine connoisseurship was Mechislav
Peliakh's *Rasskazy o vinograde* (Kishinev, 1974) and the journalistic writings of Iurii Chernichenko.
The former was part popular history and guidebook to viniculture and winemaking (particularly in
Peliakh's native Moldova), and part celebration of all things wine-related. Peliakh avoided questions
about quality and taste, even as he couched the Russian Empire and the Soviet Union as participants
in a broader European culture of wine. The edition of Peliakh's *Rasskazy* that I consulted, available at
the University of California's Northern Regional Library Facility, was inscribed by Peliakh to Maynard
Amerine, the subject of the previous chapter. Similar to Peliakh's book, albeit less comprehensive and
less scholarly, was K. K. Almashin and L. U. Niiazvekova, *Solntse v bokale* (Uzhhorod, 1975).
Chernichenko's journalism, which is cited later in this chapter, helped familiarize readers with the
different wine regions of the Soviet Union, and with the persons who dedicated their professional lives
to bettering Soviet wine production.

[7] I. K. Sivolap, ed., *Kniga o vkusnoi i zdorovoi pishche* (Moscow, 1955), 79, 108–21. The journal
Obshchestvennoe pitanie, which served the restaurant economy, was similar in this regard: it concentrated on presentation and pairing, rather than connoisseurship. See 'Eto dolzhen znat' ofitsiant'
Obshchestvennoe pitanie, no. 1 (January 1963): 56–7. My thanks to Diane Koenker and Steve Harris
for sharing this material with me. On the cookbook, see Edward Geist, 'Cooking Bolshevik: Anastas
Mikoian and the Making of the *Book about Delicious and Healthy Food*', *Russian Review* 71, no. 2 (2012):
295–313; Gian Pierro Piretto, 'Tasty and Healthy: Soviet Happiness in One Book', in *Petrified Utopia:*

that dwelling excessively on taste and quality was self-indulgent pretentiousness. According to Adam Walker and Paul Manning's work on the Georgian wine industry, the privileging of quantity over quality, which was an oft-noted feature of Soviet-style economies, fostered 'homologous logics in regimes of consumption', where wine drinkers cared more about quantity than quality.[8] Thus, the absence of a culture of wine connoisseurship in the Soviet Union was indicative of the ways that consumption was 'forcibly structured by the materiality of...production'.[9] Few people dwelled excessively on the way Soviet wine tasted, because Soviet vintners had for so long produced few wines deserving of appreciation.

Beginning in the late-1960s, however, enterprising vintners and sympathetic administrators in the wine industry, who were both inspired and alarmed by their growing familiarity with the elitist cultures of wine production and connoisseurship that existed in Western Europe and North America, sought to counter the overarching emphasis on the quantity of production by seeking to make good wine of the conventional, unfortified sort, and marketing that wine for Soviet consumers in ways that underscored its quality. They fostered a basic distinction between wine sold in bulk and wine that was labelled *marochnoe*, an adjective that is usually translated as vintage when used with wine, meaning year of harvest (which was, in fact, rarely indicated on Soviet wine labels), but was almost always used instead to refer to high-quality, mature wine that displayed varietal and/or regional distinctiveness and that was branded as such. Soviet vintners produced labels for special occasions, holidays, and celebrations, which offered a pretext for spending a bit more on production and presentation. In the Western fashion, they often labelled these and other good wines 'reserve' and gave them a label appellation (*naimenovanie*), which sometimes indicated grape origin with some degree of specificity but was more often akin to a trademark name. And they bestowed an industry-specific 'mark of quality' on domestic wines and cognacs that tasting commissions deemed unusually good.

The emphasis on making good wine coincided with a broader shift in Soviet society from the post-Stalinist thaw of the 1950s and 1960s, to the so-called developed or mature socialism of the Brezhnev years. The latter coinages, though of official origin, describe a Soviet Union that had become decidedly post-revolutionary

Happiness Soviet Style, ed. Marina Balina and Evgeny Dobrenko (New York, 2009), 79–96; Jukka Gronow and Sergey Zhuravlev, 'The Book of Tasty and Healthy Food: The Establishment of Soviet Haute Cuisine', in *Educated Tastes: Food, Drink, and Connoisseur Culture*, ed. Jeremy Strong (Lincoln, NE, 2011), 24–57.

[8] Adam Walker and Paul Manning, 'Georgian Wine: The Transformation of Socialist Quantity into Postsocialist Quality', in *Wine and Culture: Vineyard to Glass*, ed. Rachel E. Black and Robert C. Ulin (London, 2013), 202. See also Yuson Jung, 'Re-creating Economic and Cultural Values in Bulgaria's Wine Industry: From an Economy of Quantity to an Economy of Quality', *Economic Anthropology* 3 (2016): 280–92.

[9] Krisztina Fehérváry, 'The Political Logic of State-Socialist Material Culture', *Comparative Studies in Society and History* 51, no. 2 (April 2009): 433.

and acquisitive in outlook. Although the Brezhnev years witnessed a number of alarming demographic trends—rising suicide rates and alcohol consumption, and declining longevity, among others—they were for many Soviet citizens the good life, or at least a more comfortable life than what came before and after. Televisions, automobiles, and annual trips to the Black Sea became staples for educated, urban professionals. Career success, and the material rewards and status that came with it, were no longer considered bourgeois afflictions, but celebrated in film and fiction. Young people in droves abandoned the classics of Russian literature, even high culture altogether, for rock-and-roll and blue jeans. Alternative social and cultural networks flourished, encompassing everything from organized crime to dissidents and hippies. In a society that coveted electronic gadgets from East Germany and Hungary far more than the latest scholarly tome from the Institute of Marxism-Leninism, it is not surprising that good wine, and the good life that it embodied, became a priority.[10]

The story of this chapter, however, is not simply that of an increasingly wealthy society embracing a traditional trapping of European refinement. The reasons good wine became a priority in the late-1960s had a lot to do with fears that alcoholism was becoming the chief threat to public health, and with the idea, which was dubious at best, that good wine worthy of savouring and appreciation was the cure.[11] Efforts to improve the quality of wine thus underscored the emergence of an affluent, urban society that was keen to measure itself by a yardstick of Western origin, at the same time that it highlighted the failures and limitations of Soviet power. To be sure, when it came to the production of high-quality wine, these failures and limitations were often economic, a topic that is unusual in the late-Soviet years because it has been comparatively well-trodden by social

---

[10] Juliane Fürst and Stephen V. Bittner, 'The Aging Pioneer: Late Soviet Socialist Society, Its Challenges and Challengers', in *The Cambridge History of Communism. Volume III: Endgames? Late Communism in Global Perspective, 1968 to the Present*, ed. Juliane Fürst, Silvio Pons, and Mark Selden (Cambridge, 2017), 290–304; Natalya Chernyshova, 'Consumers as Citizens: Revisiting the Question of Public Disengagement in the Brezhnev Era', in *Reconsidering Stagnation in the Brezhnev Era: Ideology and Exchange*, ed. Dina Fainberg and Artemy M. Kalinovsky (Lanham, MD, 2016), 3–20; Christian Noack, 'Brezhnev's "Little Freedoms": Tourism, Individuality, and Mobility in the Late Soviet Period', in Fainberg and Kalinovsky, *Reconsidering Stagnation*, 59–76; Juliane Fürst, 'If You're Going to Moscow, Be Sure to Wear Some Flowers in Your Hair (and Bring a Bottle of Port Wine in Your Pocket): The Soviet Hippie "Sistema" and Its Life in, Despite, and with "Stagnation"', in Fainberg and Kalinovsky, *Reconsidering Stagnation*, 123–46; Diane P. Koenker, *Club Red: Vacation Travel and the Soviet Dream* (Ithaca and London, 2013); Christine E. Evans, *Between Truth and Time: A History of Soviet Central Television* (New Haven, 2016).

[11] Belief in the healing properties of grapes and grape juice, and the comparative healthfulness of wine, was at least as old as Soviet power, and in all likelihood, a good deal older than that. An early Soviet description of the 'grape cure' traced the origins of such beliefs to Pliny: see A. I. Gruzin, *O vinogradnom lechenii v Odesse s opisaniem kurorta im. Oktiabrskoi revoliutsii* (Odessa, 1928), 8. In the nineteenth century, arguments about the healthfulness of Russian wine were often made in response to contrary allegations—that wine was harmful to human health. See, for instance, *Otchet o deistviiakh Imperatorskogo obshchestva sel'skogo khoziaistva iuzhnoi Rossii v 1865 g.* (Odessa, 1865), 23.

scientists keen to identify so-called systemic flaws in the socialist economy.[12] Soviet vintners lacked important feedback mechanisms, such as the idea of profit as a marker of quality, and a pricing mechanism that corresponded to demand, which were embedded in a market economy, and which served as economic measures of taste. Yet more important from the standpoint of vintners were limitations in the realm of culture, or more accurately, the realm of acculturation. Soviet vintners were capable of making fine wine in the European sense, even in the absence of the free market's feedback loop. What they lacked, despite their best efforts, were enough consumers who coveted good wine more than sweetened and fortified *bormotukha*. More than a century after tsarist vintners had identified wine production and consumption as an essential European trait, and more than a half century after they had successfully lobbied the tsarist government for a law banning wine 'falsification', consumers had not yet been weaned from their ersatz concoctions of wine, fruit juice, grain alcohol, and sugar. As Adrianne Jacobs has argued in regard to Soviet food cultures broadly, the 1970s saw a turning inward, as Soviet citizens sought historical continuity and authenticity in their kitchens.[13] When it came to wine, this 'historical turn' was too great to surmount: the Soviet civilizing process, which had been so transformative elsewhere, foundered on the long-standing popular taste for the strong and sweet.[14]

*   *   *   *   *

Even in the Soviet Union, where so many cultural norms were dictated from above, the characteristics that made wine good were open to debate. To officials in the federal Ministry of Food Production, for whom wine was just one component of a broad administrative portfolio, quality was principally synonymous with safety and purity. Yet for vintners, particularly at factories that produced large amounts of *marochnoe* wine, quality was increasingly synonymous with taste, and the preferred taste palate was increasingly European in orientation—an emphasis on varietal and regional uniqueness, a balance between sugar, alcohol, and acidity, and most difficult outside the production of cognac, the ability to improve over time. These contradictory views of wine quality came to a head in June 1966, when the Ministry of Food Production banned 'the treatment of

---

[12] See, for instance, Katherine Verdery, *What Was Socialism, and What Comes Next?* (Princeton, 1996), 19–38; Philip Hanson, *The Rise and Fall of the Soviet Economy* (London, 2003); János Kornai, *The Socialist System: The Political Economy of Socialism* (Princeton, 1992).

[13] Adrianne K. Jacobs, 'V. V. Pokhlëbkin and the Search for Culinary Roots in Late Soviet Russia', *Cahiers du Monde russe* 54, nos 1–2 (January-June 2013): 165–86. Jacobs borrows the term 'historical turn' from Denis Kozlov: see Denis Kozlov, 'The Historical Turn in Late Soviet Culture: Retrospectivism, Factography, Doubt, 1953–1991', *Kritika: Explorations in Russian and Eurasian History* 2, no. 3 (Summer 2001): 578.

[14] On Soviet efforts to transform popular tastes for food, see Anton Masterovoy, 'Engineering Tastes: Food and the Senses', in *Russian History through the Senses: From 1700 to the Present*, ed. Matthew P. Romaniello and Tricia Starks (London, 2016), 167–91.

substandard grapes and wine materials'. This was a not very eloquent way of describing the remediation of flawed grape must with sugar (typically not from beets), or concentrated grape must through a process called chaptalization. Named for the French scientist and statesman Jean-Antoine Chaptal, who advocated the process at the beginning of the nineteenth century, chaptalization was often derided as oenological cheating, yet it was relatively common among vintners in Northern Europe—Alsace, Loire, Burgundy, and Mosel—where weather conditions were less than perfect, and where grapes often had to be harvested before peak ripeness. Because sugar levels correspond to ripeness at harvest, the percentage of must needing treatment commonly rose in years with early autumns, and fell in years with long, hot summers. In 1962, Rosglavvino, the Russian Republic's Main Administration for Winemaking, recorded that 45 per cent of the grape must under its supervision was subject to chaptalization; in 1963, the figure fell to 35 per cent, but then rose to 55 per cent in 1964. In 1966, the year the ban came into effect, industry officials predicted that the vast majority of the Russian harvest, between 250,000 to 300,000 tonnes—figures that corresponded, at the upper end, to 87 per cent of the Russian Republic's 1964 harvest—would require chaptalization. The cause was an uncharacteristically cold summer and a blight of the vine fungus powdery mildew, which delays grape ripening.[15]

For vintners struggling to produce wine of good quality, the ministry's prohibition was pure idiocy, as it was motivated by a mistaken view that good wine was synonymous with pure wine. In a letter to Nikolai Oreshkin, the deputy minister of food production and the point man for all issues concerning wine, the head of Rosglavvino pointed out that the 250,000 to 300,000 tonnes of must requiring chaptalization had natural sugar levels below 17 per cent (commonly rendered as 17 Brix), meaning they would produce wine with no more than 10 per cent alcohol, below the 10.5 per cent necessary to prevent spoilage. The finished product would have to be combined with grain alcohol and sold as fortified wine, which was so ubiquitous on store shelves that consumers joked that the adjectives 'fortified' (*kreplennoe*) and 'strong' (*krepkoe*) were Soviet grape varietals (see Figure 7.1). In the view of vintners, chaptalization was an essential part of an oenological arsenal that facilitated the production of good wine. In 1972, for instance, Magarach employees conducted a tasting to determine whether chaptalization with frozen must increased the 'quality and nutritional value' of semi-sweet table wines. The scores were unambiguous. 'Among the data in the tablets', a Magarach scientist wrote while describing the tasting results, 'pay attention to the comparatively high concentration of aromatic compounds, ascorbic acid, and nitrogen compounds in the frozen must, good sensory stimulants, and the presence of bright, varietal aromas'. The adulterated wines scored nearly a half point higher

[15] RGAE, f. 468, o. 1, d. 443, ll. 1–2.

Figure 7.1. Label for a Moldovan 'Strong White' wine, 19 per cent alcohol, 3 per cent sugar. The GOST number, 7208-70, specifies the 'general technological conditions' under which the wine was produced. It also indicates that this label was in use at some point between 1970 and 1984, when the federal State Committee on Standards issued new GOST regulations for wine production. Author's collection.

on the composite tasting scale than their semi-sweet counterparts that had suffi-cient natural sugar levels to avoid chaptalization. Science, it turned out, tasted better than purity.[16]

In the short-lived ban on chaptalization lay the challenge that ambitious Soviet vintners faced: producing good wine often meant ignoring inconvenient direct-ives from officials who knew little about wine, and acting in ways that were very un-Soviet. In 1965, the newly chartered Rosglavvino, encouraged by the results of an international competition in Tbilisi, where forty-eight Soviet entries won thirty gold and eighteen silver medals, directed viniculturalists in the Russian Federation to prune berry clusters more aggressively in the early summer. This had the effect of reducing yields and improving the characteristics of the remain-ing clusters, and was generally embraced by vintners. While cluster pruning was common practice in Western Europe, where yield had never been the paramount concern, it was virtually unheard of in the Soviet Union, where the wine industry operated in an economy that incentivized quantity over quality, and where there

---

[16] RGAE, f. 468, o. 1, d. 2807, l. 245.

was a growing chasm between the productive capacity of Soviet wine factories, which was growing rapidly, and the volume of grapes grown each year, which was growing more slowly.[17] Despite the official licence, however, growers always had to be careful not to prune too aggressively—in short, even in the eyes of sympathetic officials, the production of good wine was not an end in itself. In 1970, three wine *sovkhozy* in Moldova were chastised for letting yields fall too low, to 2,000 to 3,000 kilogrammes per hectare. While there were many reasons for the poor harvest, one was overly aggressive pruning. Similarly, there was little patience among officials in the Soviet wine industry for so-called 'old vine' vineyards, which in Western Europe were prized for their superior wine qualities and often protected by law. In 1982, the Main Administration for Viniculture and Winemaking in Ukraine notified Gosplan that it intended to pull out 244 hectares of old vines in Zaporozh'e. Lacking single-vineyard wines and, for the most part, any notion of *terroir*, Soviet vintners found it impossible to justify the reduced productivity of old vines.[18]

An important component of better wine was production equipment from the West. In preparation for the Russian Revolution's fiftieth-anniversary celebrations in 1967 and a year-long festival in Georgia for the twelfth- and thirteenth-century poet Shota Rustaveli, the Main Administration for Winemaking petitioned the Ministry of Food Production for permission to purchase the latest in French bottling and labelling technology, equipment that could handle up to 6,000 bottles per hour, and that would facilitate the production of the sort of *marochnoe* wine that was rare in the Soviet marketplace. Plans called for the release of a Matrassa, an Azerbaijani dessert wine; a Crimean Aleatico, a sweet red wine commonly produced on the island of Elba; and a cognac from Koktebel'. A wine factory in Kherson proposed a 'reserve' table wine from grapes grown near the Azov Sea. In Georgia, vintners planned a limited release—500 bottles per day—of an old cognac, which would be sold under the label Shota Rustaveli. In all, the Soviet wine industry stood to produce more than 600 appellation wines, meaning they had names (which sometimes specified region and more often varietal), and forty appellation cognacs for the jubilee year, eighteen more than in 1965.[19]

The attention to better production facilities was nowhere more evident than in the so-called Inter-Republic Wine Factory, which was located far from the vinicultural belt in Moscow. Outfitted with the latest Western equipment at a cost of 20 million roubles, it could produce 10 million decalitres (more than 140 million bottles) of wine per year when it came online in the late 1960s, making it the largest wine production facility in the world. The factory's raison d'être was improving the overall poor quality of Soviet wine. According to M. M. Kuprianov, the

[17] RGAE, f. 468, o. 1, d. 2412, l. 4.
[18] RGAE, f. 468, o. 1, d. 2412, l. 4; and TsDAVO Ukraïny, f. 5201, o. 1, d. 1136, l. 9.
[19] RGAE, f. 468, o. 1, d. 443, ll. 8, 10, 20.

Russian Republic's deputy minister of food production, many commercial organizations were refusing to accept wine shipments, citing an inability to sell wine that consumers found revolting. Dry white wine from Ukraine, for instance, was distinguished mainly by its capacity for languishing on store shelves, despite the overall economy of shortage. Kuprianov's assertion was more than useful embellishment; throughout the 1970s, industry officials often complained about commercial organizations that refused to accept shipments of dry table wine that consumers would not buy. Moscow's special status as a capital city, filled with important officials and foreign diplomats, was also cited as justification for the factory's expense. The factory was designed to represent the full vinicultural diversity of the Soviet Union. Its eleven bottling lines were organized by region, and it had specialized facilities for Madeira, vermouth, port, and cognac. With must imported by rail car, it was capable of producing nearly all Soviet appellation wines. Between 1966 and 1970, Soviet vintners hoped to increase the overall production of *marochnoe* wine by 16 million decalitres; 2.5 million would come from the Inter-Republic Wine Factory. This was extraordinary investment in the production of wine in a world where vodka was king. Similar improvements were made in the late 1960s to wine factories in Lviv, Kiev, and Dnipropetrovsk, where Western bottling lines were capable of turning out more than 5,000 labelled bottles per hour.[20]

To encourage improvement among growers, Rosglavvino began to score 'wine material' prior to the winemaking process, measuring sugar, acid, spoliation, and other characteristics that impacted subsequent wine quality. In 1963 and 1964, when poor weather beset the southern wine belt, 30 per cent of the total harvest in the Russian Federation displayed a spoilation rate higher than 10 per cent (meaning at least 10 per cent of the berries in a single cuvée had already begun to spoil, often on the vine, before the winemaking process could begin). By 1965, the spoilation rate had dropped to 1 per cent, and only 34 per cent of the harvest had insufficient sugar levels to support winemaking. The latter figure, while substantial, was historically low by Russian standards. The wine results were promising. In 1965, Abrau-Diurso scored all its wines, creating an average 'general mark' for each category of wine it produced. No category had an average score lower than 8.23 (ordinary, fortified wines) on the ten-point scale; Abrau-Diurso's vintage dessert wines scored 9.17. Rosglavvino's other winemaking facilities in the Don, Grozny, Stavropol, Dagestan, and Moscow displayed similar scores. Soviet vintners had rediscovered a winemaking rule of thumb: good wine came from well-tended grapes.[21]

Soviet vintners' attention to quality was admirable, but there were practical limits on what they could accomplish. Their emphasis on producing wines with

[20] RGAE, f. 468, o. 1, d. 103, ll. 16–17, 24; d. 2808, l. 54; d. 2412, l. 2.
[21] RGAE, f. 468, o. 1, d. 54, ll. 15, 34–5.

appellation called to mind the French *appellation d'origine contrôlée* system, geographical classifications, dating from the late nineteenth and early twentieth centuries, that linked wine with place, even though Soviet appellation lacked the French system's historically rooted regulations and traditions governing yield, varietal, production area, and alcohol content. In practice, Soviet appellation was closer to the American Viticultural Area designation, which came into use in the 1980s to ensure truth in advertising. It required that a wine specifying AVA be composed principally (no less than 85 per cent) of grapes grown within that area. But even this was an inexact parallel, since AVA designation sought to enshrine the microclimates, soil characteristics, drainage patterns, and geographies of small, sharply demarcated vinicultural areas, and thus protect property and production values, and promote a sense of *terroir*. The latter was sometimes true of Soviet appellation use. In the 1970s, for instance, Massandra sourced grapes from across Crimea, yet it produced an award-winning red port with grapes from the prestigious south-facing vineyards on the 'southern shore', which was indicated on the label (see Figure 7.2). To be sure, southern shore encompassed a huge vinicultural area of considerable diversity, especially in comparison with any single French AC or American AVA designation, but it was bound by shared climatic conditions, and it had been a region prized by knowledgeable Russian wine drinkers for nearly a century. Other Soviet wine labels also referenced place, but in ways that were far more ambiguous. Massandra produced a white port with the label 'Surozh' (azure), which was the old name for Sudak (see Figure 7.3). The fact that it was not labelled 'southern shore' meant that the grapes came from elsewhere in Crimea, likely the less prestigious steppe vineyards north of Simferopol. The same was true of the Crimean Wine Trust, which produced a 'Crimean sherry' under a label that featured a drawing of Swallow's Nest castle in Gaspra (see Figure 7.4). The Odessa Wine Trust made a semi-fortified red wine under the label 'Red Gold of the Estuary', which referred to the long, narrow estuaries that defined the shoreline of the Black Sea between Odessa and Mykolaiv (see Figure 7.5). Yet most often, Soviet appellation simply meant wine that was sold in bottles, and that bore labels indicating varietal and producer (from which place of origin might be assumed). Moldvinprom, the agency that oversaw wine production in Moldova, produced a labelled Fetească Albă and Cabernet Sauvignon, both 'ordinary' table wines made from Moldovan grapes. Its counterpart in Dagestan did the same with a dessert Rkatsiteli. In a world where the standardizing impulses of bureaucracy encroached on so much, Soviet appellation remained haphazard, implied, and vague.[22]

Soviet vintners faced other problems, as well, which would have been unimaginable to their counterparts in the West. Standard wine bottles, 500 millilitres for

---

[22] On the origins of the AOC system, see Erica A. Farmer, 'Local, Loyal, and Constant": The Legal Construction of Wine in Bordeaux", in *Wine and Culture: Vineyard to Glass*, ed. Rachel E. Black and Robert C. Ulin (London, 2013), 145–59. On appellation as a form of bureaucratic control, see Yuson Jung, 'Cultural Patrimony and the Bureaucratization of Wine: The Bulgarian Case', in ibid., 161–78.

Figure 7.2. Label for the Massandra Red Port wine from the southern shore, emblazoned with medals from international tasting competitions, c. 1970s or early 1980s. Author's collection.

fortified wines and 700 for table wines, were constantly in short supply. In 1960, the Soviet wine industry received shipments of 31.4 million new bottles. During the first eleven months of 1970, shipments rose to 42.8 million. Despite elaborate schemes to encourage Soviet citizens to wash and return bottles after consumption, and despite the import of bottles from abroad, estimates of the bottle deficit

Figure 7.3. Label for the Massandra White Port wine 'Azure', produced for the Ukrainian market, with a painting of the hills around Sudak, c. 1970s or early 1980s. Author's collection.

ran as high as 600 million per year. In Ukraine, the deficit was so severe that industry officials encouraged wine drinkers to purchase reusable three-litre, screw-cap bottles, which could be filled on demand from cisterns and barrels in wine stores. In the 1970s, Soviet industrial designers devised the sort of boxed, bladder systems that were coming into vogue in the bulk-wine market in the

Figure 7.4. Label for Crimean Sherry, emblazoned with medals from international tasting competitions in Budapest, Yalta, and elsewhere, and with a 'mark of quality' in the upper right corner, c. 1970s or early 1980s. Author's collection.

West, yet these were never embraced by the industry. It is tempting to dismiss the significance of the bottle shortage, when the vast majority of wine was sold in bulk. Yet one of Donald Raleigh's respondents in his oral-historical study of Soviet baby boomers recalled that the advent in the late 1970s of green vodka bottles with foil caps was, in retrospect, the beginning of the end of Soviet power.

Figure 7.5. Label for Red Gold of the Estuary, c. 1970s or early 1980s. Author's collection.

'It showed the authorities' huge lack of respect for the people.'[23] The hodgepodge nature of Soviet wine bottles made it difficult for producers to abide by so-called state-standard (GOST) laws, which regulated food composition, means of production, safety, labelling, and packaging. In 1970, several commercial organizations in Russia, Ukraine, and Belorussia returned shipments of wine that failed to conform to

---

[23] Donald J. Raleigh, *Soviet Baby Boomers: An Oral History of Russia's Cold War Generation* (Oxford, 2012), 277.

minimum GOST regulations. Moreover, as Soviet vintners increasingly encountered the world of Western wine, problems in presentation became more glaring. Glass bottles were of poor quality, varying colours, chipped, and often smelled of their previous contents. Labels were rudimentary, lacking in artistic beauty, poorly adhered, and often askew. If the wine inside the bottles was indeed of decent quality, as the Soviet wine industry wanted consumers to be certain, it did a very good job of hiding it.[24]

Moreover, the Soviet capacity to produce good wine, ideally for sale in bottles, gradually surpassed its ability to grow grapes for good wine. Across the Soviet Union, total vineyard area and grape production more than doubled between 1958 and 1968, to 790,000 hectares (7,900 square kilometres) and 4.45 million tonnes. However, because quality was identified, above all, as a production problem, producers saw even greater increases in capacity. Between 1917 and 1969, for instance, the Soviet state built eight new cognac distilleries. In 1969, plans were unveiled for additional facilities in Togliatti, Alma Ata, Irkutsk, Leningrad, Kazan, Vladivostok, Novokuznetsk, Minsk, Krasnodar, Belts, Simferopol, and Grozny, in effect more than doubling capacity in a few years.[25] In 1966, the Soviet authorities tried to close the shortfall in domestic grape production, caused by rising production capacity, by purchasing fresh and crushed grapes from Hungary and Bulgaria. Similarly, in 1969, they purchased 500,000 tonnes of 'wine material' (grape must), the equivalent of more than 10 per cent of the previous year's harvest, from Algeria. The Council of Ministers proposed to increase this amount to 700,000 tonnes in 1970. In total, grapes of foreign origin constituted nearly one-quarter the total processed by the Soviet wine industry in 1970. Of course, such purchases underscored Soviet support for allies in Eastern Europe and the newly independent Algeria, which was struggling with reduced access to the French market. But buying grapes also made economic sense, despite necessitating upgrades to port, railroad, and warehouse facilities in Novorossiysk and Tuapse. Unless all the factors beyond human control, such as weather and pestilence, lined up perfectly, Soviet growers were hard-pressed to produce at a level commensurate with the capacity of Soviet producers. Moreover, in areas where substantial new vineyard plantings were made, such as Armenia, the results were often inauspicious. Over the course of ten harvests, the average sugar composition of Armenian grapes (as a percentage of total volume) fell by three percentage points.[26]

In the countryside, the threats to quality wine were more familiar. Persistent shortages in copper sulphate meant that downy mildew, a fungal infection that

---

[24] TsDAVO Ukraïny, f. 5201, o. 1, d. 595, l. 113; d. 212, l. 21; RGAE, f. 468, o. 1, d. 2412, ll-2–3. For GOST regulations on wine, see *Vina vinogradnye. Obshchie tekhnicheskie usloviia. GOST 7208-84* (Moscow, 1984).

[25] RGAE, f. 468, o. 1, d. 1641, ll. 3–4.

[26] RGAE, f. 468, o. 1, d. 1641, ll. 1, 14–26; d. 2807, l. 72; Iurii Chernichenko, 'Grozd' Armenii', *Pravda*, 23 June 1968, 2.

typically manifests itself in wet weather, remained a constant threat. In some years, downy mildew was responsible for up to 40 per cent crop losses. Weather was an omnipresent concern. The 1971 harvest missed its target by 30 million decalitres of grape must, a failure attributed to an unusually dry summer in Dagestan, Krasnodar, Stavropol, Crimea, Georgia, and southern Ukraine. In 1979, an unusual spring cold spell, with temperatures as low as –6 degrees Celsius, damaged more than 230,000 hectares of vineyards in Ukraine. The Crimean steppe bore the worst of it. Contrary to viniculture in the West, phylloxera remained a persistent drain on production. In the early 1970s, Abrau-Diurso lost 600 hectares to the vine aphid. Between 1962 and 1976, 19,000 hectares of vine-yards in Crimea similarly perished. While phylloxera reappeared in Sonoma and Napa Counties in California in the 1980s, because of the widespread use of the hybrid rootstock AXR1, which displayed insufficient resistance to the aphid, Soviet losses occurred in un-grafted vineyards, which was a product of the Soviet Union's comparative isolation and poverty. Across the Soviet Union, 600,000 hec-tares of vineyards were un-grafted and vulnerable to phylloxera a full century after it was identified as the cause of the 'great wine blight'. Finally, like vineyards everywhere, Soviet vines resisted all but the most limited attempts (such as the use of conveyor belts) at harvest mechanization, despite elaborate and costly efforts to replace human labour with machines.[27]

Despite these challenges, the newfound emphasis on quality meant, at least in the eyes of industry officials, the production of better wine. This was evident not only in a slew of respectable performances in international tasting competitions at home and abroad (the subject of the previous chapter), but in the fact that quality became part of the industry's annual planning and production quotas, present in nearly every discussion about the future of Soviet wine. In 1970, when officials in the federal Ministry of Food Production crowed about the fact that Soviet wine production accounted for about 10 per cent of the world total, they also underscored the 'improvement of its quality'. As the supply of decent wine increased, so did the gradations that the industry used to market wine for Soviet consumers. By 1974, 25 per cent of all Ukrainian *marochnyi* wine, which was itself a step above the bulk wine that comprised the majority of Soviet production, and 60 per cent of all Ukrainian champagne received the so-called 'mark of quality' (*znak kachestva*). Bestowed by the Central Tasting Commission, which was con-vened annually by the federal Ministry of Food Production, the 'mark of quality' designated wines and cognacs that were deemed unusually good in comparison with their peers when judged by colour, bouquet, and taste. To be sure, there was

[27] TsDAVO Ukraïny, f. 5201, o. 1, d. 593, l. 21; d. 778, l. 40; RGAE, f. 468, o. 1, d. 2028, l. 27; B. Zabruskov, 'Kak sorvat' vinogradnuiu grozd'', *Sovetskaia Rossiia*, 30 June 1967, 2; P. Bogatenkov, 'Pomoshchnik vinogradarei', *Pravda*, 4 April 1968, 1; V. Darmodekhin, 'Chem srezat' vinograd?' *Izvestiia*, 31 August 1968, 2; A. Isaev, 'Vinograd i mashina', *Komsomol'skaia Pravda*, 31 December 1968, 4.

the usual planned-economy idiocy about the mark of quality. In January 1971, the Central Tasting Commission awarded the mark of quality to thirty-two wines, nine cognacs, ten champagnes, and ten fruit and berry wines. This was trumpeted as a great success, because Soviet vintners had earned, in total, nineteen more marks of quality than the plan had envisioned. The year 1976 was another good vintage: forty-five Ukrainian wines earned marks of quality, thirteen more than planned.[28]

For vintners, earning a mark of quality from the Central Tasting Commission was a significant honour. Retaining a mark of quality across two or more vintages was an even rarer accomplishment, because it suggested that the skills of the winemaker—rather than the vagaries of weather and harvest—were paramount. In 1974, when the Main Administration for Viniculture and Winemaking in Ukraine notified the Ukrainian Central Committee and Council of Ministers that forty Ukrainian wines had earned marks of quality, it specified which wine factories and wine *sovkhozy* had earned these distinctions: the Odessa Wine and Cognac Complex, the Artemovskii Champagne Factory, the Kakhovka wine *sovkhoz*, and others. Among these, the Crimean, Trans-Capathian, and Kherson wine *sovkhozy*, the Kharkov and Odessa Champagne Factories, and Novyi svet retained previously awarded marks of quality by submitting new vintages for 're-evaluation' (*pereattestatsiia*).[29]

The Central Tasting Commission also served as a sounding board for vintners from across the Soviet Union. In 1972, it encouraged Soviet wine factories and *sovkhozy* to release twelve new wines that it found promising, albeit not yet deserving of marks of quality, including a Massandra Bastardo, which was a Portuguese red varietal that scientists at the Magarach Institute thought ideally suited for Crimea, and a Georgian cognac. The commission lent its expertise to the task of improving the ordinary (unfortified) wine. In 1972, it convened specialists from across the Soviet Union in hopes of making Soviet table wine less terrible than it normally was. Beginning in 1976, it organized annual, industry-wide 'days of quality' to encourage vintners to eliminate bad habits, share best practices, and show greater production discipline. By 1983, 'days of quality' had been reduced to a single 'day of quality'. This signalled not a change in priorities, but the fact that quality had been widely accepted as a principal goal of production.

Yet progress toward better wine was always uneven. In 1982, the federal Ministry of Food Production took the Soviet wine industry to task for focusing its efforts toward better quality—meaning using the most modern equipment, the must with the lowest rate of spoilage and highest natural sugar content, and the most attractive bottle labels—only on *marochnye* wines, cognacs, and champagnes.

[28] TsDAVO Ukraïny, f. 5201, o. 1, l. 105; RGAE, f. 468, o. 1, d. 2412, ll. 2, 33; d. 2028, l. 4.
[29] TsDAVO Ukraïny, f. 5201, o. 1, d. 212, ll. 27–8.

Moreover, the industry's pricing system, which assigned to bottles of widely varying quality, prices that were or less the same, tended to obfuscate what was good and what was bad. This was a long-standing problem. According to the actor and novelist Iurii Chernichenko, who was perhaps the closest the Soviet Union came to producing a wine writer, not only were the price differences between *marochnye* and ordinary wines negligible, but the price gradations among the *marochnye* wines were themselves insufficient. In an interview in 1967, Petru Pascari (Petr Paskar'), the general secretary of the Moldovan Communist Party, told Chernichenko that it would be ideal if wine factories could assign their own prices to their production: after all, who knew better the differences in quality that stemmed from an especially favourable vintage (meaning, in this case, year of harvest) or vineyard microclimate? Current Soviet practice was contrary to the French experience, Pascari said, where ordinary wine was not much more expensive than mineral water, but the best wines might sell for truly astronomical prices.[30] Fifteen years after Chernichenko's interview, the Ministry of Food Production recommended that consumers be offered a greater number of clearly-marked gradations from which to choose: ordinary, middle, and high quality. The ministry's proposal drew inspiration from the French system of labelling production from consistently great and good vineyards grand cru (great growth) and premier cru (first growth), respectively. Yet it also promised to resolve an increasingly evident problem with the 'mark of quality' designation: since the International Wine and Cognac Competition in Yalta in 1970, the 'composite marks' earned by Soviet wines that won the mark of quality had been in slow decline. While such a development might have been attributed to the subjective nature of taste and growing familiarity with the wines of the West, for the Ministry it meant that wine of the highest quality had, in fact, declined in quality.[31]

*   *   *   *   *

In 1978, *Literaturnaia gazeta* ran a half-page article under the title 'Ink' (*chernila*), which was synonymous with another slang term, *bormotukha*, low-quality sweet and fortified wine. Sometimes labelled as port, Cahors (*kagor*), or vermouth, *bormotukha* was ubiquitous in the Soviet marketplace and popular among consumers because it was inexpensive. The author of the article was Vil' Dorofeev, a scientific journalist and commentator who had become something of a public scold on matters concerning alcoholism. Dorofeev asked why, after spending an evening walking the beat with local police officers in Odessa's residential neighbourhoods, it was so difficult to find dry table wine on store shelves. It was a common complaint in cities across the Soviet Union, but especially difficult to fathom

[30] Iurii Chernichenko, 'Delo chelovekom stavitsia. 1. Vino belogo aista', *Pravda*, 17 December 1967, 2.
[31] TsDAVO Ukraïny, f. 5201, o. 1, d. 1139, ll. 144–5.

in Odessa, which was the capital of an oblast with twenty-three wine factories and 40,000 hectares of vineyards. Consumers were instead offered a slew of fortified wines, adulterated with fruit juice, sugar, and grain alcohol, bearing the labels 'Maritime' (see Figure 7.6), 'Aroma of the Steppe', 'Rosé 72', and others. 'In long conversations with vintners of different ranks', Dorofeev wrote,

> I tried to clarify whether it was possible to get by without *chernila* and *bormotukha* in our winemaking industry. Is it possible to give people a sufficient quantity of dry wine, which will raise their spirits but not knock them off their feet, like all these 'aromas of the steppe', which stink of rotgut (*sivukha*)?

Dorofeev discovered that the Moldvinprom wine factory, the largest in Odessa, was scheduled to produce nearly 1.5 million decalitres (30 million 500-ml bottles) of fortified wine in 1978, but only 30,000 decalitres (almost 430,000 700-ml bottles) of unfortified, dry wine, which made little sense in a country that had been officially struggling, since 1972, against an epidemic of alcoholism. Odessa was by no means exceptional in this regard. In 1974, the wine factory in Novosibirsk reported that only 5.3 per cent of its production was dry table wine. Like so many puzzling features of Soviet life, the cause was a directive from above. According to Dorofeev, the director of the wine factory shared a document, signed by the deputy director of the Main Winemaking Administration for Ukraine, directing Moldvinprom to cancel plans to produce more than 700,000 decalitres of dry wine in 1978, and to devote those resources instead to fortified wines. Dorofeev found that the Soviet consumer was captain, and the consumer wanted sweet and strong *chernila*, even if it was dangerous to health and welfare.[32]

Dorofeev's essay was notable for reasons that went beyond his incredulity about the decrees emanating from Kiev. First, it hewed to a fairly well-established pattern about the relationship between wine, *bormotukha*, and alcoholism broadly, as similar articles appeared in *Literaturnaia gazeta*, *Sovetskaia kul'tura*, and elsewhere in the late 1960s and beyond.[33] In the absence of a wine press for consumers, newspapers such as these, with audiences that tended to be disproportionately urban and educated, could be counted on for an article every few years extolling the sublime and ineffable characteristics of wine. The articles often

---

[32] Vil' Dorofeev, 'Chernila', *Literaturnaia gazeta*, 22 February 1978, 13. On the Novosibirsk wine factory, see N. Samokhin, 'Prokhodnye gradusy "stervetskoi"' *Literaturnaia gazeta*, 30 October 1974, 11. For similar complaints about the absence of dry wine on store shelves, see Library of Congress, Anatolii Zakharovich Rubinov Papers, box 56, folder 159, 25–6.

[33] See, for instance, R. Lirmian, 'Est li istina v vine', *Sovetskaia kul'tura*, 22 August 1978, 6; 'Vopreki sprosu', *Izvestiia*, 8 January 1978, 2. The linkage between dry wine and anti-alcoholism policies was sufficiently well established in Soviet media that it caught the attention of foreign journalists in Moscow working for Reuters and *The Times*: see OSA, 300-80-1, Box 898, File: Sel'skoe khoziaistvo: vinogradarstvo, 1960–93, unnumbered pages entitled 'USSR – Russians Raise a Toast to Château Moldavia', and 'USSR—From Vodka to Wine'.

Figure 7.6.   Label for a white Maritime Port wine, one of the popular brands of
bormotukha, c. 1970s or early 1980s. Author's collection.

reproduced a dichotomy of taste and refinement that was at least a century old in
Russia. There were the banal, lowbrow tastes of the street, where consumers
looked to *bormotukha* for drunken entertainment and escape; and there were the
subtle tastes that winemakers sought to inculcate. These were characterized not
by the heat of alcohol and the sweetness of sugar, but by the interplay of sun, soil,
and varietal, all managed by the skills and intuitions of the grower and vintner. In
short, according to the oft-repeated formula, wine was not something that one
drank for the sake of inebriation, but to appreciate its complexities. Mikhail

Gerasimov, one of the Soviet Union's most eminent and internationally renowned vintners, began an article from the mid-1960s that helped establish the formula by quoting from a poem by Mikhail Iashin:

He loves dry wine / his whole life, only dry wine / dry wine does not numb the brain / it does not weigh on arms and legs / in his heart resides not malice / but love for people / not loathing for work / but the desire for creation.[34]

In Dorofeev's formulation, the winemaker was a defender of old ways. 'From time immemorial', he wrote, 'a rule has existed: under no circumstances can beet sugar be used to the raise the sugar level of grape must.' While Dorofeev's ancient rule was not exactly a hard-and-fast prohibition, especially in the Soviet Union, it had become common in Western Europe to use concentrated must in chaptalization, rather than sugar, with the thought that the additive was close in composition to the base. Yet the same deputy director of the Main Winemaking Administration in Kiev who scaled back the production of dry wine in favour of *chernila*, ordered the use of grain alcohol and beet sugar, which was a very different thing than tolerating its occasional use. 'How can such wines have proper taste and bouquet?' Dorofeev asked. The Ukrainian Ministry of Health and Gosplan could perhaps be forgiven for signing off on the decree, given their ignorance about the way wine is typically made, but the same latitude could not be granted to A. P. Demenkov, the deputy director of the Main Winemaking Administration in Kiev, who signed the decree. As a writer for *Krokodil* put it, while lampooning a similar case of adulteration that turned one barrel of wine into three barrels of *bormotukha*, such actions 'spit into the face of the master-winemaker'.[35]

Dorofeev's criticism cut to the heart of the strange politics of alcohol in the Soviet Union in the Brezhnev years. On the one hand, the Central Committee sought in 1972 to reduce the consumption of vodka, particularly among young people, by promoting non-alcoholic diversions, such as entertainment and sports, and low-alcoholic alternatives, such as beer and wine. The cause was a growing concern among people of widely varying political stripes, from communist officials to their dissident critics, about a growing societal malaise.[36] On the other hand, the value-added tax (*nalog s oborota*), which increased in proportion to alcohol content, was an important source of income for local authorities.[37]

---

[34] M. A. Gerasimov, 'Solntse protiv, "Zmiia,"' *Sovetskaia kul'tura*, 25 December 1965, 4.

[35] S. Bodrov, 'Delo o "bormotukhe,"' *Krokodil* 4 (1974): 6.

[36] Mark Lawrence Schrad, *Vodka Politics: Alcohol, Autocracy, and the Secret History of the Russian State* (Oxford, 2014), 336–55; OSA 300-80-1, Box 586, File: Napitki, unnumbered pages entitled 'K voprosu o postanovlenii SM SSSR "O merakh po usileniiu bor'by protiv p'ianstva i alkogolizma"'.

[37] The perverse incentives of alcohol taxation in Russia are a very old problem, dating to at least the sixteenth century. According to Mark Lawrence Schrad, *Vodka Politics*, 81, 'the might of the autocratic Russian state was built on a pillar of vodka'; David Christian, *Living Water: Vodka and Russian Society on the Eve of Emancipation* (Oxford, 1990), 30–39; David Christian and R.E.F. Smith, *Bread and Salt: A Social and Economic History of Food and Drink in Russia* (Cambridge, 2008), 288–326.

Consequently, as the sale of vodka was restricted in 1972, *bormotukha*, which typically had an alcohol content between 16 and 19 per cent of total volume (less than half of vodka, but about one-and-a-half times more potent than conventional wine) took its place. In Odessa oblast, the volume of apples destined for *bormotukha* was eight times greater in 1973 than in 1972, provoking severe shortages of apple preserves, sauce, and juice. In Mykolaev, the municipal food complex generated nearly 2.7 million roubles in taxes from the production of wine in 1977, principally *bormotukha*, and 77,000 roubles in taxes on non-alcoholic beverages. Between 1972 and 1976, the annual consumption of dry wine in Mykolaev increased by 1,600 decalitres, and *bormotukha* by 110,500 decalitres. Moreover, from the perspective of the food industry, fruit-infused wine was considerably less expensive to produce (in terms of labour hours) than its alternatives—jams, jellies, sauces, and preserves. In short, everyone profited from the production of *bormotukha*—local officials, who depended on the tax revenue, and factory officials, who saw it as less labour intensive than other products. As Dorofeev noted with sarcasm, everyone was able to say, 'Look, the consumption of vodka is hardly growing. People are drinking wine. We have undertaken all measures in order to fulfill the decree on the battle with drunkenness.'[38]

Despite rehashing old formulas about wine and alcoholism, Dorofeev's article stirred up immediate controversy, probably because its publication came after a few years of concerted efforts to improve the quality of dry table wine. Shortly after its publication in February 1978, the article was an item of discussion in the Ukrainian Central Committee, which solicited a response from the same bureaucrats whom Dorofeev had singled out for criticism. Their response was more *mea culpa* than defensive: 'The problems raised in the article are real', the Collegium of the Main Administration for the Fruit and Wine Industry admitted. Yet it also insisted that these problems could be resolved, because consumer demand for *bormotukha* ultimately reflected the poor quality of conventional wine. To that end, the administration was taking steps to improve the 'selection and quality' of wine, as well as its packaging and presentation. It was removing from production four fortified wines sold under an appellation, albeit the four that that were in least demand among consumers. And it planned to raise the production of dry wine across the Ukrainian Republic to 13.8 million decalitres (almost 200 million bottles) in 1979, nearly 40 per cent of total wine production; *marochnoe* wine would constitute an increasing proportion of the total. The remaining 60 per cent, of course, would be *bormotukha*, which was still a huge quantity, particularly in comparison with the wine markets of the West, yet a decreasing proportion of the overall production. Soviet consumers could not be weaned off their strong and sweet wine all at once.[39]

---

[38] Vil' Dorofeev, 'Chernila', *Literaturnaia gazeta*, 22 February 1978, 13.
[39] TsDAVO Ukraïny, f. 5201, o. 1, d. 691, l. 8.

In truth, late-tsarist and Soviet vintners had been trying to wean consumers off strong and sweet wines for a very long time, since at least the final decade of the nineteenth century, when resolving the so-called 'crisis in winemaking' caused by rampant falsification became the industry's most pressing issue. The perceived linkage between the production of quality wine and reducing rates of alcoholism was scarcely younger, although evidence that the former was in any way related to the latter was circumstantial at best. The case that wine proponents frequently made lay in the comparatively low alcohol content of conventional wine, the comparatively lower rates of alcoholism in countries such as Spain, France, and Italy, where wine was firmly embedded in local cuisines, and in the idea that good wine was a tool of acculturation to European norms and etiquette, which included stronger social taboos on drunkenness. The linkage between *bormotukha* and alcoholism was much easier to establish, even if only on an intuitive level. The screenwriter Iurii Nagibin, for instance, whose diary serves as a guidebook to the societal malaise associated with the late-Brezhnev years, noted the easy availability of *bormotukha* in Kostroma amid widespread consumer shortages and drunkenness:

> In the stores there was gray liver sausage, for which people kill, cheese (!), canned vegetables, soup in glass containers with the garish inscription 'WITHOUT MEAT,' some kind of mysterious canned fish, which no one buys. There is also vegetable shortening, fruit candy, pastila, sugar. The remaining items are in bottles: vodka and *bormotukha*. There are many drunk people on the streets, in much grief about everything.[40]

Consequently, officials in the Brezhnev-era wine industry walked an old but precarious path when they asserted that an effective policy in the fight against alcoholism would be 'raising the quality of wine', which was a euphemism for producing more conventional, unfortified wine. In 1972, officials at the Magarach Institute, noted with pride that Soviet wine production had grown to about 10 per cent of the world's total output, a figure that put the Soviet Union in third place internationally, behind France and Italy. While the popularity of fortified wine, which constituted 78 per cent of all wine output, had the effect of reducing the prominence of vodka and other grain alcohols as a proportion of overall alcohol consumption—vodka had fallen from 89 per cent in 1913 to 58 per cent in 1970—it was also crushing real and potential demand for conventional wine. Thus, Magarach scientists proposed to increase by 1990 the per capita consumption of wine to just under 20 litres per year, and the proportion of overall production devoted to conventional wine to 38 per cent. This, they argued, would further

---

[40] Iurii Nagibin, *Dnevnik* (Moscow, 1996), entry for 18 August 1978, available at prozhito.org.

reduce the prominence of vodka in the Soviet marketplace, and help rid the Soviet Union of the scourge of alcoholism.[41]

The linkage between the quality of wine and anti-alcoholism policies had the effect of making the anti-alcoholism campaign an important pretext for, and anti-alcoholism officials important allies in, efforts to invest in the production of better wine, even if it was destined to languish on store shelves because of minimal demand. In 1976, the Main Administration for Winemaking in Ukraine cited the 1972 Central Committee and Council of Ministers decree on drunkenness and alcoholism to increase the production of *marochnoe* and ordinary table wine by 1.6 million decalitres over 1972 levels. Similar increases were planned for sparkling wine, cognac, and cider. The industry tried to woo sceptical consumers with new labels, souvenir boxes, and crystal and ceramic bottles for high-end wines. Similar steps were taken in 1978, when Massandra cited the campaign against alcoholism as reason to invest in new *marochnoe* wines: White Muscat of the Red Stone, Southern Shore Tokaji, Pinot gris Ai-Danil', and others. Moreover, nearly every discussion about the production of better wine included representatives from the Commission on the Battle against Drunkenness in Kiev, as if wine had become the methadone for the heroin of vodka.[42]

In truth, efforts to present wine as a cure for the scourge of vodka were more nuanced than consumer seduction and choice. They were wrapped in a broader *kul'turnost'* campaign, orchestrated principally by the wine industry and a handful of sympathetic intellectuals, that sought to challenge and transform the tastes of the drinking public. In 1974, the Siberian humourist Nikolai Samokhin told the readers of *Literaturnaia gazeta* that many years earlier, he had been an 'unwitting participant in an experiment' that had 'dragged on for a long time before the reasons for it were fully clear.'

> For some reason, I asked in a store for a bottle of dry wine.
>
> 'It only has 9 percent alcohol, mister,' the sales clerk warned me.
>
> 'I know.'
>
> 'It's sour.'
>
> 'That I also know.'
>
> 'Well, take heed.' Then there was a pause in the conversation. 'How people drink this stuff, I don't understand.'
>
> A week later (the sales clerk had of course forgotten me) the scene repeated itself. After another week, it happened again. After about six months of this, she got used to me. I even received a nickname appropriate for a red-skinned chief—dry wine.

---

[41] RGAE, f. 468, o. 1, d. 2807, ll. 70–77.
[42] TsDAVO Ukraïny, f. 5201, o. 1, d. 329, l. 85; d. 449, l. 104; d. 692, l. 65.

'Dry wine has come!' the salesclerk loudly and sarcastically informed her coworkers when I appeared. Why did this dear, caring girl act in such a way? It was on account of her personal taste and the taste of the old man who [when offered wine] at the counter wheezes, 'Why are you forcing this kvass on me?'[43]

In Samokhin's view, his six-month experiment laid bare the lowbrow tastes of the masses. 'It is necessary to cultivate taste', he wrote in conclusion to his tale. 'Lord, is that the old truth.'

On first glance, Samokhin's account appears to be exceptional for its snobbery, as he invited readers to scoff at the sales clerk's misdirected sarcasm and unrefined palate. Yet such snobbery, particularly when tempered by humour or light-heartedness, was common in public discussions about wine in the 1970s and beyond. In 1975, for instance, the satirical journal *Krokodil* published a letter—presumably more comical than real—that was sent to the journal from 'employees of a children's library' in Velikie Luki, in response to a diagram the journal published a few months earlier that supposedly depicted the apparatus one needed to turn *samogon* (moonshine) into *bormotukha*. The anonymous authors of the letter asked the editors of *Krokodil* to share the recipe as well, since the New Year holiday was approaching. The editors, poking fun at the lowbrow tastes of the letter writers, responded that the diagram in question had been mistakenly labelled: it actually depicted an apparatus for turning *samogon* back into the sugar from which it originated, not into *bormotukha*. Similarly, in 1978, *Sovetskaia kul'tura* published a letter from a resident of Sochi who humorously advocated 'snobbism in wine drinking'. 'I am for…comfortable wine bars', the Sochi correspondent wrote, 'where it is possible to learn how to carry on proper and fine conversations about life and art. Abolish the wine bars, and people will forever gather in apartments. Enough with the attacks on wine.' [44]

Of course, dubious was the letter writer's assertion that one could find quiet, thoughtful conversation about life and art in most Soviet 'wine bars'. Wine bars were more often boisterous places for getting drunk, where inexpensive, low-quality, sweetened and fortified Port wine and Cahors were drawn from tap like beer. In his memoir of late-Soviet Leningrad, Nikita Alekseev recalled the 'one-armed devils, like something in a casino', which bartenders used to pour glasses of wine, and crowds of noisy customers who had mastered an elaborate language of handsigns and symbols to indicate what they wanted. In retrospect, they

[43] N. Samokhin, 'Prokhodnye gradusy "Stervetskoi,"' *Literaturnaia gazeta*, 30 October 1974, 11.

[44] 'Pro "bormotukhu,"' *Krokodil*, 23 (1975): 12; S. Bykovskii, untitled letter, *Sovetskaia kul'tura* (22 August 1978): 6. Fear that the 1972 Central Committee decree served mainly to hide drinking behind closed doors—or worse, make it a solitary endeavour—was not unique. See, for instance, Catriona Kelly's analysis of representations of drinking and intoxication in Brezhnev-era films: Catriona Kelly, 'Period zapoia: Kinoproizvodstvo v Leningrade brezhnevskoi epokhi', trans. Tat'iana Pirusskaia, *Novoe literaturnoe obozrenie*, no. 152 (April 2018), https://www.nlobooks.ru/magazines/novoe_literaturnoe_obozrenie/152/article/20023/.

reminded Alekseev of the feverish traders on the New York Stock Exchange. 'Every fifteen minutes cops (*menty*) entered the bar', Alekseev wrote: 'They cast their professional gaze on a crowd that was getting more drunk and more wild.' Yet in light of the anti-alcoholism campaign, *Sovetskaia kul'tura* was obliged to solicit a serious response to the tongue-in-cheek letter from a professor who taught at the Academy of the Ministry of Internal Affairs, and who advocated abstemiousness. 'As a matter of fact', the professor wrote about one of the most popular types of sweet, fortified wine, '"Aroma of the Steppe" is an enemy of humankind'. The wine snob might have agreed, albeit for different reasons: the offence Aroma of the Steppe inflicted on good taste was far greater than the offence it inflicted on human health and welfare.[45]

In its underlying premise that the chief problem plaguing Soviet wine production was one of popular taste and behaviour, Samokhin's article was by no means exceptional. Similar ideas could be found elsewhere in the public sphere, where newspaper headlines encouraged consumers, among other things, to sip rather than gulp, a life lesson with value far beyond the realm of wine.[46] For the writer Vladimir Soloukhin, professional success in the 1960s and 1970s, and the rewards that came with it, brought both greater appreciation of wine, and recognition that as a young man he did not much care for it because of his own limited horizons. 'Concerning natural wines', he wrote about his younger self,

> they seemed to me to favor only one taste—they were all sour. To perceive the astringency of a Mukuzani, the spicy bitterness of a Gurdjaani, the sunny subtlety of a Tsinandali, the rosy pleasure of a Chkhaveri, the complexity, so to speak, of the taste gamut of an Isabella, or the lightness of a Vaskevaza, to discern and savor all of these is not possible from the first sip. But if you already understand...you will never again in your life put that sweetened and fortified rubbish in your mouth.[47]

To be sure, Soloukhin made for a bit of an unusual wine snob. In his public persona, as a prominent writer in the village-prose movement and a historical-preservation activist, he was a Russian patriot and a man of the people. But just as Soloukhin avoided the hard, anti-Semitic edge of Russian nationalism, he carved out room in his self-presentation for an appreciation of the subtleties of European wine. The above passage comes from an autobiographical essay about a trip that Soloukhin took to Burma in the late 1960s or early 1970s. Sitting with a Soviet

---

[45] Nikita Alekseev, 'Piterskie khroniki', *Zvezd*, no. 12 (2006), https://magazines.gorky.media/zvezda/2006/12/piterskie-hroniki.html; R. Lirmian, 'Est' li istina v vine', *Sovetskaia kul'tura* (22 August 1978): 6. My thanks to Catriona Kelly for sharing the Alekseev article with me.

[46] V. Golovanov, S. Rostov, A. Diatlov, et al., 'Ne vypit', a popit'', *Sovetskaia Rossiia*, 15 May 1985, 6.

[47] Vladimir Soloukhin, *Olepinskie prudy* (Moscow, 1973), 142–3. Soloukhin's tale is also available, in slightly different form, in *Literaturnaia gazeta*, 14 June 1967, 16.

diplomat in the embassy compound in Rangoon, the conversation turned to wine, a passion for both diplomat and writer. After trading stories about Bulgarian varietals, the wine cellars of Armenia, and the history of Madeira production, the diplomat told Soloukhin that during an earlier rotation at the embassy in Paris, he had got into the habit of buying wine from the cellar of a famous French producer. Near the end of his assignment, the diplomat decided to purchase a bottle of old wine, from the 1900 vintage, to take back to Moscow. He asked for a recommendation.

> Our dear friend, of course we would be very happy [to do so], except that we cannot recommend to you 1900. There was a very rainy summer that year, and grapes did not develop well at all. There was too much unnecessary moisture in them, and they were watery. No, I cannot say that the wine turned out excellent. But if you, our friend, absolutely want this wine, then stick with the 1899 or the 1901.[48]

Like the accounts of Samokhin and the wine snob from Sochi, Soloukhin's story was darkly humorous. Before leaving the wine cellar, the diplomat signed a guest book, because the sales clerk was afraid that no one would ever believe his story about the rare bottle from 1901 that was on its way to Moscow. They then opened a bottle of younger wine to drink to the diplomat's purchase. And once in Moscow, the rare wine from 1901 was mistaken by the diplomat's wife as just another bottle, and taken to her brother's apartment as a courtesy gift. It was raining outside, and she could not be bothered to run to the store for another bottle instead. The diplomat's brother-in-law drank the old wine from a teacup, pronouncing it 'rubbish'.

In a country where vintage was rarely indicated on wine bottles, Soloukhin's tale was an unusual paean, nearly as rare in the Soviet Union as the old wine he described, to the cultures of appreciation and connoisseurship that surrounded wine in France. Yet it was also tinged with tragedy that went beyond the ignominious fate of the old bottle. The tragedy lay in the fact that the vast majority of Soloukhin's compatriots, including the diplomat's wife, were ignorant of the complexities fine wine, that the vast majority of Soviet consumers could experience fine wine only through literature, that the Soviet civilizing process had run aground on the shoals of taste.

The latter was not for lack of effort in the wine industry. In 1979, officials in Ukraine's Main Administration for Winemaking proposed a slew of changes to facilitate the production of 'high-quality' wine: investments in Western technology, greater attention to standardization (cuvée uniformity), more attractive labels, and so on. All of this was familiar territory. New was their attention to

---

[48] Soloukhin, *Olepinskie prudy*, 144.

acculturation. The administration opened in Kiev a Ukrainian wine tasting room (*degustatsionnyi zal*), 'with the goal of cultivating in the population a knowledgeable, medically literate, and aesthetic attitude toward wine'. It also opened a similar, albeit temporary facility in the horticultural pavilion at the Exhibition of the Achievements of the National Economy (VDNKh) in Moscow. Of course, officials hoped these tasting rooms would showcase high-quality Ukrainian wine; but they also wanted to familiarize consumers with the 'culture of its consumption': how to open a bottle of wine, how to assess whether the bottle is good, how to pour and sip wine, what tastes, aromas, and colours to expect in a *marochnoe* or reserve wine. In a world where consumers preferred wine that stunk of 'rotgut', as Dorofeev put it, such knowledge promised a different popular attitude toward wine.[49]

Natalya Chernyshova has recently argued that one of the most significant changes from the Stalin to the post-Stalin years in Soviet consumption patterns involved so-called deficit goods. In the 1930s, essentials—food, kitchen tools, sewing implements, and so on—were in shortest supply. Yet by the 1970s, the things in highest demand, and in shortest supply, were items that made life good rather than possible—they had that 'special taste', Chernyshova notes, quoting the comedian Arkadii Raikin. So often exemplifying the good, richly savoured life, wine thus stands out in the Soviet consumer universe as the exception. In a world where consumption was 'inherently political', Soviet citizens were making independent judgements about the taste and quality of domestic dry wine by refusing to purchase it.[50] It is also hard to avoid the impression that efforts to transform popular taste in wine were never much of a priority for officials beyond the wine industry, and for the small number of intellectuals who embraced wine as a hallmark of cultural refinement. Catriona Kelly has noted that behavioural advice literature was especially prominent in the post-Stalin period, as it helped assuage long-standing Soviet anxieties about materialism, consumer desire, and consumption broadly, with newer anxieties that stemmed from the comparative abundance of the final Soviet decades and from lives that were increasingly spent behind the closed doors of single-family apartments. Yet advice about wine— what to consume, how to consume it, and so on—was notable mainly for its absence: a small number of articles that targeted a very select component of Soviet society and that were characterized more by high-brow pretentiousness toward popular taste than purposeful didacticism aimed at transforming those tastes. A reader might rightly surmise that the chief case for drinking dry wine that Samokhin makes is to avoid being the object of his derision. In the latter regard, the articles about wine were fully representative of Soviet advice literature broadly: 'Late Soviet intellectuals', Kelly writes, 'so far from always maintaining an

[49]   TsDAVO Ukraïny, f. 5201, o. 1, d. 779, ll. 28–9.
[50]   Chernyshova, 'Consumers as Citizens', 4–6.

ironic distance from the process of dictating refinement, often directly involved themselves in it.'[51]

It may be the case that the civilizing process in regard to wine foundered because industry officials never really believed their own assertions that better wine would reduce demand for *bormotukha*. Whatever the case, the closer one got to vineyards and wine factories, the greater were the reasons to look askance at such claims, and even to concede the usefulness of *bormotukha*. For instance, industry officials, in their private moments, begrudgingly acknowledged that the wide availability of inexpensive *bormotukha*, which was half as potent as vodka, likely helped curtail the production of *samogon* (moonshine) after vodka sales were tightened in 1972. As a result, until the late 1980s, alcohol appears to have been less central to the Soviet second economy than in other parts of the socialist world, such as Romania, which had stricter regulatory regimes.[52] *Bormotukha* was also undeniably lucrative. Writing in 1987 about the suicide of Pavel Golodriga, a prominent vintner at the Magarach Institute, the novelist and actor Iurii Chernichenko argued that *bormotukha*, far from being a scourge, was the wine industry's golden goose, even if the industry refused to admit as much. 'What is true is true: entire regions have been corrupted by the "drunk years",' Chernichenko wrote. 'Without *bormotukha* it is impossible to think that viniculture will survive.' According to Chernichenko, a tonne of freshly harvested grape clusters could be sold at market for 280 roubles profit, made into dry wine for 512 roubles profit, or fortified with sugar and alcohol and sold as *bormotukha* for 1,709 roubles profit. Without the money generated by *bormotukha*, in short, there would no dry wine of any sort.[53]

* * * * *

The end came suddenly. In May 1985, less than two months after Mikhail Gorbachev, the 'mineral-water Gensec', came to power, and in the midst of mounting evidence that vodka posed a grave threat to Soviet public health and economic performance, the Communist Party's chief mouthpiece, *Pravda*, announced an all-out assault on alcohol. As Mark Lawrence Schrad writes in his history of Russian vodka, by 1985 Russians consumed nearly 15 litres of pure alcohol per capita annually, and the typical Russian adult male drank 130 half-litre bottles of vodka

---

[51] Catriona Kelly, *Refining Russia: Advice Literature, Polite Culture, and Gender from Catherine to Yeltsin* (Oxford, 2001), 365.
[52] See, for instance, Narcis Tulbure, 'The Socialist Clearinghouse: Alcohol, Reputation, and Gender in Romania's Second Economy', in *Communism Unwrapped: Consumption in Cold War Eastern Europe*, ed. Paulina Bren and Mary Neuburger (Oxford, 2012), 256–7. A similar point appears to be corroborated by one of Donald Raleigh's respondents, who associates the growth of the second economy for vodka with Gorbachev's policies: see Raleigh, *Soviet Baby Boomers*, 274.
[53] Iurii Chernichenko, *Muskat belyi krasnogo kamnia* (Feodosia and Moscow, 2007), 91.

each year, the equivalent of one every three days.[54] For so long, wine had been couched as a healthy alternative to vodka, and an essential component of the Soviet civilizing process. Now it was part of the problem. By October, officials in Ukraine had reduced the annual target for grape must from 58 million decalitres to 41.5 million, citing a convenient spell of cold weather as one of the reasons. In 1986, the cuts were steeper. The Main Administration for the Fruit and Wine Industry in Ukraine scaled back the production of *marochnoe* wine by 23 per cent; its counterpart in the Russian Republic cut *marochnoe* wine by 40 per cent. The production of 'ordinary' table wines and *bormotukha* in Ukraine were curtailed even more sharply, by nearly 50 per cent. Entire wine factories were converted to the production of soft drinks, such has carbonated grape juice; the Kiev wine factory, which had recently been outfitted with expensive Czechoslovakian bottling equipment, began to turn out 0.33-litre bottles of sparkling wine, less than half the typical size. To keep sparkling wine and cognac in short supply on store shelves, industry officials ramped up export targets. In 1986, the Soviet Union exported 4.7 million bottles of Soviet Champagne, 127 per cent more than in 1985.[55]

This was just the beginning. Newspaper headlines that had once waxed lyrical about grapes and wine—'Clusters of Success', 'The Generosity of the Vine', 'The Vine Reaches for the Sun'—now carried very different messages—'Not Berries for Wine, or Why Vineyards Are Being Uprooted', 'Crimea is not for Wine, but for Grapes', 'Why the Grape is More Profitable than Wine'.[56] Of course, there was a strong odour of disingenuous surrounding these headlines. Yet the crisis that they heralded was the largest to beset Soviet viniculture and winemaking since the German and Romanian occupation of the Second World War. Growers struggled to find non-alcoholic uses for their grapes, as table fruit, juice, jelly, concentrate, and compote, before bulldozers—or more likely, simple neglect—threatened vines that no longer had economic value.[57] 'Panicked rumours' circulated that Soviet officials had ordered the replacement of all Georgian vineyards with watermelon fields. Consumers complained about holidays that passed without the traditional champagne toasts, because no champagne could be found on store shelves.[58] *Komsomol'skaia pravda* reported that Queen Elizabeth was so taken

---

[54] Schrad, *Vodka Politics*, 275. See also Stephen White, *Russia Goes Dry: Alcohol, State, and Society* (Cambridge, 1995); A. V. Nemtsov, *Alkogol'naia istoriia Rossii: noveishii period* (Moscow, 2009).

[55] TsDAVO Ukraïny, f. 5201, o. 1, d. 1482, ll. 19, 110–11, 142; V. A. Shaitanov, 'Ekonomicheskii eksperiment v Donetskom proizvodstvennom ob"edinenii bezalkogol'noi promyshlennost', *Pishchevaia in pererabatyvaiushchaia promyshlennost'*, no. 4 (1986): 25–6.

[56] Iu. Chernichenko, 'Grozd' uspekha', *Komsomol'skaia Pravda*, 5 September 1980, 2; D. Suleimanov and L. Tairov, 'Shchedrost' lozy', *Pravda*, 4 November 1980, 2; V. Artemenko, 'Loza tianetsia k sol'ntsu', *Pravda*, 29 June 1981, 2; T. Konstantinova, 'Ne vinnaia iagoda', *Izvestiia*, 6 September 1985, 3; V. Kovalevskii and S. Troian, 'Krym ne vinnyi, no vinogradnyi', *Sovetskaia kul'tura*, 19 November 1985, 6; V. Tolstov, 'Milliony, obretennye zanovo, ili vinograd, kotoryi vygodnee vina', 2 August 1986, 2.

[57] See, for instance, N. Kvizhinadze, 'Lagidze protiv Bakhusa', *Sotsialisticheskaia industriia*, 22 July 1987, 4; G. Lebanidze, '"Bakhmaro" protiv "bormotukhi"', *Pravda*, 22 October 1985, 3.

[58] E. Chugunova, 'Sud'ba solnechnoi iagody', *Sotsialisticheskaia industriia*, 24 December 1986, 1; 'Tupiki', *Sovetskaia Rossiia*, 10 August 1986; 'Bezalkogol'nyi pososhok', *Trud*, 8 November 1990, 2,

with Dagestani wine, after sampling a bottle at an international trade show, that she told her aides to have several cases sent to Windsor Castle from the winery in Kizliar. The winery responded that it only had enough wine on hand to provide samples for exhibits; it no longer produced wine for consumption. Even attendees at the Seventieth General Assembly of the International Organization of Vine and Wine, which Yalta hosted in 1990, found a city devoid of wine. Whatever embarrassment the Soviet hosts felt was all the more acute because Nikolai Pavlenko, a scientist at the Magarach Institute, had been elected president of the organization two years earlier in Paris. As the 'planet's chief winemaker', Pavlenko used his keynote address in Yalta to trumpet Soviet successes in wine production.[59] The irony was lost on no one.

There were oases of comparative normality amid the general vinicultural collapse. In Georgia, because of the prominence of private vineyards and in-home production, and because *bormotukha* never constituted more than a very small proportion of the republic's output, growers and vintners did not experience the same scale of production decreases as their counterparts elsewhere. Overall, Georgian production levels stabilized in 1986, after 1.2 million tonnes of grapes were reportedly left unharvested in 1985 due to restricted access to markets in Russia and elsewhere. In an interview with John Kampfner, a journalist for *The Daily Telegraph*, Mikhail Shiukashvili, the director of a wine factory in Tsinandali, put a positive gloss on his factory's predicament: the quality of grapes that his factory used to make wine had increased since Gorbachev unveiled the anti-alcohol measures in 1985, because vintners were no longer under pressure to maximize the quantity of production above all else. Georgian vintners also began to experiment with new products, such as a half-strength sparkling wine, to regain lost markets in the north. Shiukashvili's comments appear to have been more than brave optimism in the presence of a foreigner: Kampfner noted that Tbilisi's wine stores remained well stocked, and contrary to other big Soviet cities, there were no queues to buy alcohol. Even Nikolai Pavlenko, who had the ignominious task of welcoming foreign delegates to an alcohol-free Yalta for the meeting of the International Organization of Vine and Wine, optimistically predicted in 1990 that within four to five years, the 'wine deficit' would pass. Pavlenko had in mind the time it took new vineyards to become productive, not the life expectancy of Soviet power.[60]

M. Vas'kov, B. L'ianov, M. Papovko, and B. Shestakov, 'Pochemu bez shampanskogo?' *Sovetskaia Rossiia*, 30 December 1989, 1.

[59] 'Bez vina vinovatye', *Komsomol'skaia pravda*, 9 September 1990, 2; V. Zaikin, 'Glavnyi vinodel planety', *Izvestiia*, 21 September 1988, 3; E. Nefedov, 'Dryzgi shampanskogo', *Komsomol'skaia Pravda*, 21 October 1990, 3.

[60] OSA, 300-80-1, Box 898, File: Sel'skoe khoziaistvo: vinogradarstvo, 1960–93, unnumbered pages entitled 'Georgian Wine Flows Despite Kremlin Crackdown on Drink'; Vladimir Voina, 'Sud'ba

There were instances of opposition. Kampfner and others noted graffiti on train cars deriding Gorbachev's policies: 'Mikhail will pass, but wine will remain.' In Moldova, home to nearly a quarter of the Soviet Union's vineyards, the deputy minister of viniculture and winemaking, Georgii Kozub, was sentenced in 1986 to ten years of corrective labour in eastern Siberia for accepting bribes, for the theft of state property, and for the possession of an unlawful weapon. The fact that Kozub had opposed anti-alcoholism policies that he thought heavy-handed and misguided, and the fact that he was one of the Soviet Union's most famous wine-makers, a specialist in sherry production and an 'honorary vintner of France', made him a *cause célèbre* for a press that was increasingly free to publish what it wished, and prone to see parallels in the present with the Soviet Union's repressive past. In 1989, *Literaturnaia gazeta* published a full-page article about Kozub's case, describing how he was incriminated the old-fashioned way—by an article alleging corruption in *Pravda* that had been written by the head of the Moldovan procuracy. The *Literaturnaia gazeta* writer, Kapitolina Kozhevnikova, one of newspaper's most esteemed and veteran journalists and journalist-laureate of the Soviet Union of Journalists, detailed Kozub's prosecution on trumped-up charges: for instance, the unlawful weapon that he possessed was a decorative dagger from Uzbekistan. And Kozhevnikova related the indefatigable efforts of Kozub's Moscow-based defence attorney to clear his name. In 1989, the chief investigative prosecutor in Moldova annulled the verdict, citing the 'absence of corpus delicti'. In short, the Moldovan procuracy had failed to prove that there were any crimes, much less that Kozub had committed them.[61]

After reviewing twenty-five volumes of investigative and trial material, Kozhevnikova concluded that there was either a desire within the Moldovan pro-curacy to initiate a 'huge trial' of a person connected to winemaking, or orders from above to do so.

> Why did Kozub serve two years in a [labour] colony? Why was he excluded from the party? Why did he spend time in five prisons before arriving in Angarsk? They confiscated his property, tormented his family, took away Georgii Ivanovich's health. For what purpose was this done?

While the answers were not readily apparent to *Literaturnaia gazeta* in 1988, Kozub later claimed that his prosecution had been instigated by the second secretary of the Moldovan Communist Party, Viktor Smirnov, who was a fierce opponent of

---

vinogradnoi lozy', *Izvestiia*, 20 August 1986, 2; E. Nefedov, 'Dryzgi shampanskogo', *Komsomol'skaia Pravda*, 21 October 1990, 3.

[61] Kapitolina Kozhevnikova, 'Porugannaia loza', *Literaturnaia gazeta*, 2 August 1989, 12; I. Cheban, 'Vino tvorit vinu', *Pravda*, 9 August 1986, 3.

Moldovan nationalism. Kozub was not a nationalist, yet when Kozub refused to implicate the first secretary of the Moldovan Communist Party after being questioned about transferring a collection of champagne, cognac, and wine to a vinicultural school, he had to be punished. Smirnov's downfall in 1988—ironically, on charges of accepting bribes—coincided with Kozub's rehabilitation.

While the reasons for Kozub's arrest likely stemmed from bureaucratic rivalries, many of Kozhevnikova's readers interpreted it as the silencing of a critic of Gorbachev's anti-alcoholism policies, with the latter, rather than an unjust prosecution, being the paramount issue. In November 1989, *Literaturnaia gazeta* published a follow-up article that had less to do with the injustices inflicted on Kozub, than with whether the party had been justified in restricting wine production and consumption. On this issue, reader opinions were split. A woman from Krasnoyarsk wrote that Kozhevnikova was trying to 'resurrect the stagnant theory of "cultured" drinking that blossomed under Brezhnev, and rehabilitate the idea that wine is "noble"'. Yet other readers put forth exactly this view of wine—that its production and consumption were deeply rooted in human history, and thus one of the greatest human achievements. 'The grape vine has always been a symbol of life', a woman from Kronstadt wrote, 'But now it is under the axe!' Kozhevnikova gave equal space to her critics, but her sympathies were clearly with the latter respondents. She noted that wine was essential to the identity and culture of regions like Bordeaux and Tuscany, where the success of harvest was measured not in tonnes of grapes, but in decalitres of wine. Even in the Soviet Union,

> microclimate, soil—everything affects the taste of grapes and wine from which it is made. Behind all of this stands the great professional culture [of vintners]. Not for the wretched drunk do they make wine. Like civilized people, they study and preserve wine.[62]

Of course, Kozhevnikova's defence of Soviet winemaking was for the most part disingenuous—there was no great professional culture, no appreciation of soil or microclimate behind *bormotukha*, the industry's cash cow. It constituted wine only in the broadest sense, and sometimes—when it was simply fruit juice fortified with grain alcohol—it failed to do even that. The Krasnoyarsk critic was correct: Kozhevnikova was trying to resurrect the idea that wine was a 'cultured' drink, qualitatively different from a vodka that was undeniably destructive to the social and economic fabric. Yet even during the Brezhnev era, when this idea about wine was supposedly ascendant, it never had much currency beyond a narrow group of winemakers and connoisseurs. For Kozhevnikova and the other proponents of traditional wine, this was the crux of the problem: conventional

---

[62] Kapitolina Kozhevnikova, 'Snova o porugannoi loze, a takzhe o razgnevannyhk chitateliakh i zdravom smysle', *Literaturnaia gazeta*, 1 November 1989, 11.

dry wine was an easy target, because it never constituted more than a small proportion of overall production, only 13 per cent in the late 1970s. For every Kozhevnikova who questioned the wisdom of reducing the production of dry wine, there were many other persons who grumbled about the disappearance of vermouth, Cahors, sherry, and the other 'strong' and 'fortified' wines that Soviet vintners produced in such great abundance.

Paradoxically, all the evidence suggests that Soviet vintners' attention to the quality of their production worked. There was far more good wine in circulation in the early 1980s than fifteen years earlier. The proof lay in the increasing number of labels that bore the industry's 'mark of quality' and reproductions of medals from international tasting competitions. It lay in the growing volume of *marochnoe* wine that was available to consumers, and the elaborate hierarchies the industry created to distinguish the sublime from the pedestrian. It could even be seen in the ubiquity of the *degustatsiia*, which, after a long hiatus where taste did not much matter or was too dangerous to assess, became the Soviet wine industry's characteristic venue and event. Yet the old logic of the Soviet deficit economy—if we produce it, they will consume it and like it—fractured in the face of *bormotukha*, which never disappeared from store shelves, contrary to the industry's sanguine predictions. Despite more than a century of effort, the tsarist and Soviet civilizing project foundered on the popular taste for the strong and the sweet. Once Gorbachev's reformers identified alcohol as a social evil, there could be no exemption for an industry that had learned to produce fine wine, but only as an afterthought to the sweet and strong elixir that paid the bills.

Conclusion
Rebirth
Wine after Socialism

Two decades after the Soviet Union ascended to the uppermost ranks of global wine production, and just a few years after an embarrassingly dry Yalta hosted the General Assembly of the International Association of Vine and Wine (OIV), the destruction of the former Soviet wine industry was complete. According to statistics compiled by OIV, wine production in the newly independent Russian Republic was about 3.1 million hectolitres for the five-year period ending on 31 December 1995, about the same as tropical Brazil, and roughly 5 per cent of the production levels of the industry leaders, France and Italy. In Ukraine (1.8 million hectolitres) and Georgia (1 million), the production decline was equally severe, if not worse. Moldova fared better. It accounted for about 18 per cent of all Soviet wine production in the 1970s, a proportion that had not changed much since Aleksandr Kovalevskii struggled to save Bessarabian vineyards from the 'great wine blight' a century earlier. Moldova emerged from socialism with the largest wine industry, producing about 4.4 million hectolitres between 1991 and 1995, and 3.2 million hectolitres in 2003 alone.[1] Writing about 'ExpoVin Moldova 2006', an international trade fair in Chişinău that occurred just weeks before Russia enacted an embargo on Moldovan wine, one Moldovan journalist boldly predicted that 'our wines are ready to be first'.[2] Yet as Maynard Amerine had anticipated, neither the Soviet Union nor its constituent parts would become one of the twentieth or twenty-first century's great vinicultural success stories. Those honours would go elsewhere—to Amerine's native California, of course, but also Argentina, Australia, and Chile.

The contraction of the Soviet wine industry in the late 1980s was a man-made disaster many years in the making. It reflected the failures of the Soviet civilizing process, the reality that a half century after Stalin embraced champagne as part of the good life of socialism, Soviet consumers preferred wines sweetened with sugar and fortified with alcohol. Despite the pretentious criticism of self-identified connoisseurs, the Soviet wine industry was guilty mainly of producing what it

---

[1] *The Oxford Companion to Wine*, ed. Jancis Robinson (Oxford, 3rd ed., 2006), unnumbered pages in appendix 2B; G. G. Valuiko, *Vinogradnye vina* (Moscow, 1978), 7.

[2] Angelina Taran, 'Vino & Proviant. Iskusstvo vinodeliia. Nashi vina gotovy byt' pervymi', *Logos Press*, 3 March 2006, 23.

Whites and Reds: A History of Wine in the Lands of Tsar and Commissar. Stephen V. Bittner, Oxford University Press (2021). © Stephen V. Bittner. DOI: 10.1093/oso/9780198784821.003.0009

could sell, of following what would become one of the advertising slogans broadcast on the escalators of the Moscow metro during those first post-Soviet years: the customer is captain. By the time Gorbachev became convinced that excessive alcohol consumption was an important cause and symptom of the general malaise of late-socialism, it was impossible to draw good-faith distinctions between wine as a civilizational hallmark and *bormotukha* as a cause of alcoholism. There was too little wine in the Soviet Union that represented the former, hence Mikhail Stroganov's surprise in the opening paragraphs of this book, and too much *bormotukha* that contributed to the latter.

Yet these were only the proximal causes of the crisis that befell Soviet winemaking after socialism. Since the annexation of the Black Sea territories in the late eighteenth and early nineteenth centuries, viniculture and winemaking were implicated, often in contradictory ways, in Russian and Soviet imperial politics. Wine thus offers a useful prism for disaggregating the centripetal forces that bound the empire together for two centuries, from the centrifugal forces that pulled it apart in 1991. Close on the heels of territorial annexations came vineyard surveys, the planting of European varietals, the hiring of foreign vintners, and eventually invitations to vinicultural colonists from the Swiss Vaud, Thrace, Württemberg, and elsewhere—in short, attempts to integrate indigenous wine economies and cultures into imperial political and economic structures. Yet there were always tensions between what Russia hoped to create in its new vinicultural territories, and the recalcitrance of what predated its arrival. Aleksandr Kovalevskii and Vasilii Tairov's deep-seated belief that only a science of European origin and Russian transmission might save *Vitis vinifera* from extinction and vault Russia into the first order of European wine producers was antipode to Mikhail Ballas's subversive reordering of the components that produced fine wine in his native Bessarabia. While Kovalevskii and Tairov differed in many ways on what that science entailed, they were united by the belief that modernity was Russia's principal contribution to the wine cultures and economies that imperialism had domesticated. Ballas, to the contrary, came to understand that the recipe for fine wine included more than European varietals and techniques, thus anticipating the transformation that *terroir* would undergo a half century later. While Ballas was able to look charitably at Bessarabia, he saw only backwardness on the Kakheti plain in eastern Georgia. Here wine was so ubiquitous in the daily lives of peasants that they were unable to appreciate its significance. Similarly in Crimea, Tatar growers, who were supposedly impervious to outside advice and expertise, and whose scrawny, mismatched, and unidentifiable vines produced grapes with barely enough sugar for fermentation, were convenient foils—the very embodiment of backwardness—for the grand estate vineyards that began to appear on the southern shore in the early nineteenth century. The latter vineyards, some owned by the tsar himself, would eventually produce Russia's most coveted wines. More than any other part of the empire, viniculture in Crimea became a rich man's pursuit, with landholding patterns that resembled Bordeaux, and varietals that were likely to be from Champagne, Loire, and Mosel. Here Russian wealth and non-Russian poverty coexisted.

During the Soviet years, viniculture became embedded in the economic and commercial structures that bound the union republics together, and that linked the internal empire—the Soviet Union—with the external empire—the satellite states in Eastern Europe and beyond. Grape must from across the Soviet Union was shipped by train car for processing at the world's largest winery, the Inter-Republic Wine Factory in Moscow. Located at 55 degrees north latitude, it was many kilometres north of the 10-degree Celsius isotherm where viniculture was possible. As the journalist John Kampfer reported in the late 1980s, some of these train cars may have been defaced with anti-Soviet graffiti, as official concern about the consumption patterns of Russian men in the north became the source of non-Russian nationalist grievance and economic hardship in the south. By the 1970s and 1980s, Soviet wines could be found on restaurant menus and store shelves in Eastern Europe. Soviet vinicultural scientists participated in techno-logical exchanges with their counterparts in Bulgaria, Romania, and elsewhere. The Soviet Union showed support for newly independent Algeria by purchasing huge quantities of grape must—the equivalent of 10 per cent of the total Soviet harvest—to cover the widening gap between the production capacity of wine fac-tories and productivity of Soviet vineyards.

While Russia's expansion into the Black Sea region was not motivated by wine, many important persons—from Peter the Great to Alexander III—treated domes-tic winemaking as an important fringe benefit of territorial expansion. Russia would be remade in a European fashion, in part, by wine. The sanguine predic-tion that Russia would one day join the ranks of the great European wine producers became something of an article of faith among winemakers and knowledgeable consumers in the late-nineteenth century. Moreover, the tsar's subjects—first the aristocracy and then the urban middle classes—would be acculturated to appreciate fine wine. Russia's 'passage through Armageddon' at the beginning of the twentieth century transformed but did not diminish these aspirations. Among the losers of 1917, those who emigrated abroad, confidence that late-tsarist Russia had achieved enviable winemaking successes was evident in last-ditch efforts to evacuate the contents of Crimean wine cellars before Mikhail Frunze's Red Army could seize control of the peninsula, and to profit a final time from Western European demand for wines from the southern shore. Among those who stayed behind, regardless of individual politics, was a palpable desire to build on tsarist successes with all the tools the newly activist state offered, and to widen acculturation efforts beyond the old privileged classes to the empowered working class and peasantry. Though the 1920s and early 1930s were inauspicious years for domestic winemaking, because agricultural priorities lay in the grain sector, Stalin's embrace of champagne in 1936 elevated to national importance an industry long associated with wealthy aristocrats and foreign investors. By the time Maynard Amerine arrived in the early 1970s, he found an industry that had for many years been a participant in international tasting competitions and that accepted without question his expertise and palate. Although Amerine found the vast majority of Soviet wine lacking by Western standards, his hosts—vinicultural and oenological scientists and wine industry officials—thought wine no less important than he.

As it turned out, wine advocates, wine patriots, and wine connoisseurs never went away during the Soviet years. They gathered at a vinicultural conference at the Magarach Institute in the post-war years to share a bottle of Moët that pre-dated Soviet power. They helped the new Soviet government assign prices to wines it had seized during the Civil War. They evacuated wine cellars at Massandra and Magarach, priceless national treasures, before advancing German troops could plunder them. They gathered annually in tasting commissions, naively hoping that a 'mark of quality' would entice Soviet consumers, who were more prone to buy vodka, to give wine a try instead. They wrote articles for newspapers extolling the sublime characteristics of Georgian wines and disparaging the banal tastes of the masses. They used diplomatic postings and rare vacations abroad to smuggle bottles from Bordeaux and Tuscany to dinner tables at home. They celebrated successes in international tasting competitions, adorning bottles with prize medals from even obscure competitions in Sofia, Yalta, Budapest, and the other pinnacles of the socialist wine world. These were the heirs—in patriotism, advocacy, and connoisseurship, if not in politics—to Prince Lev Golitsyn, late-tsarist Russia's most famous vintner. Golitsyn would surely have looked askance at Anton Frolov-Bagreev's 'continuous method' of champagne production, and at the whole Soviet ethos that bigger is better. Yet he would have understood the determination to make Soviet wine great. There was much more at stake than wine.

Yet if Russian and Soviet winemaking was implicated in empire, it was also in many ways dependent on empire. The economic dislocation of the 1990s was accompanied by a deregulation of the retail sector and the re-regulation of trade between the former union republics. Both were preconditions for Russia's 2006 ban on Georgian and Moldovan wines. Russia's Chief Sanitary Inspector used the new international border to curtail a chaotic, unregulated trade in alcohol, in which counterfeits and adulterated wines were the rule. He alleged that chemical testing had shown that Moldovan and Georgian wines were compromised with pesticide and grain alcohol. Behind the embargo was official Russian dismay with Georgia's Rose Revolution, which brought a pro-American president, Mikheil Saakashvili, to power, and which would eventually lead to Russia's war on behalf of Ossetian and Abkhazian separatists in 2008. Moldovan policy toward the Russian-speaking Transnistria region was another sore point in Moscow. Banning the sale of Georgian and Moldovan wines in Russia, which was the largest export market for both countries, was an easy way to retaliate. It did not matter when the vice-president of the Moscow League of Winemakers, Nikholai Mekhuzla, publicly cast doubt on the allegations, arguing that peasant viniculturalists in both countries were too poor to afford pesticides.[3] Georgian industry officials tried to combat the allegations by submitting their wines to European laboratories for testing. They set about replacing the lost Russian market with commercial forays into Ukraine, Europe, and the United States. The Georgian defence minister did not help his country's efforts when he claimed that quality mattered little in Russia, because Russian consumers would buy even 'fecal matter'.[4]

In the months following the wine embargo, Russian newspapers assured readers that even powerful people 'in the presidential administration' were curtailing their wine consumption.[5] Compliance was couched as a form of patriotic sacrifice, which meant feigned indignation followed an investigative report showing the Russian Orthodox diocese of Ekaterinburg continued to trade in a Cahors-style wine produced in Moldova. The wine was transported into Russia by private automobiles registered to a hegumen known to be friends with the archbishop of Ekaterinburg, and then sold to parishioners via church stores.[6] During the first weeks of the ban, the journalist Aleksei Korshunov found that Moldovan wine imported through a company in Cyprus could still be found on store shelves in Moscow. Korshunov's investigation showed that the Cypriot importer had long-standing commercial connections to a company called Trading House Garling, whose street address happened to be same as the Moldovan Embassy's. 'It seems, if not for a few alarming circumstances, that this is not commerce, but a beautiful pastoral', Korshunov wrote sarcastically.[7] While the Russian government lifted the ban on Georgian wine not long before Saakashvili left office, it renewed the ban on Moldovan wine that same year, after Moldova signed an association agreement with the European Union. Even in the post-Soviet years, the politics of wine were never just about wine.

The latter was especially evident in the aftermath of Russia's occupation and annexation of Crimea in 2014, which occurred after protests in Kiev forced Viktor Yanukovych from office. Consonant with the broader economic crisis of the 1990s, Crimean production collapsed in the immediate post-Soviet years. Its predicament worsened during the real-estate boom of the early 2000s, when many long-standing vineyards on the southern shore were uprooted to accommodate residential and commercial construction. That fact that much of this construction was for wealthy and powerful people, such as the former speaker of the Crimean

---

[3] Leonid Gordeli, 'Chto tam v vine?' *Severnyi Kavkaz*, 5 April 2006; Ol'ga Gorelik, 'Eshche raz pro vino', *Novye izvestiia*, 3 April 2006, 3.

[4] S. Repov and A. Fufyrin, 'Iz vina: konfetku', *Argumenty i fakty*, 3 May 2006; Igor' Baikov, 'Skandal. Ministr "Bormotukhi"', *Tribuna RT*, 28 April 2006, 10.

[5] Kira Remneva, 'Vina net i ne budet', *Gazeta*, July 3, 2006, 9.

[6] Mikhail Pozdniaev, 'Kak by ne vino', *Novye izvestiia*, 17 September 2008, 1.

[7] Aleksei Korshunov, 'Riskovoe vinodelie', *Nasha versiia*, no. 12 (27 March 2006): 16.

parliament, Anatolii Gritsenko, and that it occurred despite laws prohibiting the sale or rezoning of agricultural land belonging to *sovkhozy*, struck many observers as corrupt. But it also raised questions about vinicultural provenance and truth in labelling. As Sergei Mikhailechko noted, 'nearly every tourist' to Crimea went home with a bottle of Massandra wine, understanding that Massandra was a unique 'national achievement' inextricably tied to Crimea. Tourists purchased their wines with the understanding that the source grapes were Crimean in origin—Crimean sunshine in a bottle, as a Soviet-era advertising slogan put it. But this was no longer a sure thing, as Massandra compensated for declining Crimean production with grapes from distant Bulgaria. One of the largest winemaking facilities in Odessa oblast faced a similar predicament—it had come to rely almost entirely on grapes from Macedonia. Moreover, as Crimean production shifted away from the southern shore amid skyrocketing real-estate values, the region around Bakhchisarai, long seen as vinicultural backwater because it was north of the tempering effect of the coastal range, became the peninsula's de facto winemaking capital.[8] A free market in real estate, not climate change, was reordering the geographies of Crimean viniculture.

Russian sovereignty in 2014 brought hope for something better, at least according to a press that knew it was dangerous to question the politics and repercussions of annexation. One observer noted that Crimean wines stood on the cusp of 'terroir...the acme of winemaking', because of changes in Russian law that lowered the licensing fees on small producers. The assumption was that small producers were better positioned to foster a sense a *terroir* in their wines because their cuvées often comprised grapes from single, geographically distinct vineyards. The comparatively flush Russian government also sought to reverse two decades of decline in the vinicultural economy by offering subsidies of up to 80 per cent of the costs for the planting of new vineyards. Government largess tended to benefit investors and corporate entities as much as plucky, aspiring vintners. During the first few months of 2016, a publicly-traded company called SVZ-Agro planted 69 hectares of new vineyards in the hills outside of Sevastopol, one of the first instalments in what was expected to be 500 hectares of new vineyards near Sevastopol over the course of 2016.[9] These efforts engendered the sort of optimism about the future of Russian winemaking that had characterized the final tsarist decades: Russia had proven itself capable of producing high-quality wines; Russia possessed large swathes of territory that were climatically suitable for viniculture; and Russia increasingly 'followed international wine trends', meaning that the Russian palate for wine was becoming more or less indistinguishable

---

[8] Valentina Samar, 'Dilemma drakonova Iaitsa', *Zerkalo nedeli*, no. 12 (30 March 2012): 6.

[9] Rafael Zalian, 'Terruarnye vina: vershina vinodeliia', *Krymskaia pravda*, 8 July 2016, 2; 'Vinogradarstvo i vinodeliia: novaia kontseptsiia razvitiia', *Slava Sevastopolia*, 21 July 2016, 3.

from the European standard. *Bormotukha*, it seems, had finally lost its hold on the Russian consumers.[10]

Indeed, Russian revanchism aside, there was growing acknowledgement after 2000 in both Russia and Ukraine that *bormotukha*, which was as much a civilizational scourge as health risk, was on the wane, particularly among young people. Adulterated wine was not long for a world where young, educated, and increasingly wealthy and worldly urban consumers drank craft beers, dined in organic, farm-to-table restaurants, and could pull up Robert Parker's reviews of the latest Bordeaux vintage on their iPhones. Inexpensive, comparatively high-quality wine from Australia, Argentina, and Chile could be found at the corner market, along with domestic standbys like Abrau-Diurso and Shabo and (after 2013 in Russia) Georgian wines, all of which were much improved in quality since Soviet times. At stores specializing in wine, knowledgeable salesclerks were happy to explain why a 2015 Barolo was better than a 2013 Barbera d'Asti. Finally, the wine regions themselves—once places of myth and imagination for Soviet consumers—became popular destinations for long, epicurean weekends. Wine had come a long way since Mikhail Stroganov unexpectedly encountered two bottles in a liquor store in Tver in the early 1980s.[11]

Domestic producers were quick to capitalize on the changing tastes of wine drinkers. In 2005, the Russian government—working in conjunction with the Union of Viniculturalists and Winemakers—adopted a nomenclature for wine quality and provenance that resembled the French AOC. At the lower end, corresponding to vin de pays, were wines marked with the phrase 'with appellation by origin' (or by the acronym NP), which indicated that all grapes came from a specified area. At the upper end, corresponding to the French AOC, were wines marked with the phrase 'with controlled appellation by origin' (KNP), which indicated that the winemaker had conformed to regionally specific guidelines to assure quality and composition.[12] *Bormotukha* was legally reclassified as a 'wine-based beverage', which contained not less than 50 per cent wine, but up to 22 per cent alcohol. Below the middle vin de pays classification, table wines, 'sweet' wines, sparkling wines, and Russian champagne were formally defined by production process and acceptable additives. Generally, any sugar or alcohol that was added during production had to be derived from grapes. Some industry officials began to lobby for a 'geographical marker' on wine labels that indicated the place where the source grapes were grown; the place where the grapes were

[10] Sergei Taranov, 'Novorusskii Bakhus: kak vinodelam zavoevat' svoi rynok', *Novye izvestiia*, 3 April 2018; Ol'ga Vandysheva, 'Chestnoe russkoe vino', *Ekspert* 49 (5 December 2016): 24–8.

[11] See, for instance, Mariia Solovichenko, 'Proshchai, bormotukha!', *Russkii kur'er*, 7 July 2004, 1; Aleksandr Rybakov, '"Sovin'on" vmeste "777"', *Severnaia Osetiia*, 25 December 2007; Vladimir Chopenko, 'Nevinovnoe vino', *Zerkalo nedeli*, no. 12 (30 March 2012): 1; Anon., 'Kabernet protiv bormotukhi', *Dagestanskaia pravda*, 23 January 2013.

[12] 'Konets bormotukhi', *Zolotoi rog*, 1 November 2005.

crushed, fermented, and aged; and the place where the resulting wine was bottled.[13] When the *New York Times* sent its Moscow correspondent, Neil MacFarquhar, to Crimea to report on changes in the post-annexation wine industry, MacFarquhar found a 'boutique' winery producing 50,000 bottles a year of 'high quality, fresh, elegant wine' in the hills above Sevastopol. The vintner was a former sommelier from Moscow's posh restaurant scene. In Georgia, an American artist-turned-vintner, John Wurdeman, set about making wines in the traditional Georgian way, leaving must in contact with grape skins, which in white wine produces a deep amber colour, and fermenting the maceration in clay amphorae (*kvevri*) lined with beeswax and buried in the ground. Wurdeman's wines, sold under the label Pheasant's Tears, are highly coveted by wealthy wine drinkers who are bored by the high-quality monotony and easy drinkability of Napa Cabernets and Bordeaux Clarets, and by health-conscious consumers who have come to believe that old foodways are superior to the new. Larger Georgian producers, such as Teliani Valley and Château Mukhrani, which produce wine in the conventional European fashion, have benefitted from Western investment and technology, not to mention the increasingly astronomical prices that wines from famous French and Italian producers command. For adventurous consumers in Europe, North America, and especially China (which is now Georgia's third largest export market, after Russia and Ukraine), the oldest world of winemaking, with its strange, unpronounceable, and ancient varietals, offers bottles of pedigree at comparatively inexpensive prices.[14]

With better quality domestic wine and relatively easy access to the wine economies and cultures of the West came a new literature of connoisseurship. Newspapers and journals in Russia, Ukraine, Georgia, Moldova, and Belarus hired wine critics and writers, who helped novice wine drinkers and aspiring connoisseurs navigate wine lists in restaurants, not to mention the perilous moment when the sommelier uncorked a bottle of wine. They described how to swirl a freshly poured glass of wine to open its bouquet. They advised on proper food pairings. They explained elusive concepts like *terroir* in terms that were almost mystical and religious. They helped with proper French, Italian, and Spanish pronunciation.[15] To be sure, some persons bristled at the apparent snobbery sur-

[13] Aleksei Aronov, 'Vino otdelili ot bormotukhi', *Izvestiia*, 30 June 2010, 3; Irina Dronova, 'Bormotukha zachisliat v napitki?', *Nizhegorodskie novosti*, 15 November 2011; Aleksandr Mel'nikov, 'Pravila vinodelov', *Argumenty i fakty*, no. 46 (16 November 2011): 90.

[14] Neil MacFarquhar, 'Crimean Winemakers Look to Shed the Rot Gut Label', *New York Times*, 19 October 2017; Esther Mobley, 'Yes, Georgian Wine Is Worth the Hype and Yes, You Should Be Drinking It', *San Francisco Chronicle*, 21 August 2019; David Williams, 'Why Georgia is a Hotspot for Natural Wines', *The Guardian*, 25 February 2018; 'Andrew Jefford on a New Era for Georgian Wine', *The Financial Times*, 3 August 2018, https://www.ft.com/content/2d0e77f8-951b-11e8-b747-fb1e803ee64e; Andrew Jefford, 'Georgian Wines: Older and Wiser', *The Financial Times*, 2 August 2013, https://www.ft.com/content/7307e952-f50b-11e2-b4f8-00144feabdc0.

[15] Ivan Kaverin, 'Restorannyi znatok vin, ili Kto takoi somel'e', *Vladivostok*, 5 September 2003; Viktor Iakimov, 'Chem pakhnet vino?' *Zolotoi rog*, 22 January 2004; Vera Koniukhova, 'Vino dlia

rounding wine, which had not been unknown during Soviet years, but was now amplified many times over. Wine prices that varied little by producer and quality before 1991, were now glaringly 'undemocratic', as one writer put it.[16] A fine French wine might command 100 times the price of a respectable bottle from Shabo.

There is little doubt, however, that wine became more firmly entrenched than ever as a hallmark of *kul'turnost'* among a young, worldly, and upwardly mobile professional class that associated vodka and *bormotukha* with Soviet times. A civilizing process, which began at the behest of Peter the Great, which once enjoyed the patronage of Alexander III, which was embraced by an aristocracy and urban middle class keen to consume in ways that were recognizably European, which for many decades enlisted all the tools the Soviet government had at its disposal, paradoxically succeeded in the chaotic atmosphere of post-socialism, in the absence of empire, and without much state support at all. The world of wine was no longer a costume ball that required these uncouth 'northerners', as Théophile Gautier derisively put it 150 years earlier, to pretend to be something they were not.

gurmanov', *Vladivostok*, 25 May 2007; Aleksandr Mel'nikov and Irina Pavlova, 'Vinnaia karta', *Argumenty i fakty*, no. 52 (23 December 2009): 50; Angelina Taran, 'O prevrashchenii vinograda v vino', *Logos press*, 25 November 2011.

[16] Viktoriia Popova, 'Vino sredi liudei', *Belarus' segodnia*, 17 June 2008.

Acknowledgements

Significant funding for the research and writing of this book was provided by the National Council for Eurasian and East European Research, the Kennan Institute for Advanced Russian Studies, the National Endowment for the Humanities Fellowship and Summer Stipend programmes, the School of Social Sciences at Sonoma State University, and California State University's Research, Scholarship, and Creative Activities Program. I am deeply grateful to these organizations, without whose support this book would not exist. In 2019, Senator James Lankford of Oklahoma singled out my NEH Fellowship, which allowed me to take a year-long sabbatical and write an initial draft of this book, as a particularly odious example of wasteful government spending. For this ignominious distinction, I am thankful too, even if I respectfully disagree with Senator Lankford's estimation of the importance of wine and winemaking in Russia.

Research for this book was conducted in libraries and archives in five countries and one region that has since become contested. Thanks go to the many librarians and archivists who steered me toward relevant collections and who made sure my books or documents would be ready for me as soon as I arrived. I am especially grateful to Axel Borg, Distinguished Wine and Food Sciences Bibliographer at the University of California, Davis, who alerted me to Maynard Amerine's encounter with Soviet winemaking long before I understood Amerine's significance in the world of wine, and to Michael Cook, Head of Collections at Cornell University's Albert R. Mann Library, who facilitated a trip to Ithaca to consult a rare item. Over the years, I have presented portions of this book at workshops, seminars, and wine tastings at Birkbeck College, London; Georgetown University; the University of California, Berkeley; the University of California, Davis; the University of Illinois; the University of Michigan; the University of Texas; the University of Toronto; and the University of Wisconsin. Thanks go to the participants in these events, who carefully read my work and responded with encouragement and gentle criticism. I am also indebted to Ian Campbell, Johanna Conterio, Michael David-Fox, Victoria Frede, Krista Goff, Steven Harris, Yoshiko Herrera, Mary Neuburger, John Randolph, Yuri Slezkine, Alison Smith, and Lynne Viola for their generosity and hospitality in arranging these talks. At critical junctures, David Brandenberger, Juliane Fürst, Steven Harris, James Heinzen, Almas Musakyzy Ismailova, Polly Jones, Catriona Kelly, Scott Kenworthy, Nadieszda Kizenko, Diane Koenker, Rachel Koroloff, Aleksandr Popov, Erik Scott, Alison Smith, Tricia Starks, and Willard Sunderland generously shared with me their expertise or materials I would not have found on my own. Where appropriate, I have acknowledged their specific contributions in the footnotes. Thanks are also due to my colleagues in the Department of History at Sonoma State University, who have always accommodated in good cheer the many absences from teaching and university life that this book required of me, and to Robert Faber, now retired from Oxford University Press, who solicited a book proposal from me after we met by chance at a reception at where I knew almost no one. Finally, Juliane Fürst, Catriona Kelly, Ethan Pollock, Lewis Siegelbaum, and the anonymous readers at Oxford University Press, *Past & Present* (where an abbreviated version of chapter 2 first appeared), and *Kritika* (an abbreviated version of chapter 6) offered advice on the manuscript in whole, or on its (not always successful) individual parts. I hope all of you recognize your positive influences in these pages.

For my family—Christel, Mia, and Ethan—who have lived with this book and the demands it has placed on me for many years, a simple thank you is inadequate. I hope instead you will see that our shared lives among the vineyards and wineries of Sonoma County were the book's first inspiration and the fuel that kept me determined to finish. Historians naturally mark the passing of time through the publication of their books. When I wrote the acknowledgements for my first book, a four-year-old Mia and two-year-old Ethan were playing outside the door to my home office, anxious for me finally to be done. Now Mia is on the cusp of university, and Ethan stands 6 feet 2 inches tall. Where did the time go? Much of it, I can see now, went to this book.

I dedicate this book to my parents, Rodger Vincent Bittner and Barbara Jean Bittner. After all these years, my mother remains my first proofreader and editor.

Santa Rosa, California

Archives and Abbreviations

DAOO	State Archive of the Odessa Oblast
f. 5	Administration of the Temporary Governor-General of Odessa
f. 22	Imperial Society for Agriculture in Southern Russia
GAARK	State Archive of the Autonomous Republic of Crimea
f. 156	Tauride-Ekaterinoslav Committee for Viniculture and Winemaking
GARF	State Archive of the Russian Federation
f. A442	State Joint-Stock Company for the Production and Trade of Wine and Vodka (Vintorg)
f. R130	Soviet of People's Commissars RSFSR
f. R356	Administration for Trade and Industry of the Supreme Command of the Armed Forces in Southern Russia
f. R393	People's Commissariat of Internal Affairs RSFSR (consulted at the Hoover Institute, Stanford University)
f. R1318	People's Commissariat of Nationalities RSFSR
f. R1726	Commission of the Council of Labour and Defence for the Reporting and Realization of State Funds
f. R4085	People's Commissariat of the Workers' and Peasants' Inspectorate RSFSR
f. R5446	Council of Ministers USSR
f. R8300	Ministry of State Control USSR
f. R8350	Main Concessionary Committee of the Soviet of People's Commissars
f. R9415	Main Administration of the Police of the Ministry of Internal Affairs USSR
OSA	Open Society Archive
PSZ	Full Collection of the Laws of the Russian Empire
RGAE	Russian State Archive of Economics
f. 468	Ministry of Food Production USSR
f. 738	Central Administration of the State Wine Trade
f. 8543	Ministry of Food Production USSR
STA	Central State Archive of Georgia
f. 243	Plenipotentiary of the Minister of Land Affairs in the Caucasus
f. 351	Administration of the Inspector of the Crown Estates in the Caucasus
f. 354	Administration of the Crown Estates
TsDAVO Ukraïny	Central State Archive of the Supreme Authorities of Ukraine
f. 4182	Odessa Administration for State Viniculture and Winemaking
f. 5201	Main Administration of the Horticulture, Viniculture, and the Winemaking Industry of the Ukrainian SSR
UCD	Special Collections, UC Davis Library

Index